REALITY
FICTIONS

The great seal of Cambrai, Centre historique des Archives nationales, Paris.
Photo: Collection of the photographic studio, Centre historique des Archives nationales.

REALITY FICTIONS

Romance, History,
and Governmental Authority,
1025 – 1180

ROBERT M. STEIN

University of Notre Dame Press

Notre Dame, Indiana

Manufactured in the United States of America

Library of Congress Cataloging-in-Publication Data
Stein, Robert M., 1943-
Reality fictions : romance, history, and governmental authority,
1025–1180 / by Robert M. Stein.
p. cm.
Includes bibliographical references and index.
ISBN-13: 978-0-268-04120-5 (pbk. : alk. paper)
ISBN-10: 0-268-04120-2 (pbk. : alk. paper)
1. Romances—History and criticism. 2. Historiography—Europe—
History—11th century. 3. Historiography—Europe—History—
12th century. I. Title.
PN671.S73   2006
809.1'33—dc22

2006004487

∞ The paper in this book meets the guidelines for permanence and durability of the
Committee on Production Guidelines for Book Longevity of the Council on Library Resources.

For Marilyn and Emma

diligentia diligere dicta

CONTENTS

Abbreviations   ix

Introduction   1

chapter one   Sacred Authority and Secular Power: 13
                 The Bishops of Cambrai

chapter two   Narrating the English Nation after 1066   65

chapter three "Dreaming of Other Worlds":   105
                 Romance as Reality Fiction

chapter four   From Romance to Epic   161

Epilogue: Sovereignty and Governmentality   207

Notes   211

Works Cited   263

Index   285

ABBREVIATIONS

BHL   Bollandists, *Bibliotheca hagiographica latina antiquae et mediae aetatis,* Subsidia Hagiographica 6 (Brussels: Société des Bollandistes, 1949), and its supplement, *Bibliotheca hagiographica latina antiquae et mediae aetatis: Novum supplementum,* ed. H. Fros, Subsidia Hagiographica 70 (Brussels: Société des Bollandistes, 1986), no. 3289

PL   Patrologiae Cursus Completus, Series Latina, ed. J.-P. Migne (Paris: Garnier, 1844–)

CCSL   Corpus Christianorum, Series Latina

INTRODUCTION

Es ist dem philosophischen Schrifttum eigen, mit jeder Wendung von neuem vor
der Frage der Darstellung zu stehen. [It is a characteristic of philosophical writing that with each new turn it must again take up the question of representation.]

Walter Benjamin, *Ursprung des deutschen Trauerspiels*

This is a book about literary innovation. It has long been a commonplace of literary history to observe that in the twelfth century, first in the French-speaking
territories controlled by the Anglo-Norman and Capetian ruling families, and
especially within the milieu of the English royal court, antique and chivalric romances appear simultaneously with a new kind of historical chronicle driven by
contemporary affairs. In short order historiography and romance, whether written in Latin or in the vernaculars, become culturally dominant genres of narrative expression throughout the rest of Europe.[1] This simultaneous appearance
and spread within the same cultural milieu, which has frequently been remarked,
suggests a deeper intimacy that I propose to examine here.[2]

The appearance of a new form of writing is an event of literary history and
a question for literary theory. As Bakhtin's work has shown with great clarity,
new forms disrupt old systems and create new areas of meaning and new para-
digms of meaningfulness; they also alter the significance of already existing
modes of literary expression and change the whole constellation of literary
forms. Yet why a new kind of writing appears at a particular time, or even appears at all, is not a question that literary theory can answer. To understand the
changes in the literary constellation that the emergence together of history and
romance effects requires us to consider the structure of literary production
as a whole in its relation to the world from which it emerges and to which it

responds. Who writes? and to what end? I suggest in this book that the provocation to romance writing is the same as the provocation to history: they grow
out of the same cultural need and intend to do the same cultural work. To put
it as briefly as I can, this is the need to make the secular world intelligible as
driven by secular imperatives, no matter how mediated through varieties of religious discourses the process might be. This similar provocation and identical
cultural task is the basis of the relation of history and romance to each other
in their simultaneous appearance, the rapid development and wide spread of
their reception, and their formal affinities. Moreover, this cultural need is not
our own theoretical abstraction: it was urgent for those who were most practically and immediately involved with secular processes, the literate clerks who
produced the texts, served in the courts of royal and territorial administrators,
and advised noble elites. In the rearrangements of power that were part of the
state-making designs of Capetian and Anglo-Norman ruling families, new imaginative and conceptual entities became matters demanding serious representation, often in new discursive configurations, and often for the first time—the
boundaries between self and other, the experience of eros, the differentiation
of public from private life all took on new contours. These matters are new
urgencies demanding practical knowledge. Thus while artistic activity is never
directly reducible to the political sphere, it is nevertheless to the domain of political and social transformation that we must look in order to understand artistic innovation. At the same time, our account of artistic innovation can shed
light directly on the process of social change.

    While I am writing about a political process and its connection with liter-
ary innovation, I am not concerned with narrating the trajectory of political
change in itself. I intend rather to deal directly with the pressures on modes
of representation that are correlative to changes in the structure of political
power. Above all, I do not see the political process as a static or knowable fac-
tual context in which to situate artistic change in order to explain it. To para-
phrase what Marx refers to as the guiding idea of all his inquiry, it is the sphere
of culture in the largest sense in which people become conscious of changes
in their existence and in which these changes are fought out. They are fought
out theoretically in the realms of political theory, theology, and philosophy and
in the realm of literary representation that is the subject of this book. They are
also fought out practically in war, internecine battle, and other types of armed
struggle and unarmed social conflict—but even in the towns, fortified strong
houses, and castles in the midst of conflict it is only through protocols of rep-

resentation that people decide to take sides, take action, understand and assert the significance of the action they take, and justify themselves to themselves and to others. Thus changes in the structure of representation are themselves primary phenomena, and their analysis can provide us with as direct an entry point into the lives of real social actors as quantitative or other hard evidence can.

I am particularly concerned with changes in political power related to the process of state formation in the *longue durée*. In thinking about this process, I am much indebted to the analytic model developed by Charles Tilly in a series of extremely important studies.[3] Tilly's notion of state formation (a term he introduced to political theory to counter the teleological implications of phrases such as *nation building*)[4] has the great advantage for medieval studies of drawing attention to the wide variety of governmental entities that exist besides the national state and their very fluid possibilities of development and change. For Europe around the year 1000, Tilly signals three basic forms of many diverse organizations of power: petty military despotisms, city-states oriented to trade and the exploitation of their surrounding countrysides, and empires "concatenating central military organizations, thin regional administrations, trading networks, and organizations of tribute in which local and regional rulers—often maintaining cultural identities distinct from that of the empire's center—enjoyed great autonomy in return for collaboration in the collection of tribute and support in the empire's military campaigns."[5]

None of these organizations of power are *pre*-states or "primitive" states, or necessarily on their way to become states, although in each type we can find a process of state formation—the process of centralization and territorialization of rule and the monopolization of the means of coercion into an organization distinct from any other in the same territory. Moreover, these three basic systems of political consolidation overlap with other kinds of consolidation and territorial identities such as languages, religions, trading systems, and tribal and ethnic unities in a way that defies simple mapping.[6]

During the long twelfth century, some ruling elites in western Europe did nevertheless manage, more or less successfully and with an impact on other competing claimants to local authority, to centralize territorial administration, to exercise clear dominance over other competing claimants to local authority within the territory that they administered, and especially to find more efficient ways of extracting capital and military service from subjects under their control. This new efficiency, which has been much studied, was especially dependent on writing, and it brought with it a new class of clerically educated, literate and numerate intellectuals who transformed writing from a primarily liturgical instrument into a potent instrument of secular power.[7] Yet state formation *as a process* within these territories, as important as it is, is one social process among others. It is in conflict with other countervailing tendencies and with other centers of power, and it is by no means destined to become victorious.

My task here is thus to consider the history of state formation without relying on the narrative of the inevitable rise of the state. The traditional narrative of western European development still sees state formation as the paradigmatic postmedieval signifier.[8] In what follows, I treat state formation as something going on within the sphere of governmental power and against other kinds of sovereignties, and my intention is to take it into account without a teleology— without a story of the ultimately successful rise of the state or the sense that the state is the inevitable and proper outcome of the conflict of sovereignties. And while the chapters in this book are arranged in a generally chronological order, this arrangement is merely a convenience for the reader. I am more concerned with tendencies within the *longue durée* that come to light at particular moments when they become visible for us in particular texts. These changes cannot be ordered into a single trajectory of change over time without doing much violence to the range of their implications. In 1980 Michel Foucault famously remarked, à propos the tendency to treat the state as the natural and "real" form of sovereignty, that political theory still needed to cut off the king's head.[9] Foucault made that remark at a moment in which liberal democracy in the form of the western European welfare state already seemed to have definitively deposed the king in practice: it seemed, that is, to have put an end to the unique power of centralized coercion. In that context Foucault saw the need to understand scattered hegemonies, microsystems of power, and governmentality directly, without the mediation of state theory.[10] The way I see this task now inevitably arises from our own contemporary situation in which nonstate actors— whether multinational corporations, the drug cartels and money-laundering operations that are their illegal counterparts, or international terrorists—have become important historical agents even as the fragility, if not the outright failure, of the secular state has become increasingly apparent while the state is in no great rush to disappear from the historical arena.[11]

The nationality of the modern national state has always been an ideological fiction in the service of a political program. Whether part of the rhetoric of the demand for statehood by ethnic minorities within larger sovereignties, by former colonial subjects, or by "nationalities" otherwise conceived, or part of the rhetoric of already hegemonic political entities promoting or enforcing the dominance of one set of cultural idioms over others, what Homi Bhabha refers to as the "pedagogic,"[12] appeals to nationality are always an act of construction.[13] Even the most homogenous of modern European states are and have been quite diverse—polyglot, composed of diverse regional cultures, and always containing minority religions. That the medieval state is fissured with difference does not make it the Other of modernity. Yet the fact that a political boundary is not an epistemological boundary is obscured for us both by conditions of universal statehood and by the enormous weight of the nation in our contemporary disciplinary structures. Our university departments and the hiring and specialization codes of our learned societies and granting agencies are all organized by the idea of national literatures and national history. For most of medieval Europe, the nation is simultaneously too small and too large to be a useful analytic unit. We need only think of the career of Anselm, born in Lombardy, abbot of Bec and archbishop of Canterbury, or reread Robert Bartlett's fine chapter on the aristocratic diaspora of the eleventh to the thirteenth centuries[14] to remember how frequently people moved around in Europe through marriages, work, or warfare and carried cultural practices with them as they moved and how central displacement, relocation, migration, and cultural friction were to medieval experience. We can recall the powerful international ecclesiastical culture and its social organization in archiepiscopal dioceses that often crossed political boundaries of all sorts or the allied monastic houses that did the same. And we can remind ourselves as well of the unification of secular culture across national lines and within national territories that occurred not only among the elite, who intermarried, were educated within a similar curriculum, and shared a common political experience, but also among ordinary people, who, in the ancien régime, led overwhelmingly similar lives in labor-intensive cultivation of the land, different as local practices may have been. These large-scale international phenomena that characterize the Middle Ages also do not make it modernity's Other.

The large variety of overlapping institutional, epistemological, and practical structures of power that the European Middle Ages presents to us in fact provides us with a great opportunity to explore the ways that dislocations and transformations of power are registered in the consciousness of those who live through them. I set out to do this within the disciplinary framework of literary criticism by reading a set of exemplary texts. Some of these texts are very well known; others have rarely been discussed. I read these texts here to understand how changes in formal representational practices not only witness but participate in the structure of power by their play of complicities and resistances to change. Hence my interest throughout this book in material related to structures of governance that are not reducible to state borders as well as in material that emerges from the Anglo-Norman or Capetian court, and in various kinds of narratives of resistance as well as in the self-justifying narratives of those in power.

For an inquiry of this sort, a survey of many texts is less useful than a few carefully selected examples that can be read closely and in full. I take my texts from borders rather than political centers, and always from contested or ambiguous territory.[15] The border between the Holy Roman Empire and Capetian France, the border between England and other sovereignties on the island of Britain, territories such as the Champagne or Brittany—these margins of sovereignty are the centers of narrative innovation.[16] One could, I am sure, accomplish my ends by choosing other examples, and these examples need not be either European or medieval. I do think the European medieval examples have their own special weight in that they make the process of representation and its transformations available to us in a highly visible way. This is not because the European Middle Ages form the starting point for a continuous narrative of the development of our modernity, the origin of all that comes later, but rather because of the precise and multiform relation of medieval expression to a variety of practices of representation that are themselves continuously reconfigured, reaccented, and endowed with new meaning in later moments of Western narrative practice. Among them are oral storytelling, the rhetorical curriculum derived from Roman civic education, and the privilege of the book as a special location of truth.

Accordingly, my first chapter begins with a consideration of the historiographical project undertaken by Gerard I, bishop of Cambrai. The conjoint Diocese of Arras-Cambrai bridged imperial and Capetian territory and was itself crossed by two linguistic frontiers, and the bishop was simultaneously an imperial appointment, a member of the emperor's entourage, and, as suffragan of the archbishop of Reims, a member as well of the Capetian ruling elite. Because of its strategic importance, the diocese was riven by serious and prolonged internal disputes when in 1024 Bishop Gerard commissioned the compilation of a huge three-part historical chronicle, the *Deeds of the Bishops of Cambrai,* tracing the history of Cambrai from its mythical founding by its first bishop, St. Gerí, to his own time. Along with the composition of the chronicle, Gerard ordered the construction of the textual archive on which the chronicle was based. Among the new texts created for this archive was a life of St. Aubert, one of the patrons of the city, and Gerard seems to have commissioned no less than Fulbert of Chartres to write it. These texts are not only important witnesses to contemporary affairs; they are themselves assertions of power, political weapons in the bishop's attempt to achieve supremacy over his secular and ecclesiastical rivals. At the very moment when secular lords were becoming capable administrators, the bishop of Cambrai claimed an ever wider authority over ever more intimate aspects of secular life and asserted his own right to rule by using the full panoply of coercive spiritual weapons at his disposal. This strategy of control thus opens intimate aspects of secular life to serious representation. At the same time, the bishop's appeal to the authority of traditional spiritual practices for nontraditional uses puts a tremendous strain on the traditional forms and techniques of narrative representation. In turn, an analysis of these narrative complications reveals the fault lines of his own authority in opposition to other claimants.

The second chapter turns from a consideration of narratives in the service of centralizing power to an exploration of narratives of opposition to the rapid growth of Norman central administration in Britain after 1066. I begin with an examination of the eleventh- and twelfth-century chronicle accounts of the death of Harold Godwinson, the last Anglo-Saxon king. In their attempt to make the stunning defeat and death of the king comprehensible, some of these texts are complicit with political orthodoxy and the contemporary array of power, while others, such as the remarkable *Vita Haroldi,* enact a serious kind of opposition in which Harold's military defeat is transformed into victory. In the process Harold becomes a new kind of saint, England becomes a nation, and hagiography becomes romance. Like the body of Harold, the figure of Waltheof, Earl of Northumbria—enemy, captive, collaborator, traitor, English patriot, local hero, and ultimately saint—takes on a spectral life in the various accounts of William the Conqueror's struggles to control the northern border territories in the 1070s and becomes a powerful engine for narrative invention. In these texts, Waltheof's inner life and private experience, like Harold's in the *Vita Haroldi,* move from the margins of interest to displace what began in both instances as the central political story of the rise of Norman power. By this very act of displacement, these narratives of resistance allow us to understand processes that cannot be seen when narrated from the top down as the story of the triumphant rise to power of the Norman regime.

The texts of the first two chapters emerge from political borders; they also continuously operate on a narrative border that, however fluid, also marks a real distinction—the border between history and hagiography. In their efforts to make secular life comprehensible, these texts continually come up against a historiographical impasse: the truth that the historian seeks seems always about to appear in time—sometimes as the revelation of the secrets of a soul, sometimes as the revelation of a Last Judgment—but it remains always hidden away beyond the historian's ken. Whether we consider historians' prefaces or their actual practice, it is clear that medieval historians worked under the same principal constraint that historians labor under today—not to narrate beyond the evidence, even if their canons of truth and their sense of what the evidence provides are separated from our own by an epistemological divide. It is clear, too, that medieval historians' claim to a truth-telling intention, even when their canons of truth had more to do with probable argument and pedagogical efficacy than with narrating the past "as it actually was," required the reader's assent to the mimetic truth value of their narrative. Yet it is equally clear that the effect of mimetic truth value is produced by the historian's use of the full repertoire of fictional narrative techniques and that fiction and history effectively merge in historiography even while medieval readers recognized some generic and functional distinction between them.[17] In my third chapter, I thus turn from the border that history shares with hagiography to the border that history shares with romance, first by examining the Latin prose of Geoffrey of Monmouth's pseudohistorical *Historia regum Brittaniae* and then by very close readings of two well-known texts, canonical for all discussions of romance: Chrétien's *Chevalier au Lion* and Marie de France's *Guigemar.* I argue in this chapter that romance emerges from the desire to seize directly and with the same narrative techniques the kind of truth that seems always just outside the historian's knowledge, but above all to seize this kind of truth for historical understanding. Similarly, I argue that even when they are most overtly fantasies, romances are immersed in the contemporary secular world. Just as historians absorbed the techniques and narrative voicings that we associate with fiction, writers of romance used pseudohistory to explore the same tensions that provoked the writing of history. Their formal affinities thus derive from identical desires to master experience and make it an object of knowledge.

Finally, my readers will recognize my homage to Sir Richard Southern's brilliant conclusion to *The Making of the Middle Ages* in the title of my last chapter, "From Romance to Epic."[18] Southern wanted to see the relation between epic and romance as developmental and progressive—romance brought new experience to consciousness, brought new matter to representation, and elaborated a new sense of life that Southern saw as a change for the better. It was dynamic, energetic, looking toward the future. I argue here that we need rather to understand the relation between romance and epic as dialectical and thoroughly mediated by historiography. The epic is addressed to the same experience as romance, presenting it as equally dynamic though ultimately in a very different configuration, and it is always in dialogue with the romance writing.[19] As romance and historiography become the dominant genres of narrative representation, writing in older genres takes on new meanings and is used for new functions. The chansons de geste as we have them do not in any way preexist the chivalric romances. They are their contemporaries. The same forces that provoke the elaboration of new narrative forms are reflected in epic as its traditional aura is used in the service of nontraditional ends. Whereas both historiography and romance ground their authority to convey truth in the fact that they are written documents, the epic claims to speak the truth of the past directly with the voice of tradition. The apparent formal naiveté of the chanson de geste, I argue, is a mere appearance deployed for quite complex purposes of understanding and critique. In the process, tradition itself ceases to be something static and merely at hand, and history becomes a weapon under continuous construction wielded by those who would resist change by invoking precedent.

Medieval techniques of reading and composition, such as monastic meditation and its allied pedagogy derived from Roman topical invention, led to a sense of narrative as a structure of emotionally powerful scenes that could provoke chains of rich textual and experiential associations in the reader. In her studies of memory and invention, Mary Carruthers calls these powerful scenes "cognitive fictions" to draw attention to the fact that their value consisted in their pedagogic or ethical efficacy and that, sensuously vivid as they were, their vividness had nothing to do with mimetic truth value but rather with their memorability. Thus paintings of Jerusalem in Beatus commentaries changed from copy to copy of the same original to reflect changing architectural tastes—the knowledge that the image intended to effect depended, not on its faithfulness in representing the architectural details of the actual Jerusalem, but on its memorability as a starting place for meditation. But to stay with Mary Carruthers's example, the very changes in architecture—for example, that Spanish copies show Mozarabic arches while later English copies show gothic points—demonstrate the dependence of cognitive fictions on a claim, however construed, to mimetic truth. I call this book *Reality Fictions* to underline the deep entanglements of the texts under discussion with the secular reality that they variously engage. Historical writing is thoroughly dependent on the techniques of fiction to represent the reality of the past; epic and romance imagine worlds that never were in order to make the world their readers inhabit available for practical knowledge.

▉ It is a great pleasure to acknowledge the generosity of colleagues and friends without whom this book would not exist. Early research was enabled by a grant from the National Endowment for the Humanities, and time to reflect and write was supported by several generous grants from the Purchase College Foundation. I am especially grateful to Felice Lifshitz for introducing me to the arcana of hagiographical research and for sharing the materials she gathered on the life of St. Aubert. Brigitte Bedos-Rezak first showed me the great seal of Cambrai that graces the cover. Chloë Wheatley, my dear friend, was the best of research assistants during a crucial period of discovery. The staff at the Columbia University Library, where I did most of my research, have been uniformly welcoming and helpful. I am extremely grateful to past and present members of the New York medievalists' work-in-progress group—Christopher Baswell, Christine Chism, Sealy Gilles, Charlotte Gross, Joan Haahr, Robert Hanning, Sandra Pierson Prior, Anne Schotter, Paul Strohm, Sylvia Tomasch, Peter Travis, and Jocelyn Wogan-Browne—who have heard a great part of this manuscript over the last several years. Their enthusiastic responses, hard questions, careful reading, and serious advice have done much to make this book what it is. Working with Barbara Hanrahan and the University of Notre Dame Press has been a special pleasure: D. Vance Smith and the anonymous reader read the manuscript with the kind of attention one always hopes for and rarely receives. I thank them for their discerning comments, editorial suggestions, and high praise. The book benefited greatly from the sharp and practiced eye of Elisabeth Magnus. Of my colleagues at Purchase College, I owe special debts of gratitude to Wayne Te Brake, Louise Yelin, Ronnie Scharfman, and Gari Laguardia. I have had the pleasure to present parts of this work to the Columbia University Seminar on Medieval Studies, to the Princeton University Medieval Studies Association, and to the History Seminar at Johns Hopkins. I thank all their members for their warm hospitality and lively engagement with my work.

Three fellow historiographers deserve special thanks. I have benefited immensely from Gabrielle Spiegel's foundational work in historiography, her intellectual friendship, and her encouragement at various stages of this project. Nancy Partner has been a lifelong intellectual companion in the vineyards of historiography and my ideal reader. Above all, I want to thank Robert Hanning, my colleague, friend, and first teacher: in many ways this book is a continuous meditation on his work. Finally, of the very many people who have also contributed to this project and who all deserve mention, let me single out Susan and Russell Garrett, Wen Chao, Harriet and Dennis Surdi, and Sheri Duxin.

Chapter One

SACRED AUTHORITY
AND SECULAR POWER

The Bishops of Cambrai

The City

Prologue

In 1023, after a decade of tumultuous and contentious rule, Gerard, bishop of
Cambrai, began a project he had dreamed of since the day he first entered the
city in February 1012.[1] Finally free from enemies at home and abroad, he began
to rebuild the Cathedral of Notre Dame in Cambrai. Fearful of never finishing
the great task that circumstances had forced him to defer for so long, he was
especially grateful for what he considered to be the miraculous discovery of
two quarries of beautiful stone a mere quarter-mile from the city, and the work
was completed in only seven years. In November of 1030 the church was ready
for consecration, and Gerard planned an extraordinary ceremony. Gerard and
Richard, abbot of St. Vaast, each dressed in his most splendid robes, entered
the church carrying in solemn procession the relics of St. Gerí, founding bishop
of Cambrai. And while the clergy and people, weeping with joy, sang the *laudes*
to greet the saint, Gerard placed him directly on the bishop's throne. To his
right and his left the relics of the sainted Merovingian bishops Aubert, Vindicien, and Hadulf had already been arranged as if to assist St. Gerí in officiating
at the ceremony, and in their midst was the bishop's staff that had belonged to
St. Vaast along with that saint's physical remains. Around the altar, in order
according to their rank, were all the sainted dead of the diocese — martyrs,
confessors, virgins — so that they all appeared to join the living members of the

congregation in the holy ceremony: "Who is able to describe worthily the splendor of such glory, or who—even the most eloquent—could encompass such a great office in words? When you see the bodies of the saints in a single congregation with the clerics and people of our diocese; and the chorus of monks mixed with the voices of the canons; and not only the inner city but even the whole surrounding countryside overflowing with crowds of men and women." [Quis enim tantae gloriae pompam digne sufficit enarrare, aut quis dicacissimus verborum ambitu tantam dignitatem poterit cohibere? ubi videlicet sanctorum corpora nostrae dioceseos cum plebe et clero in unum congregata, ubi choros tam monachorum quam et canonicorum catervatim commixtos, ubi etiam non tantum urbem interius, verum et campos exterius passim utriusque sexus multitudine pernatare videres] (3.49.40–45).[2] The chronicler presents this dedication ceremony as a culminating vision of the unity and hierarchy of the world manifest in the community of Cambrai. The whole history of the diocese participates with the living congregation in a display of order, continuity, hierarchy, and just power. In the miraculously completed building, the founding bishops seem to live again to officiate for a congregation that joins the dead with the living, the clergy with the people, monks living under a rule with secular canons, the urban population with the rural, men with women. The sainted dead of the diocese, each in his own rank, make hierarchy and order visible and present. In this powerful ideological representation the community is imagined as the outcome of a continuous past overseen by an unbroken succession of just authorities stretching from the founders of the town to its current bishop. Of course, this representation is a dream. And like all dreams it speaks also in spite of itself: by summoning up its vision of order and social harmony it tells us, too, of social division, competing interests, and conflict—between cleric and lay, canon and monk, man and woman, city and country, the old and the new, the bishop and his flock. And these are not the only conflicts within Cambrai at the turn of the eleventh century.

Cambrai

By the year 1000, the old Gallo-Roman city of Cambrai stood at the climax of a complex political and economic development. Strategically located on the banks of the Escaut, right on the line of division between the two halves of the Carolingian Empire, Cambrai had passed from Francia into the eastern empire in 925. In 948, the emperor granted the bishop comital rights over the urban domain, and in 1007 over the Cambrésis as well, effectively ousting the Caro-lingian urban and provincial counts, the secular lords with whom the bishop had shared power. As prince of the church, the bishop oversaw the more than eighty religious communities of his diocese.[3] And as secular prince he coined money, administered justice, regulated markets,[4] and controlled defense. He was surrounded by a court, originally his hall servants, who by the eleventh century became a distinct urban nobility. In the Empire, the bishop of Cambrai was a great secular lord with no secular peers in his realm. He was an impe-rial functionary, dependent directly on the emperor for his election and an-swerable to the emperor, in whose name he collected taxes, enforced the law, and organized military defense. Like Liège at the same moment, Cambrai around the year 1000 had become an ecclesiastical principality, and the bishop-count was its prince.[5]

At the same time, the Diocese of Cambrai and its bishop were equally part of a completely different sphere of power. As head of one of the most exten-sive dioceses within the thoroughly French Archdiocese of Reims, the bishop of Cambrai was a figure to be reckoned with, not only in the contentious ec-clesiastical politics of Reims but also in the secular affairs of the Capetian world.[6] Moreover, the Diocese of Cambrai was also until 1094 conjoined to the Diocese of Arras, a smaller but economically and strategically equally important terri-tory, and the Artois had never been other than part of France.[7] In brief, Cam-brai was an imperial diocese and an imperial principality, and its bishop was an imperial appointment and great prince of the Empire, but in political culture, economic development, kinship ties, and language Cambrai was equally a part of France.

Some were very aware of the complex identity of Cambrai and attempted to exploit it in the interests of French domination. In 1024, Robert the Pious was put off from invading the Cambrésis—and only by the receipt of lavish gifts and tribute from Bishop Gerard. Baldwin IV, Count of Flanders, eyed the borders of Cambrai eagerly. He erected castles in the border territories and attempted to put up fortifications even within the Cambrésis. In his attempts on the territory, Baldwin made use of a new political force in the person of the castellan of the city. First mentioned in documents in 972,[8] the castellan was officially a non-noble dependent of the bishop, in charge of overseeing those secular matters prohibited for the bishop by ecclesiastical law—such as man-ning the fortifications of the city and overseeing urban defense. His control of weapons, money, and above all a standing garrison of soldiers, however, made his position a powerful point of independent opposition to the authority of the bishop.[9] In effect, the castellan was virtually identical in power to the former secular lord, the urban count of Cambrai. Historians have long noted the significant emergence of castellans in France in the last decades of the tenth century. Officially they are representatives of more distant, legitimate authority—indeed, documents often designate them as *vicarius, vicedominus,* or *vicecomes.* But from their castles or strong houses in strategic locations, they easily dominated the surrounding countryside, which they treated as their own possessions. They set themselves up as arbiters of local justice and collectors of local revenue for themselves and equipped themselves within one generation with titles such as *comes,* with regalia, and often with a genealogy tracing their ancestry back to a mythical or Carolingian origin as signs of their territorial legitimacy. They were men of power, essentially kings in their own realm, whose territorial control they were able to pass on to their offspring.[10]

By the time Gerard came to power, the castellany of Cambrai had become essentially a hereditary office belonging to a Vermandois family with ties to the counts of Flanders. The castellan, Walter of Lens, was subordinate to the bishop in theory but in practice was a creature of the Count of Flanders and entirely out of the bishop's immediate control.[11] He was powerful enough in fact to have seriously disrupted the funeral of Gerard's immediate predecessor, Bishop Herluin, and even to have occupied the bishop's house, using it as a stronghold before Gerard's arrival. Indeed, Emperor Henry II appointed Gerard days before the death of the seriously ill Herluin precisely to avoid what was shaping up to be a coup by a candidate specifically chosen by the castellan and Baldwin IV. During the early years of his reign Gerard used several strategies to gain power over his castellan. Too weak for outright coercion himself, and with his neighbors such as King Robert unwilling or unable to be relied on for aid,[12] Gerard managed to make a kind of peace by binding Walter and his immediate associates into a web of mutual personal obligations and dependencies. In what the chronicler calls "a new custom," Walter was made to swear a series of oaths of personal loyalty to the bishop and to pledge under threat of excommunication to administer justice to the city and people of Cambrai and provide for their defense under the bishop's direction. In return for these oaths the bishop pardoned Walter for all previous offenses against his sovereign rule. The oaths were sworn on relics in the presence of witnesses and were repeated in several venues. There was an exchange of hostages. The agreement, carefully recorded verbatim and preserved, included some of the most powerful people in the Capetian world as witnesses: among others involved in the elaborate public occasions were the bishop of Noyons, the counts of Burgundy and Flanders, and King Robert the Pious himself (3.42.40–43). Georges Duby recognized exactly what this all amounted to: in a ceremony that was only just beginning to be used in France for similar purposes, Gerard made Walter his vassal.[13] The decision to rebuild the Cathedral of Cambrai was clearly prompted by what seemed at the time to be Gerard's decisive victory over his castellan.

To this point it would seem that I have been simply filling in background, describing a state of affairs around the year 1000 and a set of events that led up to the rebuilding of the cathedral in 1024. What I have actually been doing, in fact, is retracing the main narrative line of the strikingly rich text that both presents the events that I have been narrating and, more significantly, was itself an active intervention in them. And in simply retracing this account, I virtually unwittingly tell the story from a very particular position—that of the bishop's secular legitimacy. For the power to have his own particular account of experience written, disseminated, and preserved was itself among the most important weapons in the arsenal of the bishop. Accordingly, in 1024, along with the rebuilding of the cathedral, Gerard embarked on a huge, and I think unprecedented, historiographical enterprise: he began to have compiled the historical rights of the bishops of his diocese. Or shall we say he began to have them invented? The centerpiece of this enterprise is the single work of historical composition whose narrative I have been tracing, the *Gesta episcoporum Cameracensium,* the *Deeds of the Bishops of Cambrai,* and it is therefore to the historiographical argument of this text that we must now turn our attention.

The Deeds of the Bishops of Cambrai

Begun in 1024, the *Gesta episcoporum* is disposed in three books. The first traces the history of the city from its primitive founding to the consecration of Gerard I in 1012. The chronological framework of this first book is provided by the succession of bishops, the spiritual and temporal power being handed from one to the other genealogically, as if in an unbroken chain. At the beginning of this chain stand the sainted founders and patrons of the city, and at the culmination stands Gerard. The second book self-consciously interrupts the chronological presentation to survey, as if by means of an itinerary, the wide network of monasteries and monastic foundations subject to the Diocese of Cambrai. The third book returns to chronology and is entirely occupied with the present on which the historical narrative of the first and the geographical exposition of the second converge, namely the deeds of Bishop Gerard himself. The book begins with his consecration and ends, as originally planned, with his triumph over Walter the Castellan and the rebuilding of the church.

As we now have it, the *Gesta episcoporum* is the product of two rewritings. The exhaustive researches of Erik van Mingroot have demonstrated that the whole work—that is, books 1 and 2 and book 3 to chapter 50—was planned and executed between 1024 and 1025 by a single writer, a canon of Cambrai, personally close to Bishop Gerard, who remains still otherwise unidentified. Around 1036 the chronicle may have been updated to include the events of the decade after 1025. This updating was very likely done by the original writer. Later, during the reign of Bishop Lietbert, who succeeded Gerard in 1049, a *Vita Lietberti* was added to book 3 to create the text as we find it in all the eleventh-century manuscripts. To make the addition seamless, van Mingroot argues, around 1055 the writer of the *Vita Lietberti* rewrote the chapters following chapter 50 of book 3. The notice of the beginning of the rebuilding of the cathedral in 1023 was certainly part of the original chapter 49; the description of the dedication in 1030 had to have been added later, most likely in the original updating.[14]

Along with the composition of the *Gesta episcoporum,* Gerard ordered the construction of the textual archive on which the book was based. For the work demanded a library. Existing material needed to be gathered together for the benefit of the writer of the chronicle, while new texts needed to be composed to fill gaps in the historical record. Thus the writer of the *Gesta episcoporum* began, under Gerard's instruction, in 1023 by first writing a life of St. Gerí, the city's founder.[15] And at the same time Gerard also commissioned the writing of several other saints' lives and miracle collections relevant to the enterprise, including the *Life of St. Aubert,* which I shall discuss in the second part of this chapter.[16] Digested in the *Gesta episcoporum,* the newly composed lives appear as if they were ancient and venerable texts that long ago recorded the origins of the authority of the bishops of Cambrai.

The climactic moment of the *Gesta episcoporum* is reached with the dedication of the church and the display of order, continuity, hierarchy, and power that it celebrates. This moment is first of all a narrative climax—all opposition is quelled, the bishop is firmly in control, and the building that had been begun in fear is completed in joy. More importantly, it forms the climax of an argument that has been pursued in different modalities throughout the extremely various events narrated by the chronicle. The argument most centrally concerns the relation between sovereignty and justice. In brief, the text uses a variety of strategies to contend that the achievement of justice on earth is due to the providential coming into being of a hierarchically ordered society—specifically Christian society, ruled over by a bishop. Modern acquaintance with the chronicle has largely been shaped by Georges Duby's powerful examination of trifunctional social taxonomy in *The Three Orders*, which carefully analyzes Gerard's speech against the proponents of the Peace of God as the chronicle represents it. This speech, we remember, provides a very early instance of the proposition that human society is naturally divided into three reciprocally dependent orders—*oratores, bellatores, laboratores*. In his reading of the speech, Duby was, for various reasons, most concerned with its immediate occasion, Gerard's opposition to the so-called Peace of God.[17] The emergence of the peace movement is undoubtedly an extremely important stimulus to the historiographical concern with the bishop's power, but the peace movement is by no means a primary interest of the chronicle. It enters as a small part of a rather extensive concern not with peace but with the nature of sovereignty. The narrative ends with the dedication of a church. Where does it begin?

It does not begin with Adam as Gregory of Tours does, for example, or with a story of foundation by an eponymous relative of Aeneas, a story that will become virtually the standard procedure of later medieval chroniclers. The *Gesta episcoporum* opens rather with a general account of why people began to live in cities. Men at first, writes the chronicler, lived scattered and wandered like wild beasts. They were uncivilized, having no social life (neque mos neque cultus), and, neither being ruled by reason nor knowing anything of the divine, they were dominated entirely by blind desire. After some time, they built protective walls for themselves, and having thus come together they learned to keep their word and to serve justice and became accustomed to submitting their own desires to the desires of others (fidem colere et iustitiam retinere discerent, et aliis parere sua voluntate consuescerent). Indeed, writes the chronicler, they thought it right not only to labor for the common good but even to sacrifice their own lives for it (ac non modo labores excipiendos communis commodi causa, set etiam vitam amittendam estimarent). Thus the prudential building of the city is the immediate cause for the coming into being of a just civil society obedient to imperatives higher than blind need (1.1.25–40).

Now, this "hard" primitivist myth of the naturally savage state of humanity is a commonplace of classical antiquity[18] very rarely found in medieval texts, first of all because it conflicts with the Genesis version of the original human state on the literal level—Adam is placed in paradisal garden, not in a savage wasteland—and more importantly because it conflicts with the moral readings commonly made of it. Indeed, Lactantius's *Institutiones,* from which the chronicler seems to have taken this account, his text often echoing it verbally, presents the classical myth precisely as an illustration of the folly of classical philosophy. Lactantius uses the myth to argue that classical philosophy has no knowledge of the true relation between God and humanity and therefore no insight into the meaning of justice. For Lactantius, justice, piety, and mercy are part of the original human essence: what needs to be explained is not why people help others and seek help from them but why they refuse.[19] Because the hard primitivist myth derives justice from something external to the natural condition of humanity, it has exactly the opposite explanatory force: whereas Lactantius imagines justice as an origin and an essence from which humanity has unnaturally fallen, the hard primitivist myth posits rather fear, suspicion, and mutual aggression as the natural state of humanity and justice as a historically fragile prize that humanity painfully seeks to attain.

With a simple change in explanatory direction, the chronicler seems to go out of his way to answer Lactantius's argument by taking the words out of Lactantius's mouth. For, says the chronicler, this change in the human condition, and the building of cities that brought it about, is providential in itself. Exactly what Lactantius called a base and absurd fantasy—that wild and dangerous people hiding in fields and foliage became thus gentle and civilized as an outcome of prudential activity—not only is explicitly embraced ("non enim vile aut absurdum fuerat, homines agris et tectis silvestribus abditos ex feris et inmanibus mites reddi ac mansuetos," writes the chronicler) but even more profoundly is said to signify much higher things (longe altior rerum causa portendebatur). Unknowingly these builders of cities "usefully served a future posterity; namely, that by these walls they thought to construct nothing but what I might call royal edifices. But soon the future holy mother church would obtain in them the principal fortress of its dignity and its apostolic seat." [superventurae posteritati utiliter ministraret; videlicet ut ipsis suis moenibus nihil aliud pretendere viderentur, nisi quaedam ut ita dicam regia aedificia construere, in quibus mox futura sancta mater aecclesia principalem suae dignitatis arcem et apostolicam sedem obtineret] (1.1.37–40). The ternary figure that so intrigued Duby is already articulated here at the beginning of the chronicle—not, however, as a social typology of simultaneously dependent functions but rather as a diachronic chain of social production. Humanity labors, institutes secular order, and in building the secular city creates the conditions for a radically new future. The appearance of the church transforms the royal city into its own "principal fortress and apostolic seat" and thus provides human work with its true cause and ultimate goal. At the end of the process the church emerges as sole governor, described in military and imperial language. Like Gerard's ceremonial dedication of the Cathedral of Notre Dame, this myth of origin gathers up all of humanity in a single representation that materializes the double significance of the word *ecclesia:* the material building itself and the lawful structure of the community that it calls into being to assemble there in ritual celebration of itself. In the process, the emperor and his sovereignty over the bishop disappear. The bishop is supreme over all.

Violence and Historical Time

One reason for the appeal to the writer of the *Gesta episcoporum* of the rarely invoked classical commonplace of primitive society is undoubtedly its evocation for him of the devastation following the Viking raids of the tenth century, a social trauma that was still part of living memory. As such, the primitivist myth serves psychologically to contain violence by locking it away in a past absolutely other than the present — it is savage, pagan, unruled.

The first book of the *Gesta episcoporum* is filled with origin stories of the various institutions connected to the diocesan governance of the bishop of Cambrai. Abbeys are founded, churches are erected, shrines fill the landscape. The text is accordingly peppered with miracles — the blind see, the lame walk — that manifest the spiritual gifts of founding individuals and the sacred presence of the places they found. Procedures that are institutional and routine in the present of the chronicle are thus represented at their origin as exceptional performances by charismatic individuals. The sudden eruption of the sacred into ordinary life creates the past qua past, utterly different from the present that charisma inaugurates, and this separation gives birth to history. The third book of the *Gesta episcoporum,* being occupied entirely with the present, is at pains to stress the absolutely routine and institutional basis of the bishop's power. From the perspective of power derived from election and public rituals of consecration, charisma is disruptive and dangerous. Indeed, charismatic individuals appear in the third book only as enemies of social order, whether they claim to have a "letter from heaven," like the proponents of the Peace of God, or claim access to a special revelation outside the institutional church, like the so-called Manicheans who appeared in Arras in 1025.[20]

The chronicler negotiates the passage from charismatic founding to contemporary legitimacy by filling time and making it continuous. Historically full and unbroken time is the mark of the continuous presence of the sacred in the institutional regularity of the church and its governance by the bishop. The charismatic act is once for all, exceptional, and constitutive; the continuity of the church is its guarantee. In no place is the significance of chronological continuity for social legitimation more apparent than in the chronicler's treatment of the death of St. Vindicien, third bishop of Cambrai after Vaast, precisely because here we find one of the only places in the first book where the regular chronology of the narrative breaks apart. Prompted immediately by the historian's anxiety over present social disorder and violence, the narrative rupture leads to a lament for lost time. When he reaches the moment to tell of Vindicien's death, the chronicler addresses his reader directly to deplore the absence of written records about the sainted bishop. Much writing has surely been lost, he says, on account of the civil violence (seditionibus procellosis) by which the church has been frequently shipwrecked. And he poignantly goes on to insist that a large volume must once have existed, containing an account of Vindicien's life and miracles. This volume, he imagines, has disappeared, its leaves disbound and scattered to the winds [Fieri enim potest, ut cum tantis subversionibus aecclesiarum una etiam volumina, quibus series vitae et miraculorum huius sancti viri continebatur, auris quidem ridentibus, disperirent] (1.28.48–51). All we know about Vindicien is that he is buried in a church on Mount St. Eloi (1.28.56–58).

At this point, the narrative suddenly leaps forward several hundred years to the tenth century to tell of the discovery of Vindicien's tomb. The young sons of a nobleman of Arras, being educated in letters, are sent into the woods by their writing master to make ink. Picking their way through the dense growth of thorns and brambles, the boys come upon the ruined church. While the older boys pray, the younger investigate the interior. One of them begins to dig below the church floor when suddenly he is struck blind. He screams for help and says that he is being punished because of his violation of the tomb. Vowing to become a monk, the young boy soon recovers his sight and returns home "thoroughly chastised" [puer haud mediocriter castigatione rediit] (1.29.60). The news of the event spreads throughout the region, and people spontaneously begin to venerate the place. Finally, the whole affair is reported to the bishop, who has the body raised and rebuilds and reconsecrates his burial place as a monastic church.

The motif of blindness and sight is elaborated in two following miraculous cures at the newly created monastic shrine. A young blind boy is cured when he is taken to Vindicien's altar; a blind noblewoman, about to depart on pilgrimage to Rome, has a vision the night before and goes instead to Vindicien's tomb, where she miraculously gains her sight. These two thoroughly conventional miracles remind the chronicler of a third, and the narrative makes yet another sudden and even more unexpected leap forward to the chronicler's own days and the year 1006.[21] Emperor Henry II, Robert the Pious, and Richard, Duke of Normandy, form an alliance to aid Baldwin IV in a struggle with the Count of Valenciennes. Richard's Normans arrive in the Artois, and they raid the monastery in a scene of horrific violence. The Norman soldiers mercilessly slaughter the monks and pillage the treasury, even stealing the ecclesiastical vestments. When they begin to divide the treasure among themselves, however, they are suddenly struck down miraculously in a scene reminiscent of romanesque paintings of the torments of hell:[22] "Some were seized by a demon and twisted; some had their tongues on fire; some bit themselves, others were folded back on themselves, their thighs burned out, a miserable torture." [Plerique arrepti a daemonio torquebantur; alii linguis adusti, alii proprio morsu precisis, plerique cruribus exustis, misero cruciatu plectebantur] (1.33.38–40). The soldiers flee, and on his return to Normandy Duke Richard orders an inquisition into the affair "sub sacramento" and demands restitution of everything taken. One of the men secretly keeps a little bell and afterwards becomes paralyzed. He confesses his guilt, makes double restitution, and is completely cured.

This sequence of stories begs to be read as a meditation on history itself. The discovery of Vindicien's burial place, including the motifs of clearing away the undergrowth and digging into the ground, and the series of miraculous cures is entirely about the process of bringing the buried past to light and preserving it in writing. Yet, as Monika Otter has taught us to see,[23] the desire for the past is not without peril: in the story of discovery, the boy who dug into the tomb because he wanted to see what was there committed an outrage in the process and was "thoroughly punished" for it by the inability to see anything at all. That danger is surmountable by the proper reverence: by devoting himself to the saint he has so irreverently found, his vision is restored. Similarly, the soldier paralyzed for wanting to keep a bit of spiritual treasure for himself is cured after doubly restoring it to its rightful place. But these surmountable dangers are merely screens for a much greater fear: the fear of present violence that threatens the historiographical scheme and triumphal structure of the chronicle itself. Violence refuses to stay safely buried in the prehistoric past. It erupts again and again into the historian's consciousness of the present. Things fall into ruin, books disappear, churches are pillaged and destroyed, and it is not only Franks and Vikings — whom the chronicler tellingly lumps together as *gentilitas* — but above all the Christian princes of the contemporary world who turn cities into wastelands and cause people to live like beasts. Who can govern them?

The Power of the Prince-Bishop

The answer to the crisis of violence that the chronicle proposes with ever increasing urgency is clear. The hybrid figure of the prince-bishop in whose daily activities the sacred is institutionalized and routinized is the last and only hope for secular peace and justice. It is thus the secular affairs of the bishop that are dwelt on with great attention in the third book. The language is entirely conservative — Bishop Gerard is said to reform deteriorated institutions to their former prosperity and spiritual dedication or to restore good customs that have been long in disuse. He is presented as standing last, heir to the long accumulation of spiritual goods that he wisely invests. But what is in fact narrated is a record of great political innovation. More and more, the bishop uses the full panoply of coercive spiritual weapons at his disposal to rule and regulate secular affairs. In the process, there emerges a new being for the church — it becomes identical to secular society — and a new sense of the meaning of Christianity itself, as the bishop claims an ever wider authority over ever more intimate aspects of secular life.

I have already remarked on the negative light in which any instance of spiritual privilege is treated in the third book, and I have attributed this to the need to ground the bishop's power in institutional legitimacy. It is not the charismatic gifts of the individual bishop but rather his legitimate election and consecration that invest him with the power to rule. What makes him a good bishop are his abilities as a good governor.[24] Accordingly, with only one exception the third book is entirely free of the miraculous.[25] And that exception is telling precisely because the miraculous here opens entirely new and unexpected spiritual territory. During the account of Bishop Gerard's efforts to reform the Abbey of St. Ghislain, at the time part of the possessions of the Count of Mons, there is a cluster of three miracles. Only the first of these miracles is in the chronicle's main narrative line; the other two are prompted by the first and reported immediately after it as stories that Bishop Gerard liked to tell. All three are stories of miraculous punishments, and all three are involved rather with the bishop's relations with lay people and his control of a nexus of institutional procedures—penance, excommunication, burial, and above all the offering of the Eucharist—than with the revelation of special spiritual gifts. Together, the three stories form a very concentrated inventional place, pulling into a single thematic unity various aspects of ecclesiastical power. Let me summarize the three stories briefly.

1. A thief, dependent on Count Rainer of Mons, who is described as "himself a thief accustomed to cherish thieves" (ipse raptor raptoribus favere consueverat) is in the habit of despoiling the Abbey of Saint Ghislain at Celles. (One desperately wants to look *through* the text here—I take it that what is being described is the collection of taxes by a knight acting as the agent of a secular lord. The monastery, however, claims the land to be immune.) He is arrested by Bishop Gerard, handed over to the bishop of Utrecht for a year, and then released after the intercession of his relatives. He swears (promittentem videlicet et sancte deierantem) to Bishop Gerard "that he will withdraw from his thievery and remain faithful to the church with all devotion" (quod rapinis se subtraheret, fidelis aecclesiae cum omni devotione mansurus) and then goes back on his oath. He dies, and again at the intercession of his family and unbeknownst to the bishop, he is buried in the monastery's cemetery. Two years later, his tomb is opened for another burial, and, except for one shoe, not a trace of his body or clothes is found there (3.20).

2. In the days of Bishop Adalbaldus of Utrecht (1010–27), the Maritime Frisians had the custom of not taking the Eucharist on Easter. Offered the Eucharist, one of them, "prompted by the Devil" (instinctu diabolico agitatus) says he would rather have a big glass of beer than "that banquet from the celestial table" (illud celestis epulum mensae) and says that anyone who eats of it will surely die during the coming year. All the people depart in fear, and he goes to the local tavern to drink. Coming home drunk, he falls off his horse, breaks his neck, and dies. The

"blasphemer"—that is all he is ever called—because of his stature in the town, is buried in the cemetery (in atrio). Bishop Adalbaldus hears of this while he is in Saxony with Emperor Henry and is outraged. He orders the body to be disinterred, but since no one will do it out of fear of retribution from the family, the bishop makes the journey home himself, orders a rope put around the feet of the corpse, and has the body dragged from the tomb to a place along the roadside out of town. Dragged for the space of a mile, the dead man, although already buried for fifteen days, vomits up the prodigious amount of beer he drank on Easter (3.21).

3. Albert of Vermandois, brother of Count Odo of Vermandois, character-ized as a liar, perjurer, and blasphemer, is struck with a grave illness, and at the urging of Waleran, provost of the Monastery of Saint Hune-gonde, becomes a monk. As his health improves, and at the urging of his mother and friends who think he is insane to have given up wealth and power, he goes back to secular life. His health deteriorates again, and when he is at the point of death "stupid canons" (stulti canonici) bring him the Eucharist. When he tastes it, Albert cries out with his last breath, "The sword that the clerics brought me has killed me" (Fer-rum, inquit, quod mihi clerici detulerunt, me occidit). Waleran and other bystanders pry his mouth open with a knife and show his mother and friends that his tongue has been incinerated (moribundum os diffi-cillime cultello reclusit, et linguam usque ad palatum, miserabile visu, crematam matri ac fratri et ceteris adstantibus aperte monstravit). The chronicler comments on the appropriateness of the punishment for one who had always used his mouth to lie and swear falsely (3.23).

All three stories narrate vivid acts of retribution against lay people who re-fuse to be subject to the sovereign bishops whom the chronicle presumes they are supposed to obey. Significantly, the stories do not involve the bishop's posi-tion within the closed world of the church; all three rather involve secular lords who have defied him, and they present a conflict between ecclesiastical and secu-lar structures of power, which are represented as if they were strictly sepa-rable: powerful families and territorial princes on the one hand, bishops and monastic foundations on the other. All three assert the bishop's right to regu-late the conduct of secular life and secular individuals from a position of power that extends even beyond the grave. At the very moment that various ecclesiastical reform movements were beginning to attempt to create the sharpest possible separation—legal, sexual, and so forth—between the clergy and the laity (to "clericalize the church," as Jo Ann McNamara recently remarked),[26] the church begins to claim for itself an ever larger arena of secular power and to assert itself as the authoritative governor of the conduct of secular life. In the ensuing conflicts with other structures of secular power—familial, territorial, political, and so forth—with which it is in fact entirely entangled, the secular power of the church is conceptualized by ecclesiastical writers as occupying the highest position in a hierarchical ladder of power, and the secular power of the bishop is posited as absolute.[27] Although the *Gesta episcoporum* is entirely occupied with his daily affairs, the prince-bishop comes before us not as an imperial functionary but as a transcendent entity. Created by his ordination and anointing, he is himself a "twinned being" like Christ.[28] His power centers on his special relationship to the institutional practices represented in the cluster of stories I have just paraphrased: excommunication, the imposition of public penance, and the regulation of proper burial are all at this time being put to intensive and new uses. At the very center of this conceptualization is the Eucharist, one of the two sacraments with biblical precedent, which the bishop alone can offer or deny. By the end of the century, innovative formulations about the nature of the Eucharist and innovative uses of it as a real social practice will eventuate in a transformed sense of secular society as the *societas christiana*. Like the church building in which the congregation gathers to see it displayed, the Eucharist is a figure of the bishop's sovereignty.

The Eucharist and Power

As Miri Rubin among others has pointed out, until the eleventh century and the famous dispute between Berengar of Tours and Lanfranc over the real presence of Christ in the Eucharist, eucharistic practices and theological issues such as "the nature of sacramental change, the nature of Christ's presence, the moment of transformation, the symbolic link between matter and God"[29] remained rather loosely formulated. Rather than theological inquiry into the nature of the sacrament, tenth-century questions regarding the Eucharist tend to be raised concerning practice and appropriate use. For example, Gerbert, archbishop of Reims, wrote three times about eucharistic matters in his letters: once regarding the question of the seriousness of excommunication,[30] once protesting that the judgment of the pope against the archbishop of Sens was illegal and therefore

could not separate him from the sacrament no matter what the pope said,[31] and
the third time acknowledging that reconciled penitents ought to be allowed com-
munion.[32] Scholars have, however, remarked a discernable drift in the course of
the tenth century toward realism in the general notion of the Eucharist's substance.[33] It seems to me that this drift in the direction of realism—sufficiently
marked that when the dispute between Berengar and Lanfranc arose the realist
Lanfranc took up what had clearly become the orthodox position—is inseparable from the need to distinguish the bishop's power from the power of any
other secular lord on ontological and absolute grounds. And the need for the
bishop to make this distinction is urgent, for this moment when the bishop has
become institutionally identical to any other secular lord is the moment when
various secular lords are themselves becoming able territorial administrators.
Rather than looking to the few strictly theological discussions of the sacrament,
one needs to consider its deployment in bishops' lives and other historical and
hagiographical writing. Deployed in the miracles we have been considering, the
Eucharist acts as a powerful conceptual center, not only symbolically demonstrating the authority of those who are empowered to administer it,[34] but physically bodying it forth as a fully materialized spiritual presence with all-too-real
material effects.

   In the miracles under discussion, the power of the Eucharist is visible
entirely in the context of excommunication and in its baleful effects on those
who doubt its power or partake of it without being worthy. Rather than leaving
the material world behind to show forth spiritual presence in visions of bodily
transformation such as the famous Gregorian miracles of a baby rising above the
altar or a finger floating in the glass of wine,[35] the power of the Eucharist manifests itself in the real bodily effects of spiritual retribution against those who
contemn it or doubt its power. Albert of Vermandois, for example, experiences
the taste of the host as a sword, and its effect is to incinerate his tongue. This
is, of course, a direct literalization of the common Latin idiom for war, *ignis
atque ferrum:* the warfare by which he lives kills him. Similarly, the excommunicated knight of the first miracle is fully obliterated in the tomb he wrongfully
occupies—nothing remains of him save one shoe. I think it is telling that we
find proverbial usages, comic effects, and vernacular elements in the vocabulary
of these stories,[36] as well as the appearance of folk beliefs, such as the Frisian's
fear that anyone who eats the host on Easter will die during the year. They witness precisely the oral, secular currency of these stories that manifest the awesome power of the Eucharist and of the bishop who controls access to it.

The Eucharist shares this special power with the representation of the church building itself as a sacred place where the community, of which the Eucharist is both sign and manifestation, assembles to see it displayed. This is a place that one violates at extreme peril.[37] We have already discussed the spectacular vengeance meted out to the Norman soldiers who despoiled Arras. Individuals similarly laying claim to what abbeys or churches claim as their own property or privileges meet similarly dire fates if they ignore excommunication.[38] Worst of all is the case of Bishop Berengarius. Wrongfully appointed, he behaves like a warrior, makes and breaks oaths of alliance to secular lords, pursues one of his enemies into the very church he should protect, and kills him there with his own sword. Berengarius dies a horrific death when the founding bishop of Cambrai, St. Gerí, rises up from the dead to strike him down (1.83).

The context of all these stories, as I said a moment ago, is the rapidly increasing use of excommunication as a tool of governance of lay society. To be effective, the mysterious power of the Eucharist had to become an object of fear and desire, its deprivation a matter of great consequence to the lay population. It thus became no mere symbol of spiritual union but the very place where the spiritual intersects with the material world, its proper use a matter of literal life or death. That the transformation was in fact successful is nicely attested by the *Gesta episcoporum*'s Aquitanian contemporary Adhemar of Chabannes. He writes of the "new observance" employed by the bishop of Limoges in the last years of the tenth century: to punish the depredations of warriors and the oppression of the poor (*rapina militum et devastatione pauperum*), the bishop ordered the cessation of "the divine service and the holy sacrifice" in all the monasteries and churches of his diocese — an act, Adhemar adds, that was considered excommunication.[39] As Richard Landes points out, this new observance is the old practice of the interdict, here put to the new use of coercing a secular lord "through arousing the innocent to protest"[40] by depriving them of the sacrament, a protest unthinkable in earlier centuries before the Eucharist had become so ardently desired.

The realism implied in the punitive miracles of the chronicle is forcefully asserted in the voice of Bishop Gerard himself in the record of Gerard's inquisition of the heretics who appeared in Arras in 1025. Composed most probably for the bishop by the writer of the *Gesta episcoporum,* it is distributed in the form of a letter to a certain Bishop R.[41] At the heart of the heresy is an attack on the efficacy of the church, of its personnel, and of the sacraments. Gerard answers their contentions at great length.[42] His argument presents a detailed explanation of the power of the Eucharist, much of it taken fairly directly from Paschasius, that fully takes up the realist position, along with a demonstration of the sanctity of the altar, the priesthood, the anointed bishop, and the church building itself. The exposition traces the same historical course that we have seen several times in the chronicle. The sudden and exceptional eruption of the divine into the secular world that happened once only in the distant past is reiterated by the routine offering made daily by the priest in the church, and its spiritual effects are visible in day-to-day material life. Secular history thus becomes the privileged sphere of spiritual performance. The spiritual presence, invisible in itself to the ordinary eye, is both made visible and made real by the routine performance of the rite that only the priest can perform in the sole place where it can be performed. In passage after passage the series "Eucharist, bishop, church, salvation" is reiterated.[43] At one point the series is brought together in a passage that could be read as an explication of the ceremony of consecration that began this chapter. The church building is the place where a multitude of oppositions is unified—the past with the present, angels with humanity, God with his angels, humanity with God—and where a diversity of people become united (unanimes), free from all that might divide them, into a single community. Sanctified by the bishop, the community passes from secular experience to a direct contemplation of the majesty of God (maiestatis Dei):

> Indeed, for this reason the house itself has the name *church,* since it contains the Church—that is to say, the people called together by him who unifies them so that they may dwell in the house. It is sanctified by the bishop so that angels might arrive, and men entering it would know that it holds them free from all base speech, and scurrility, and useless thoughts. . . . Thus entering the house of God, the church, where God and His angels are, we must take off the shoes of mortal deeds and think about the conversation of angels and the present majesty of God, and we must invoke the name of the Lord in fervent hymns and spiritual psalms, so that what the psalmist said will be complete in us: "Strengthen, O God, what you have wrought in us; to your holy temple, which is in Jerusalem [etc.]" (Psal. 67).

> [Porro ipsa domus idcirco vocabulum habet ecclesiae, qui continet Ecclesiam, id est populum convocatum ab eo, qui facit unanimes habitare

in domo. Quae ideo sanctificatur ab episcopo, ut in ea velit esse adventus angelorum, et homines in eam introeuntes ab omni turpiloquio, et scurrilitate, et inutili cogitatione norint se continere. . . . Intrantes igitur domum Dei, ecclesiam, ubi Dominus et angeli eius sunt, oportet nos exuere mortuae actionis calceamentis, et cogitare de conversatione angelorum, et de praesentia maiestatis Dei, et assiduis hymnis et psalmis spiritualibus invocare nomen Domini, ut illud compleatur in nobis quod ait Psalmista: "Confirma hoc, Deus, quod operatus es in nobis a templo sancto tuo, quod est in Jerusalem" (Psal. 67).][44]

The building is the place of full presence, but to narrate it the writer traverses a series of hierarchies. There is an outward ascent in the place itself that passes from humanity at large to the bishop, then to angels, and finally to God, and an inward, contemplative ascent that doubles the first (oportet . . . cogitare de conversatione angelorum et de praesentia maiestatis Dei), passing from the local church to Jerusalem.[45]

Reality Fictions

In considering the miracles of the *Gesta episcoporum,* I have at several points called attention to them as inventional places. Monastic pedagogic and meditational practice, as is well known, developed from Roman topical invention. Images—the more vivid the better—form nodal points that can connect long chains of textual and experiential associations, making them memorable and forming powerful emotional starting places for further associational activity.[46] Vivid scenes of retribution and punishment, for example, furnish prime instances of rhetorical *enargeia* and beg to be read as what Mary Carruthers has called "cognitive fictions" with no stake in their literal or mimetic truth. The classic instance of this distinction between cognitive and mimetic truth can be found in those visual representations of the New Jerusalem in Beatus commentaries in which architectural detail varies from copy to copy of the same original—a copy from Spain, for example, shows mozarabic keyhole arches, while a thirteenth-century English copy of the very same original shows gothic points.[47] The truth of cognitive fictions lies in their pedagogic or ethical efficacy, not in their mimetic value. The sacraments and elements of the liturgy serve similar pedagogic purposes as starting points for meditational exercises intended to end in an

intuition of the absolute that lies beyond all such images. And the church building itself is a generally useful receptacle and indexing system of commonplaces
for a variety of memory systems.[48]

Yet in the *Gesta episcoporum* these strikingly efficient memory places cannot be simply called "cognitive fictions," for their inventional and associational
efficacy depends on their claim to mimetic truth value, just as the Eucharist is,
in these texts, not merely symbolically efficacious as a starting point for meditation on Christ's incarnation and sacrifice but their real reiteration. In the *Gesta
episcoporum* and in the *Acta synodi Attrebatensis,* the church building is a meditational place precisely because it is also a real building. One entering it is
prompted to meditate on "the conversation of angels and the majesty of God."
But it is also more than a memory place: it is the literal place where the heavenly hierarchy of angels and the society of men meet and find their proper habi-
tation. The emphasis thus falls on the literal truth of the cognitive image.

The *Acta synodi Attrebatensis* returns to the church as literally both a material and a spiritual entity in the discussion of ecclesiastical administration and
the significance of ordination. For the Church consists, Gerard argues, of both
men and angels (Sancta Ecclesia . . . ex angelis et hominibus constat), each organized in a hierarchy and each linked with the other: "Part of the Church, made
from men enjoying the angelic society, which is ranged in distinct orders, already reigns with God in heaven; the other part, also in distinct orders, is still
in exile on earth, and it longs for the heavenly society, where, according to the
Apostle, its tabernacle is not constructed." (Quae, partim ex hominibus soci-
etate angelica in ordinibus distinctis perfruens, iam cum Deo regnat in coelo;
partim vero in ordinibus distinctis adhuc peregrinatur in terra, et ad supernam
societatem suspirat, ubi, secundum Apostolum, tabernaculum est non manu-
factum.) In this heavenly tabernacle, sitting on the right hand of the Father, is
Christ in majesty: "through whom kings reign, and founders of the law discern
justice, who rules the heavenly and earthly realm, that is the whole republic,
and disposes and governs the whole army, the heavenly and spiritual as well as
the earthly and temporal, in distinct orders, and presides over the supernal and
earthly courts. In a wonderful order he manages the ministry of angels and men
through the variety and occasions of time." (per quem reges regnant, et con-
ditores legum justa decernunt, coelestem ac terrenum principatum, cunctam
videlicet rempublicam regens, et universam militiam, tam coelestem et spiritualem quam terrenam et temporalem, distinctis ordinibus disponens ac mod-

erans, et supernae atque mundanae curiae praesidens, miro ordine angelorum hominumque ministeria pro temporum varietate et opportunitate dispensat.)[49] The meditational chain culminates in the real body of Christ, of which the church, the Eucharist, and the consecrated bishop are all real figures. It ties the earthly world of time and space to the spiritual world in an ontology. Meditation on earthly order or earthly rule does not begin with a "cognitive fiction"; the symbolic connection between earth and heaven is epistemologically efficacious precisely because it traces the real.

To support the ontological connection between the heavenly and earthly orders, Gerard directly refers to the authority of both the Old and New Testaments and then continues: "And so the blessed Dionysius the Areopagite, namely the bishop and venerable father, just as he learned from the apostle Paul, who was rapt up to the third heaven, saw the heavenly secrets, and wrote two books about the angelic and the ecclesiastical principality." (Unde beatus Dionysius Areopagites, antistes videlicet et venerabilis pater, sicut didicit a Paulo apostolo, qui raptus est usque ad tertium coelum, vidit coelestia secreta, duos libros de angelico et ecclesiastico principatu scripsit.)[50] M.-D. Chenu has discussed the importance of Pseudo-Dionysian ontology for Victorine meditation and pedagogy, and Gabrielle Spiegel has drawn attention to it in the historiographical schemata of Suger's *Life of Louis the Fat.*[51] What I want to underline here is that this same ontology that takes the "varietate temporum" as both symbolic and more than symbolic—a real reflection of divine unity—provides an essential groundwork for the eleventh-century writer of history. I do not at all maintain that Pseudo-Dionysian ontology causes the writer to take historical change seriously, rather the reverse: the urgent need to render comprehensible the ever more complex transformations in secular order prepares the writer to understand the implications of Pseudo-Dionysius for his own task.

Thus the city of Cambrai—reflection on its temporal order is a vehicle for perceiving mystically the order in heaven. In the historical vision of the *Gesta episcoporum,* Cambrai stands symbolically for Christianity itself. Its emergence from a past that is imagined alternatively as pagan and as bestial is a promise of a future in which all humanity will be saved because all are Christian. The city ruled in historical time by its bishop is a temporal symbol of the New City, the heavenly Jerusalem ruled without mediation by Christ in the reality of his majesty. In the present of the text, Bishop Gerard is the central figure, not because he is exceptionally endowed with charismatic grace, but precisely because through his ordination and consecration he holds the keys to inclusion in this promised future.

Yet the Pseudo-Dionysian ontological connection between the local and the universal is a two-way street. If its ontology allows the writer to assert the universal truth made manifest by secular history, only in the secular history of Cambrai is such truth made visible. Cambrai can never be entirely a sign. To bear its symbolic weight, Cambrai is always the historical Cambrai where the bishop coins money, grants privileges to the merchants, collects revenue from his dependents, judges malefactors, and struggles for supremacy with all the resources available to him against those who effectively challenge his power. And in this Cambrai, the bishop's supremacy qua bishop is not a universally held certainty: it is a polemical position wielded by the bishop himself in his struggle with others. To show him repeatedly triumphing over his adversaries is at the same time to show him constantly being challenged by other powers. Even in the affairs of the church, the bishop is in constant struggle, not only with his colleague bishops over questions ranging from succession to the Peace of God, but with his manifest inferiors. For example, the chronicle contains a long letter—itself a small legal treatise on excommunication—addressed by Gerard to the archdeacons of Liège, angrily reminding them that when a bishop excommunicates someone, he *stays* excommunicated even if he should go to another diocese. For it seems that Gerard had excommunicated for incestuous marriage a certain Erlebaldus, who, upon leaving Cambrai, returned with his wife to his ancestral domain in the Diocese of Liège, where he enjoyed the privileges of his wealth and power and was subsequently ceremoniously buried "inter fideles" (1.28). To win in these constant struggles required very powerful weapons such as those we have been considering here: first of all, a magnificent building, where the bishop could sit in public display on a splendid throne and make the claim of his own authority visible to the assembled community; second, the power over a sacrament that was imagined to be no mere symbol but a vehicle of the most awesome might; third, the city itself—not only the institutional position of sacred authority legitimated by divine sanction but the control of an effectively coercive governmental apparatus that could administer land, collect income, extract labor, mount defense, hand down judicial rulings, and intimidate those who would prefer not to listen; and, not least important, a big book that tells this very story and a library of precedents to support it.

THE FOUNDER

The Life of Bishop Aubert

The new life of the Merovingian bishop St. Aubert, along with St. Gerí, one of the patrons of the city of Cambrai, was an important part of the archive compiled by Bishop Gerard for his massive historiographical project. According to the *Gesta episcoporum,* in which it is epitomized as if it were an ancient and venerable source, the *Vita Autberti Cameracensis et Atrebatensis*[52] was written at the order of Bishop Gerard of Cambrai by Fulbert, "doctor clarissimus." This "outstandingly learned Fulbert" has almost universally been taken to be the famous Fulbert, bishop of Chartres. There are many good reasons for making the identification: it was by no means unusual in the eleventh century to want to commission a famous author to write a new saint's life or to revise an old one.[53] In fact it was highly desirable, for the fame of the writer lent immediate credibility to the truth claims made by the text. Fulbert of Chartres was a perfect candidate for Bishop Gerard. He was an experienced hagiographer,[54] Gerard and Fulbert were educated together at Reims by Gerbert, and they both remained part of the same clerical intellectual circle. Gerard was likely to have been especially desirous to have the life of St. Aubert, a patron of the city, written by someone of immense prestige.[55] As we shall see, the text is indeed "outstandingly learned."

The *Vita Autberti* had to have been written some time after 1015, the date of Aubert's translation and third year of Gerard's episcopacy, which is mentioned in the text, and before 1024, the year of the composition of the *Gesta episcoporum,* which contains its epitome. There are thus two contexts for the production of the *Life of St. Aubert.* The text may have been written to be part of the consecration of the new church housing the saint's relics. Whether written in time for the inaugural feast or not, it is certainly written to be part of the permanent celebration of his cult. Read on his feast day, December 13, as part of the divine office, it provides a point of reference for the community, whose worship thus centers on the spiritual treasure administered to them by the bishop, Aubert's successor. Second, it is part of a politically useful historical record, for from its inception it is intended to be in Gerard's historical library, where it is a central piece of the justification for the bishop's rule. Just as the second book of the *Gesta episcoporum* gives an account of the founding and subsequent dependence of monastic houses on the governance of the bishop, and does so in the manner of an itinerary, the *Vita Autberti* demonstrates the connections between the bishop and the founding of those same houses in the manner of a lineage: the founding bishop who consecrates the monastic house becomes the father of a spiritual family of monasteries that remain subject to his governance, and the power of governance is handed along from one bishop to the next as his spiritual patrimony. This spiritual patrimony comes accompanied by a temporal patrimony, revenue and power that are real enough and absolutely necessary for the effective rule of the city. In this way the life of one of its founding bishops organizes the geographical, economic, and cultural landscape around Cambrai, and a historical narrative of spiritual authority functions as the basis of its territorial organization. The *Vita Autberti* makes yet another and more all-encompassing political claim—a claim for the absolute difference between the two anointed governors, bishops and kings, on the one hand and all other human beings on the other. Only the anointed figures, the *Vita* claims, have the right and indeed the duty to govern. Thus, just as the three books of the *Gesta episcoporum* articulate a history, an institutional survey of monastic dependence, and a presentation of a contemporary struggle for secular governance and its legitimation, the *Vita Autberti* organizes itself around the same three topics.

The contemporary public reading of the life keeps the saint present in memory to the members of the community that already has a special relationship to him.[56] For the convenience of such public reading, the text of the *Vita Autberti* is divided into a prologue and four chapters, clearly marked as such in several manuscripts.[57] Each chapter contains a single session of reading aloud. Such division is also part of the text's internal structure: each chapter constitutes a complete narrative unit with a clear beginning and end and with no explicit narrative link to the material that precedes or follows it. Since each section stands narratively on its own, it is easy to break the text into its independent sections, and it is accordingly often broken.[58] The independence of the sections makes it also as easy to lengthen as to shorten the text.[59] Finally, the *Gesta episcoporum Cameracensis* contains, as we noted above, an epitome of the *Vita Autberti,* clearly made from Fulbert's text.[60] Epitomized in the chronicle, the life is removed from its liturgical purpose and has become purely historiographical.

The *Vita Autberti* is useless as a historical source for Merovingian life. Entirely a product of the eleventh century and obedient in its interests to eleventh-century imperatives, it is a pastiche of other lives written between the ninth and eleventh centuries in which Aubert happens to appear. Faced with the necessity of composing a new life of an old saint whose life had never been written, Fulbert pieced together as much as he could from whatever material he could find. In a similar circumstance, the receipt of the relics of the sainted Anglo-Saxon King Oswald by the monks of Bergues-Saint-Winnoc, as Baudouin de Gaiffier notes, the contemporary hagiographer was able to turn to Bede's *Historia ecclesiastica* for an already continuous narrative of Oswald's life that he could use with only minor changes.[61] Here, in the absence of a single source narrative, Fulbert found scattered mentions of Aubert in many lives, including Alcuin's *Life of St. Vaast*,[62] and in the *Vita Fursei, Vita Waldetrudis, Vita Aldegundis, Vita Landelini, Vita Ghisleni, Vita Vincentii Madelgarii,* and *Vita Vulmari,* and he wove them all together to make the fabric of the text.[63]

Each of the four chapters is, as I have noted already, a separate narrative, and in each Aubert plays a part in someone else's life. In the totality of the process, Aubert becomes a peculiar kind of hagiographical hero whose saintly exemplarity is visible not so much in what he does as in what he inspires or authorizes in others. The first two chapters are each based on a preexisting biographical narrative. Chapter 1 virtually reproduces the life of Landelin of Lobbes, for whom Aubert provided a warning in a vision, while chapter 2 presents material from the circle of St. Ghislen, including first an episode from the life of St. Ghislen himself and then the stories of Vincent Madelgarius and Waldetrude, a noble husband and wife who each became monastics under Ghislen's influence. Aubert examines Ghislen's teachings and after finding them not to be heretical consecrates his oratory. He then counsels Vincent on the superiority of monastic over secular life and finally veils Waldetrude as he previously veiled Waldetrude's sister Aldegund. The last two chapters of the *Vita Autberti* are narratively quite different from the first, although they ultimately serve similar historiographical ends. Chapter 3 presents Aubert's translation of St. Vaast's relics to the monastery of St. Vaast at Arras, and the fourth chapter tells of successive translations of Aubert's own relics. After burial outside the walls of the city in the Church of St. Peter, which he is said to have founded, Aubert is translated in 888 to the Cathedral of St. Mary inside the walls of Cambrai to keep him safe from the Norman raids. Finally, in 1015 the body in Cambrai is returned to its newly refurbished and newly consecrated original burial place, now inside the walls on account of the growth of the city.

In treating Aubert this way, primarily as a secondary character in other people's lives, the writer is in the first instance simply making do with what his source material provides. Nevertheless, while Aubert is less a character than a narrative position—that is, while he is represented neither as the sum total of his words and deeds nor as the texture of his wishes, dreams, and desires—he remains the central narrative interest in the text. This narrative centering performs a comprehensible and intentional historiographical function: Aubert is the origin and center of a web of personal dependencies traced precisely by his actions. He counsels, inspires others to make choices for themselves, examines their teachings and pronounces on the orthodoxy of their beliefs, builds their churches, consecrates their oratories, and prays for their success. These actions create a web of personal dependencies that provide historical justifications precisely for the dependence of a set of monastic establishments on the spiritual and temporal benefits of Cambrai and of its bishop. These include Vaucelles, Lobbes, Mons, and Hautmont. In this way the *Vita Autberti* clearly is at one with Gerard's project of consolidating the spiritual and temporal authority of the bishops of Cambrai. In fact, a good part of the third book of the *Gesta episcoporum* is devoted to Gerard's attempt to reestablish his authority over these same monastic houses.

Rewriting the Life of Landelin

The *Vita* carries on its historiographical project by a series of extremely complex narrative and exegetical strategies with far-reaching effects. The first of these strategies consists in the rather wholesale rewriting and reaccentuation of the source text. The first of these rewritings tells the story of Landelin, a child of a noble family given to Aubert at baptism to be educated. After an exemplary youth, Landelin is "tempted by Satan" beginning in his early adolescence [ut autem in virilis animi robur adolescens evasit, quae aetas liberior ad quaeque audendum semper videtur] (543). While the language of temptation is highly erotic, reminiscent of language found in the lives of the desert fathers, where the first temptations after taking up the eremitic life are typically sexual, the content of the temptation is simply Landelin's recollection of his family heritage and his longing for a life that will no longer be his. He begins to recall "the memory of his earthly patrimony, the nobility of his birth, the numerous dignities of his family, the glory of his property, and the other charms of a rather pleasurable life" [nunc quidem inmmittens ei memoriam terreni partrimonii, generis nobilitatem, familiae numerosam dignitatem, rerum gloriam, et reliqua vitae lascivioris blandimenta] (543). Indeed, spurred on by his relatives' persuasions that a "handsome young man [egregiam juventutis formam] ought rather to imitate the ancient virtues of his family, who won great glory in affairs by the arts of secular warfare, than to occupy himself with service in the church [ecclesiasticis cultibus]" (543), Landelin leaves the monastery. Changing his name to "Maurosus," he gathers a band of young men like himself around him and proceeds to live by private warfare, which for the author of the life is simply theft and rapine. In this way, the *Vita* insists, Satan attempts to spoil Aubert's spiritual victory by keeping Landelin away from the monastery. But Aubert prays for the rescue of his young disciple, and the power of his prayer is ultimately victorious. One night, greatly distressed by the death of one of his comrades, Landelin sees a ghastly vision of the tortures visited on the dead man in hell. An angel appears and tells him that this vision was granted him by the strength of Aubert's prayers and that he should instantly change his life, for worse tortures otherwise await him. Terrified, Landelin returns to Aubert, where he grows in virtue, becomes a priest, and in the end founds the monastic house of Lobbes in the very place in the wilderness where his hideout used to be.

Up to this point, the *Vita Autberti* follows its source, the *Vita Landelini,* rather closely, developing it by the well-practiced rhetorical technique of *amplificatio.* Here, for example, is the presentation of Landelin's vision of his dead comrade in the *Vita Landelini:* "And when it was night, in which they were hurrying to complete their nefarious work, it happened, by God's disposition, that one of his crew, taken by death, breathed his last breath. Meanwhile Maurosus, deeply affected by the death of his companion, when he had gone to rest, saw the soul of that wretched man led away to hell by demons." [Cumque adesset nox, in qua tam nefarium opus perficere festinabant; accidit Dei dispositione, ut quidam ex sodalibus ejus, morte deprehensus, spiritum exhalaret. Interea Maurosus, dolore soldalis sui vehementer afflictus, cum se dedisset quieti, videt miseri illius animam a damonibus ad infernum deduci] (459).[64] And here is what happens to it in the *Vita Autberti:*

> And when black night rose up with its spreading shadows, while they
> were hurrying to finish their nefarious work, it happened, by the pious
> disposition of God, that one of the above-mentioned thieves, being taken
> by death, breathed his last breath, and the Devil took his soul, freed from
> its corporal prison, to the infernal cloister, since his sins were beyond
> measure. At his exequies, while his companions, who lacked any de-
> votion to religion, were keeping watch, Maurosus, vehemently afflicted
> with sadness for the dead man, went off alone to rest out of weariness

and sadness, and by both the divine will and the supporting merits of Blessed Aubert it was given to the young man to see with how many pains that wretched soul was being tortured in hell, with how many vengeful flames he was burning. And this was given to the errant youth by divine will to be an exemplum of fear, so that from this consideration he could gather that as great a punishment menaced his own crime as called to account one of his band.

[Cumque jam incumbentibus tenebris nox tetra inhorresceret, qua illi nefarium opus perficere festinabant, pia Dei dispositione contigit unum ex supradictis furunculis morte deprehensum, spiritum exhalasse, cujus animam corporeo carcere resolutam peccatis exigentibus diabolus secum ad infernalia claustra traxerat. Ad cujus exequias dum inani religionis studio socii excubarent, et Maurosus defuncti dolore vehementer afflictus, se ex lassitudine et tristitia paululum daret quieti, divina voluntate et suffragantibus meritis beati Autberti, datum est adolescenti videre, quantis poenis illa miserrima anima in inferno cruciabatur, quantisve ultricis flammae incendiis urebatur; ac si erranti juveni ex divina voluntate hoc daretur ad exemplum formidinis, ut videlicet ex hac consideratione colligeret, quanta reatus sui poena instabat, quem ex consortio criminis similis culpa accusabat.] (544)

The comparison provides an extraordinarily clear example of compositional technique. Amplification of this sort makes the scene vivid and memorable in ways that Mary Carruthers has taught us to recognize and appreciate.[65] Such memorability, while also serving other important ends, creates meaning. It is motivated by a forensic intention that lies at the heart of rhetorical practice: to put the case vividly before the eyes of the jury so that they will see the situation in exactly the way the advocate wants them to see it and judge it accordingly. In this instance, the whole description is in the service of praising St. Aubert by moving him into the center of narrative activity, and the emphasis on the vision's horror makes his power appear all the stronger. What follows, an angel's address that comments on this scene, makes this shift in emphasis abundantly clear. First, here is the whole of the angel's speech in the *Vita Landelini*:

O Landelin, now you see the reward of your labor; with what punishment the soul of your companion is led away to an infernal place. See therefore what would be better for you, to be led with such torment into the pit of Gehenna, or to be forever with us in the mansion of heaven. So put away the work of the Devil, and join the army of Christ. Tear away from yourself the blindness of a dark heart so that you can gaze on the bright light of Christ. Refuse the service of the ancient enemy so that you can reign after death with Christ. Hear the blessed Bishop Aubert, and recognize that he is your spiritual father; receive from his mouth the warnings of heavenly teaching. After teaching him these things and many others, that angelic spirit sought the heavens.

[O Landeline, modo conspice remunerationem tui laboris: cum quali poena socii anima deducatur ad inferni loca. Vide ergo quid tibi melius sit, cum tali tormento deduci in baratrum gehennae, an nobiscum perfui coelesti mansione. Derelinque igitur opera diaboli, et assume militiam Christi, abscinde a te tenebrosi cordis caecitatem, quo possis intueri clarissimum Christi lumen. Refuge jam nunc hostis antiqui servitutem, quo possis cum Christo regnare post mortem. Audi ergo B. Audbertum Antistitem, et recognosce tuum esse spiritualem patrem: suscipe ab ore ejus monita coelestis doctrinae. Haec vero aliaque multa eum edocens supernus ille Angelicus spiritus, coelos petiit.] (459)

In the *Vita Autberti* the speech begins with a long apostrophe, a fifteen-line elaboration of "See here the reward of your labor." With this apostrophe the angel acts like an advocate, driving home the point of the vision to Landelin by *amplificatio*. The point is made by a set of rhetorical questions that summon Landelin to think about which is his true identity, the Landelin whom Aubert educated or the Maurus whom Landelin willfully became: "For were you named Maurosus, anointed Maurosus, reborn Maurosus? Aubert had you inscribed with us in the book of life as Landelin; the devil inserted Maurosus to be with him in a contract of destruction." [Numquid Maurosus signatus es, Maurosus unctus, Maurosus renatus? Landelinum nobiscum in libro vitae Autbertus obtinuerat adscribi, Maurosum diabolus secum inserit chirographo perditionis] (544). The next passage in which one can easily follow the author's procedure of phrasal substitution and rhetorical opening is directly based on the source:

For you would have been tortured with the punishment of such great burning if the intercession of Aubert your advocate had not mitigated

the avenging anger of the judge. A fire of even greater torment was
already prepared for you and lit, but the tears of blessed Aubert ex-
tinguished the flames; and now that you are informed, know what you
would rather choose, to be led with torment into the pit of Gehenna
or to enjoy the vision of heaven with Aubert. But this choice would have
been too late if Aubert had not already intervened. Therefore, let go of
your wretched band of thieves, and, joining the army of Christ and hearing the blessed guardian, imitate your leader Aubert and recognize your
spiritual father, your guardian, your redeemer from eternal death. Receive these warnings of heavenly teachings from him, and having been
made more faultless by them, you will deserve to receive from that same
intercessor the garment that you lost. These things having been said,
the angel disappeared.

[Quod tanti peonam incendii cruciandus subieras, nisi intercesso Autberti advocati tui ultricem iram judicis mitigasset. Tibi paratus ignis
cruciatorius accenditur, sed beati Autberti lacrimis flammae ejus extin-
guuntur; vel nunc expertus intellige, quid potius eligas, cum tormento
duci in baratrum gehennae, quam cum Autberto frui coelesti visione. Sed
sera ista deliberatio fuerat, nisi Autbertus praevenisset. Relinque igitur
execranda consortia latronum et Christi militiam assumens, ducem tuum
imitare Autbertum audiens beatissimum Praesulem, et recognosce tuum
spiritualem patrem, tuum protectorem, tuum ab aeterno interitu redemptorem. Suscipe vero ab eo monita coelestis doctrinae, quibus emenda-
tior factus, merearis stolam quam perdideras recipere ipso intercessore.
His dictis continuo angelus disparuit.] (545)

Substituting Aubert for the angel in the vision of heaven is a daring maneuver: "See therefore what would be better for you, to be led with such torment
into the pit of Gehenna, or to be forever with us in the mansion of heaven" becomes "Know what you would rather choose, to be led with torment into the
pit of Gehenna or to enjoy the vision of heaven with Aubert." And this substitution continues in various modalities throughout the passage and becomes even
more daring. Thus the emotional imperatives in the *Vita Landelini,* "Tear away
from yourself the blindness of a dark heart so that you can gaze on the bright
light of Christ" and "Refuse the service of the ancient enemy so that you can
reign after death with Christ," are rewritten to emphasize Aubert's continual

presence as mediator and his ultimate responsibility for Landelin's fate: "Leave the evil band of thieves and, joining the army of Christ and hearing the blessed Guardian, imitate your leader Aubert and recognize your spiritual father, your guardian, your redeemer from eternal death" (545). The grammatical structure of the Latin period makes the strikingly christological language of the last phrase—"tuum spiritualem patrem, tuum protectorem, tuum ab aeterno interitu redemptorem"—refer unequivocally to Aubert. This rewriting of the angel's speech is of a piece with the whole rhetorical strategy of the chapter. The changes to the source make Aubert the agent of all the action. In this way what began as the life of Landelin becomes the life of Aubert, a record of his deeds and their fruit, and the language that served in the source to indicate Landelin's integrity—that is, his dependence on Christ rather than on the Devil— here indicates Landelin's complete dependence on Aubert.[66] The first fruit of Aubert's intercession is in fact Landelin's return to Aubert because of this vision, his penitence as a secular under Aubert's spiritual direction, his tonsure as a monk, and then his ascent through the *cursus honorum* of the ecclesiastical hierarchy as he becomes first a deacon and then a priest. Finally, "informed by the ways of his teacher and strengthened by the habit of his customary way of life" [Magistri moribus informatus, et exercitatae conversationis usu roboratus] (545), he takes himself to a distant place on the banks of the Sambre, lives for a time as a hermit, and then founds the monastery at Lobbes in the spot where his hideout used to be. He does this precisely as the culmination of his penitence: "And thus to erase the stain of his prior life, he constructed monasteries in the places that he had prepared as a refuge and gathering of thieves, establishing ministers to do the divine service, and he made those men who previously had been his partners in crime sharers in the divine mysteries." [Ad evacuandam igitur prioris vitae maculam, in locis quae sibi ad refugium et receptacula latronum paraverat, monasteria construsit, statuens ministros in executionem ecclesiasticae institutionis, et quos ante socios habuerat criminum, postmodum fecit cooperatores divinorum mysteriorum] (545–46).

Although there are many more events in the *Vita Landelini,* including notices of a pilgrimage to Rome and the founding of a network of monastic houses, the *Vita Autberti* concludes the chapter here, adding only one piece of further information about Landelin "as a sign of his outstanding labors": Lobbes has been greatly enriched by imperial donations. It has been given a "treasure of villages and households" [villarum familiaeque replevit copia] (546). Indeed, it has received so much royal munificence that "the congregation of brothers serving there lacks nothing said to be appropriate for monks" [fratrum congregatio ibidem serviens non egeret his, quae monachis feruntur esse congrua] (546).

The historiographic purpose of concluding the narrative at this point is obvious: once the dependence of Lobbes on Cambrai and on the Empire has been demonstrated, there is nothing more to say about the relation of Aubert to Landelin. In the *Vita Landelini* the pope plays a role both in the founding of Lobbes and in Landelin's establishment of several other houses, a role that the *Vita Autberti* simply never mentions. This is a silence easily understandable in the context of the contemporary monastic reform that pursued a policy of tying monastic establishments directly to Rome in order to break their dependence on local lords, both secular and ecclesiastical—indeed, on such local lords as the bishop of Cambrai. And the threat posed by the reform is visible in the very force of the text's rhetoric. The argument of this text is made precisely in opposition to the Cluniac program; it represents the dependence of a monastic house on a local lord as beyond question.[67] The monastery takes its place in a natural hierarchical relation of universal dependence. Aubert is Landelin's spiritual father, his protector, his redeemer: from the moment of its foundation Lobbes owes its existence to Aubert. To assert the institutional dependence of Lobbes on Cambrai, that is, the text pursues a rhetorical strategy that first conceptualizes institutional authority as a personal dependence and then asserts the personal dependence of Landelin on Aubert to the point of making Aubert the hero of Landelin's life.[68] This rhetorical substitution of a personal dependence for institutional authority is an instance of the general representation of public authority as private lordship, a central feature of eleventh-century political life.

Rewriting the Life of Waldetrude

A similar rhetorical strategy continues into the next chapter, where Aubert's centrality to other people's experience is similarly asserted. Thus the narrative shows how Aubert comes to stand at the center of an elaborate network of personal relations among Aldegund, Waldetrude, Vincent Madelgarius, and Ghislen, a personal network that traces the institutional dependences of at least ten monastic houses on Cambrai. As in the first chapter, the narrative continually asserts Aubert's to be the primary agency, but it does this here by some fairly drastic changes to the plot of its source. Thus, to consider only one example, in the *Vita Waldetrudis* Waldetrude, already a recluse living in the oratory of St. Peter that she had built in the wilderness, on the advice of Ghislen, her spiritual advisor, goes herself to receive the veil from Aubert: "Meanwhile Waldetrude, the beloved handmaiden of Christ, burning in spirit and more and more sighing with celestial desire, according to the admonition of the man of God Ghislen, of whom we made mention above, went to Bishop Aubert and asked that she might merit accepting the holy veil, and this was accomplished immediately." [Interea dilectissima Christi famula Waldetrudis, fervens spiritu et magis magisque coelesti desiderio anhelans, juxta viri Dei Gisleni, cujus superius mentionem fecimus, admonitionem, ad Beatissimum Autbertum Episcopum accessit, et ut velamen sacrum accipere mereretur petiit, et citius impetravit] (444).[69] In the *Vita Autberti* she is sent by Ghislen to Aubert while she is still living at home (in seculari adhuc habitu posita) taking care of the house, children, and property after her husband has left and become a monk: "Ghislen, sacred to God, of whom we made mention above, admonished her with sweet speech, that she ought to go to blessed Aubert, to get counsel and precepts of salvation from him, how informed by the example of a good husband, and following the footsteps of holy women, she might merit pleasing her heavenly spouse. Hearing these things, the handmaiden of Christ went to the venerable bishop. Having taken from him the counsel of holy admonition, she began little by little to set aside the cares of the world and long with heavenly longings." [Quam sanctus Dei Gislenus, cujus superius mentionem fecimus, dulci affatu monuit, ut ad beatum Autbertum ire deberet, quo ab eo consilium et normam salutis acciperet, quatinus boni conjugis exemplo informata, et sanctarum feminarum imitata vestigia, sponso coelesti mereretur placere. Quibus auditis Christi Famula ad venerabilem pervenit Episcopum. Quae accepto ab eo sacrae monitionis consilio, coepit paulatim curas mundi postponere et desideriis supernis inhiare] (551). The sentences of the source are active, charting Waldetrude's desires, her decisions, and the actions that she takes to implement them; here Waldetrude is put in a passive position throughout. In the process, Aubert becomes the immediate agent of her spiritual growth. She ought to go, Ghislen says, "to get counsel and precepts of salvation from him." And by means of free indirect discourse, the counsel that Aubert will give to Waldetrude is immediately insinuated into the purpose clause of the sentence—"how informed by the example of a good husband, and following the footsteps of holy women, she might merit pleasing her heavenly spouse." And when she hears this counsel from Aubert (accepto . . . consilio), she begins the spiritual growth that will end personally in monastic commitment and institutionally in monastic governance—"she began little by little to put aside the cares of the world and to long with heavenly longings"; the words are a repetition of the source with very simple variation, but the temporal location in Waldetrude's spiritual life has been entirely changed. The journey to Aubert, which in the source was the culmination of her spiritual journey, is here the first step. And it is her one and only action, placed neatly between two sentences of masculine advice: advised by Ghislen, she goes to Bishop Aubert to be advised.

Throughout the *Vita Waldetrudis,* Waldetrude is entirely in control of her own life and spiritual destiny; the *Vita Autberti,* on the other hand, consistently places her in the position of extreme spiritual passivity. Thus the source text represents the beginnings of her spiritual growth according to the biographical pattern of the lives of early Christian women such as St. Cecilia. Since she is born to a noble household and is herself beautiful to look at [pulchra facie decoraque aspectu] (441), Waldetrude's parents arrange a very favorable marriage for her "according to the ancient ordinance of God and the example of the patriarchs" [secundum antiquam Dei ordinationem et Patriarcharum exemplum, ad nuptias viro tradere debuissent] (441). Yet "by the hidden disposition of God" [Domini Dei occulta dispositione] (441) Waldetrude begins to desire to live a perfect life. She dedicates herself to helping the poor, widows and orphans, and captives and pilgrims "in order entirely to root out vices not only from the acts of her body but even from the impulses of her heart" [vitia quoque non solum ab actu corporis, sed etiam a cogitatione cordis funditus extirpare] (441). Moreover, not simply content with her own spiritual growth, she takes pains to inspire her husband to the desire for God and a perfect life. She lectures him daily, and she desires to renounce all sexual activity, not, says the narrator of her life, because she does not want to have children, but because she sees that sexual desire blunts the edge of spiritual intention [quia carnalis affectus intentionem mentis multum diverberare ejusque aciem obscurare solet] (441) and because of the teaching of the Apostle: "A woman unmarried and virgin thinks about the things of God, so that she is holy in body and spirit: a married woman thinks about things of the world and how to please her husband. And so, desiring to be free for God alone, she feared carnal marriage as an impediment, and with tears and sighs she prayed daily that it might be undone by the will of God and be in itself the will of the Lord." [Mulier innupta et Virgo cogitat quae Domini sunt, ut sit sancta corpore et spiritu: quae autem nupta est cogitat quae sunt mundi quomodo placeat viro. Ideoque soli Deo vacare desiderans, veluti quoddam impedimentum, carnale conjugium pertimescebat: atque ut nutu Dei solveretur, et in se Domini voluntas fieret, quotidie cum lacrymis et gemitu exorabat]

(441). And Waldetrude gets her wish. The section concludes by telling us that God placed these desires in her heart (again through his "occulta dispositione") precisely so that he could powerfully help her fulfill them. Her husband, Vincent, on fire with divine love, dissolves the marriage and goes himself to live in a monastery, where he can complete the course of his temporal life in holy acts [in sanctis actibus temporalem hujus vitae peregit cursum] (441), thus opening the way for Waldetrude's own renunciation of the secular world.

Throughout the narrative, the text consistently places Waldetrude in direct relationship to God, and, prompted by her desires alone, she moves herself to ever increasing degrees of spiritual intimacy. The frame of this narrative, importantly, is her daily activity in the secular world—the key word *quotidie* is repeated strategically throughout the passage—first as a wife and then purely as *Christi famula*. Yet her daily activity is always the same—filled with spiritual longing she prays and counsels. The passage begins with her praying to her husband daily: "With sweet and salving speech she took pains to excite her noble husband Madelgarius to the love of God, desire for the heavenly fatherland, and the preservation of purity, and she strove to ignite his mind with the fire of charity with which she herself sweetly burned." [Nobilem scilicet virum Madelgarium, ad amorem Dei et coelestis patriae desiderium ac castimoniam conservandam, blandis quotidie ac salutiferis sermonibus excitare curebat et igne caritatis, quo ipsa suaviter flagrabat, illius mentem accendere satagebat] (441). And at the end of the passage she prays to God daily to dissolve her marriage [quotidie cum lacrymis et gemitu exorabat] (441). She desires daily to ignite her husband's mind with the fire of charity, and she prays daily that God will untie the knot of her marriage so that she may be perfect. Essentially, this is the same prayer, and it is successful. In the event, Vincent dissolves the marriage, "set on fire by the torches of intimate love" [accensus facibus amoris intimi] (441). Whereas in the *Vita Autberti* Waldetrude is admonished to follow the good example of her husband, in the corresponding passage in the source it is Waldetrude whose spiritual life is exemplary and who spurs her husband forward by daily prayer. In brief, Waldetrude prays, admonishes, and acts as an intimate of God. She is the authoritative center of her own and her husband's life.

The *Vita Autberti*, on the other hand, places Aubert directly in this same position: as bishop he prays, admonishes, and acts always as a mediator of divine authority and judgment, to the point that the unmediated divine presence effectively disappears from the narrative altogether. The most manifestly striking transformation of the source material is the replacement of Waldetrude by

Aubert in Vincent's story. As the *Vita Autberti* tells it, Vincent, a high-ranking
member of the royal court, discontent with his life as a knight [jam se a negotiis
militaribus cogitabat longe facere] (550), goes to Aubert and asks him "that he
might merit hearing healing words in very secret conversation" [ut ab eo secre-
tioribus colloquiis salutis verba mereretur audire] (550). And Aubert complies,
as the narrator says, " to irrigate a dry field with the flood of his saving argument"
[et sitientem agrum imbre salutiferae praedicationis irrigare] (550). Whereas
in the *Vita Waldetrudis* Vincent is set on fire by the "salutiferis sermonibus" of his
wife, here it is the flood of "salutiferae praedictionis" from Aubert that has the
same result: "[The bishop] set the man on fire with the fervor of heavenly love"
[virum superni amoris fervore accendit] (550). In the one text the words of his
wife, in the other the words of the bishop set Vincent on fire with heavenly love.
She is replaced by official authority.

Nor is the gender shift accidental. In the context of official authority,
which is necessarily masculine, his wife is merely one of the many treasures
that Vincent possesses and that he leaves behind for a better life. The court is
amazed at what he has renounced—"such great glory of property, inestimable
honor, love of children, a wife especially glorious in being of the royal family,
riches sought with great labor" [tam magna rerum gloria, inaestimabilis digni-
tas, amor filiorum, uxor praesertim regio genere gloriosa, et magnis laboribus
quaesitae divitiae] (550). His renunciation of so much immediately inspires
many men of the royal court to follow him into the monastic life. This demonstration of the superior power of the spiritual, incarnate in the person of the
bishop, over the secular life is the real work of Aubert. This is work that takes
place purely in the masculine world of court and monastery. Waldetrude is
for the moment left at home—"Vincent's wife, the blessed Waldetrude, as yet
placed in secular life, taking care of her own household, nobly ruled her offspring and the estate conferred on her by her father" [Uxor vero praedicti Vincentii, beata scilicet Waldetrudis, in saeculari adhuc habitu posita, domus pro-
priae curam gerens, proles, praediaque sibi a seniore collata nobiliter regebat]
(551)—until Aubert releases her also from the cares of household and children, and in her subsequent conversion she too becomes a sign and witness to
Aubert's spiritual power.

The wholesale transformation of Waldetrude's character, which I have argued is a result of placing Aubert in the position of central authority in her life,
points to the central narrative problematic of this complex text. I said earlier
that Aubert is less a character than a narrative position. I want to insist that we

cannot simply attribute the lack of narrative interest in Aubert's inner life or in the details of his character as a moral agent to an absence of detailed presentation in the source material, for, as we have seen, Fulbert constantly rewrites his sources. Moreover, as we have already seen in discussing Landelin's vision and Vincent's discontent with his noble circumstances, the text stages the inner life as virtually the exclusive scene of significant action. Spiritual longing and interior unrest are central both to the narrative content of the text and to its rhetorical efficacy. It seems to me that the real *aporia* here—that Aubert is simultaneously the central point of narrative presence and an absolute narrative opacity—is a result of the text's historiographical burden. Like the *Deeds of the Bishops of Cambrai,* the *Vita Autberti* argues that the authority of the bishop is based on his being qua bishop and not on his charismatic gifts as an exceptional individual. In the climate of monastic reform and the Peace of God, these texts make the strong argumentative claim that the bishop's authority is institutional and routine, not personal and exceptional, a result of the consecration that is its efficacious sign. As in the *Gesta,* the *Vita Autberti* narrates the secular activity of the bishop exclusively: Aubert advises, prays, and intercedes on behalf of others. Yet Aubert is more than a bishop. He is a saint, and by the eleventh century he had long been recognized as such. That is, Aubert occupies an official status within the cultic life of the church; he is listed on the liturgical calendar for December 13; his body is a relic; and his life is the subject of a particular kind of narrative, written for a particular kind of reading, that proposes him as an example for emulation and as an object for meditative contemplation because he is a special and unique conveyance of special grace. The hagiographical form, pressed into the service of this particular historiographical argument, is here under considerable strain.

Form as Argument: Two Lives

In much conventional hagiographical narrative, the saint's exceptional merit is manifest already in prophecy before his birth, in his deeds while alive, and in the efficacy of his relics after death. This schema is a particular adaptation and deployment of the order of praise in the *narratio* of an epideictic oration as set forth, for example, in the *Rhetorica ad Herennium.*[70] The *narratio* follows the "order of nature": that is, the order of the exposition is chronological, which importantly serves to double the order of events in experience, to create the illusion that reading is transparent and provides the audience direct access to the experience being narrated. The rhetoricians say that the life should seem to be being lived before the very eyes of the audience. The oration of praise thus constructs an argument for merit by stringing a set of value-saturated events along the lines of a biographical plot, and by this means the value embodied by the life seems to speak for itself. The deeds of the subject of praise are construed as legible signs of the subject's special excellence. In hagiography, the prophecies before birth, the events of the life, and efficacious acts performed by the relics are not merely indices of the subject's special merit; they are miraculous signs. They are recognizable as such because they are extraordinary occurrences[71] but more importantly because they are events pregnant with figural implications. These events therefore belong to an order of sacred history that the saint's peculiar destiny both furthers and witnesses. Thus the paradox of hagiographical biography: the biography insists on the uniqueness of the saint's life precisely by demonstrating that the life is patterned exactly like the lives of all other saints. The claim to sainthood is made by the life's repetition of earlier narratives whose elements it self-consciously redeploys. Moreover, the life is a continuous reiteration of itself, for every moment reveals the full significance of the life being narrated. The saint's life uses a temporal form—a narrative of a life from birth to death and beyond—and in so doing it organizes time around the living presence of the saint. Time in the narrative consists of a period of preparation before the birth of the saint (during which his coming is prophesied) to a period of fulfillment in acts after the saint's death (by which the permanence of his presence is demonstrated and guaranteed). Yet although it invariably uses a temporal form, the saint's life is never the narrative of a temporal development. It is rather always, as de Certeau nicely puts it, the representation of a destiny.[72] The whole life in time consists of a single manifestation of blessedness, a plenitude reinstantiated at every moment of its being. To this I would add the following corollary: although the biography insists on the uniqueness of the saint's life, the life as such is entirely without interest; it is narrated as a means to represent the permanent and unchangeable truth that it signifies. That is, the conventional structure of hagiographical narrative is itself an interpretative procedure; the narrative creates its own significance by means of its representational strategies.

A consideration of two lives roughly contemporary with the *Vita Autberti* can demonstrate just how radical Fulbert's writing becomes under the weight of its historiographical argument for the bishop's authority. Odo of Cluny's *Life of Gerald of Aurillac*[73] and Rodolphus Glaber's *Life of William of Volpiano*[74] are both from the Cluniac milieu. Each in its own way is anomalous in relation to hagiographical tradition, yet each nevertheless creates its meaning by deploying the conventional design of hagiographical narrative. The *Life of Gerald of Aurillac* is the biography of a pious lay lord, celebrated for founding a Cluniac monastery. It mobilizes a wide range of hagiographical conventions to transform Gerald's primarily secular public activity into the fully unequivocal sign of monastic piety. Thus the fact that Gerald never becomes a monk—not even in extreme old age—is narrated as an argument for his great humility: he shuns the monastery as a way of avoiding spiritual pride. And thus Gerald's noble lineage—witnessed by the extent of his landholding and the number of serfs in his possession (94)—is transformed by a visionary narrative into a sign of Gerald's spiritual election: his father, while still at this point childless, sees a vision of his own descendants growing from his body in the form of a tree of Jesse (95). Spurred on by this vision, he visits his wife in the night, and Gerald is as it were miraculously conceived. More signs follow. Gerald cries out from the womb nine days before his birth, and in his youth he differentiates himself from his companions by his physical beauty and especially by a measured demeanor that makes him seem destined for greatness. Sickly as a boy, he is taught to read and begins to devote himself to letters. Even when he recovers his physical strength and is remarkable for his great physical prowess, he prefers reading to the exercise of military skills. Thus in its beginning the life of Gerald follows the schema of early medieval lives of men of noble families destined for monastic life, such as Bede's life of St. Cuthbert. The topics of praise common to secular epideictic oratory—the nobility of family, early signs of greatness in childhood, the exploits of youth, the theme of the *puer senex*—are deployed here to create a structure of prophetic signs subtended as much by typological hermeneutics as by the rhetorical tradition.

Although the prophetic structure of these early chapters points unequivocally to a monastic vocation, Gerald remains a secular lord to the end of his life. It is a life occupied primarily with the activities of the tenth-century warrior aristocracy. Yet, by deploying biblical citation and typology, miraculous events, and a homiletic style that transforms outer activities into signs of inner grace, Odo inscribes these activities into the register of monastic piety. Thus Odo first presents Gerald's military exploits as tokens of humility—he is led on not by love of praise but by "love of the poor who were not able to protect themselves"—and then as an ascetic project "lest, if he become sluggish through an indolent patience, he should seem to have neglected the precept to care for the poor" (100). And in this project Gerald is miraculously victorious, for

> he commanded his men in imperious tones to fight with the backs of their swords and with their spears reversed. This would have been ridiculous to the enemy if Gerald, strengthened by divine power, had not been invincible to them. And it would have seemed useless to his own men, if they had not learnt by experience that Gerald, who was carried away by his piety in the very moment of battle, had always been invincible. . . . For it was a thing unheard of that he or the soldiers who fought under him were not victorious. But this also is certain, that he himself never wounded anybody, nor was wounded by anyone. For Christ, as it is written, was at his side [Ps. 117:6], who seeing the desire of his heart, saw that for love of Him he was so well-disposed that he had no wish to assail the persons of the enemy, but only to check their audacity. (100)

The miraculous nature of the victory simultaneously witnesses both Gerald's inner personal virtue and the justice of God's deeds performed outwardly through him. In this way the narrative becomes a generalization, a homily extolling secular power in the service of a vision of world peace and divine justice. In the course of the homily, Gerald's actions take on sacramental force: efficacious in their own right (he is always victorious), these actions are also signs manifesting the real and continuous presence of Christ both within him and in the world.

Gerald's own motivation is thus adequated to a vision of the world-historical progress of divine justice. In the following passage, the homily moves continually back and forth between a presentation of Gerald's personal motives—humility, devotion to God, love of his fellows, simplicity of heart—and a notation of the progressive victory of justice over injustice, of "the cause of God" in the world. In the course of the argument Gerald becomes universalized, always simultaneously a sign to be understood, a manifestation to be wondered over, and an example to be imitated:

> It was lawful, therefore, for a layman to carry the sword in battle that he might protect defenceless people, as the harmless flock from ravening wolves according to the saying of Scripture [Acts 20:29], and that he

might restrain by arms or by the law those whom ecclesiastical censure was not able to subdue. It does not darken his glory, then, that he fought for the cause of God, for whom the whole world fights against the unwise [Wisd. 5:21]. Rather is it to his praise that he always won openly without the help of deceit or ambushes, and nevertheless was so protected by God, that, as I said before, he never stained his sword with human blood. Hereafter, let him who by his example shall take up arms against his enemies seek also by his example not his own but the common good. For you may see some who for love of praise or gain boldly put themselves in danger, gladly sustain the evils of the world for the sake of the world, and while they encounter its bitterness lose the joys, so to speak, which they were seeking. But of these it is another story. The work of Gerald shines forth, because it sprang from simplicity of heart. (101)

By means of a catena of biblical citations and a constant play between reading Gerald's acts as signs of his inner spiritual grace and examples of just social action, aristocratic private war is placed into the order of the miraculous as a manifestation of God's continual presence in the world. The enabling ground of this rhetorical procedure is monastic piety itself. In the *Life of Gerald of Aurillac* monastic piety provides the sole criterion by which any action or any human being is measured and judged to be good. Indeed, although he remains a secular lord to the end of his days and the narrative registers his activities as a judge, landholder, and warrior, the *Life* insists that inwardly, which is the location of the only reality that counts, he is a monk. Odo puts it succinctly: "If therefore one considers his desire, he was true to the monastic profession through his devotion to Christ" (145). He is chaste; he eats and drinks abstemiously when not actually observing fast days; he performs the divine office, singing through the Psalter daily; he dedicates his life to the divine service. Because in his inner life Gerald has fully withdrawn from the world, all his behavior in the world becomes a sign of his inner transformation. Thus, quoting Matthew 12:34, "Because he gave himself wholeheartedly to the desire of heaven, his mouth was so filled from the abundance of his heart that the law of God sounded almost continuously on his lips" (144). Or, quoting Psalm 1 and Psalm 15, "His speech and his silence were such that his mouth declared the praise of the Lord and the meditation of his heart was always in His sight" (145). The superiority of this inner withdrawal from the world is finally represented in the trope of blindness: toward the end of his life Gerald is blind for seven years, but "in proportion as he was not able to gaze on the face of the world, by so much he contemplated more clearly the true light of the heart" (163). The life of a great secular lord here enacts monastic piety. It is an example, as his *Vita* would have it, to be emulated by secular lord and monk alike.

Having thus presented the prophetic signs of his special vocation, his deeds, and his particular virtues, the life proceeds to authenticate itself by a recital of the many miracles performed during Gerald's life and after his death. Odo says that "although the time of Anti-Christ is now at hand and the miracles of the saints ought to cease" (141) these miracles occur especially to "honor him in the sight of men who honored God" (141). They are primarily miraculous healings, often at one remove, as for example by means of the water in which Gerald washed his hands. There are also several examples of miraculous meals on the model of the multiplication of the loaves and fishes. The obvious and conventional typological structure of these miracles is precisely what makes them legible as miracles. Performed during his life, the miracles point forward to the visions and miraculous cures that occur around his tomb after his death. In life and in death Gerald is a manifestation of the power of monastic virtue even though the scene of his life is secular action: through him the divine witnesses its own permanent presence and singularity, and divinity irradiates all of secular life.

Odo's *Life of Gerald* is the story of a lay lord, yet for all intents and purposes it is the story of a monk; Rodolphus Glaber's *Life of William of Volpiano* is the story of a monk, but one whose significant claim to the attention of his contemporaries is his activity as a lord. A powerful member of the complex, differentiated structure of Cluniac monastic governance and an intimate of kings, his deeds are primarily those of a governor and administrator. Like Odo, Glaber begins his life in the expected place with a presentation of the greatness of William's ancestry. His grandfather is a poor Swabian refugee who arrives in Italy fleeing the vengeance of those who hate him. There he becomes very rich, and his son, William's father, who is an intimate of the Lombard king, marries a woman of noble birth, "outstanding for the manner of her life" [morum honestate praecipua] (258), who quickly gives birth to a son. Soon after, she has a vision of her son's being carried up to heaven by angelic beings. As a boy William distinguishes himself from other children by his admirable character, and he amazes his teacher by the speed and depth of his learning. When he is brought to an old woman to be taken care of, her "breasts, which hung pendulously with wrinkled skin, swelled suddenly and poured out milk copiously" as she embraces him (258–60). Continuing to excel in his studies, William has more and more of the duties of monastic governance entrusted to him. After the death of his mother, he convinces his father to enter the monastery. There follows a period of *errance* during which William is tested. He leaves the monastery at Pavia, where, according to Glaber, the rule has become too lax for his character, and travels to St. Michele in the Alps. His journey is shadowed with signs and wonders. On the way, for example, his horse slips and falls into a terrible chasm but emerges unscathed: "Quae res gesta plurimus admirationem prebuit atque indicium sanctitatis eius" (264). Thus the first part of the life is organized as a set of prophetic signs of William's singularity and future greatness.

The main body of the life begins at Cluny, where William is placed under the tutelage of Abbot Mayol. He distinguishes himself by his mode of life there, and he is later chosen to be abbot for a variety of houses, each of which he reforms. Throughout his travels from house to house the blessedness of William's life is correlated with the success and power of his leadership. William is a powerful founder of new abbeys and a successful reformer of old institutions because he is himself blessed, and the success of the reform is a sign of the blessedness. Blessed himself, he makes the world blessed. His outer activities and inner worth are thus permanent manifestations of a single truth, the power of God.

A recital of his miracles should typically follow the narrative of William's great deeds, and Glaber accordingly complies with the expected pattern with an introductory passage that inscribes all William's activities into the register of the miraculous:

> Nor does it seem that we should pass over the fact that while, through the encouragement of Father William there were many whose spirits were renewed, there were many too who were restored in body by his touch, revived by his prayers, comforted by his presence and strengthened by his blessing. And in the matter of raising which is very little heard of nowadays, but which was once quite usual amongst the followers of Christ, we will speak of a few cases from amongst many in which we had witnessed the Lord working through him.

> [Nec pretereundum nobis videtur, dum patris Willelmi alloquio multi fuerint in mente recreati, plures etiam in corpore tactu eiusdem redintegrati, oratione refocilati, uisitatione confortati ac benedictione firmati.

Et quamuis nunc minus audiatur, quod olim Christi sequacibus usui fuit, suscitare mortuum, pauca tamen e pluribus, ut testati sumus, quae Dominus per eum operatus est dicemus.] (292)

The rhetorical gradation from comforting, to curing, to raising the dead (in mente recreati . . . in corpore tactu eiusdem redintegrati . . . suscitare mortuum) makes explicit the typological parallel to the sequence of miracles in gospel narrative. Yet what the narrative actually presents in this section are all secular examples, acts of magnanimous clemency exercised by a great and powerful lord. William prays, comforts with visits, and makes strong with blessings primarily in scenes of merciful intercession for people accused of secular crimes or victimized by excessive taxation. The principal example of William's "raising the dead" is a spectacular example of narrative transformation: William comes across a thief sentenced to hanging, pushes his way through a crowd of excited spectators, cuts him down from the gallows, and in full view of the astonished onlookers revives the shocked victim. The other scenes of "raising the dead" arise from even more extreme interpretative maneuvering: they all show William's interceding, generally in a court scene or in a prison, *before* the death penalty can be executed or imposed in the first place.[75] As in the *Life of Gerald,* William's actions as a lord and governor are placed firmly into a hagiographical frame by narrative procedures that inscribe secular action into a typological order of the miraculous.

The *Life of William* ends with a narrative of the circumstances of his death.[76] William revisits "all his people," traveling from Italy into Gaul and from monastery to monastery. At Fécamp, the scene of one of his greatest earlier triumphs as a reformer, he dies quietly. The narrative specifies the exact time of death at great length and with the utmost precision. His soul departs happily to heaven, "leaving the holy body of that friend of God, a lamp of the world passing to eternal and sacred light, his own people lamenting but the angels rejoicing" (299). He is buried in the heart of the church "so that each day they should have before their eyes as an example to them this father whom they had had as a teacher to help them win the eternal reward of justice. By his prayers and merits may they be able to receive the kingdom of eternal life and glory with all saints, through the gift of Our Lord Jesus Christ who with the Father and the Holy Ghost liveth and reigneth world without end. Amen" (299). Thus William, whose great deeds in life are acts of intercession, leaves his body after death to be a site of merciful intercession for the monastic community that he governed. In this way, the period of his governance becomes merely a moment in his permanent embodiment of the presence of divine mercy.

Both these *Lives* ultimately abolish time. Gerald's and William's deeds—deeds of warriors, princes, monastic administrators—ultimately erase any possible distinction between the sacred and the secular. It is the special destiny of each saint to witness through the multiplicity of his or her deeds the permanent presence and unchanging reality of the divine in human affairs. All secular events thus become signs of the singularity of divine truth.

Hagiography as Historiography: Monastic Piety and the Bishop's Life

Fulbert, too, begins his *Life of Aubert* with devices drawn from epideictic invention that put the conventions of hagiography directly into play. His preface is a direct and knowing imitation of the preface to Sulpicius Severus's *Life of St. Martin*. By the eleventh century the *Life of St. Martin* had become the paradigmatic life of a confessor-saint, and it is particularly appropriate here, since Martin was a bishop. Fulbert's rewriting of this preface draws the sharpest distinction possible between writing secular biography and writing the life of a saint. "The lives of Aeneas and of Turnus are worth nothing to Virgil and to those like him when their bodies have been given to the worms and their souls to raging fire" [Quid enim Dardanius Ductor aut Rutulus ferox suo Maroni, aut iste contulit illis, cum corpora vermibus, animas dedere saevis ignibus] (538); the only lives truly worth contemplating are those whose deeds manifest the divine, since their contemplation will prepare eternal life for the writer. The introduction that follows is a classic *captatio benevolentiae*. Following virtually all of the commonplaces listed in the *ad Herennium*,[77] Fulbert writes that it is good in itself and practical to think about the deeds of men whose holiness makes them worthy to be imitated; that he will not rely on his own strength to do this but will seek the aid of the Holy Spirit; that he has learned of Aubert's deeds by "the relation of very truthful men or found them written here and there in sacred pages"; and that he writes these things solely for the benefit of the community so that they might have them "for the praise of their founder . . . and to make progress in the emulation of his holy works" (539). And he continues with the expectable modesty topos, begging forgiveness for this own inadequacies as a writer and referring praise to his patron for ordering the life to be written rather than to himself for writing it.

At the very moment of transition to the *narratio,* precisely where we would expect to begin the chronological presentation of the significant events

of Aubert's life, we find instead Fulbert's absolute and knowing refusal to narrate a life using the conventional hagiographical plot. And since the refusal is
made by means of the trope of *occupatio,* the conventional narrative procedure
is invoked in the very act of setting it aside: "Nor should the curious reader demand from us that the deeds of the blessed man be written in a contiguous
order—namely, that he arose from such and such a birth, that his holy infancy
had such and such beginnings, that his adolescence was outstanding by means
of such and such a miracle—when the reader understands that the greatest
and highest part of his miracles lies hidden from our notice." [Id vero lector a
nobis curiosius requirere non debet ut beati Viri gesta continenti ordine scrib-
antur, videlicet quibus oriundus natalibus, quibus initiis ejus sancta infantia,
quibus adolescentia miraculis claruit, dum intelligat miraculorum ejus sum-
mam et maximam partem a nostra notitia latere] (539). The biographical plot
is set aside in favor of a narrative of apostolic succession that seems to open a
full-fledged history of the church.[78]

> When God and Our Lord Jesus Christ, having pitied the fate of human
> destruction and having brought to completion the sacraments ordained
> by the Father, was about to return to heaven and present before the
> paternal face the new glory of victory over the flesh, he chose new
> guardians for the newborn Church, to whom he delegated the care of
> the firstlings of his flock. Radiant with the light of faith and enriched by
> the treasure of the Holy Spirit, they lit up with the light of truth the
> world blinded by the darkness of ignorance, and they constantly weeded
> out the poisonous seeds of the ancient seducer from the field of the
> Church. The disciples were the first executors of this holy instruction,
> and then their successors were the holy doctors whom divine providence
> preordained to tend the minds of the faithful till the end of the aged
> world.

> [Igitur humanae perditionis sortem miseratus Deus et Dominus noster
> Jesus Christus, paternae dispositionis peractis sacramentis, ad coelum
> rediturus, novamque victricis carnis gloriam paternis vultibus praesen-
> taturus, novos nascentis ecclesiae cultores, quibus novelli gregis cura
> mandaretur, elegit; qui lumine fidei irradiati, Spiritus Sancti munere di-
> tati, mundum ignorantiae tenebris caligantem veritatis lumine illustrar-
> ent, et virulenta antiqui seductoris semina de agro Ecclesiae constanter

resecarent. Hujus Dominicae institutionis executores primi discipuli, deinde successores eorum, sancti scilicet Doctores extiterunt, quos in finem senescentis mundi ad excolendas mentes fidelium providentia divina praeordinavit.] (540)

The passage begins with a moment of temporal fulfillment that is also the origin of a history of salvation, and it ends with history's end. Jesus is visualized at the moment of his withdrawal, his work having been brought to completion (per-actis) in "the new glory of victory." Yet this moment of thorough completion serves as the singular origin of the Church, which here is placed at the beginning of a historical trajectory through a triple metaphor of birth—the Church is a child at birth, a flock of newborn lambs, a newly seeded field. Because it requires instruction, shepherding, and cultivation, the Church's coming into being at the moment of Christ's withdrawal also requires a succession of governors, stretching, as the image has it, from the beginning of a new temporal dispensation to "the end of the aged world" (in finem senescentis mundi).

In the passage that immediately follows, the phrase "the treasure of the Holy Spirit" receives a full-fledged allegorical development via the parable of the talent. History is the progressive gathering of all humanity into the single Church: "Accepting the talent of spiritual gifts from their high Paterfamilias, and investing it in the business of preaching for an interest of souls, they yearned so much the more to increase it as they were the more certain of remuneration by their bestower and terrified by the sentence of damnation for the lazy servant in the gospel. And in their number the holy man of God and most just priest of Christ, Aubert, shone forth at the time of Dagobert, the outstanding King of the Franks." [Qui spiritualium talenta donorum a summo Patre-familias accipientes, et praedicandi negotio ad usuram animarum ex-pendentes, tanto impensius amplificare studuerunt, quanto certiores erant de remuneratione largitoris, et ex Evangelica sententia conterritit de damna-tione torpentis servi. De quorum numero sanctus vir Domini Autbertus et sacerdo Christi probatissimus, refulsit temporis Dagoberti, Francorum regis incliti] (540). In the source for this passage, Alcuin simply placed Vaast in the multitude of Christ's successors; Fulbert places Aubert at a point of culmina-tion along with Dagobert, the Merovingian king so important for Capetian royal propaganda.[79] Bishop and king shine forth as unique embodiments of au-thority, the guardians of all humanity gathered up into the community of the Church.

Aubert's early life is then quickly summarized from boyhood to high ecclesiastical office, but merely in one short sentence. There are no miracles, no
prophecies, no signs of charisma, no narrative development: "From the years of
his sacred boyhood, inspired by supernal grace, he surpassed his contemporaries
in his way of life. Given over to letters and informed sufficiently in canon law,
advancing step by step, he grew in excellence by increments until he was carried to the height of priestly honors." [Qui ab ipsis sacrae pueritiae annis, su-
perna gratia aspiratus, annosos viros sanctis praeibat moribus. Litteralibus
denique studiis traditus et ecclesiasticis sanctionibus decenter informatus, per
gradus singulos proficiens, succedentibus virtutum incrementis provectus est
ad culmen sacerdotalis honoris] (540). This sentence is the beginning and end
of chronologically ordered, biographical writing in the text. Its culmination
is the very point reached in the rehearsal of sacred history (the moment when
Aubert shines out). The life of Aubert and the history of church governance are
then seen again from a visionary perspective outside either history or biography: "The maker of human salvation indeed foreknew that the ancient enemy
would persecute the human flock so much the more ardently as the end of the
world drew closer, since he would know that nothing more would then remain
exposed to be attacked by his arts. Against the strong force of this tyrant he
therefore prepared a strong defense, giving us Aubert to be a most vigilant
shepherd of his flock and most faithful guardian of his souls." [Porro humanae
salutis auctor praescius antiquum hostem tanto ardentius gregem dominicum
insecuturum, quanto vicinius instante fine seculi sciret nihil superesse quod ad
tentandum artibus suis ulterius patuisset, adversus tyrannidis ejus impetum
validum defensionis paravit obstaculum, dans nobis Autbertum, videlicet gregis
sui pastorem vigilantissimum et custodem animarum fidelissimum] (541). As
the register changes from history to biography to apocalypse, the bare narrative,
stating no more than that Aubert excelled in his education, learned ecclesiastical law, and became bishop of Cambrai, is made to signify matters of the highest
consequence: Aubert's succession to the episcopal throne becomes a point of
presence whose consideration gathers up the whole history of salvation. Not
merely the culmination of sacred history, or even its resumé, but all of history
is complete and wholly present in his life. His becoming bishop enacts Christ's
victory over Satan that is both the origin of sacred history and its end. The threefold rhetorical transformation that we have been observing in this brief passage
shifts the narrative register from that of the historical life of the Church in time,
to the individual life of Aubert, and finally to the dynamic of salvation where

Christ and Satan are the only actors. *The Life of Aubert* thus begins not by assimilating individual moments in Aubert's life to typological models but by invoking one of the principal interpretative mechanisms of biblical reading, a three- or fourfold correspondence between the literally narrated event, the sacramental history of the Church, the moral life of the individual, and the events of the last days.[80]

The beginning of this narrative puts into play a process of symbolization far more demanding and far more radical than anything we should expect to find in conventional hagiography. Every moment in the bishop's life becomes a meditational place that conveys the highest of mysteries. The most ordinary set of events in the life of the bishop is made here to carry an enormous burden of symbolic weight. There are no signs and wonders. For those who demand signs, Fulbert writes, "need to ponder the words of evangelical faith that the very author of signs said: 'Who believes in me, the works that I do even he will do, and he will do greater than these' [quoting John 14], so now that the exterior miracles that formerly carnal eyes and weak listeners used to need have ceased, at last they do not ponder the signs but discern the life, which is far more profitable for the emulation of virtues than is the demonstration of miracles." [fidei Evangelicae verba pensarent quae ipse Auctor signorum dicit: "Qui credit in me, opera quae ego facio et ipse faciet, et majora horum faciet," ut videlicet cessantibus exterioribus miraculis, quibus olim carnales oculi et infirmi auditores indigebant, jam tandem discerent vitam et non signa pensare quae longe melius proficit ad aemulationem virtutum quam ostensio miraculorum] (542). And of what does this life that needs to be discerned consist? As we have seen, it is the routine life of an eleventh-century bishop: Aubert prays, advises, educates, pronounces on questions of orthodoxy, and consecrates churches.[81] These ordinary events are not miraculous signs; they are the very life of the church, and their significance is revealed, as we have seen, in the lives of those others whom Aubert affects, each of which is a moment in the progressive unification of the world into the single community of Christendom. "The greatest and highest part of his miracles lies hidden from our notice," writes Fulbert. Spiritual truth, from the beginning to the end of his *Vita* is hidden away in the deepest recesses of Aubert's self, yet the whole history of the world signifies him.

The one explicitly visionary passage in the *Vita* deepens the hiddenness. Like Ezekiel, who in a vision foresaw the reconstruction of the Temple in Jerusalem, Aubert suddenly sees a man measuring out the place where a new church should be built in Arras to house the translated remains of St. Vaast. Aubert's vision is given an elaborate, allegorical development in a long, homiletic digression that uses the interpretation of Ezekiel's vision current in contemporary Cluniac meditational literature in which each architectural detail of the Temple is given a complete exegesis.[82] Fulbert's exposition hinges on the Pauline aphorism "Vos estis templum Dei vivi" (2 Cor. 6:16), and in this passage Aubert simultaneously occupies the positions of the wise architect who constructs the temple, the temple itself, and the God housed within it whose works, namely the other people's lives that compose his own *Vita*, are his signs. What Aubert finally teaches, as the homily concludes, is the whole process of sacred history. He teaches it because he incarnates it: "There are many other things, which it is not necessary to rehearse individually lest it be too long. Each of these individual things has its own measure and order, and the grace of virtues and of the sacraments conforms to these same measures. Blessed Aubert, like a wise architect, suited the moral observance of our work and the whole plan of our conversation to their example, teaching us to go from the carnal to the spiritual, from the Synagogue to the Church, from the old to the new, from the earthly to the heavenly." [Sunt vero multa alia, quae omnia recensere singillatim ne nimis longum fit, non oportet, quorum singula mensuras et ordines suos habent, et iisdem mensuris consequens est Sacramentorum et virtutum gratia, ad quorum exempla beatus Autbertus et moralem nostrae operationis observantiam, et totam conversationis rationem ut sapiens architectus conformavit, docens nos de carnalibus ad spiritualia, de synagoga ad ecclesiam, de veteribus ad nova, de terrenis ad coelestia transire] (558).

There is no death scene, for we do not know the "largest portion of his virtues" [maximam virtutum eius partem a nostra memoria sustulerunt] (561). But he has left the trace of his body, and the narrative of its history concludes the *Life.* There are still no miracles, no cures, no visions. But the body itself stages again the significance of its holiness. The body is first buried in the Church of St. Peter outside the walls of Cambrai and is then brought inside in the year 888 to keep it safe from the Norman raids. Then Aubert's relics are fragmented and partially translated. For when the Holy Roman Emperor Otto I creates Magdeburg as an archiepiscopal seat (this would have been 968) as an outpost against the Saxons, he wishes to make a gift of the bodies of Sts. Gerí and Aubert for the consecration of the cathedral. Reluctant to refuse the emperor, but equally reluctant to deprive Cambrai of the presence of its two patrons, the bishop of Cambrai temporizes and sends Otto two other bodies, along with "certain small bones" (articuli) from the bodies of Gerí and Aubert, thus satisfying the imperial request while also keeping the patron bishops at home in Cambrai. The body thus becomes coterminous with the Empire itself: "Plainly it was not without the counsels of the divine will that the city of Cambrai, which marked the border separating his empire from France, and the city of Magdeburg, which under his reign expelled the Slavs from Germania at the other border, each fortified with the protection of the blessed man, would stand guard like a strong wall for an enclosed city." [sane non sine nutu divini consilii, scilicet ut Cameracensis civitas quae confinium imperii ejus a Francis disterminat, et Magadaburc, quae alio confinio sub regno ejus Sclavos a Germania eliminat, beati Viri munitae praesidio, tanquam forti circumdatae muro tuerentur] (563). Finally, in 1015 Gerard has Aubert translated back to his original burial place in the Church of St. Peter, now enclosed in the new walls of the city. The paradox of the Christ, enclosed in the womb while himself enclosing the world, is the final figure for Aubert. Aubert, himself the temple of the living God; Cambrai, a figure of the celestial city; the Empire, enclosed by Cambrai and Magdeburg, and thus enclosed by Aubert like a city by its walls — all are signs and more than signs of the process of sacred history, a process visible in the most ordinary events of ordinary life, performed by the routine work of the bishop in what Fulbert considers the extreme old age of the world.

But there is an excess, an irreducible remainder that escapes the intense pressure of the exegetical writing in this text. That remainder is everyone's restlessness and dissatisfaction with their lives. Landelin in the monastery longs for the life of the warrior nobility, and as a warrior he has hellish visions that drive him back to the monastery. Ghislen, a young Athenian nobleman cultivated in the liberal arts, leaves home, wanders first to Rome, and then, summoned by a voice, winds up a hermit in a wild place near Cambrai. Vincent walks away from court; Waldetrude sets aside her family. The characters surrounding Aubert live lives of inner turmoil. Driven by spiritual longings, they wander restlessly and far from their secular homes. That excess, too, is Aubert's story.

Chapter Two

NARRATING THE ENGLISH NATION AFTER 1066

THE LAST ENGLISH KING

The rapid growth of Norman power in France and the sudden hegemony of the Normans in England and in Italy in the eleventh century have been subjects of fascination to modern historians.[1] This chapter considers contemporary accounts of the Norman reign in Britain. Exploring narratives in the service of Norman centralizing administration together with narratives written in opposition to it allows us to understand processes obscured by the conventional story of Norman power and its dramatic rise. I begin with contemporary treatments of October 1066 by focusing not on William's victory but on the defeat of King Harold. In the second half of this chapter I proceed to the next decade and turn to Earl Waltheof of Northumbria and his historians. These narratives place the multiple relations of state formation to national identity in very high focus.

Medievalists, it is generally presumed, study the time before the state, yet they do this, if they are literary scholars, as part of the historical study of national literatures. The departmental structures of our universities, as well as the "specialization category codes" of our professional associations and granting institutions, are organized by the idea of national languages, literatures, and history. This disciplinary organization rests on the fundamental assumption of philology, that the essential ethnic characteristics of a nation are embodied most profoundly in the deepest characteristics of its language. In these linguistic characteristics the truth of the nation progressively realizes itself and becomes most profoundly manifest in its literature and in its law.[2] Philology so construed requires the identification of the state with the nation, an imaginary structure that maps political sovereignty onto ethnic and linguistically homogenous territories.[3] Philology, if I may say it this way, recapitulates an ontology. Hence, for medieval literary studies, the great privilege granted to writing in the European vernaculars. And hence, too, the emphatic assertion—despite all evidence to the contrary—that the European vernaculars are themselves linguistically homogenous entities. For it long went without saying that creoles and pidgins belonged to the polyglot, lawless, disorderly world of the darker races, the races "without history" who needed to be ruled.[4] The orderliness that once was asserted to signify culture itself[5] was also manifest in the orderliness of the map: the division of the world into ethnically and linguistically bordered national states began in Europe, when the "not yet modern" medieval associations coalesced into the early modern state, and thence spread by the "modernizing" and "civilizing" imperial project to the rest of the world.[6] In several recent studies John Ganim has reminded us of a forceful image of the homology of the medieval and the colonial in the narrative of modernity: in the Paris Exposition of 1899, the icon of modernism, the Eiffel Tower, rose majestically over reproductions of medieval European and contemporary South East Asian villages placed at its feet. History is nothing but the history of modernity; all the rest is the not-yet-modern that possesses a history insofar as it can be read as a prelude to modernity.[7]

When we turn to the case of England, it is easy to see why the Norman Conquest has been enough of an embarrassment for English historical self-consciousness that much of insular historiography over the last two centuries has had a stake in its disavowal or, to use Clare Simmons's telling formulation, its reversal.[8] While Victorian nationalist and imperial investments are surely the principal determinants of the nineteenth-century historiography of the Middle Ages, we need too to consider the various kinds of complicity, as it were in advance, of medieval social, political, and ideological processes with the imperial project.[9] The outlines of the same colonial discourse that lives on into modern historiography are already implicit in the source texts' own methods of constructing the categories of ethnicity, the nation, and the individual subject that the Conquest provokes. Walling off the Middle Ages from early modern colonialism—as Other—hides this complicity and is itself a part of it.

The death of Harold Godwinson, the famously last Anglo-Saxon king defeated by William the Conqueror at the Battle of Hastings, was the subject of a wide variety of contemporary representations. Best known, of course, is the illustration in the Bayeux tapestry showing Harold killed by an arrow to the eye. As historical pictures tend to do, whatever their actual degree of visual representational skills, the Bayeux tapestry presents itself as a simple and unmediated representation of reality: Harold is depicted with an arrow in his eye because, the tapestry seems to say to us, he was shot in the eye by an arrow. Let us, however, remind ourselves, as a way of beginning, that modes of representation, including conscious and unconscious decisions about what to represent and what to gloss over, are always driven by a variety of considerations and that blinding, for example, was a frequent punishment for a variety of crimes from theft to multiple arrest.[10] Harold may well be depicted in the Bayeux tapestry with an arrow in his eye because it is a legible sign of the justice of his defeat at Hastings rather than because it is what "actually happened to him" on the battlefield.[11] When we turn to the narrative sources, we find that, rather than clarifying the question of "what happened," the multiplicity of sources throws the problematics of representation into very high relief.

The Official Story

William of Jumièges, a principal source for almost all later medieval historical treatments of the Norman ruling families, does not narrate the scene of Harold's death at all, merely noting that Harold was among those killed during the first engagement.[12] In this lack of detail, his account is similar to what seems to develop as an English tradition. Both the *Peterborough Chronicle* and the *Worcester Chronicle,* for example, merely note the death of Harold without narrating the circumstances; Florence of Worcester notes, with a sigh of lament, that Harold dies on the first day at twilight, but he too does not narrate the circumstances.[13]

For more elaborate eleventh-century descriptions we need to consider Norman and French sources. In many ways closest to the event was Guillaume de Poitiers, whose social position and intellectual affiliations are summed up by Raymonde Foreville as "l'écho direct de la cour anglo-normande et du clergé lettré et réformateur qui entourait et assistait le prince normand."[14] In his life of William the Conqueror, composed probably in 1075, the death of Harold and the events leading to it are presented as the unequivocal enactment of God's judgment, a continual demonstration of the justice of William's claim to the English throne. In this text too, the actual death scene is not narrated; rather, after a long praise of William's valor — William is Achilles and Aeneas to Harold's Hector and Turnus — and a set of brief, vivid descriptions of William's force and agility in battle, we are presented with a number of substitutes for a description of Harold's death. Guillaume's narrative first of all jumps to the aftermath of the fighting at the end of the first day, where it takes up for a moment the point of view of the vanquished English; as they come to understand the extent of their devastation, they see that their king, his brothers, and a great part of the nobility lie dead.[15] There is a decisive last battle, for the English—"prompt to arms" because descended from the Saxons, "the most savage of men"[16]— rally after they have become aware of Harold's death, and then the narrative redescribes the same scene, this time from the point of view of the Normans. William surveys the battlefield with mixed emotions: he laments the carnage and the loss of the "flower of English nobility and youth" but recognizes the outcome of the battle as just.[17] He recovers Harold's mutilated body with difficulty because it is no longer recognizable by its physical appearance but only by "some signs" (quibusdam signis). After first rejecting a generous money offer from Harold's mother and then absolutely refusing to turn Harold over to her freely when so many others lie unburied, William gives the body to a certain William Malet to be buried near the sea because, he says mockingly, it is fitting for Harold now to be the guardian of the shore.[18] Guillaume concludes this narrative sequence in his own voice, apostrophizing Harold in his tomb by the sea. The narrative here moves into a distinctly moral register, and Harold becomes in the process a universal example of political excess: driven by vice to try to increase his own considerable power, Harold in his tomb bodies forth the perils of ambition for all future generations, whether English or Norman: "We do not boast about you, Harold, but together with the devoted victor who has lamented your fall we pity and weep over you. You have been conquered in an outcome worthy of you: deservedly, you have fallen in blood; you lie in your tomb on the shore; and you will be an abomination to succeeding generations both English and Norman." [Nos tibi, Heralde, non insultamus, sed cum pio victore, tuam ruinam lachrymato, miseramur et plangimus te. Vicisti digno te proventu, ad meritum tuum et in cruore jacuisti, et in littoreo tumulo jaces, et posthumae generationi tam Anglorum quam Normannorum abominabilis eris] (2.25).

If Guillaume de Poitiers' narrative is the official Norman version of the battle, The Carmen de Hastingae proelio, a Latin verse chronicle probably written by Guy of Amiens before May of 1068,[19] provides in many ways the voice of William's French allies. We owe to the Carmen the earliest description of the death of Harold. Far from being among the first to fall, Harold is among

the last: his death in the poem brings the fighting to an end. Four principal Norman nobles — William himself; Eustace, Count of Boulogne (the actual hero of
the poem); Hugh of Ponthieu; and a certain Giffard — rush Harold in the midst
of his heroic resistance, and each carves off a significant piece of Harold's body.
Not a random shot by an anonymous archer but a choreography of noble vengeance brings about Harold's death: William kills Harold directly with a blow
to the chest; next Eustace of Boulogne decapitates the body, then Hugh stabs him
in the stomach, and finally Giffard cuts off a piece of his thigh (the editors draw
attention to the likely euphemism of this description) and takes it away. As well
as a choreography of noble action, the discourse presents itself as a formal spec-
tacle of value — the royal blow occupies a whole elegiac couplet:

> The first one breaking his breast with the point of his sword through
>   the shield
> Pours out a shower of blood on the ground
>
> [Per clipeum primus dissoluens cuspide pectus,
> Effuso madidat sanguinis imbre solum].

The decapitation takes up a long line:

> The second with a sword cuts off his head under his helmet
>
> [Tegmine sub galeae caput amputat ense secundus]

The less noble thrust to the stomach occupies a pentameter:

> And with his weapon the third pierces the organs of his stomach
>
> [Et telo uentris tertius exta rigat]

Finally, the thigh wound is presented in a half-line:

> The fourth cuts off his hip
>
> [Abscidit coxam quartus]
>   (34–36)

The English are immediately vanquished just as the body has been fragmented. Yet later William gathers up the pieces of the dismembered body and in a manner has it made whole: wrapped in a purple cloth (sindon purpurea), it is buried in a noble tomb high on a cliff to become the guardian of the shore.

The poem describes Harold's burial by the sea, but while Guillaume treats the suggestion that Harold be guardian of the shore as mockery, the *Carmen* takes it very seriously indeed, making it the epigraph for his burial stone. William, "iratus," has refused Harold's mother's request for the body and declared that Harold belongs on the shore. The poem continues:

> And so, as it was witnessed, the body was ordered to be
> Enclosed in the earth on a high promontory.
> Immediately, a certain man, part Norman and part English,
> A companion of Harold, was ordered and did it freely,
> He quickly took up and buried the body of the king
> And placing a stone, he wrote an inscription:
> "By order of the duke, you lie here, King Harold,
> To be the guardian of the shore and of the sea."
>
> [Ergo uelut fuerat testatus, rupis in alto
> Precepit claudi uertice corpus humi
> Extimplo quidam, partim Normannus et Anglus
> Compater Heraldi, iussa libenter agit.
> Corpus enim regis cito sustulit et sepeliuit;
> Imponens lapidem, scripsit et in titulo:
> "Per mandata ducis rex hic Heralde quiescis,
> Vt custos maneas littoris et pelagi."]
>
> (38)

The veneration that the writer shows to the body of Harold owes much more to the Capetian milieu and the developing sense of sacred kingship than to any residue of Viking burial customs among the Normans.[20] Harold has been justly defeated, but he remains always an anointed king. He also becomes in the process a complex ideological entity: he is a king, to be sure, but a king subject to the commands of a duke (Per mandata ducis rex hic Heralde quiescis). He is buried by a peer (compater Heraldi), but one who already is both English and Norman. And in his subjection by conquest he becomes also a guarantee of the inviolability of England, the guardian of its shores and of the sea. The fact of conquest is, in the body of Harold, both proclaimed and disavowed, a contradiction at the heart of William's own ideological program: William claimed the English throne first of all by descent, then by election, and finally by feudal right.[21] The Conquest is not, as it were, a conquest, but both the recovery of what was rightfully already William's own and a continual manifestation of the justice of that recovery, a judgment of God in a large-scale aristocratic trial by combat over the rights of land tenure. In fact, Eadmer, writing at the end of the eleventh century, says that it is the French who call the Norman victory a judgment of God: "Even now the French who were there say about this battle that although there was such various fortune on the one side and on the other, yet nevertheless there were so many wounds and such flight on the side of the Normans that their victory must truly and without doubt be entirely ascribed to a miracle of God, who in thus punishing the crime of Harold's perjury shows that he is not a God who will allow iniquity." (De quo proelio testantur adhuc Franci qui interfuerunt, quoniam, licet varius casus hinc inde extiterit, tamen tanta strages et fuga Normannorum fuit, ut victoria qua potiti sunt vere et absque dubio soli miraculo Dei ascribenda sit, qui puniendo per hanc iniquium periurii scelus Haroldi, ostendit se non Deum esse volentem iniquitatem.)[22]

A very different version of Harold's death and burial, already current by 1125,[23] is narrated in the chronicle of Waltham Abbey, *De inventione sancte crucis*.[24] Written sometime between 1177 and 1189,[25] the chronicle interlaces two traditions of Waltham: the discovery, translation, and miraculous activity of an *imago Christi* brought to Waltham by Tovi le Preud, the first founder of the church; and, after Tovi's lands came to him by inheritance, Harold's refounding and endowment of the church with his own college of twelve secular canons. According to the chronicle, Harold is at Waltham when he hears of the landing of the Normans, and when, before heading out for the engagement, he prostrates himself in the form of a cross (in modum crucis prosternens) before the life-sized crucifix, the stone image of Christ bows its head in sorrow for his fate.[26] Fearing this sign, two canons follow Harold, observe the battle, and afterwards beg William for the body, promising him a large amount of gold for it. William at first refuses, telling the canons that he has vowed to erect a church on the battlefield in penitence for all the blood shed on both sides and that Harold would be more fittingly buried there.[27] William later relents, nobly refusing all offers of repayment. The canons therefore proceed to the battlefield to retrieve the body, but to their dismay they cannot identify it among the large number of mutilated corpses. One of the canons finally brings Edith Swan-neshals, Harold's concubine (cubicularia), who "knew the secret marks on the king's body better than others did, for she had been admitted to a greater intimacy of his person" (Secretiora in eo signa nouerat ceteris amplius, ad ulteriora intima secretorum admissa),[28] and upon her identification the body is taken to Waltham and buried. The writer concludes by telling us that he saw the body there with his own eyes when it was translated, and he notes that the wounds Harold suffered were visible even on his bones (plagas ipsis ossibus impressas).[29]

Finally, in 1125 William of Malmesbury fashions what seems to be a narrative synthesis of these various accounts. Harold is killed by an arrow that pierces his brain (iactu sagittae uiolato cerebro procubuit) and then has his thigh deliberately slashed by a soldier whom William later punishes for the "shameful and cowardly action" (rem ignauam et pudendam). William then freely and magnanimously gives Harold's body to his mother for burial at Waltham.[30]

Each of these early representations employs hagiographical procedures, not least the narrative pattern of *inventio* and *translatio,* and in each of them Harold's corpse occupies the spiritual position of a relic—found, transferred, and installed in a privileged space, its rightful home, where it serves as both a sign and an effective means of commemoration—although none of the narratives under consideration, including the *Waltham Chronicle,* has any intention of sanctifying Harold in the strict sense. Rather, in all cases the body of the defeated king serves as the sign of spiritual victory: it manifests the permanent presence of divine justice in a secular order, no matter how transient, arbitrary, or unjust the saeculum might seem to be. As such, Harold's body and the permanent presence of his tomb make the event historically comprehensible and permanently legible. In all these texts, Harold's body thus commemorates not so much William's victory as God's made manifest in the secular sphere.[31] In this way, as different as are the details of the events from text to text, all the texts are united in their complicity with the contemporary array of power: whether treating Harold's body as a sign of English inviolability (as if the Conquest—that is, a violent transfer of regimes—were not a political fact), or as a sign of the just succession of the Norman regime (as if the Norman regime were the outcome of ordinary principles of routine succession and not a break with the past), or as a commemoration of the pious behavior of a great landholder (whose secular failure is transmuted by his gifts to eternal success), each of these texts deploys hagiographic procedures in the service of what we might call political orthodoxy.

The Alternative Version

Yet contemporary with these texts, and circulating in the oral tradition, is another entirely alternative story—namely that Harold did not die at Hastings at all. Indeed, the writer of the *Waltham Chronicle* knows of it and is at some pains to refute it, and traces of its existence show up in various ways in a rather large number of texts in various genres composed in the twelfth century. This alternative version is a species of oppositional narrative: the story of the rightful king, lurking in obscurity, who will return to rally his loyal followers and claim his due. That story became the basis for an astonishing life of Harold written much later. The *Vita Haroldi* was written at Waltham during the early thirteenth century in highly elaborate Latin prose, and around the beginning of the fourteenth century it was copied into a codex, now Harley 3776, in which manuscript alone it survives, along with other material relevant to the founding and history of Waltham Abbey.[32] Before turning to it, however, I want to examine three texts written during the reign of Henry II: Aelred of Rievaulx's *Vita Edwardi confessoris et regis,* Wace's *Roman de Rou,* and Gerald of Wales' *Itinerarium Cambriae.* Like the texts we have been examining, each of these narratives works out a complex ideological rapprochement between representing and disavowing conquest as a political fact. The particular ideological investments of the court of Henry II place a heavy burden on the representation of Harold's death and the violent transfer of power attendant upon it, and each of the three texts is in its own way cognizant of the alternative story of Harold's possible survival.

Aelred's *Life of Edward* was written around the time of Edward's translation in 1163 and seems to have been commissioned for the occasion. Like the translation, the *Vita* was one of the principal instruments for the royal policy that transformed Edward into a saint. Very widely circulated, it became the basis for the many later accounts of the life and miracles of the royal saint. Aelred constructs Edward primarily as a figural and material double of Henry Plantagenet, a celebration and guarantee of the legitimacy of his rule. The ideological work begins in the preface addressed to Henry II and continues throughout the life. Aelred presents Henry as a fulfillment of Edward's prophecies, the king signified both by Edward's very existence and by all his words. He is to be a consolation for the English and a "cornerstone" uniting the English and the Normans in one political edifice, since he himself, like Edward, unites England and Normandy in his body. Edward was the child of Aethelred, descended directly from Alfred, and Emma of Normandy; Henry Plantagenet's mother, Mathilda,

great-great-granddaughter of Edmund Ironside, returns the English blood to
the king's otherwise Norman body.[33] Aelred thus reads Edward's famous deathbed prophecy—that England shall be well only when a green tree shall be cut
through the middle and when the part cut off, after being carried the space
of three acres from the trunk, shall become again united to its stem, bud with
flowers, and bear fruit—as referring precisely to Henry I's marriage. The three
acres of distance are the three perforce illegitimate kings—Harold, William I,
and William Rufus forming together a kind of "antisuccession"—and the fruit
is the birth of Henry II.[34] Thus Edward's life ends, not with his death, but rather
with the accession of Henry II. In the body of Edward, England was already
Norman before William's arrival; in the body of Henry, England again becomes
English through Mathilda, herself Norman and English. By such narrative
means, Henry becomes the direct descendant of Edward, and the Conquest is
thus entirely effaced, told literally in a parenthesis. Aelred tells how Edward,
seeing Harold beat his brother Tostig when they were children, prophesies that
the one brother will triumph over the other. This leads to a very brief narrative of Harold's victory at Stamford Bridge, the fulfillment of the prophecy,
followed without further elaboration by the notice of Harold's presumed death at
Hastings. This is all there is of the Conquest: "In that same year, Harold himself,
having despoiled the realm of the English, either died wretchedly or, as some
people think, fled to live in penitence." (Eodem anno Haroldus ipse regno spoliatus Anglorum aut misere occubuit, aut ut quidam putant poenitentiae tantum reservatus evasit.)[35]

Whether Harold lives on or dies is irrelevant to Aelred's purposes. The
sole importance is the unity of England and Normandy in Henry, for which the
Conquest, as Aelred narrates it, need not have happened. For in all the ways
that matter most, Aelred asserts the unity of England and Normandy as already
manifest in Edward's body and therefore in his reign. Henry II's reign is in this
way a manifestation of the justice proclaimed by Edward's existence, and it appears to arise directly from it without a break. His reign thus recuperates the
devastation brought upon England by Harold himself, a devastation manifest precisely as a conquest for which Harold bears the sole responsibility:

> Finally they understood that the holy king had prophesied these things and
> did not make them up himself when King Harold, who proceeded against
> his oath that Duke William would be made king, was defeated in battle by
> the duke and thus made an end to English liberty and a beginning to servi-

tude. And so some people say that this prophecy was an advance warning that he was made king wrongly, especially those who greatly lament that the whole nobility of the English have perished to the point that they scarcely discern anyone descended from this people in England — neither king, nor bishop, nor abbot, nor governor of any sort.

[Experti sunt tandem regem sanctum haec non de suo spiritu prophetasse, quando rex Haraldus qui contra jusjurandum quod Willielmo duci fecerat regnum invaserat, ab ipso victus in praelio Anglicae libertati finem dedit, initium servituti. Unde quidam praemissam similitudinem dicunt, pro impossibili regem statuisse, illi maxime qui totam Anglorum nobilitatem sic deperisse lugebant ut ex ea gente nec rex, nec episcopus, nec abbas, nec princeps quilibet vix in Anglia cerneretur.][36]

The language celebrating Henry's accession to the throne is a virtually verbatim repetition of this list, without the negative particles: "Now England has a king from the English people, and has from the same people bishops and abbots, governors, and even the noblest knights who from the joining of both seeds have been born as an honor for some and a consolation for others." (Habet nunc certe de genere Anglorum Anglia regem, habet de eadem gente episcopos et abbates, habet et principes, milites etiam optimos, qui ex utriusque seminis conjunctione procreati aliis sunt honori, aliis consolationi.)[37] Thus the Conquest is undone. With Harold's disappearance, Henry has become Edward's son and heir.

The *Roman de Rou* enacts a similar unification of Henry II's reign with Edward's, but while Aelred's narrative procedures are primarily prophetic and exegetical, Wace writes in the voice of a secular historian. He narrates the events of the Conquest at length and with great circumstantial detail, blending the wide variety of sources that we have been examining and amplifying them for the sake of verisimilitude by means of the elaborate fictional procedures characteristic of contemporary historical narrative.[38] Moreover, Wace frequently intervenes in the narrative to tell his readers what he is certain about and where he has doubts or missing information. As Wace tells it, Harold is hit in the eye by an arrow during the earliest phase of the battle, when the Norman archers, realizing that they are not getting anywhere shooting at the well-armored English, decide to shoot high into the air. Harold is not killed but grievously wounded, and since no one knows whose arrow it was, many take credit for the shot: "And many boasted with great pride / that they pierced Harold's eye."

(e mult les mist en grant orguil / qui al rei Heraut creva l'oil.)[39] The battle rages for almost eight hundred lines more before Harold, in great pain from the arrow, is killed by an anonymous soldier and cut in the thigh by another (8811–18). After narrating the death of Gyrth, Harold's brother, at the hands of William himself, Wace returns to Harold and emphasizes the devastation of his defeat and the anonymity of his assailant:

> They threw the standard to the ground
> And they killed King Harold
> And the best of his companions.
> They captured the gonfalon of gold.
> There was such a crowd when Harold was killed
> That I cannot say who killed him.

> [L'estandart ont a terre mis
> e le rei Heraut ont ocis
> e les meillors de ses amis
> le gonfanon a or ont pris
> tel presse ont a Heraut ocire
> que jo ne sai qui l'ocist dire.]

(8829–34)

The burial takes place after William spends the night on the battlefield, eating and drinking among the dead. Wace tells us that the noble women of the realm came to find their husbands, brothers, fathers, and sons and carried them to their towns for burial. He then turns to the king:

> King Harold was taken away
> And was buried at Waltham
> But I don't know who took him away
> And I don't know who buried him.
> Many were left lying on the field,
> Many fled from there by night.

> [Li reis Heraut en fu portez
> a Watcham fu enterrez
> mais jo ne sai qui l'enporta

ne jo ne sai qui l'enterra
Maint en remest el champ gesant
maint é en ala par noit fuant.]
(8967–72)

What is striking about this narrative sequence as it stretches over hundreds of lines is the accumulation of confessions of ignorance around Harold's body: Wace says that he does not know who shot him, who killed him, who disfigured the body, who took him from the field, or who buried him. This amounts to a wholesale dismissal of the significance both of Harold's death and of the victory, a victory for which no one is responsible and no one can claim credit. Instead, the real victory lies elsewhere, neither on the battlefield nor in heaven but in the council chamber. Immediately after the battle, William's reign is inscribed by the narrative into two versions of secular justice. William is first of all a feudal lord who receives homage and fealty and appropriately invests his vassals—"He received fealty and homage / and so gave them their heritages" [e feelté en prist e homages / si lor rendi lor eritages] (8982–83)—and indeed he is exemplary in his generosity:

To many who were with him
And who had long served him
He gave castles, gave fortifications
Gave manors, gave counties;
He gave lands to vavasors
And gave many other incomes.

[As plusors qui l'orent sui
e qui l'orent longues servi
dona chastels, dona citez
dona maneirs, dona contez,
dona terres as vavasors
dona altres rentes plusors.]
(8991–96)

But more importantly, William is a lawgiver who is himself governed by law.[40] In one of the strangest and most important scenes of the poem, a scene without analogue in any other narrative source, William asks his feudal council composed of both Normans and English to choose what laws they would live under and thus to choose their ethnic identity:

> Then he had all the barons sent for
> And all the English assemble
> And had them choose what laws they would hold
> And what customs they wanted,
> Whether Norman or English.

> [Poist fist toz les barons mander
> e toz les Engleis assembler
> a chois les mist quels leis tendreient
> e quels costumes li voldreient
> ou des Normans ou des Engleis.]

(8997–9001)

They choose the laws and customs of King Edward, a choice that William confirms:

> And they said of King Edward
> They would hold and preserve his laws
> The customs that they knew
> And that they were accustomed to hold from the time of Edward
> Those they wanted, those they requested
> Those pleased them, those they prized
> Those were what they desired
> And the king granted these to them.

> [E cil distrent del rei Ewart
> les soes leis lor tienge e gart
> les costumes qu'il conoisseient
> qu'al tens Ewart tenir soleient
> celes voldrent, celes requistrent,
> celes lor plorent, celes pristrent.
> Issi lor fu a volenté
> e li reis lor a graanté.]

(9003–10)

Wace and Aelred converge in a radical denial of conquest as such. Norman history is made English as the Normans become themselves English,[41] choosing to live under the customs and laws that they all declare to date from the time of their own King Edward.[42] In the process Harold has disappeared into a cloud of speculation. He is replaced by a return to a past identity that is no longer identical to itself: the Anglo-Norman present here has colonized the English past.

Both Aelred's *Life of Edward* and the *Roman de Rou* elide the Conquest by figuring the post-Conquest period as a recuperation of the pre-Conquest past. There is a further elision here that remains always unmentioned but is inextricably linked to what we have been observing. In representing Henry II as the direct heir of Edward or—and this amounts to the same thing—in making the Normans responsible for introducing English law to England, the whole period of civil war and the reign of Stephen of Blois are entirely passed over. Just as William is the heir and elected successor of Edward, his own son Henry I produces Henry II, and a series of violent and discontinuous transfers of power are represented as if there were an unbroken chain of legitimate succession. The result of this process is routinely figured as a dual identity or hybrid body. Gerald of Wales foregrounds this process in an extraordinary passage of his extraordinary book.

Arriving in Chester, Gerald notes that it purports to be the burial place of the Emperor Henry V, who did penance by living there secretly after abdicating his throne. Similarly, he says,

> King Harold is buried there. He was the last of the Saxon kings in England, and, as a punishment for his perjury, he was defeated by the Normans in pitched battle at Hastings. He was wounded in many places, losing his left eye through an arrow that penetrated it, but, although beaten, he escaped to these parts. It is believed that he led the life of an anchorite, passing his days in constant attendance in one of the local churches, and so came contentedly to the end of life's journey.

> [Similiter et Haroldum regem se habere testantur: qui, ultimus de gente Saxonica rex in Anglia, publico apud Hastinges bello cum Normannis congrediens, poenas succumbendo perjurii luit; multisque ut aiunt confossus vulneribus, oculoque sinistro sagitta perdito ac perforato, ad partes istas victus evasit: ubi sancta conversatione cujusdam urbis ecclesiae jugis

et assiduus contemplator adhaerens, vitamque tanquam anachoriticam
ducens, viae ac vitae cursum ut creditur, feliciter consummavit.][43]

At this point Gerald immediately begins telling stories of monstrosities and
hybrids. In Chester, he writes, he saw cheese made from deer's milk;[44] he tells
of the appearance of a deer-cow (vacca cervina), the offspring of a deer and a
cow, which had the forequarters of a cow but the hindquarters, hair, and color-
ing of a deer; he tells also of a litter of puppies born of a dog that had coupled
with a monkey. These were apelike in front but doglike behind, and they were
killed with a stick by a countryman scandalized by the monstrous appearance
of their hybrid bodies.[45] Finally he tells of a woman without hands but whose
toes were so finely articulated that she could sew as well as other women. Gerald's narrative typically moves by such seeming inconsequence. It is hard, however, not to read this strange passage as a figure for the political mythology of
Henry II's court that celebrates the unity of England, a political mythology constructed by historiographic and hagiographic procedures in which political violence and social rupture are here displaced onto a narrative series of absences,
elisions, monstrous couplings, hybrid bodies, and, in the case of the countryman
and the dog-monkeys, the violent wielding of the *baculum,* the sign of secular and
ecclesiastical power.

Harold Sanctified

The narrative development of the *Vita Haroldi,* too, hinges not on a manifestation, which, as I discussed in the first chapter, is perhaps the defining characteristic of hagiography,[46] but on an absence—the body absent from its own death
scene at Hastings and above all absent from the tomb at Waltham—and therefore on a transformation of the significance of place and of the miraculous associated with it. Yet we will be much misled if we think of the absent body and
the empty tomb in the *Vita Haroldi* as having any kind of figural significance.
Rather, while retracing the development of the standard hagiographical narrative pattern modeled on the *Life of St. Martin,* the text shifts the scene of the
sacred entirely, from the place rendered holy by the manifestation of the divine presence in the miracle-working body into the psychological territory of
repentance and change. In the process, the *Vita Haroldi* transforms Harold into
a new kind of saint while transforming itself into a romance. Yet it does not

come before its readership as a mere fiction. The writer stakes his all on his own particular abilities and his claim to being a truth teller.

Let me briefly summarize the story. After a preface, the text begins with a quick presentation of the rise of Godwin to preeminence in the kingdom and then notices signs of Harold's distinction in youth. When he comes into his own, Harold leads a triumphant military campaign against the Welsh, but afterwards he suffers from what seems to be an incurable paralysis until he goes to Waltham and makes certain vows to its cross. Miraculously cured, Harold "leaves Waltham in body but not in spirit" and fulfills his vows by giving it great treasure. He becomes king but is immediately cast down. Left for dead on the battlefield, his body is found almost lifeless by some women who take him to Winchester, where he remains incognito in a cellar for two years and is cured by the ministrations of a Saracen woman. He then tries unsuccessfully to recruit first the continental Saxons and then the Danes to his cause. Finally, giving up on political action and family alliance altogether, he makes a pilgrimage to Jerusalem. Upon his return, now under the name of Christian, he takes up residence as a solitary on the Welsh borders, where he not only undergoes the kinds of ascetic discipline typical of the genre but, in an act of singular self-abasement, allows himself to be continually robbed and beaten by the wild Welshmen over whom he was once victorious. He never goes out without covering his face completely with a cloth. Over time, the Welsh become pacified by Christian's suffering and begin to venerate him, at which point he leaves and, again covering his face, goes to Chester, where after several years of confinement in another hermitage he dies after a deathbed confession: "It is true that I was formerly the King of England, Harold by name, but now am I a poor man, lying in ashes; and, that I might conceal my name, I caused myself to be called Christian." The text ends by telling us that the priest who has heard this confession tells everyone about these last words.

The text insists on a split between inner and outer experience that results in a complete redefinition of hagiographic exemplarity: Harold is an exemplary figure of Christian life, but his sanctity lies in the actual life and unique experience that is his story alone and can be replicated by no one else, his rise to power and rapid fall into suffering and repentance. Harold, after his cure, leaves Waltham "non corde sed corpore" and returns to the court, where he, or more properly his body, is welcomed into a series of social relations—as brother, soldier, and companion. Yet his experience, the text asserts, is not that of his body in society; it takes place elsewhere, in his heart, where he still stands in the presence of the cross. The hagiographic procedures of this text are thus in sharp contrast to what we have seen in the earlier representations of Harold's life. There Harold's identity was played out precisely in a context of family and status and thus was integrated directly into social being: even in the *Waltham Chronicle* Harold was venerated as a founder and gift giver and thus as a standard part of the aristocratic economy of gift exchange. In the *Vita Haroldi,* however, family, status, and social being are precisely what mask identity and what must be renounced, voluntarily or by compulsion, for real experience to be achieved. They are what must be seen through for real experience to be narrated. When Harold gives up all his political aspirations and returns from pilgrimage as Christian, he becomes "Christian," an example of generic Christian suffering, but only on the most starkly individualized and subjectivized terms. These are terms that are entirely dependent on significances developed in Harold's unique past. First of all, he fulfills the Pauline injunction to put on the armor of God by literally putting on his own armor: he wears his armor next to his skin to mortify his body, and thus his outer appearance no longer signifies the particular strength of a warrior but is "translated" into what I would like to call an efficacious sign of abjection and penitential torment. Like a sacrament, that is, his armor is both a metaphor and more than a metaphor:

> All the armor of the warrior, the whole adornment of this mighty man, is either left off altogether, or else worn for the abjection and punishment of the penitent. Not only is the breastplate not thrown off from his shoulders, arms, loins, and side, but it is brought closer to his body; for the inner garments being taken off and thrown aside, the roughness of the metal is next to the bare flesh. Thus when awake, he walks, not indeed armed so much as imprisoned in armor. Thus when he sleeps, a bed does not receive him, but he is embedded in a cuirass.[47]

> [Omnis armatura fortis totus potentis ornatus vel abdicatur penitus aut in abjeccionem transfertur: et penitentis penam. Nam humeris lacertis lumbis et lateri: lorica solum solita non adimitur sed proprius admovetur. Abstracta siquidem et abjecta interula: nude carni claibis duricies copulatur. Sic vigilans non armatus sed incarceratus incedit ferro, sic dormientem non thorus excipit sed thorax includit.] (40)

Similar, too, is Harold's decision to take up residence on the Welsh borders. Thus not only does Harold enclose himself, but, by enclosing himself there, he transforms the scene of his former triumph into an instrument for self-abasement. He encloses himself, that is to say, in the landscape and in the very clothes, the signs, that signified his earlier being. He is simultaneously entirely other than what he was and curiously the same.

The narrative of complex interior transformation is plotted by means of a series of romance motifs. The *Vita Haroldi* is precise in noting spatial movement and enclosure, but always as an image for development in time or interior growth. Harold leaves on pilgrimage and returns as Christian, the name change being simultaneously a disguise and a revelation of his real identity. As in the contemporary romance, there is a strong tendency toward doubling figures and a double plot: Harold's pilgrimage is an imitation of a pilgrimage by an older hermit whose pilgrimage is narrated first. Similarly, Harold lives enclosed in a cellar, enclosed in a hermitage in the forest, and enclosed finally in Chester, and each of these enclosures and movements from one enclosure to the next not only doubles previous ones but also doubles the experiences of past residents in those same places, whose adventures are also narrated. As in the courtly romance, these doublings ultimately construct a structure of difference, one that serves to deny the transferability of experience and to insist on the unique value of its difference not only from all others but also from the hero's earlier self. Yvain's adventure, to take a well-known example, doubles Calogrenant's so that what is made clear are all the ways in which Yvain's experience is not that of his uncle, and it doubles his own adventure as well, so that the Yvain who approaches the Lady of Landuc for the second time is a changed man from the one who came to her at first. So in the *Vita Haroldi* Harold's adventure as Christian is meaningful both in relation to other Christian lives—not least, the *Life of Martin*—and especially in relation to his earlier life as Harold.

There is a marked difference between the miraculous in the *Vita Haroldi* and in the texts on which it is modeled. If Harold is a place where the divine intersects with the secular world, the divine becomes manifest only in his suffering and never in his deeds—*in corde* and not *in corpore:* Harold performs no miracles but rather moves through a landscape of marvelous signs that are miraculous in the way they point to him and to him alone. He is cured of a mysterious paralysis by the wonder-working cross at Waltham, the stone Jesus later bows its head to him, the great oak in Rouen under which he swore fealty to

William withers on the instant of his defeat at Hastings. The landscape is similarly organized around the hero, as if long prepared for his coming: his jour-
neys take him from the height of kingship to Jerusalem to a series of enclosures
where he lives among hermits, and his final journey takes him, accompanied by
angelic voices, to a hermitage already prepared to accept him, where he will
reveal his identity as Harold and then die. This is remarkably like the landscape
of the vulgate Lancelot,[48] and it shares with the Lancelot, as well, the structure
of its adventures, a structure odd in comparison to that of the twelfth-century
courtly romance: the hero suffers, he does not act; and he experiences a set of
events that seem to have been long waiting for his presence but whose significance is available only to a privileged interpreter. This is a landscape simultaneously apocalyptic and hermetic: events long ago foretold are rapidly being
fulfilled, time is coming to an end, but the fullness of time reveals itself in a manner private, shut away, deeply personal. And the hero needs continually to be in-
structed in the meaning of his own life. He lives surrounded by a forest of signs,
but they are ambiguous, fraught with meaning but never transparently legible.

In the vulgate cycle the forest is populated with hermits who instruct the
hero in the meaning of the adventure;[49] in the *Vita,* Harold is himself a hermit
in the forest, but there is no privileged interpreter of the signs. The task de-
volves to the writer, whose authority exists only in a field contested by the versions of other writers and by the inevitability of other interpretations. Why
does the stone Christ bow its head? Is it a sign of the defeat of the English or
of the immense task of purification about to be undertaken by Harold? And the
great oak at Rouen? Does it wither because Harold violated his oath or to make
manifest the enormity of William's violently extracting Harold's oath under a
threat of death? All signs are thus ambiguous, and the necessary task of interpretation places the ingenious activity of the writer squarely in the foreground
of the text: Harold suffers silently while the writer weighs the evidence, constructs long and elaborate arguments, criticizes earlier interpretations. Thus
he writes a chapter in which he criticizes by name the "threefold error of William of Malmesbury," who had reported that Harold was killed by an arrow, cut
by a sword, and buried by his mother; and in another chapter criticizes the official Waltham version of the discovery of Harold's body, telling us that Edith,
misled by the rumor of Harold's death and ashamed not to recognize the body
of her lover, randomly chose a body to protect her own reputation. Finally, he
criticizes the way the anonymous writer, whose account of Harold's last days

he appends to his own text, assigns motives. The *Vita Haroldi* thus ends twice: the death of Harold is narrated in someone else's voice, but first the writer of the *Vita Haroldi* ends his own text, not with a narrative, but with a set of rejoinders to the final narrative, and then with a short treatise on how difficult it is to extract the truth from old accounts:

> But let this little book in its last sentences implore the benevolent reader to deign to make allowance for the excesses of the author by holy prayers, and assisted by the intercession of the pious King Harold, let him take him in his company to the harbor of eternal safety; may he grant pardon for the garrulousness of the writer of this present work when he sees how very difficult it was to patch up and make new again the materials at his command, torn and misplaced as they are by the studies of former authors, and to guide into the wished-for haven the boat, old and shattered, amid the ill-famed rocks of histories, while the tongues and writings of calumniators are, as it were, winds fighting against it. But all glory and honor be to God our helper, who alone, the Trinity and Unity, is King, blessed, worthy of praise, glorious and highly exalted for ever. (196–97)

> [Benivolum vero lectorem in sui calce libellus iste finali clausula semper habeat exoratum quatinus sui auctoris excessus piis precibus dignetur expiare secumque sancti Regis Haroldi opitulante intercessione ad portum salutis eterne ipsum pariter optineat pervenire. Multiloquio etiam in presenti opusculo scriptoris eo clemencius indulgeat veniam quod difficilius fuisse conspicit propositum materiam tot prius veterum studiis auctorum discissam multipliciter et dilaceratam resarcire quodam modo et innovare ac vetustam ut ita dicatur cimbam et conquassatam inter famosos hystoriarum scopulos in adversum eciam undique nitentibus tanquam ventis obtrectancium linguis et litteris ad destinatam perduxisse stacionem. Sit autem Deo adjutori nostro omnis honor et gloria qui trinus et unus solus imperat benedictus laudabilis gloriosus et superexaltatus in secula amen.] (92–93)

The very ingenuity that the writer needs simply to do his work becomes itself a source of anxiety. Thus the preface begins by reworking the themes of the preface to the *Life of Martin,* where the emptiness of telling stories about

secular heroes is contrasted with the glorious commemoration of spiritual perfection.[50] The emphasis in both prefaces is placed directly on the act of writing and on the writer's relation both to the community that requested him to
write and to the posterity that will receive it. Yet even in following the wishes
of his community to write the book, the writer of the *Vita Haroldi* fears that he
may be succumbing to temptation and a lesser reward: "Although to have looked
for the reward of transitory praise for one's labor on one's work is to have lost
one's trouble and one's task, in the same way to accept the attraction of a favor,
not indeed sought for, although freely bestowed, is to have deprived one's self of
the reward of internal self-consciousness and of the praise of the eternal Judge"
(104). [Ceterum quovis pro labore aut opere. laudis trasitorie expetisse merce-
dem: operam perdidisse est et impensam. Non solum autem sed nec nullatenus
expetite ultro tamen ingeste adquievisse favoris illecebre interni testis et eterni
judicis seipsum retribucione et laude privasse est] (4). From this perspective,
even serving the needs of the community and of posterity may put the writer
in a precarious moral position if his motives are not pure. The writer's concern
for his own "internal witness" (interni testis) mirrors his sense of the elusive and
hidden truth of Harold's experience.

What, then, is this ever elusive truth that the writer is so anxious to extract? In the historical chronicles the truth that Harold's defeat guaranteed
was the sense of the continual presence of God and the triumph of justice. In the
Vita Haroldi the truth always seems to lie just out of reach, always betrayed by
the simultaneous surplus and absence of meaning that writing and its dissemination produce. Harold, once King of England "but now a poor man, lying in
ashes," remains opaque at the very place where the genre most needs to understand him—in his exemplarity. This sense of truth's being always visible just as
it disappears or always just out of reach saturates the *Life,* but it is never more
apparent than in the image of the veiled figure. Harold/Christian never leaves
his enclosure except veiled, but the text cannot say why without equivocation—
perhaps, the narrator says, it is to keep from being recognized so as not to be
venerated, or perhaps to spare others the repulsive sight of his mutilated face,
or perhaps to prevent the sight of worldly vanities from entering his eyes. This
will to know and need to tell the truth, to reveal once and for all what lies beneath the veil by knowing the meaning of the veil itself, continually gives rise
within the narrative to the sense of a character whose experience always exceeds knowledge and to the sense of a truth that always ultimately escapes signification. It lies forever elsewhere—far beyond what can be told and buried

deep within, in the heart: thus this narrative seems always about to find that place where one's experience is finally one's alone, free from all traces of social being and all considerations of political right or divine justice. It seems always about to tell the secrets of a soul.

AFTER THE CONQUEST

Any current textbook of English history echoes the schema found in many of the chronicles written shortly after 1066. As we have seen, the daylong Battle of Hastings marks the decisive passage from one English regime to another. After the battle William consolidates his power in the south and, shortly before Christmas, approaches London, pacifies the city, and by means of the coronation ceremony takes possession of the England that he won on that single day. Chroniclers' general elision of the two months that separate the battle from the coronation is as striking as it is widespread. Representative is this passage from the *Hyde Chronicle*:

> On the day before the Ides of October, a Saturday, war was made in England between the Normans and the English, and although at first its outcome was indecisive for both sides and there was no respite from dying, finally, by a manifest judgment of God, on that same day King Harold, rushing to his death, brought an end both to the war and to the reign of the English. Count William, having won the victory, on Christmas Day following, was elevated to the kingship in London, and the reign of the English ended and the reign of the Normans began.

> [Pridie idus Octobris, ipso die Sabbati, factum est bellum in Anglia inter Normannos et Anglos, in quo bello quamvis varius in primis utrimque fuit eventus et nulla morientium requies, tandem manifesto Dei judicio eodem die rex Haroldus, corruens morte sua et bello et Anglorum regno finem imposuit. Willelmus igitur Comes, potita victoria, ipso sequenti die Natalis Domini apud Londoniam elevatus est in regem, finitumque est regnum Anglorum et inchoatum regnum Normannorum.][51]

To be sure, something happened in November and December. The chronicles speak of resistance before the coronation and especially after. In the west and especially in the north of the island, there were holdouts who had to be especially appeased, and even acts of open rebellion against the Conqueror during the following decade. These William would put down with the kind of spectacular violence he had already practiced in his drive to power in Normandy. By the end of 1075 he achieved unquestioned power over the whole of England, thus completing the logic of what had begun in 1066. William, as we discussed earlier in this chapter, claimed the English throne by descent, by election, and by feudal right. From this perspective, the Battle of Hastings signifies the recovery of what was rightfully already William's own while also manifesting the justice of that recovery. Hastings, as staged in the writings of the Conqueror's apologists such as William of Poitiers, is a trial by combat that demonstrates God's justice, and the Christmas coronation celebrates the regular passage of dominion from one legitimate sovereign to his lawful successor. Even this bare entry from the *Hyde Chronicle* is structured by the discourse of legitimacy and the regularity of succession. There is first of all the direct statement that these events were a "manifest judgment of God." But even in deeper structural layers the language of the text is saturated with this discourse. The Battle of Hastings and the Christmas coronation, for example, are each given a single sentence. In the first sentence, the grammatical subject and agent of all the action is King Harold. Everything in it is rendered as the attendant circumstances of three acts that King Harold actively performs: the first, his death, is subordinated to the latter two, which he performs as it were, post mortem. Rushing to his death, he puts an end both to the war and to the reign of the English (rex Haroldus, corruens morte sua et bello et Anglorum regno finem imposuit).[52] These are his last official acts as king, and they fully embody royal legitimacy: Harold, the last English king, brings *pax et iustitia* to his realm: he ends the war and in so doing ends English rule, "by a manifest judgment of God." If the first sentence is thus Harold's, the second sentence belongs entirely to William. In it, Count William becomes king (Willelmus igitur Comes . . . elevatus est in regem). But in this, his only action, William properly does nothing: the main clause of the sentence is in the passive voice, and the rest is made entirely of circumstantial and temporal constructions only loosely connected to him. The two sentences could not be more different. The first, Harold's sentence, is entirely controlled by the actions of the king; the second marks the precise moment when William becomes king and will be able to act henceforth. To this point, action (potestas) belongs to King Harold alone; afterwards, it belongs to William. In its tendency to treat the battle as the politically decisive moment of William's succession, the mainstream of modern historiography is, like the Hyde chronicler, entirely complicit with the official French version of the story. It takes William's side, even if it intends to deplore the event as a conquest.[53]

What I want to underline here is the unquestioned assumption at the heart of the story of the Conquest, that England—the England that William rightfully or wrongfully conquered—preexisted the Conquest and would outlive its immediate transformations. The metaphor of the Norman yoke, for example, combines the Whiggish sense of history as progressive with the assertion of the primary Englishness of enlightened institutions. It thus demands that before the Conquest there be an England whose essential nature may be recovered afterward. As Christopher Hill summarizes the notion in its general outlines: "Before 1066 the Anglo-Saxon inhabitants of this country lived as free and equal citizens, governing themselves through representative institutions. The Norman Conquest deprived them of this liberty, and established the tyranny of an alien King and landlords. They fought continuously to recover them, with varying success."[54] The patriotic sense that "there will always be an England" easily slides into the historical assurance that there always was an England.[55] The chronicle sources self-consciously deploy the Roman language of state, administration, and sovereignty and speak of what happened at Hastings as a transfer of regimes over an identical territory. The Hyde chronicler, for example, speaks of the end of the English and the beginning of Norman dominion as happening on the day of William's coronation. Sometimes the analogies with Roman politics are explicit: William of Poitiers, as I mentioned earlier, compares the Conqueror to Achilles at several points in his narrative, and William of Malmesbury compares him to Caesar.[56] At other times the analogies are an inescapable function of latinity: *gens, natio, princeps, regnum,* and *respublica* map the affairs of the eleventh century onto ancient Roman notions of the public sphere. And modern conditions of universal statehood make this ancient notion appear to be all the more naturally and unquestionably appropriate to the reality of the eleventh-century world being represented.

More painstaking modern scholarship, of course, paints a somewhat different picture from that of medieval and modern popular narratives, if only by acknowledging the rather tenuous hold that the Anglo-Saxon monarchy had on its borderlands to the north and west and the necessity for a continual negotiation with the Danes, who were an all but separate political and legal entity in the east.[57] Nevertheless, even quite precise local scholarship is often shadowed by a narrative marked by a strong teleology not all that different from the popular historiography of Hastings. The master narrative is of the rise of the Norman state in England, and an English state is thus both the precursor and the preordained outcome of the story. Hence the examples of political violence in the west and north between 1066 and 1075 are invariably conceptualized as rebellions against the king of a state that seems already to exist prior to its actual political existence.[58]

Waltheof and the Construction of England

I turn now to the process by which the state-making designs of William and his kin are represented in the chronicle sources as the story of the state of England. To do this, I will consider the narrative career of Earl Waltheof of Northumbria—enemy, captive, collaborator, local hero, traitor, English patriot, and ultimately saint. Resistance to and complicity with William's particular political designs and strategies in the north are narrated in the sources as the heroic story of native English opposition to the Norman colonial invader. In this story a complex of motives for opposition and collaboration is finally and uniformly reduced to a single essentialized ethnic struggle. This reduction produces three related transformations that I will discuss: there emerges a new, interiorized political space represented as a personal psychological struggle among conflicting loyalties; England becomes conceptualized as a continuous essential political entity whose present abjection in conquest is a sign of future political triumph; and the Christian *gloria passionis* is assimilated to secular heroism—not the victory of the warrior but the suffering of the political prisoner is the material token of both universal justice and the inevitable triumph of right.

Waltheof, son of Siward, Earl of Northumbria, and Aelfleda, a descendant of the house of Bamburgh, the most powerful family in the territory, appears only three times in the *Anglo-Saxon Chronicle*.[59] The first is in the *Worcester Chronicle,* where Waltheof, titled earl, is mentioned as being among the notables—including Archbishop Stigand, Edgar Aetheling, and the earls Edwin and Morcar—whom William took with him as hostages on his return to Normandy in the spring of 1067. Both the *Worcester Chronicle* and the *Peterborough Chronicle* place him among the leaders who fought against the king at York in 1069, and both chronicles single him out from among the others in the opening line of the entry for 1070: "In this year Earl Waltheof made his peace with the king." Finally, both chronicles name Waltheof as a conspirator against the king in the so-called wedding plot of 1074, for which, as both note, he was beheaded at Winchester.[60] But these sparse notations of the opposition and reconciliation of a small player on the very big stage of post-Conquest England give no hint of the huge quantity of narrative that Waltheof spawns over the next century: besides commanding significant narrative space in virtually all the major twelfth-century Latin histories,[61] Waltheof is the subject of two Old Norse poems;[62] several genealogies and quasi-hagiographies written in Latin,[63] in Anglo-Norman,[64] and, if we can believe the Anglo-Norman hagiographer, in English as well; an enormous Anglo-Norman romance of over 22,000 lines;[65] and the thirteenth-century *Crowland Chronicle,* purporting to have been written by the twelfth-century Abbot Ingulf.[66]

The engine of Waltheof's narration is fueled by a primary contradiction: all these narratives manifest the desire to heroize Waltheof as a resister even as they simultaneously want to exonerate him from treason against the king. Florence of Worcester's development of the *Anglo-Saxon Chronicle* provides us with the outlines of the process by which Waltheof becomes the main character of his own story.[67] According to Florence, at the wedding between Ralph, Earl of East Anglia, and the daughter of Roger, Earl of Hereford, Waltheof is surprised by the two principals and "compelled" to join a conspiracy against King William [comitemque Waltheofum suis insidiis praeventum, secum conjurare compulerunt] (10). Later he goes to Canterbury and confesses to Lanfranc, who gives him penance and demands that he go to the king in Normandy and throw himself upon the royal clemency.[68] This Waltheof does, but on the king's return in 1075 — Roger and Ralph having meanwhile been decisively defeated by an alliance of what looks like the whole population, seculars and ecclesiastics, bishops and abbots, Normans and English [tam Anglorum quam Nortmannorum] (11) — Waltheof is imprisoned and then executed. Florence concludes the episode with a direct address to the reader, calling on Lanfranc as a witness to both Waltheof's innocence and the vigor of his penitence:

> This man, while yet in the enjoyment of his life, being placed in close confinement, lamented without ceasing and with extreme bitterness the unrighteous actions of his past life. He earnestly sought to appease his God by vigils, prayers, fastings, and almsgiving; men desired to blot out the remembrance of him on earth; but we firmly believe that he is now rejoicing with the saints in heaven, on the testimony of archbishop Lanfranc of pious memory, from whom he received the sacrament of penance after his confession, who declared that not only was he guiltless of the crime

laid to his charge, the conspiracy mentioned above, but that, like a true Christian, he had lamented with tears of penitence the other sins which he had committed. (303)

[Hic cum adhuc temporali frueretur vita, arta positus in custodia, ea quae gesserat inique incessanter deflevit et amarissime: vigiliis, orationibus, jejuniis, et eleemosynis Deum studuit placare; cujus memoriam voluerunt homines in terra delere, sed creditur vere illum cum sanctis in coelo gaudere, praedicto archipraesule piae memoriae Landfranco, a quo, confessione facta, poenitentiam acceperat, fideliter attestante; qui et impositi criminis, supradictae scilicet conjurationis, illum immunem affirmabat esse, et quae in caeteris comminem affirmabat esse, et quae in caeteris commisisset, ut verum Christianum, poenitentialibus lachrymis deflevisse; seque felicem fore si, post exitum vitae, illius felici potiretur requie.] (12)

I want to underline three properties of Florence's treatment. First, there is absolutely no attempt to connect the wedding conspiracy and Waltheof's role (or nonrole) in it to Waltheof's earlier public or private life. It is narrated as an entirely independent narrative unit, beginning with his surprise at the wedding and ending with his penitence and execution. The second property is the genre shift that closes the scene. A public episode in a series of other public episodes in the chronicle continues beyond the conspirators' military defeat and moves into the psyche of its main character. What begins in the world of public power closes as a story of personal penitence and individual salvation. But let us note very carefully that Florence imputes no motives to any of the action—neither personal, nor political, nor ethnic. As Florence tells it, this is not a story about the quest for personal power, nor is it one of rivalry between the independent lords of the north against the centralizing designs of the monarchy in the south. And it is most certainly not a story about English resistance to Norman hegemony. Although the episode ends in the interior world of guilt, confession, and repentance, it is built out of nothing but notations of external actions. We know nothing from this text about why Ralph, Roger, and a great many other guests at the banquet form a conspiracy; nor do we know anything at all about Waltheof's motives for assenting or seeming to assent or about why the king offers him clemency but nevertheless later has him arrested and orders his execution. All actions are opaque, yet Waltheof in the process takes center stage.

As soon as writers do try to dissolve the opacity of this set of events, Waltheof's story grows more thick with implication. In Simeon of Durham, in William of Malmesbury's *Gesta regum* and *Gesta pontificum,* and especially in Ordericus Vitalis's *Historia ecclesiastica,* Waltheof's story becomes a central way to think through the significance of William's regime. The pertinent section of Simeon of Durham's *Gesta regum Anglorum*[69] is for the most part a simple transcription of the *Worcester Chronicle,* but there is one big difference. When he arrives at the year 1072 and the accession of Waltheof as Earl of Northumbria, Simeon breaks the annalistic form and adds a long digression in which hybridity, ethnic ambiguity, and the making and breaking of personal loyalties play the principal parts. The digression traces the descent of all the lords of Northumbria from the time of their last king (in the year 949) to the accession of Waltheof in 1072. This is essentially the story of a violent contest for local power extending over four generations, a private feud between the powerful ruling house of Bamburgh and two families of Danish raiders. At the same time it registers a political struggle between the local hereditary rulers and the imperial designs of Cnut and his son Hardecnut, a struggle the Danes pursued by the systematic assassination of the Bamburgh men and strategic marriage with the Bamburgh women.[70]

Let me present this story of succession in outline: with the consent of Cnut, the Danish king of the English, the Bamburgh earl Uchtraed is killed by Thorbrand, a Danish warrior; upon succeeding his father, Uchtraed's son Aldred kills Thorbrand in revenge, and when Aldred is himself later assassinated in turn by Carl, Thorbrand's son, Aldred's brother Eadulf succeeds him as earl. On his way to a meeting of reconciliation with Hardecnut, Eadulf is killed by Hardecnut's henchman Siward, who himself becomes earl and marries Aldred's daughter, Aelfleda, the Bamburgh heiress.[71] Their son Waltheof is thus the literal embodiment of the historical process that gives him two separate claims to the Earldom of Northumbria: he could claim it by the normal process of agnatic inheritance from his Danish father, Earl Siward; or he could claim it by customary inheritance from his English mother, Aelfleda, daughter of the Bamburgh earl Aldred. In the event he becomes earl by a third means: he is given it by King William when, upon returning from negotiations with the Scottish King Malcolm, William sets aside the Bamburgh descendant Cospatrick as punishment for an old offense and hands the earldom to Waltheof.[72] Simeon does not mention what other chroniclers will not fail to include: the earldom is part of the marriage property that comes to Waltheof along with the king's niece Judith.

Just as Aldred kills Thorbrand after coming to power, the first of Waltheof's reported acts after the wedding with Judith is the assassination of the four sons of Carl, by which, as Simeon writes, "he cruelly avenged the death of his grand-father earl Aldred" (145). By this act, Waltheof publicly dissociates himself from his powerful father, the killer of Aldred's brother, and identifies himself with the Bamburgh house; and in doing so he becomes at this moment En-glish. What I am suggesting here is that part of the fascination that the twelfth-century chroniclers have with Waltheof is due to Waltheof's own deliberate self-staging in strategically performing now one, now another of his own possible identities.[73] For immediately after this strategic performance of himself as the rightful English heir of an ancient English house, Waltheof begins privately to gather all his father's Danish allies around him in a bid for autonomous rule in the territory.[74] Absolutely dependent on William for his creation as Earl of Northumbria, a creature of the centralizing rule of the south and through his marriage a member of William's immediate kin group, Waltheof's earldom—indeed, Waltheof's usefulness to William—is thoroughly rooted in the history of local power. In attempting to manipulate the local enmities that had always driven the familial-political history of the North, Waltheof capitalizes exactly on his own personal authority as the Bamburgh heir even as William would co-opt it. The result is, of course, a spectacular failure. Simeon's description of the wed-ding plot and its aftermath is taken directly from the *Worcester Chronicle,* and the story of collaboration and resistance moves inward to resolve in penitence and transcendental justice.

William of Malmesbury's treatment of this episode in his *Gesta regum Anglo-rum*[75] is very different. It is brief, yet its wealth of detail and outward reference severely complicate the multiple currents of the longer accounts. William's narrative procedure here is very fluid. He centers the narrative on the events of 1074, filling in the antecedent action by a variety of narrative devices. He begins by noting both Waltheof's distinguished lineage and his having won im-mense favor from the king. The passage immediately moves into free indirect discourse to present the king's judgment: he was inclined, says William, to con-sider Waltheof's earlier opposition a sign rather of his military excellence than of disloyalty [magis illas uirtuti quam perfidiae attribuebat] (3.253.1). And there follows a complex single period of eroticized gazing, moving from Waltheof's body in heroic action, to a lingering on his physical endowments, and culmi-nating in the magnificence of his Danish paternity, the implicit source of his courage and bodily perfection: "For in the battle of York Waltheof had cut down many of the Normans single-handed, beheading them one by one as they emerged from the gate; he was strong of arm, powerful in his chest, robust and noble in his whole body. He was a son of Siward, the most magnificent earl called Digera in Danish, which means 'the strong.'" [Siquidem Waldefus in Eboracensi pugna plures Normannorum solus obtruncuerat, unos et unos per portam egredientes decapitans; neruosus lacertis, thorosus pectore, robustus et procerus toto corpore, filius Siwardi magnificentissimi comitis, quem Digera Danico uocabulo, id est fortem, cognominabant] (3.253.1). This is the voice of William of Malmesbury, to be sure, but it is equally a representation of the king's love for this powerfully attractive powerful man, the cynosure of his eye even as he cuts down the king's troops one by one. The love is made manifest by two gifts: William gives Waltheof both his "private friendship" (privata amicitia) and his niece Judith in marriage. This is the immense favor [multam familiaritatem novi regis] (3.253.1) with which the passage began—Waltheof's proud lineage and heroic opposition connect him in the closest possible bonds to his new king. And no sooner are these bonds narratively established than they are badly broken. Waltheof, says William, unable to restrain his "depraved mind" [pravum ingenium] (3.253.2), involves himself in the conspiracy of Ralph of Gael. There are no details, there is no wedding scene, no confession to Lanfranc or begging the king's clemency; the plot is merely named, and the narrative continues to center directly on Waltheof. William of Malmesbury seems to understand his "pravum ingenium" as a sort of epic *démesure,* since he is careful to note that all Waltheof's former allies who thought it right to resist have by this time either been killed or conquered [Compatriotis enim omnibus qui existimarant resistendum cesis aut subiectis] (3.252.2). Waltheof, having resisted, breaks his ties to the king and continues to resist. The result is personal disaster: "But the plot was detected; Waltheof was arrested and held for a long time in chains. Finally, he was decapitated and buried at Crowland." [Sed coniuratione detecta comprehensus diuque in uinculis tentus, ultimo spoliatus capite Crolando sepultus est] (3.252.2).

End of story. Yet there is a supplement. William reports another opinion, an opinion that he immediately discounts as a "mere" self-interested excuse while simultaneously seeming to subscribe to it himself: "Some, however, say it was the force of necessity and not inclination that made him join the traitors. This excuse is given by the English, for Normans assert other things, but they are Englishmen who stand out for their trustworthiness. And Divinity seems to support their assertion, since it has manifested many miracles at his tomb, and those of very great importance; for they say that while in chains he purged his misdeeds by daily tears." [Quidam dicant necessitate interceptum, non uoluntate addictum, infidelitatis sacramentum agitasse. Anglorum est ista excusatio (nam cetera Normanni afferunt), Anglorum qui plurimum ueritate prestent. Quorum astipulationi Diuinitas suffragari uidetur, miracula multa, et ea permaxima, ad tumbam illius ostendens. Aiunt enim in catenas coniectum cotidianis singultibus perperam commissa diluisse] (3.252.3). This self-interested excuse is "English"—the language "Anglorum est ista excusatio" is strongly dismissive—but it is offered by Englishmen who "stand out for their trustworthiness" (veritate prestent), and, says William, it seems to have divine sanction. I don't think we can dismiss this sentence as purely ironic, although I don't think we can entirely dismiss the possibility of irony either. William equivocates. Yet one thing is absolutely clear: his equivocation maps Waltheof's resistance and death as an ethnic conflict. The English excuse him by asserting the force of necessity; the Normans condemn him as depraved and disloyal. In the process, Waltheof becomes an English hero, and his resistance becomes one instance of a general struggle between the native inhabitants of England and a "foreign" king.

William revisits this event two years later in his description of Crowland in the *Gesta pontificum*.[76] The narrative repeats most of the *Gesta regum* version verbatim, but in place of the equivocation William begins by wishing in his own voice for Waltheof's innocence—telling us that many pilgrims coming to Crowland in our time find there a martyr who was, they say, innocently killed, and here William uncharacteristically enters his own narrative exclaiming, "Would that this were true" (Invenerunt quoque nostra tempora quem consecrarent martirem, quod innocenter cesum fama pronuntiet, quae utinam a veritate non dissideat). And he ends with a self-critique: "In the *Gesta regum* I set down the opinions of the Normans that he was bad. Here, I will not be silent about the different judgment that the English assert." (Opiniones Normannorum in malum in Gestis Regum posui. Hic Angli quid e diverso afferant, non tacebo.) Englishmen of the highest trustworthiness say Waltheof was surprised at the wedding banquet; he agreed to the plot with his lips but not with his heart; he immediately confessed to Lanfranc, did penance for his "false assent" (desimulato consensu), and laid out the whole affair both to Lanfranc and to the king. And after noting the miracles at his tomb and his tears in chains in language identical to that of the *Gesta regum,* William provides a final witness: "The prior of the place told me that, stirred by the miracles, he examined the body, which was untouched by wounds on all sides, and he saw the head, attached to the rest of the body, showing only a red line, as if a sign of the wound. On account of this, he said that he had no hesitation in calling him saint in every sermon and giving prayers and offerings in his name to those seeking the place." (Michi prior loci narravit se miraculis commotum corpus nobile ab omni labe immune contrectasse, caput reliquo corpori compaginatum, rubra tantum quasi linea signum cedis ostentante, vidisse. Quapropter non se dubitare illum in omni sermone Sanctum appellare, in illius nomine orationes et benefitia loci petentibus dare dicebat.)

Desire for Waltheof pervades all of William's writing about him. The Norman king gazes at the heroic body of the resisting warrior and offers him himself and his family; the English prior gazes at the uncorrupt, noble body and offers pilgrims prayers and gifts in the name of the uncorrupt soul that it signifies. And William himself flows with those same currents of desire, from whatever side they originate. Highly conscious of himself as both Norman and English,[77] William imaginatively heroizes Waltheof as Norman and English as well. And is it an accident that William, an immensely learned and careful latinist, uses the relatively rare word *compaginatum* to describe the joining of the head to the body (caput reliquo corpori compaginatum)—which I note in passing may well suggest to our ears that Waltheof's body is a text, a manuscript *pagina* rubricated at the wound (rubra tantum quasi linea signum cedis ostentante)—since *compaginatum* is used in classical Latin only to mean erasing a border (for example, joining two fields into one or uniting two states)?[78]

Vital Angligena

Depraved and disloyal while also a noble English patriot resisting the rule of foreigners even beyond his death, Waltheof commands significant narrative space in what is now the fourth book of Orderic Vitalis's *Historia ecclesiastica.* Written in 1125, this fourth book was originally the second that Orderic wrote in what was commissioned as a history of the Abbey of St. Evroul in Normandy, where Orderic spent his life as a monk.[79] While writing this second book, Orderic realized he was actually writing and wanted to write something much larger, a history of the Normans and their rapid conquest of what was for him much of the world—England, Italy, and the East. In the course of Orderic's presentation of William's conquest, Waltheof moves gradually to the narrative center. Finally Waltheof's story takes over even from the Conqueror himself. The brief first appearances of Waltheof already trouble the categories of ethnic distinction and the moral judgments attendant upon ethnic distinction that Orderic carefully constructs. Waltheof appears first as English on the list of English notables whom William took with him to Normandy after his coronation; he appears for a second time as a Dane, a leader in the battle against William at York, a battle that Orderic treats as a full-fledged Danish invasion. In his third appearance he is in the list of Normans enriched after the failed uprising of Earls Edwin and Morcar. Orderic treats William's redistribution of the land as an expropriation of the natives' wealth by the foreign invaders.[80] The list ends by drawing the starkest contrast between the English and Normans: foreigners are said to have taken over English wealth, and the English, born of the land, are murdered or driven out to wander as exiles in foreign lands: "So foreigners grew wealthy with the spoils of England, whilst her own sons were either shamefully slain or driven as exiles to wander hopelessly through foreign kingdoms." [Sic extranei diuitiis Angliae ditabantur, pro quibus filii eius nequiter interficiebantur, uel extorres per extera regna irremeabiliter fugabantur] (266). Yet Waltheof is prominent in the midst of the redistribution, where the text situates him in his patriarchal lineage, names him as a powerful Englishman (Siward's Danish family and alliance with Hardecnut being silently glossed over), and resituates him in the king's friendship (amicitia): "King William gave the county of Northampton to Earl Waltheof, son of Siward, one of the greatest of the English, and married him to his own niece Judith to strengthen the bonds of friendship between them; later she bore her husband two beautiful daughters." [Rex Guillelmus Gualleuo comiti filio Siuardi potentissimo Anglorum comitatum Northamtoniae dedit, eique Iudith neptem suam ut firma inter eos amicitia perduraret in matrimonio coniunxit; quae duas filias speciosas marito suo peperit] (262). Waltheof disrupts the coherence of this list, which otherwise is devoted to cataloguing and lamenting absolute injustice—the rape of the country and the transformation of its natives into foreigners by their foreign rulers. It is this very contradiction of Waltheof's identity—he is simultaneously English and not English, of the place and not of it—that makes him a point of fascination for Orderic himself. Indeed, the vocabulary of foreignness (the series extranei . . . extorres . . . extera regna) here resonates sharply with Orderic's own poignant self-representation in the narrative.

Orderic mentions himself in his history rather frequently, much more frequently than is the norm for his historian contemporaries, who tend to be silent even about their own well-known participation in public events. At two key moments in his writing career Orderic writes at length about his own life.

The first is at the beginning of the fifth (originally the third) book, where he acknowledges the change in his plan from writing a local to an imperial history and states his awareness of having embarked on a great work. The second is at the very end of book 13, an epilogue to the work that has occupied the now sixty-seven-year-old monk for most of his life. Both places rest on the same memory of childhood trauma and abandonment, narrated in almost the same words. Worn out with age and desiring to finish his life's work (Ecce senio et infirmitate fatigatus librum hunc finire cupio), Orderic tells us that he is English (*Angligena,* about which more in a moment); was baptized by the local priest, Orderic, who gave him his name; and at age five was put into the hands of his spiritual father, Siward, in Shrewsbury to learn Latin. The strong coincidence of names such as this—Waltheof's father and Orderic's own father-surrogate both being named Siward—is never without consequences in the unconscious. Orderic remained with Siward for five years until suddenly the boy's father reappeared to offer the ten-year-old Orderic as an oblate to St. Evroul in Normandy: "So, weeping, he gave me, a weeping child, into the care of the monk Reginald, and sent me away into exile for love of thee and never saw me again." [Rainaldo igitur monacho plorans plorantem me tradidit, et pro amore tuo in exilium destinauit, nec me unquam postea uidit] (6.552). There follows a remarkable sentence in which Orderic begins by comparing himself to Abraham, commanded by God to leave home and family, and ends by becoming Isaac, about to be sacrificed by his father: "And so, O glorious God, who didst command Abraham to depart from his country and from his kindred and from his father's house, thou didst inspire my father Odelerius to renounce me utterly, and submit me in all things to thy governance." [Iccirco gloriose Deus qui Abraham de terra patrisque domo et cognatione egredi iussisti, Odelerium patrem meum aspirasti ut me sibi penitus abdicaret, et tibi omnimodis subiugaret] (6.552). The loss of connection to friends, family, and locality is also the loss of language: "And so, as a boy of ten, I crossed the English Channel and came into Normandy as an exile, unknown to all, knowing no one. Like Joseph in Egypt, I heard a language which I did not understand." [Decennis itaque Britannicum mare transfretaui, exul in Normanniam ueni, cunctis ignotus neminem cognoui. Linguam ut Ioseph in Aegipto quam non noueram audiui] (6.554). And there he loses his English name as well: "In place of my English name, which sounded harsh to the Normans, the name Vitalis was given me." [Nomen quoque Vitalis pro anglico uocamine quod Normannis absonum censebatur michi impositum est] (6.554).

Orderic's identification with his English-born self and with the historical process of Norman power that he narrates is multiform and complex. Announcing his new subject at the beginning of book 5, he summons this same traumatic memory as he also announces that he will begin narrating the deeds of the Normans in 1075 because it is the year of his own birth. [A prefato nempe anno placet inchoare presens opusculum, quo in hanc lucem xiii kal' Martii matris ex utero profusus sum] (3.6). As a stranger, an Englishman from the extreme borders of Mercia, he writes the deeds of the Normans for the Norman natives: "And so as a ten year old English boy I came here from the extreme borders of Mercia, and as a foreigner, uncivilized and unknown, I was mixed in with cultivated natives. With the inspiration of God, I am trying to bring forth in writing the deeds of the Normans and the outcomes of those deeds for the Normans to read." [Tandem ego de extremis Merciorum finibus decennis Angligena huc aduectus, barbarusque et ignotus aduena callentibus indigenis admixtus; inspirante Deo Normannorum gesta et euentus Normannis promere scripto sum conatus] (3.6).

The desire to return, to undo his exile, is profound. Throughout the text Orderic never names himself Vital without appending *Angligena,* thus ironizing his French name (Vital) with the epithet from his birthplace and birth family. He deploys similar terms, *Angligena* and *Francigena,* particularly in the context of ethnic displacement, to talk about Normans in England—and his own strong desire to be among them is obvious throughout the text. That is, the Norman invaders and settlers in their own displacement enact the re-placement that Orderic deeply wishes for himself. And around 1118 it was, in a way, Waltheof himself who granted Orderic's wish: relations between Crowland and St. Evroul were intimate, and Orderic was invited to Crowland Abbey for a five-week stay. There he read the *Life of St. Guthlac,* which he epitomized in his own history, saw Waltheof's tomb, and collected the stories of Waltheof's miracles that would play a prominent part in his own book. And there, too, he—and here again Orderic names himself Vital Angligena—was invited to write Waltheof a verse epitaph to decorate the tomb.[81]

Saint Waltheof Angligena

Orderic's version of the events of 1074 stages them entirely as an English attempt to recover their lands from the foreign usurper. Roger and Ralph, the one Norman, the other Breton by family and land holding—are named, for example, as "powerful English lords" [Duo potentissimi Anglorum comites Rogerius Herfordensis, et sororius eius Radulfus Nortiwicensis] (2.310) and identified by the insular territories they hold. And while Orderic is by no means sympathetic to their enterprise—it is, for him, an act of treason against their divinely ordained and consecrated king—he dramatizes their organizing of resistance in a set of imaginary speeches of great power. These speeches essentially repeat the same moral and political condemnation of William and his Norman henchmen that we earlier saw Orderic himself make—their speech to the nation details William's invasion of England, the incredible violence unleashed by land redistributions, the devastation to the English people, their impoverishing, murder, and exile. To Waltheof they propose "reversing the Conquest, returning England to the good laws and customs of King Edward" [Volumus enim ut status regni Albionis redintegretur omnimodis sicut olim fuit tempore Eduardi piissimi regis] (2.314). Waltheof, they say, will thus be a savior to the English now prostrate in slavery [omnique genti tuae quae prostrata est salutiferos] (2.314).

Waltheof refuses to join them, and Orderic writes him a speech stressing the sacredness of his bonds to William as his king, lord, and kinsman via marriage. In it, Waltheof cites Achitophel and Judas as examples of treason, as well as detailing how the Lord has delivered him from many dangers, and he compares himself to David delivered from the hands of Goliath, Saul, Adarezer, and Absolon. There is no need here to analyze this fascinating list in great detail beyond noting that it is a minefield of conflicting loyalties and conflicting claims of relationship—external enemies, hostile kings, and rebellious sons are thrown together. Ralph and Roger bind him not to reveal their plot, and then rebellion breaks out all over England.

Orderic at this point narrates three outcomes based on the three principal characters: Ralph goes into exile, forfeits his English territory (and presumably his English identity, since Orderic now names him Ralph of Gael for the first time); Roger also loses his English identity as Earl of Hereford when he is imprisoned under Norman law, also having forfeited all his property; in prison he continues to defy William to the end. Orderic then begins a moving meditation on the transitoriness of worldly power: "Where now is William fitz-Osbern, earl of Hereford, regent of the king, steward of Normandy, and warlike master of his army? He was truly the greatest oppressor of the English and harshly supported a huge following, which caused the ruin and wretched death of many thousands." [Ubi est Guillelmus Osberni filius, Herfordensis comes et regis uicarius, Normanniae dapifer et magister militum bellicosus? Hic nimirum primus et maximus oppressor Anglorum extitit, et enormem causam per temeritatem suam enutriuit, per quam multis milibus ruina miserae mortis incubuit] (2.318). His only son, Roger, just five years after his own death, brought discord and rebellion to England, "as it had stirred the men of Shechem against Abimelech whom they had made their leader after he slew the seventy sons of Jerubbaal" [qui Sicchimitas contra Abimelech quem occisis LXX filiis Ierobaal sibi praefecerant commouit] (2.320). The fitzOsberns are thoroughly obliterated so that they no longer possess even a foot of English land [Guillelmi progenies eradicata sic est de Anglia ut nec passum pedis nisi fallor iam nanciscatur in illa] (2.320).

The third outcome is Waltheof's becoming definitively English and sentenced to death under English law. His execution is performed before dawn, while the people sleep, out of fear that the citizens, sympathetic to their fellow countryman (compatriotae), will rise up and murder the royal guards (regios lictores trucidarent).[82] Waltheof divides his garments among the witnesses and begs from the executioner a moment to recite the paternoster on his own and on the executioner's behalf (ut dicam pro me et pro uobis orationem dominicam). He kneels and, with his eyes turned to heaven and his hands stretched out, begins the prayer (et flexis tantum genibus oculisque in coelum fixis et manibus tensis "Paternoster qui es in coelis," palam dicere coepit), but when he gets to the line "Lead us not into temptation" he breaks down completely (Cumque ad extremeum capitulum peruenisset, "Et ne nos inducas in temptationem" dixisset, uberes lacrimae cum eiulatu proruperunt, ipsumque preces inceptas concludere non permiserunt.) The impatient executioner instantly strikes off his head with a single blow, and the severed head "in a clear voice in everyone's hearing finishes the prayer: 'But deliver us from evil. Amen.'" (Porro caput postquam praesectum fuit, cunctis qui aderant audientibus clara et articulate voce dixit "Sed libera nos a malo amen.") The body is thrown unceremoniously into a ditch and is later, at the request of Judith, taken to Crowland for burial. This is the moment that Ordericus tells of coming to Crowland and proceeds to insert the history of that abbey into his chronicle. Beginning with the *Life of Guthlac*, Crowland history as Ordericus tells it is a celebration of English unity against internal dissension and foreign invasion.[83]

During the abbacy of Ingulph, English born [Hic natiione Anglicus erat] (2.344), but educated in Normandy and sent back to be abbot of Crowland, there is a great fire in the monastery. When Ingulph orders that Waltheof's remains be brought into the main church and reburied near the altar, the body is found to be uncorrupt, the head reunited with the trunk, with only a thin, red line signifying his execution [Sed postquam sarcofagi opertorium ruolutum est, corpus xvil. dormitionis suae anno integrum sicut in die quo sepultum fuerat et caput corpori coniunctum repertum est. Filum tamtummodo quasi pro signo decollationis rubicundum uiderunt monachi et laici quamplures qui affuerunt] (2.346). There are cures from the water used to wash the corpse. In 1109 miracles begin occurring at Waltheof's tomb, and it becomes a destination for pilgrims. Orderic tells how a visiting Norman monk mocks the pilgrims for their devotion to a traitor; he dies a couple of nights later at his own house, St. Alban's Abbey, dedicated fittingly to the first English martyr (2.348). On the same night Crowland's Abbot Geoffrey has a vision: he sees "himself in a vision by the coffin of Earl Waltheof, and two saints of God, Bartholomew the apostle and Guthlac the hermit, standing beside him arrayed in shining white. The apostle, so it seemed, perceiving that the earl's head was joined once more to the body, said, 'Headless no more.' Guthlac who was standing at the foot of the coffin said in reply, 'That was Earl heretofore,' and the apostle completed the verse with the words 'Now is king evermore.'" [mox in visu se astare loculo Walleui comitis uidet, sanctosque Dei Bartholomaeum apostolum et Guthlacum anacoritam in albis nitentes secum astare uidet. Apostolus uero ut uidebatur caput comitis corpori redintegratum accipiens dicebat, "Acephalus non est." Aecontra Guthlacus qui ad pedes stabat, respondit, "Comes hic fuit." Apostolus autem inceptum monadicon sic perfecit, "At modo rex est."] (2.348). Miracles continue to multiply. Orderic, as I mentioned a moment ago, is commissioned to write the epitaph for the tomb, and the episode closes fully in the realm of monastic hagiography, with Waltheof's uncorrupted and integral body standing over against the corrupt and fragmented realm.

Yet the victory is not only symbolic, and Waltheof's kingship is in a certain sense made to become literally true. Orderic adds another paragraph to say that William was blamed by many for the killing (interfectione) of Waltheof and that "by the just judgment of God" [iusto Dei iudicio] (2.350) many rose against him. Indeed, in the thirteen years that remained to William after Waltheof's execution, he never again enjoyed lasting peace or "drove an army from the field of battle, nor succeeded in storming any fortress which he besieged" [armatorum aciem de campo non fugauit nec oppidum obsidens bellica uirtute cepit] (2.350). Thus the English are avenged through the miracle-working body. The story of William's conquests ends as the story of Waltheof's victory, the body made whole in fragmentation and the English nation powerful in abjection.

Chapter Three

"DREAMING OF OTHER WORLDS"

Romance as Reality Fiction

HISTORY AND ITS OTHERS

The previous chapters have examined historical narratives written in periods of rapid transformations in secular governance. Impelled by the desire to understand the process and outcomes of those changes, each text that we have considered has been devoted to finding an explanation and justification in the past for the state of present affairs. In each case, we have seen that this very provocation to history opens new territories of significant experience—either represented as lying deeply within experiences of personal change or imagined as lying beyond history at the end of time, at once history's fulfillment and its annihilation. Thus the writing of history continuously opens into a glimpse of meaning that looks either like history's vital inner essence or like its other. In either case, the provocation to write history, to chart the process of change from the past to the present of the secular world in order to explain it, finally leads to an impasse that is tantamount to the abandonment of history altogether in the desire to articulate a tangible truth that history promises while never delivering. In the writing of history that we have so far been occupied with, the visible, social world is ultimately devalued as such while being observed and narrated at great length and with an extraordinary attention to detail. In the *Deeds of the Bishops of Cambrai* secular life becomes the mere outward scene of spiritual performance, where the real repository of value is to be found; in Orderic's *Historia ecclesiastica,* Waltheof's inner life, like Harold's in the *Vita Haroldi,* his penitence, suffering, and ultimate salvation, displaces what began as the central political story of the rise of Norman power. William's systematic takeover of the whole of England finally seems to be merely the background for something intensely private but infinitely more important to tell about, the salvation of a soul and the justice witnessed by a realm in abject defeat. Ever out of bounds, beyond a horizon, behind a veil, the truth that the historian desires seems always about to appear as he narrates the succession of time in the visible world. This place of a truth, lying deep within, where it seems to be the secret of a soul, or far beyond, where it will appear once and for all in the revelation of the Last Judgment, a truth that is always on the verge of appearing in time but never does, has classically been the preserve of hagiographical writing. In its peculiar search for exemplary experience in a singular life, a life that is exceptional in its occurrence yet a model for all, hagiography marks exactly the place of the historiographical desire for truth while setting its attainment out of bounds. To understand the limits under which the medieval writing of history operates, it is in fact as necessary as it is impossible for us to draw a firm border between historiographical and hagiographical writing in this period.[1]

When we turn to consider vernacular composition during this period, it is equally impossible to draw a firm line between historiography and romance. I argue in this chapter that romance is an attempt to seize directly the significance that in history appears only as a disappearance, the meaning at the heart of events that seems always about to announce itself but remains ever out of reach, and to seize it directly as a matter of historical understanding. I put it this way to avoid the false appearance that narratives of interiority, of personal development, or of personal salvation such as those that have claimed our attention in historical texts are examples of "romance influences" or "romance elements" in historiography—as if such a thing as romance existed all along to lend out its features at need. Rather, in the rearrangements of power attendant upon the state-making designs of Capetian and Anglo-Norman ruling families, new imaginative entities and new discursive configurations of the boundaries between self and other, or between public and private social formations, become new urgencies demanding knowledge and therefore new objects for representation.

It is no accident that the great twelfth-century source text for the legend of Arthur and for vernacular romance in general, Geoffrey of Monmouth's *Historia regum Brittaniae,* is a work that invents Latin prose fiction by modeling it so directly on contemporary historiography that the two cannot be told apart using purely narrative criteria.[2] A medieval critic of the *Historia regum,* at pains to denounce the work as fraudulent, gives us a real insight into what Geoffrey has truly accomplished. Using Bede's text as an authoritative account of the chronology of British history from Caesar's conquest to the Saxon takeover, William of Newburgh argues in the first few pages of his *Historia rerum Anglicarum* that there is simply no available time for much of Geoffrey's narrative to have taken place;[3] he argues moreover, that since Arthur's deeds, as Geoffrey narrates them, surpass even those of Alexander the Great, and Merlin's prophecies surpass those of Isaiah, we would expect to find them at least mentioned in Bede or in the works of other historians, especially in those of the historians whose realms Arthur is said to have conquered. Of course, we find no such notices of any kind. William exclaims, "Or does he dream of another world, containing infinite realms, in which these things took place . . . ? Surely, no such things had ever happened in our world." [An alium orbem somniat infinita regna habentem, in quo ea contigerunt . . . ? Quippe in orbe nostro nunquam talia contigerant] (17). In this rhetorical outburst William means to say that Geoffrey's book is simply a lie, for the events that he narrates never could have happened. If this characterization of bad history is put positively, however, it becomes a perfect definition of good fiction: fiction is the narrative representation of an invented place, the invention of a dream world containing infinite realms in which to locate events that can be narrated and analyzed for their significance *as if* one were writing history—but without history's constraints. For even medieval historians, whose narratives are composed using imaginary speeches, developed by means of rhetorical commonplaces, and notoriously filled with invented scenes, portents, and prodigies outrageous to our contemporary canons of plausibility—even medieval historians nevertheless labor under the same prohibition as any working historian today: not to narrate beyond what the evidence provides. Hagiography escapes from history by treating the secular world as a pure symbolic surface bodying forth the permanent and unchanging truth of the spirit;[4] fiction immerses itself in history by inventing pseudohistorical narrative.[5] By narrating beyond the evidence, fiction returns to history the power to locate secular experience in the secular world and thus to make it knowable—precisely what Aristotle sees as the function of mimesis.[6]

In placing medieval fiction in this relation, I want to draw emphasis away from the features that are usually and correctly used to characterize romance—individualized quest narratives, interior monologue or interior debate, the structure of adventure, motifs of exile and return, and double plotting on the side of form; a concern with chivalric honor and detailed, realistic scenes of courtly festivity, of erotic play, and of one-to-one combat on the side of content. And in beginning with a piece of Latin prose fiction, I obviously mean to override the connection between composition in verse and in the vernacular—*mise en roman*—that gave romance its name in the first place.[7] I will have occasion to discuss all of these features in due time. For now, I want first to discuss Geoffrey's *Historia regum* to locate the kinds of narrative occasions that give rise to what we conventionally think of as romance material and that necessitate its particular formal treatment.

Romance in History

The high point of Arthur's power, as Geoffrey of Monmouth narrates it, is the achievement of peace as a result of his conquest of all the kingdoms neighboring the Britons. The last of these is his conquest of all Gaul. Having held court in Paris, at which he distributes what is tantamount to the Angevin continental territory—that is to say, the continental holdings of Stephen of Blois and his cousin Geoffrey Plantagenet—to his household vassals, he returns to Britain for a grand ceremonial crown wearing. This is a fully imperial occasion to which " he brought together kings and dukes subordinate to him to that same feast so that he could solemnly celebrate it and renew a very firm peace among his nobles" [reges etiam et duces sibi subditos ad ipsam festiuitatem conuocare ut et illam uenerabiliter celebraret et inter proceres suos firmissimam pacem renouaret] (109).[8] Indeed, one of the reasons for holding it at the City of Legions, Geoffrey explains, is its strategic location on a wide and navigable river and not far from the sea "so that kings and princes from across the sea who were coming could be carried there by ship" [per quod transmarini reges et principes qui venturi erant nauigio aduehi poterant] (110). The list of those attending includes the Twelve Peers of France, an obvious assimilation of Carolingian imperial preeminence to the Arthurian achievement. This celebration of Arthur's imperium is a powerful declaration of his political legitimacy: in the huge body of political theory provoked by the Gregorian reform, for example, writers arguing on behalf of both the imperial and papal parties claim that world peace is a result of unitary sovereignty, which is the only legitimate sovereignty—a single emperor who can unite all into the single body politic of Christendom just as the bishop of Rome is the supreme head of the spiritual body.[9] The Gelasian "two swords" remains at the heart of the mainstream of medieval political theory, and this mainstream is always thoroughly imperial even when the papal apologists place the emperor in a position subordinate to the bishop of Rome. Opposing this theoretical unity between *sacerdotium* and *regnum,* each conceived of as a totality and a singularity, the real multiplicity of political entities, each claiming some form of sovereignty within particularly defined territories, poses a problem, variously solved by notions such as that of the king being an emperor—that is to say, a supreme commander—within his own realm.[10] These solutions are each in their own way scandals for theory: they perform a strategic and necessary negotiation between the ideal demand for a single secular realm corresponding to the body of the individual and to the single spiritual community of the Christian Church on the one hand, and the justification for an existing geopolitical order on the other. Multiple sovereignty for theory always signifies a breakdown in order; it is a sign of the fallen world. Hence Arthur's justification for conquest is precisely imperial: that in his name he has brought *pax et iustitia* to the territories he has conquered is its own justification. Later he will say that he "liberated" these territories from Roman subjection. His greatness consists in, is proclaimed by, and in the last analysis is justified by the augmentation of his realm, an augmentation that would ideally continue to the limit of world conquest.

To develop the vision of peace, Geoffrey catalogues the vast and expansive number of political figures, dependents who come to pay court to Arthur at his crown wearing, and he narrates the celebration in great detail. In these details we find exactly what we generally think of as the hallmarks of romance, and they are all in the service of representing Arthur's political power and its claim to imperial legitimacy. Geoffrey remarks on the splendor of the court, the men and women in separate chambers, since the Britons keep the "ancient Trojan custom" [antiquam nanque consuetudinem Troie servantes Britones] (111) of separating the sexes in these kinds of festivities. They are each served innumerable dishes and rare wines by thousands of servants in identical livery whose fashioning is specifically and lovingly described.

The description of the feast leads to a moment of narration that pulls the contradictory drives of eros and aggression into the single configuration that lies at the heart of chivalry and forms the basic problematic of what nineteenth-century scholars named for all time as *l'amour courtois:*

> At that time Britain had arrived at such a state of worthiness that it excelled all other reigns in the abundance of riches, the wealth of ornaments, and the elegance of the inhabitants. Any knight outstanding for his excellence used to dress in clothes and arms of his own single color.

And elegant women wore similar colors and thought it unworthy to have a lover who had not proved himself three times in battle. Thus they made themselves chaste and better women, and the knights were more worthy in battle by their love.

[Ad tantum etenim statum dignitatis Britannia tunc reducta erat quod copia diuiciarum, luxu ornamentorum, facecia incolarum cetera regna excellebat. Quicunque uero famosus probitate miles in eadem erat unius coloris uestibus atque armis utebatur. Facete etiam mulieres consimilia indumenta habentes nullius amorem habere dignabantur nisi tertio in milicia probatus esset. Efficiebantur ergo caste et meliores et milites pro amore illarum probiores.] (112)

Geoffrey's attention to style and the surface elements of social behavior are in the service of a kind of secular morality: in this display of wealth and prosperity and through their amorous play, he notes, the women become more chaste and the knights become more worthy. After the feast, there are games, including a tournament described in a tableau that bodies forth this same social transaction in the visual image that Robert Hanning has aptly named the chivalry topos:[11] "The knights who knew equestrian games devised a mock-battle; the women, watching on the height of the walls, provoked them to passionate love in their playful way." [Milites simulachrum prelii sciendo equestrem ludum componunt; mulieres in edito murorum aspicientes in furiales amores flammas ioci more irritant] (112). The men fight in the fields while the women watch from the walls and provoke them to the love that is itself the provocation to their martial excellence: the male game of battle is simultaneously a game of heterosexual desire in an endless, self-contained ring of provocation. And the fighting is entirely without consequences, for it is a fiction, a *simulachrum prelii*. In this process, the romance world seems to stand forth as an independent and enclosed world, a continual performance of an ever-increasing self-worth, with only self-development at stake in the game. The real consequences come rather in the political realm that is in truth never absent from this world of romance. Indeed, it is the political realm that calls the romance world into being, even if the romance world appears as a private space of private play. For whatever else they are, the feasting and games are strategic performances of Arthur's wealth and power. They proclaim the imperial strength of his court even as they instantiate it, and they do so to all the dependent lords invited there to celebrate, which is to say, to know it, bear witness to it, and fear it. Yet the imperial dream is interrupted by the brute fact that Arthur is a power among other powers. A message arrives in the midst of the feasting from the Roman emperor, Lucius, demanding Arthur's submission to his own superior right and power.

Among the many things that could be said about the whole confrontation between Lucius and Arthur, it is only necessary for us to observe here that Arthur and Lucius mirror one another in as many modalities as Geoffrey can imagine. Each side's argument for domination of the other is countered by exactly the same argument seen from the other side. The letter from Lucius, for example, details Arthur's conquests in a virtual repetition of the triumphant narrative of Geoffrey's previous chapters. What Geoffrey presented without question from Arthur's perspective as a narrative of Arthur's victories, culminating in the celebration of just victory and peace, is in Lucius's letter represented in the manner of a criminal indictment of the neglect by a subordinate of his customary obligations and of his depredations in private war. Arthur, he writes, has unjustly neglected paying tribute to Rome, customary since the days of Julius Caesar, and he has unjustly seized—*eripuisti* is repeated three times in an ascending period—Roman territory in Gaul, a violation of Roman *potestas* and public order: "You have seized Gaul from the empire, you have seized the province of the Allobroges, you have seized all the islands of the ocean whose kings paid tribute to my ancestors while Roman power prevailed in those territories." [Eripuisti quoque illi Galliam, eripuisti Allobrogium prouinciam, eripuisti omnes occeani insulas quarum reges dum Romana potestas in illis partibus preualuit uectigal ueteribus meis reddiderunt] (113). This sequence is a simple rewriting of the outer narrative of Arthur's triumphs; what was in the main narrative presented as the liberation of the subject peoples of Gaul and their formation into a vast and legitimate political realm is here in the letter narrated as a simple, opportunistic land grab. Similarly, just as Lucius adduces Caesar's conquest of Britain as a historic justification for British dependence on Rome, so Arthur claims Brennius's capture of Rome as an equally good argument for Roman dependence on Britain. And Geoffrey reminds his readers here that the founding stories of the two realms mirror each other as well: Arthur and Lucius, each incarnating British and Roman sovereignty, are equally legitimized by their descent from the same Trojan royal family in the figures of their ancestors Brutus and Aeneas. Geoffrey recalls the founding stories by reinserting them into his narrative twice at this very point: the first place is his notation of the "ancient Trojan custom" followed by the Britons after the crown wearing; the second is in a deliberate echo, in Arthur's first address to his court, of Aeneas's address to his followers outside Carthage.[12] The effect of this mirroring is to underline the absolute impossibility of finding any criterion other than superior force with which to legitimate either Roman or British sovereignty. The criteria typically used to legitimate sovereignty are each brought forward in this conflict only to be undone: imperial conquest, genealogy, custom, descent, rituals of consecration. In this impasse, any claim to the transcendental sovereignty of the state over other forms of power, or any claim that any one state is a singular power unlike any other, collapses into tautology—the state is the superior power, as it were, because it is superior. And this tautology is further emphasized when Geoffrey's text, in narrating the military confrontation, drives the two sides into a representation of extreme ethnic and racial difference, such as we find in narratives of the First Crusade, even as the two sides continue to mirror one another in all respects: Lucius's followers are made up of African and orientalized Eastern peoples whose exotic and decidedly non-Christian names are extensively catalogued twice, once as they are summoned (116) and again as they go into battle (125) and then several times briefly thereafter during the fighting; Arthur on the other side fights with an alliance of what is basically a combination of the insular and continental holdings of the Anglo-Norman ruling elite combined with the overseas possessions of King Cnut, a comfortingly domestic dream of an imperial and Christian Britain.[13]

This kind of ethnic differentiation is an act of narrative desperation, the last attempt to find a way to differentiate the one side from the other, this time on absolute grounds, and it is an attempt that Geoffrey's text entirely undermines even while making. The two sides remain identical: they mirror each other even in the syntax of the battle scenes: "On this side Arthur, as was said, while striking the enemy, repeatedly exhorted the Britons to stand fast. On that side Lucius Hiberius admonished his Romans and led them time and again into outstanding worthy deeds." [Hinc autem Arturus sepius et sepius ut predictum est hostes percutiens Britones ad perstandum hortabatur. Illinc vero Lucius Hitberus Romanos suos et monebat et in preclaras probitates multotiens ducebat] (128). The battle, narrated at length, is indecisive; strength is matched with strength, weakness with weakness, and the advantage seems to shift constantly from one side to the other (quia quandoque Britones quandoque Romani versa vice prevalebant).

In the midst of the battle, the world of romance seems again about to thrust historical action into the background. Suddenly, Gawain, who with Hoel has been pushing ever closer to the emperor, breaks through the lines and finds himself confronting Lucius. The narrative here is entirely in the register of praise, the characters becoming objects of fascination for the reader: Gawain and Hoel each outdo the other in bravery and daring to the point that they merge into a single iconic representation of chivalric virtue: "It was impossible to determine which one was superior to the other" [Non facile diffiniri poterat quis eorum alterum excederet] (127). The moment of confrontation between Gawain and the emperor is introduced in a carefully crafted rhetorical ladder by a lovingly lingering description of Gawain's activity: "But Gawain, fervent with fresh strength, was always striving to meet with Lucius. Like the bravest knight, he rushed forward striving, and in rushing forward he laid waste the enemy, and in laying them waste he moved forward." [At Gwalgwainus semper recenti virtute exestuans nitebantur ut aditum congrediendi cum Lucio haberet. Nitendo ut audacissimus miles irruebat, irruendo hostes prosternebat, prosternendo cedebat] (127). Gawain is propelled by desire for the emperor. "Indeed, Gawain, moving forward through the troops, as was said, finally found whom he desired and rushed up to the emperor and met him." [Porro Gwalgwainus cedendo turmas, ut predictum est, inuenit tandem aditum quem adoptabat et in imperatorem irruit et cum illo congressus est] (127). And the emperor becomes at this moment a knight among others, desirous of nothing more than demonstrating his own prowess in a chivalric encounter with an opponent worthy of his strength: "But Lucius, flowering in his first youth, had much audacity, much strength, much prowess, and desired nothing more than to meet with such a knight who desired to test him and see how brave he was in knighthood. Standing against Gawain, he rejoiced marvelously at his meeting, and he gloried in the knowledge that he had so much fame." [At Lucius prima iuuentute florens multum audatie, multum uigoris, multum probitatis habebat nichilque magis desiderabat quam congredi cum milite tali qui eum coegisset experiri quantum in militia ualuisset. Resistens itaque Gwalgwaino congressum eius mire letatur et gloriatur quia tantam famam de eo audierat] (127). Here in the midst of a battle being fought over the largest question of world governance, both Lucius and Gawain are presented to the reader as objects of wonder. They are in all personal respects comparable, and the emperor "rejoices" and "glories" in the lucky chance that has brought him an opponent of such fame. The political story that has brought them to this confrontation becomes at this moment nothing more than a background, an occasion for self-worth and self-measure. The combat is an occasion for emotional experience and self-display for its own sake—for the experience of joy in combat and glory in its performance. Indeed, Geoffrey begins to narrate the chivalric combat in pure adventure terms: "The battle was long between them. Giving strong blows and holding their shields against the blows, each one labored to threaten the other with death." [Commisso diutius inter se prelio dant ictus ualidos et clipeos ictibus preponendo uterque neci alterius imminere elaborat] (127–28). This perfect first sentence promises a long and suspenseful battle, one that in the end will reveal the perfect knight by means of the defeat of the worthiest of opponents. Here, however, this perfect first sentence is the last sentence; the chivalric duel goes no further, as both Lucius and Gawain are swallowed up in the general combat, and we hear no more of their meeting. Their personal experience—and the reader's admiration that it is meant to evoke—is at this moment entirely disengaged from the political world that has called it forth and that is its only occasion. At this sudden encounter, it has become for the moment entirely irrelevant that Lucius is the emperor of Rome or that Gawain is among the most important of Arthur's court and his family. At the same time, the chivalric glory of the confrontation is equally irrelevant to the urgent political circumstances that brought it about and of which it is a part.

The war finally ends with the sudden, anonymous death of Lucius [cuius-dam lancea confossus interiit] (128–29). In my previous chapter, I considered the similar anonymity of Harold's death as it is presented in the *Roman de Rou*: Wace says that he does not know who shot Harold at first, who killed him afterwards; who disfigured the body, who took him from the field, or who buried him. There I argued that Wace's treatment amounts to a wholesale dismissal of the significance both of Harold's death and of the victory, a victory for which no one is responsible and for which no one can claim credit. In the *Roman de Rou*, the victory lies neither on the battlefield nor in heaven but in the council chamber where the legitimacy of William's rule is established through deliberation and law and where the new regime forms an indelible link with the past. Here, too, the military victory is similarly devoid of any meaning transcending the triumph of force. It is neither a trial by combat eventuating in the judgment of God nor an example of the providential ordering of the world. It demonstrates nothing beyond the fact of Arthur's superior forces. That Arthur's victory is no demonstration of God's justice is made all the more plain by Geoffrey's ironic flirtation with the language of transcendental justice. In a gesture reminiscent of the historiographical practice of his contemporaries, Geoffrey makes one of his very rare explanatory interventions in the narrative. It begins in the language of providence [quod diuine potentie stabat loco] (129), as if Geoffrey were about to declare that the British victory was a sign of God's justice; in the event, he rather makes the purely down-to-earth observation that the British were motivated to fight for their liberty because their earlier conquest by the Romans was unjust. What begins in the language of transcendence ends in the rough justice of pure secular rationality; the British fight the Romans out of historical memory and resentment over their past treatment at Roman hands. Historical action is here fully secularized: it demonstrates its own processes and nothing more.

No sooner is the war over than Arthur buries the dead—a scene narrated as a long catalog of the fallen. He extends his conquest into the countryside and immediately gets the news that "Modred his nephew, to whose care he had committed Britain, had crowned himself with his crown as a tyrant and traitor, and that Queen Guenevere, having violated the oath of her first marriage, was sleeping with him in unspeakable lust." [Modredum nepotem suum cuius tutele permiserat Britanniam eiusdem diademate per tyrannidem et proditionem insignitum esse reginamque Ganhumeram violato iure priorum nuptiarum eidem nephanda uenere copulatam fuisse] (129).[14] The devastating civil war that follows is narrated in the same mirroring syntax that Geoffrey uses in the Roman episode, and it tracks the Roman episode so closely as to become its narrative double. Double plotting of this sort serves among other things to emphasize difference: here, although Arthur ultimately slays Modred, the death of the leader on the battlefield, slain by his opposite number, neither demonstrates nor solves anything. Where the Romans immediately fled on hearing of Lucius's death, Modred's men continue to resist; Arthur's men continue to fight. The battle ends rather in mutual exhaustion than in decisive victory. Geoffrey ends the section and the episode with two catalogs of fallen leaders, Modred's men and Arthur's. In the retrospective light of these catalogs, the catalog of the dead in the Roman episode is proleptic. In fact, the whole Roman episode points to the narrative of the civil war that follows it narratively and is its immediate result. Among the dead on Arthur's side is Arthur himself, no longer a transcendental singularity but a suffering body among the wounded and a soul for whom to pray: "But here the outstanding King Arthur was lethally wounded. For the healing of his wound he was taken to the Island of Avalon, and he yielded the crown of Britain to Constantine, his cousin and son of Cador, Duke of Cornwall, in the year of the incarnation of God 542. May his soul rest in peace." [Set et inclitus ille rex Arturus letaliter uulneratus est; qui illinc ad sananda uulnera sua in insulam Aualonis euectus Constantino cognato suo et filio Cadoris ducis Cornubie diadem Brittanie concessit anno ab icarnatione Domini .dxlii. Anima eius in pace quiescat] (132).[15] The civil war thus rewrites the political story of the Roman confrontation as a family tragedy, an act of domestic betrayal that ends in devastation and death. What was political alliance in the one is incestuous joining in the other. The breaking of ties of political subjection, appealed to as the desire for liberty by both Romans and Britons, is in the domestic plot the breaking of the familial bonds and ties of "natural" affection between a nephew and his uncle and a husband and his wife.[16] The narrative supplies no motive for Modred's disloyalty and, more surprisingly, supplies no explanation for Modred's ability to attract a mass and loyal following except for personal dependence and personal loyalty. Both Modred's followers and Arthur's court are thus evoked in the register of the personal, and in this register they too mirror each other: the loyalty of the men of each side even in the face of disaster is finally represented in mirroring catalogs of the dead in which the sense of belonging implicates the reader in a familial, private, and intimate mourning for the losses suffered on both sides. This sort of inner experience presents itself as an absolute value — or it is nothing at all. After the civil war, the Britons enter into a period of political decline and ultimate disaster, even though Modred dies at Arthur's own hands and the crown has passed to a legitimate successor.

What I am suggesting is that in the Arthurian sections of the *Historia regum Brittaniae,* which form a climax to the story of the rise and imperial expansion of the Britons, we can see the appearance of romance in its full implication with secular history writing. In the festive scenes that preface the devastating Roman war and civil uprising, the whole panoply of romance motifs makes its appearance in the precise context of the performance of political power. The private world of erotic play and self-fashioning is entirely in the service of a political agenda, whether acknowledged by the players or not. The atrocious warfare that follows and brings the Arthurian realm to an end can be read as the emptying out of all transcendental ways of asserting historical meaning: what remains looks like a set of personal ethical motives and behaviors and their respective violations — loyalty and affection on the one hand, betrayal and vengeance on the other — and these alone act as the motor of historical change.

Romance at the End of History

In Geoffrey's narrative the collapse of the Arthurian enterprise marks the absolute collapse of the British state; British territory and sovereignty are henceforth fragmented, and political experience consists of permanent internecine, ethnic, and familial warfare. In the midst of this state of emergency, inner experience and its pathos are simultaneously a substitute for history and its last hope. After Arthur's realm is destroyed by the double violation of personal affection in the incestuous alliance between his wife Guenevere and his nephew Mordred, the Britains seem to be living suspended in a permanent aftermath. The betrayal marks the moment of total defeat, even if it will take several generations for the whole story to unfold and for the Saxons to achieve hegemony. For Geoffrey, the Saxon conquest of the British signifies nothing beyond itself; it is what it is, without a larger political or spiritual meaning. The conquest is certainly not the result of British moral degeneracy, as Gildas argued (although Geoffrey does give the Gildas complaint to various of his characters to voice tactically at strategic moments), and it is certainly not the providential triumph of an evangelizing Christianity, as the Saxon conquest of the Britons signified for Bede.[17] The loss of British sovereignty means nothing outside the pathos of its immediate experience, and to represent this state of permanent waiting in a static present outside history Geoffrey moves the narrative into experiential territory that seriously transgresses the borders of historiographical representation. The reign of Cadwallo, for example, begins with his uncanny doubling by the Saxon Edwin, his virtual twin, who finally defeats Cadwallo in what is simultaneously an ethnic conflict, a civil war, and a family quarrel, and it ends with the interring of Cadwallo's embalmed body inside the oddest of reliquaries, his life-sized equestrian statue erected on the West Gate of London so that the grace of his spiritual presence may protect the city. That is to say, the reign of Cadwallo, narrated at greatest length of all the reigns after Arthur, is composed of dreamlike material that continually mobilizes unconscious processes or otherwise produces uncanny effects that disturb the surface of what is no longer a purely political story. Nested within Cadwallo's story is the brief narrative of the exemplary deeds of Brian, the king's nephew, advisor, and companion. His devotion to Cadwallo is as great as was Mordred and Guenevere's betrayal of Arthur. The narrative is constructed entirely of the elements that become canonical for romance.

Brian's story consists of three discrete episodes and a coda. He is introduced in an iconic portrait of grief-stricken devotion. While Cadwallo's and Edwin's men are on one bank of the River Douglas negotiating the possibility of Edwin's consecration as northern king, Cadwallo is sleeping on the other bank, "in the lap of a certain nephew of his whom they called Brian" [in gremio cuiusdam nepotis sui quem Brianum appellabant] (137). On hearing news of the debates at the council, Brian begins to weep, bathing the face and beard of the king. The king looks up, wakened by the tears, and asks why he is weeping. Brian replies with a summary narrative of British disasters and Saxon betrayals that he presents as the permanent substance of British history: "The British people and I must weep perpetually" [Flendum est michi gentique Britonum perpetue] (137).

Brian's second appearance is the famous episode on the channel isle of Guernsey (138–39). Trying to get to Brittany, Cadwallo is washed ashore after a terrific storm that destroys all his companion ships. There he falls into deep mourning over the loss of his men: he takes to his bed and does not eat for three days. On the fourth, the king expresses a great desire for game, and Brian immediately goes hunting; coming home empty-handed, he is heartsick over his inability to grant Cadwallo's wish (maximis cruciatus est angustiis quia domini sui subvenire nequiret affectui). Fearing the king's imminent death, he slices off a piece of meat from his own thigh, roasts it, and feeds it as game to the king (et ad regem pro uenatione portauit), who instantly begins to feel better and recovers completely within three days. This second episode deepens and develops the first iconic portrait of loving piety. The christological elements of self-sacrifice extend even into the narrative texture: not finding any game, Brian is unable to have what he seeks (nec id quod querebat acquireret); yet he satisfies Cadwallo's unsatisfiable yearnings, giving him something greater than he seeks by feeding "his lord" (domini sui) from his own body. The scene is narrated in a purely affective register—Brian's acts grow from and deepen his ties of personal, not social, dependence. This is not a demonstration of ethnic or regnal solidarity: Brian is deeply pained (maxime cruciatus) by the pains of his lord. He does all within his power—to the extent of sacrificing his own flesh—to appease his lord's deep desires. Brian expects no reward, and the king never knows what he has done. The rewards are secret, buried within the realm of feeling, in Brian's own self-awareness of the extent of his devotion. The psychic material that the text engages here is extremely volatile. This scene that dramatizes the devotion of a man to his lord in terms of feeding him with his own flesh is easily reversible; a very slight change in perspective transforms the event into the story of predatory monarchs eating their subjects, as indeed we find in the story of the Giant of Mont-St.-Michel.

The volatility is neutralized in the third episode, the most complex of the three in its plotting (140–41). In a little romance plot, Brian's devotion to Cadwallo, the British, and their cause is in the forefront of the narrative action, even as his obligations to the state enter a possible conflict with obligations toward his family. These family obligations are raised only to be exorcised from the plot. While Cadwallo seeks aid from the Bretons, Brian secretly travels to York on a dangerous and self-imposed mission. Disguised as a pilgrim beggar, he assassinates Edwin's Spanish court magician, Pellitus, by stabbing him with his pilgrim staff as he circulates among the beggars and pilgrims demanding royal alms, and then disappears into the crowd. This episode includes a classic recognition scene between Brian and his sister, whom Edwin carried off on an earlier raid. On meeting her, Brian bursts into tears, and she almost faints with joy. Although they arrange an escape for her and a reunion in a crypt outside the city, the plan fails. Edwin, terrified by the assassination, has palace guards stationed at all the exits, and her escape is thwarted essentially by Brian's success (141). We hear no more about the sister or their plan as Brian instantly leaves York. In a little coda to this episode, Brian goes to Exeter, sends messengers to Cadwallo informing him of the successful assassination, and prepares the Britons for their king's arrival with Breton reinforcements. The episode ends as Peanda, king of the Mercians, with a great many followers, arrives to besiege Exeter. At this point Brian, too, disappears from Geoffrey's narrative. The romance of Brian's story is made out of the ruins of politics; this is the last refuge of public value played out in absolute privacy.

Just as Geoffrey's political narrative moves inward to become the substance of private experience, so too does it move to that other border of historical experience, eschatology. In both of these moves, Geoffrey draws on the resources of hagiography, but it is a secularized hagiography that transforms political loss and personal abjection into the sites of present value and signs of possible future glory. Thus the end of Geoffrey's narrative is marked by several of the most unequivocal declarations that British historical experience has come to an end. King Cadwallader hears a divine voice forbidding him to attempt a British resurgence, and instead of returning from Brittany to Britain as he had planned he goes to Rome, where he does penance and dies. The British retreat before the inexorable Saxon advance, and their name is changed to Welsh (Geoffrey gives several possible etymological explanations for the change). They are now nothing like their noble British ancestors, says Geoffrey, and they never again recover sovereignty in the island. That sovereignty has passed to the Saxons is underlined by the sentence describing the acts of the newly ruling Saxons, an echo of the description of the British at the beginning of their rule.[18]

The end of British sovereignty is doubled by Geoffrey's insistence on the end of his historical task. In the Bern MS Geoffrey ends by delegating the task of writing about more recent Welsh history to Caradoc of Llancarfan, his contemporary, and hands Saxon history over to William of Malmesbury and Henry of Huntingdon. The ending of the so-called first variant version is briefer and perhaps even more dismissive: "I, Geoffrey Arthur of Monmouth, leave the acts of the kings who succeeded from that time in Wales and their fortunes for my successors to write. I have taken pains to translate this history of the Britons from their language into ours." (Regum autem eorum acta qui ab illo tempore in Gualliis successerunt et fortunas successoribus meis scribendas dimitto ego, Galfridus Arthurus Monemutensis, qui hanc hystoriam Britonum de eorum lingua in nostram transferre curaui).[19] The passage strongly implies the discontinuity between the acts and deeds left to his successors and "this history" that Geoffrey has taken pains to translate. With the loss of British sovereignty and the historical discontinuity that it marks, Geoffrey's task thus comes to a definitive end.

At the same time the narrative also transforms this unequivocal passage of dominion and historical finality into a messianic assurance of future recovery. The divine voice forbidding Cadwallader to return to Britain also speaks of an end time when all the relics of British saints, hidden on account of the invasion, will be revealed and the Britons will regain their lost kingdom [Tunc demum reuelatis etiam caeterorum sanctorum reliquiis quae propter paganorum invasionem absondite fuerant amissum regnum recuperarent] (146). This is the moment, says the divine voice, prophesied by Merlin to Arthur;[20] and Geoffrey goes on to say that Cadwallader scrutinized various books of prophecy to discover that in fact they all agreed. Thus the loss is a gain; Cadwallader's renunciation of the world results in his personal salvation [inter sanctos annumeraretur] (146) and marks the eventual triumph of the British together with their saints at the end of time. From the eschatological perspective, however, the present remains out of history: the past is lost and present time is mere prolongation. It waits for the inevitable end that never comes.

Geoffrey's medieval translators, Wace and Lawman, each writing in a linguistic context—Anglo-Norman and archaized English—in which the triumph of Saxon hegemony cannot help but recall the further passage of dominion from those same Saxons to the Norman ruling elite, play this double ending of historical loss and personal and eschatological triumph differently. Lawman's ending emphasizes the eschatological leap out of history. He represents the time of a prophesied British resurgence as a finality out of time, narrated by means of golden age motifs, in which the relics of the redeemed Cadwallader will be translated to a redeemed "Brutlonde" that he himself redeems. The secular world, a domain of meaningless grief and never-ending flux, is, as it were, left behind.[21] Wace emphasizes Cadwallader's personal story, amplifying its original account by a pathos-filled description of his death and burial, but Wace also re-politicizes the outcome and insists on the continuity of dynastic succession. On deciding to go to Rome, Cadwallader makes Yvor and Yni his heirs and sends them to Wales, as lords now, not kings, so that the British will not be dishonored in lacking a leader:

> "Go," he says, "into Wales
> And be lords of the Britons
> So that they do not descend into dishonor
> for default of a lord."[22]

> ["En Guales," dist il, "passerez
> E des Bretuns seignurs serrez
> Que pur defalte de seignur
> N'algent Bretun a desenur."]
>
> (14821–24)

The British thus continue "without dishonor" but as a tributary people, sovereignty having passed to a new elite. Like Geoffrey, Wace ends by turning to his own work as a writer but with a very different emphasis that asserts historical continuity and avoids any suggestion of a messianic politics. Dating his own work *anno domini* has the effect of placing the story of the Britons into a larger secular historical continuum that holds the past together with the present and grants no regime a special place in the history of salvation:

> So ends the deeds of the Britons
> And the line of the barons
> Who derive from the lineage of Brut
> Who long held England.
> One thousand one hundred fifty-five years
> After God became incarnate
> For our redemption
> Master Wace made this romance.

[Ci falt la geste des Bretuns
E la lignee des baruns
Ki del lignage Bruti vindrent,
Ki Engleterre lunges tindrent.
Puis que Deus incarnatiun
Prist pur nostre redemptiun
Mil e cent e cinquante cinc anz,
Fist mestre Wace cest romanz.]
                    (14859–66)

"Ki Engleterre lunges tindrent" is especially interesting at this historical moment. Wace deemphasizes the messianic rupture in favor of historical continuity of land and sovereignty. Heir comes after heir within a single lineage; and then one lineage yields to another in the successive possession of a single territory. This ending is a thematic repetition of Wace's opening lines that also speak of those "who held England" to stress genealogical continuity in ways very different from the emphasis on dynastic disruption and disaster in Geoffrey's original:

Who wants to hear and wants to know
from king to king and heir to heir
who they were and from where they came
who England held first
What things happened there in order
Which first and which came after
Master Wace translated it
Who tells the truth about it all.

[Ki vult oïr e vult saveir
De rei en rei e d'eir en eir
Ki cil furent e dunt il vindrent
Ki Engleterre primes tindrent,
Quels reis i ad en ordre eü
Ki anceis e ki puis i fu,
Maistre Wace l'ad translaté
Ki en conte la verité.]
                    (1–8)

Manuscript compilations containing the *Brut* enact the same story of continuous succession: two manuscripts, for example, place Geoffrey Gaimar's *Estoire des Engleis* directly after the *Brut* and then conclude the sequence with Jordan Fantosme's chronicle of the conflict between Henry II and his son and its ultimate resolution.[23] The three works together thus tell the story of a sovereignty that begins at its single point of origin in the deepest past—the founding of Britain by Brutus—continues through the Saxon and then Norman regimes, and culminates in a historical present that joins Norman, Celtic, and English identity in the body and secure dominion of Henry II Plantagenet and his pacified barons.

Geoffrey's fictional examination of the possibilities of writing secular history within purely secular limits thus culminates in a double-edged vision of world-historical collapse and the pathos of conquest. It also continuously opens throughout the whole narrative into realms of interiority—intense emotional experience sometimes crossing over into outright perversity, such as the famous episode of Locrinus and Estrildis (16–17), or transgressing the bounds of political caution, such as Vortigern's desire for Renwein (67). Much as transgressive desires are independent objects of writerly and readerly fascination in these famous scenes, they nevertheless function primarily as what we might call historical engines, since they have immediate and usually negative political consequences. Not unlike the Dido episode in the Aeneid, such scenes provide a way to think through complex individual motivations and their complex relation to social outcomes. They are in this way among the many forms of historical explanation that Geoffrey deploys throughout his text. Indeed, Geoffrey might well have discovered in his extremely close reading of Virgil, from whom he obviously learned so much, this very way of conceptualizing the relations between interior experience and political change on a large scale.[24]

What we have been examining, in the Arthur section and its aftermath, is a complex treatment of inner experience that seems to break away from the public realm altogether and demand a different scale as a measure of value even as it is thoroughly implicated with publicity. As the confrontation between Gawain and Lucius is narrated, it no longer seems to matter that there is no political outcome: the joy experienced by the participants seems to stand over against its military occasion, and their prowess is evoked as something precious to behold. Similarly, in the full description of Arthur's crown-wearing festivities, the narrative is doubled between public display and private self-fashioning: on the one hand the crown wearing is a thoroughly political event, instantiating imperial power by proclaiming and celebrating it; on the other, it is an occasion for erotic pleasure and private self-display valorized along lines completely different from imperial success, even as they need each other to exist. In seeing inner experience in this way as something standing over against the public realm and thus potentially in conflict with it, Geoffrey seems to be making use of the resources provided by Ovid's powerful example, for in his amatory verses Ovid stands the public world of Roman imperial celebration on its head in just this way. In the *Ars Amatoria,* for example, what Virgil narrated as the fulfillment of Rome's world-historical destiny, the achievement of universal peace through world conquest, becomes primarily an occasion for picking up sexual partners: the triumph, says the narrator, is a nice place to take a date or to strike up a conversation with a stranger. In the *Heroides,* Ovid rewrites Homeric and Virgilian narrative from the perspective of the women left behind. Their pathos overrides and undercuts the official glory of male heroism. Perhaps most daring, in the *Metamorphosis* Ovid rewrites the epic boast, saying that his work will be read and remembered wherever the Roman imperium has carried the Latin language and as long as it shall last—Roman conquest is thus significant because it makes Ovid a global celebrity. In all three cases, Ovid presents the reader with a radical revaluation of Virgilian high seriousness: the public world, the world fit to be represented in grave epic measure, becomes a mere background for an action and a subject valorized on a different scale.

The episodes in the *Historia regum* that we have been examining can, I believe, certainly be read as instances of this kind of Ovidian disenchantment.[25] But they emerge from very different social circumstances and operate within the terms of a social logic very different from anything imaginable in the context of Augustan Rome. Writing in the midst of a ferocious battle over a dubious royal succession,[26] Geoffrey's evacuation of transcendental significance from historical narration and his scrutiny of immanent, secular causes for secular ends is an instance neither of royal ideological self-justification nor of Ovidian disenchantment nor of pure learned parody. As his narrative opens into realms of interior activity and private motivation, they are posited as the real locations of historical transformation and at the same time take on existence and value independent from the vicissitudes of the public world whose causes they are. These are areas of psychic extremity and social experience accessible by the techniques of fiction, the creation of an alternate world as a simulacrum of lived experience, an alternative world that can be explored fully by narrative means. This alternative world, too, has a necessarily double existence: it is at once an escape from history (for it has no existence other than as narrative, no reality other than as an effect) and an attempt to see into history's secret causes and most intimate truth (for the aim of Geoffrey's fiction is to find an adequate representation of the way the world goes "in reality"). There is no possible resolution between the two impulses, and the result, it seems to me, is profoundly unsettling. In its light it is no wonder that Geoffrey's work immediately inspired so much new writing and rewriting, especially writing in the vernacular that elaborates the very material that we have been looking at.

THE GAME OF TRUTH

Romance as I have presented it is inseparable from the consciousness of social and political processes in the secular world. Traditionally, of course, romance has been discussed as the fantasy genre par excellence, an illusionary escape from the social and political world. In his great essay in *Mimesis,* for example, Erich Auerbach insisted on the complete disengagement of the material of romance from historical reality and saw this disengagement as the result of a crisis of class consciousness. Auerbach's first characterization of romance adventure assimilates it entirely to fairy tale and stresses its unmotivated quality, just as he stresses the magical quality of the landscape in which things float free of a sociopolitical reality. This kind of adventure is what Arthurian knights must do to be knights: "All the numerous castles and palaces, the battles and adventures of the courtly romances—especially of the Breton cycle—are things of fairyland: each time they appear before us as though sprung from the ground; their geographical relation to the known world, their sociological and economic foundations, remain unexplained. Even their ethical or symbolic significance can rarely be ascertained with anything approaching certainty."[27] Auerbach draws this sense of romance adventure from a long tradition of historical medievalism that begins with the early Romantics, who saw the Middle Ages as a repository of inwardness and the last possibility of genuine feeling before the emergence of the crushing regularity of the administrative state and the tyranny of bourgeois society.[28] More recent approaches, such as those influenced by the work of Erich Köhler, which situated the rise of romance in the particular political world of the Angevin empire, have seen it as reflecting the particular social plight of the *juvenes,* the younger sons of the nobility who needed to make a social place for themselves. Typically this was done through marriage, which thus provided them with a wife and a domain. Köhler's approach, while no doubt correct in locating the social situation of the romance and especially in fore-grounding an important part of its audience, nevertheless continues to see the romance plot as a fantasy escape from the real social dilemma faced by those excluded from the lines of inheritance. Thus the social world remains in much of this work merely a static context that explains the particular imaginative escapism of romance.[29]

Auerbach was surely right in positing adventure as the essential element of romance. It characterizes both its material setting—"a chivalrous world of magic . . . in which fantastic encounters and perils present themselves to the knight as if from the end of an assembly line"[30]—and its formal centering on the quest of an individual knight. I want to dwell on Chrétien's great romance to consider those aspects of it that Auerbach did not read, for if, as Auerbach says, the sociological and economic foundations and even the symbolic significance of the elements of the romance plot cannot be "ascertained with anything approaching certainty," their articulation of a political dynamic, I want to argue, most certainly can, and not merely as an explanatory context but as an immanent part of its substance. The political dynamic appears neither all at once nor as the property of single elements in isolation but rather as a result of a continuous rewriting and reevaluation, a continuous search conducted by formal textual means for the immanent significance of the narrated event. Let me simply note here that this is a process inseparable from the medium of writing and especially from the inescapable fact that inscription always involves reinscription. We shall return to this point later.

The texture of adventure throughout Chrétien de Troyes' *Chevalier au Lion* is created by a set of immanent relations among elements whose significance emerges only gradually and over the course of the plot. Ultimately, this dynamic process takes us back to the secular world from which the text emerges and of which it is a part. Its task is to restore that world to historical comprehensibility, and it accomplishes that task by a process of progressive revelation. To understand the full significance of both the content and form of romance adventure, we need to take Auerbach's brilliant analysis of the beginning of *Le Chevalier au Lion*—Calogrenant's recounting of his failed adventure—as a starting point and not as the conclusion of an argument.

Le Chevalier au Lion: *The World of Romance*

From the moment that Calogrenant starts to speak, the motivating episode of the magic spring is presented in a continuous double perspective: Calogrenant's officially "adventurous" version, narrated in the first person, is in a dialogic relation to other versions developed progressively from the beginning of the text.[31] The most obvious of these other versions is the main plot of the romance itself, beginning with Yvain's decision to avenge his uncle by succeeding in the adventure in which Calogrenant has failed. Yet even before the main plot begins, Calogrenant's perspective is already confronted with others, including the disenchanted perspective of the single knight who defeats him, a perspective given in the knight's own direct discourse that Calogrenant's frames. In Calogrenant's narrative, the knight appears unexpectedly at the end of a set of virtually mechanical steps—Auerbach's metaphor of the assembly line seems particularly appropriate here—that were indicated by the *vilan* whom Calogrenant encountered along the way and who pointed him toward the spring: the *vilan* explains that if one arrives at the spring and pours water on the rock, there will be a terrific storm; Calogrenant continues the *vilan*'s explanation by saying that afterwards, the weather clears and birds sing. Calogrenant's story, like the version told him by the *vilan,* is narrated entirely under the sign of the marvelous: the landscape is a magical machine whose operation produces terror in the beholder followed by untold joy: "And when I saw the pure bright air I was entirely secure in joy because joy, if ever I knew it, makes great troubles be completely forgotten." [Et quan je vi l'air cler et pur, / de joie fui toz asseür / que joie, s'onques la conui, / fet tot oblier grant enui] (455–58).[32] The meaning here, as Calogrenant narrates it, is entirely exhausted in Calogrenant's emotional experience: the storm induces fear such as he has never experienced before; the bright aftermath fills him with joy. Yet when the knight appears the scene is given another meaning. His challenge to Calogrenant fully disenchants the "adventure," taking it out of the context of the marvelous by framing it as private war, an attack on the woods and town in his governance. The language of his challenge is fully legal and political: it alleges violations of traditional conflict resolution procedures and proper vassalic ties (490–516), for Calogrenant's attack was not only unprovoked but also undeclared, done "sans desfiance" (490). Thus the violence and the ensuing peace that Calogrenant has presented in the aesthetic register is reinscribed in the knight's direct address into the language of unjust private war. In this frame of reference, the knight's fight with Calogrenant amounts to the resolution of the private conflict by the legal procedure of trial by battle.[33] That the knight wins and Calogrenant is overthrown is, from this point of view, clear evidence of the justice of the knight's complaint (*plaindre* is played on continually in the passage in question), and it serves to further a problematic that will be elaborated in a rather large variety of contexts throughout the romance — the place of violence in governance.

For indeed, the text has already engaged this very problematic in the representation of the *vilan*. Asked what he is doing in the woods, he tells Calogrenant that he guards the beasts in the forest, and when Calogrenant protests their ungovernability in such a location — "I don't believe that anyone could keep a wild beast in a plain or wood or in any other place in any way unless it was tied or enclosed" [ne cuit qu'an plain ne an boschage / puisse an garder beste sauvage, / n'en autre leu, pro nule chose, / s'ele n'est lïee et anclose] (335–38) — the answer is that he governs them by coercion and fear:

> "I keep and rule them so that they will never leave this place."
> "How? Tell me the truth."
> "Not one of them dares move when it sees me coming, because when I can hold one of them, I squeeze it so hard by the two horns with my hard, strong fists that the others shake with fear and gather around me as if to beg for mercy. And no one else could be as bold as me, because if anyone came among them, he would be killed right away. Thus am I lord of my beasts."

> [— Je gart si cestes et justis
> que ja n'istront de cest propris
> — Et tu comant? Di m'an le voir.
> — N'i a celi qui s'ost movoir
> desque ele me voit venir,
> car quant j'en puis une tenir,
> si l'estraing si par les deus corz,
> as poinz que j'ai et durs et forz,
> que les autres de peor tranblent
> et tot en viron moi s'asanblent,
> aussi con por merci crïer;

ne nus ne s'i porroit fïer,
fors moi, s'antr'eles s'estoit mis,
qu'il ne fust maintenant ocis.
Einsi sui de mes bestes sire.]

(339–55)

Just as in retrospect we can see that the *vilan*'s answer looks forward to the episode of the magic spring, so Calogrenant's actions there look back to this scene while also pointing forward to many other moments of the romance: the adventure is not simply *there* for Calogrenant, and the "natural violence" that he unleashes—the storm and whirlwind—is in fact not entirely natural at all, for the forest is not exactly a natural place. Its meaning lies in its relation to the surrounding farmland and its nearby fortified town.[34] When the storm wreaks havoc on the forest, as the avenging knight points out in his complaint, it destroys his property and potentially causes a governmental crisis. This crisis is already shadowed here in the narrative when the storm makes the animals, which the *vilan* is able to govern under normal conditions, stampede and become as ungovernable as Calogrenant thought they were by nature. Later in the romance, as we shall see, the kind of destruction caused by Calogrenant's behavior at the magic spring is assimilated directly to the devastation of the countryside caused by siege warfare, and the consequences for governance will be similarly disastrous. For contrary to immediate appearances, the world of romance is not composed of castles and palaces that seem to have sprung out of the ground in the midst of the forest of adventure; rather, the world of romance is composed of towns and castles that exist in complex relations to their surrounding countryside and that pose the continuous problem of governance and its relation to aggression both public and private.[35] This is the problem investigated dynamically through multiple perspectives developed throughout the various elements of the text as a whole.[36]

Constant variation is the fundamental principle of romance structure. When Calogrenant's adventure is narrated, the experience of the magic spring is already a repetition of the motifs present in the encounter with the *vilan,* and no sooner is it narrated to the court than the adventure is repeated yet again in the text as both Yvain his nephew and Arthur his sovereign decide to visit the magic spring.[37] In this further repetition, the duality already manifest in the episode between the marvelous adventure and its disenchanted opposite provides a starting point for further textual development in which the sociopolitical stakes are significantly raised. Yvain takes Calogrenant's defeat as a slight to familial honor and thus to him. That is, he strongly desires to go to the spring in order to further pursue the private war.

> By my head, says Sir Yvain, you are my first cousin; we have to love each other . . . ; and so, if I can, and if I am allowed, I will go avenge your shame.

> [Par mon chief, fet mes sire Yvains,
> vos estes mes cosins germains;
> si nos devons molt entr'amer;
> .   .   .   .
> que, se je puis, et il me loist,
> g'irai vostre honte vangier.]
>   (581–83, 588–89)

Similarly, when Yvain leaves ahead of the court, he goes "to avenge, if he could, the shame of his cousin before he would return" [qu'il vangera, s'il puet, la honte / son cosin, einz que il retort] (748–49). Arthur, on the other hand, wants only to see the marvelous happenings and makes no mention of the fight with the knight:

> The king heard them gladly, and made three solemn oaths by the soul of Utherpendragon, his father, and by his son, and by his mother, that he would go see the spring, within two weeks, and see the storm and the marvel, so that he would arrive on the eve of the feast of Saint John the Baptist, and spend the night; and he said that anyone who desired could go with him.

> [Li rois les oï volantiers
> et fist trois sairemanz antiers,
> l'ame Uterpandagron son pere,
> et la son fil, et la sa mere
> qu'il iroit veoir la fontaine,
> ja einz ne passeroit quinzaine,
> et la tempeste et la mervoille,

si que il i vanra la voille
mon signor saint Jehan Baptiste,
et s'i panra la nuit son giste,
et dit que avoec lui iroient
tuit cil qui aller i voldroient.]
(661–72)

Arthur's way of characterizing the adventure is the same as the *vilan*'s and is blind to the precise political meaning that Yvain has determined as his own, the familial context of Calogrenant's encounter and the guilt that his defeat has revealed.

This difference between Yvain's and Arthur's reactions not only functions as an ironic comment on Arthur's wisdom — the king sees the adventure in the same terms as the churl — but also stands in dialogic relation to Calogrenant's narrative. If we read Calogrenant's story not as the account of an adventure that happens to be narrated according to the conventions of twelfth-century romance but rather as a deliberate discursive act by someone who, like the queen, "bien et bel conter li sot," then we might consider that his making the story into a judgment on his own character by expressing shame and confessing his own folly may be a deliberate attempt to exculpate himself from the legally based dishonor that Yvain makes his own affair.[38] He confesses shame, that is, to avoid confessing guilt. The world of romance is always under construction. No account is ever definitive; each is always partial and interested. And indeed perhaps Arthur's reading of the event is a similarly motivated discursive act: in the eyes of the court, which has every interest in seeing itself as the sole dispenser of governance and justice, the pursuit of family honor is a crime.[39]

While the text narrates Yvain's eagerness in prospect to see everything that Calogrenant described (696–717), his actual journey is presented quite perfunctorily. Everything that Calogrenant described is, as it were, ticked off one by one without any indications of Yvain's reactions to the experience. What Yvain solely wants is to vanquish the knight who guards the spring, not to experience wonders or marvels. In fact, Yvain's primary reason for desiring to experience the adventure alone and thus for departing ahead of the court is his certainty that when the court arrives Arthur will give the battle to Kay or Gawain (684–88) and not to him, although he is Calogrenant's nephew and claims the battle as his right. Unspoken in Yvain's certainty is what everyone knows—that both Kay and Gawain are of Arthur's family and Yvain is not—and this silence, too, raises a fundamental question of governance in yet another light. What is the place of family in Arthur's court? How does one define private right as opposed to public law-driven procedures if the king's court can be construed as simply one family among others? Ultimately, of course, Yvain becomes himself the guardian of the spring and triumphs over Kay—at once a proclamation of his own worth against his defamer, the final vindication of his family, and a halt to Arthur's potentially imperial design.

Yvain's success at the spring is already formally complete when he not only vanquishes its guardian, now named Esclados Le Roux,[40] but possesses the domain and the woman whom the dead knight left behind and with whom he has fallen in love. That this ending to the adventure is as scandalous as it is happy is put as baldly as possible by the text:

> Now Sir Yvain is lord, and the dead man is totally forgotten. He who killed him is married; he has his wife and they sleep together; and the people love and esteem the living man more than they ever did the dead one.

> [Mes or est mes sire Yvains sire,
> et li morz est toz oblïez;
> cil qui l'ocist est marïez;
> sa fame a, et ensanble gisent;
> et les genz ainment plus et prisent
> le vif c'onques le mort ne firent.]
> (2165–71)

The sexual scandal—"he [Yvain] has his [the murdered man's] wife and they sleep together"—is surrounded by notations of absolute injustice. In this passage Chrétien's language is based on a distinction that will be formalized in the next century but that already has a very long history in medieval law, for *morz,* as Howard Bloch explains, can designate the worst kind of killing, "an unemendable crime, involving the concealment of the victim's body" or the doing of the deed in secret and especially without warning.[41] This moment marks the real end of the prologue. The rest of the romance can be read as an investigation of various possible relations among the volatile elements of this officially

happy resolution: erotic desire (sa fame a, et ensanble gisent), political marriage (cil qui l'ocist est marïez), lordship (est mes sire Yvains sire), and social
reputation and the ideology of adventure, where the victor's worth is denoted
precisely by his being the victor (les genz ainment plus et prisent le vif c'onques le mort ne firent). We will take up each of these relations in turn.

Discourses of Desire

The story proper begins with a shift in register in which the prologue events
become both a metaphor and a discursive shadow of the events that will ensue.
Not only does the adventure of the magic spring lead to Yvain's falling in love
with the Lady of Landuc,[42] but it provides the very terms of the amatory discourse: she has avenged her lord, says the narrator, by wounding Yvain with
the wound of love, which is worse than the wound of lance or sword [Bien a van-
giee, et si nel set, / la dame la mort son seignor; / vangence en a feite greignor]
(1365–66).[43] The metaphor, which is here more than a metaphor, since the
Lady of Landuc is now officially lord of her domain and therefore responsible
for rendering justice, is further elaborated during the Pasme Avanture, in which
the lord's daughter is presented by the narrator as a supreme object of desire
for whom the god of love himself would become man and wound himself with
his own weapons (5374–89). This observation then opens into a disquisition
on power and on love as a wound. From the moment when Yvain sees the Lady
of Landuc reading her Psalter and lamenting the death of her husband, the
narrative is always internally doubled: familial vengeance and territorial control played out against the interests of the court will continue to shadow even
the most intensely private moments of Yvain's story, sometimes seeming to
be their false outside, sometimes merely their occasion, and sometimes even
their inner truth.

When Lunete brings Yvain to her lady, the encounter unfolds as simultaneously a scene of homage and fealty, a scene of confession, and a scene of judicial interrogation.[44] The whole structure of their encounter is thus created
by a combination of three discourses, each related to the others through their
common concern with the inner motives for social action: the bond of love
that ties together vassal and lord, the bringing to light and governing of one's
impulses, and the intentions that define the meaning of one's acts.[45] It thus
appears that the real action is taking place inside in the irrational world of

passion; the rest is all external and "merely" ideological. The private interview between Yvain and the Lady of Landuc culminates in a declaration of love in language that tries to name inner truth as passing beyond any imaginable outer situation:

> —Love? And whom?
> —You, dear lady.
> —Me?
> —Really, truly.
> —In what way?
> —In such a way that there can be no greater. In such a way that my heart will never stir from you, nor will I find it anywhere else; that I cannot think of anything else; that I give myself entirely to you; that I love you more than myself; that, if you please, I wish to live or die totally for you.

> [Amer? Et cui? — Vos, dame chiere.
> —Moi? — Voire voir. — An quel meniere?
> —An tel que graindre estre ne puet;
> en tel que de vos ne se muet
> mes cuers, n'onques aillors nel truis;
> an tel qu'aillors pansser ne puis;
> en tel que toz a vos m'otroi;
> an tel que plus vos aim que moi;
> en tel, s'il vos plest, a delivre
> que por vos vuel morir ou vivre.]

> (2024–34)

The opposition between social appearance and inner reality is played on explicitly in the immediate context of this encounter: Lunete uses exactly what I call the ideology of adventure—that success indicates worth—to convince her lady that she should accept Yvain as her lover and husband: she argues that since success in combat goes to the better man, the man who killed her husband will prove to be a better husband. Lunete couples this outrageous reasoning with real and urgent prudential counsel—Arthur's court is coming to the spring, and the Lady of Landuc therefore needs a champion.[46] Since Lunete uses real prudential considerations to manipulate the situation for other, unspoken ends, her counsel becomes simultaneously true and a ruse, and when she is later imprisoned for giving this counsel, the imprisonment will be similarly both deserved and unjust.

The Lady of Landuc then uses these same prudential considerations to talk herself into doing what she already desires, namely falling in love with Yvain. In brief, the erotic is produced in and by the very social discourses over against which it seems to stand. It thus appears as transgressive and opposed to all the discursive situations that bring it into being. For all the overt behavior of Yvain and the Lady of Landuc is a screen for their private urges — the really real appears to be latent, deep within, disguised even from the characters themselves, who talk themselves into seeing the situation as they want or need to see it. This opposition between the public excuse and the secret meaning comes to a head in the ensuing council scene, where the Lady of Landuc's counselors are manipulated into urging her to marry. The scene is composed of the continual repetition of the motif — "she agreed to do what she would have done anyway": "And their requests did not grieve her at all; but they moved her and supported her heart to do what she wanted to do." [Et les proieres rien n'i grievent, / einz li esmuevent et soulievent / le cuer a feire son talant] (2145–47).[47] Throughout the scene the action of the heart and the provocation of desire are absolutely paramount, and they are stirred further by the entreaties of the counselors. The whole scene is thus fashioned as a provocation to desire, aroused for prudential reasons that are always both genuine and false — genuine, for the Lady of Landuc does indeed need someone to defend her territory; false, because the situation comes up short of the desire, whose acting out remains still exorbitant. She wants to sleep with her husband's killer, and she wants to do it immediately. That is the desire of her heart. Yet the need for a lord, used here as an excuse, is equally real and urgent.

The exorbitance of desire is figured in various other episodes throughout the romance. In the attack of the giant Harpin de la Montagne on a baron helpless to withstand his ravaging of the territory under his governance, sexual desire takes the form of a sadistic fantasy of domination and degradation. What the giant demands is the baron's daughter, not as a wife for himself, but rather so that he can have the pleasure of watching her submitted to naked, louse-ridden kitchen boys:

> He would give her to his flunkeys as a whore, because he neither loved
> nor esteemed her so much that he would deign to abase himself for her;

she would always have a thousand slave boys around her, louse-ridden
and naked, like kitchen boys, who would all put in their contributions.

> [. . . et a sa garçonaille
> la liverra a jaelise,
> car il ne l'ainme tant ne prise
> qu'an li se daingnast avillier;
> de garçons avra un millier
> avoec lui sovant et menu,
> qui seront poeilleus et nu
> si con ribaut et torchepot,
> que tuit i metront lor escot.]
>   (4110–18)

In this fantasy the giant is a figure of the aggressive instincts out of control by
either chivalry or the restraints of the social world, instincts that are otherwise
an undercurrent in other scenes of enamorment and that the romance has depicted already let loose in the famous episode of Yvain's madness.[48]

In the entertainment for Arthur's court, Yvain's victory celebration and
public proclamation of his new status as husband and lord, are two further reflections of the transgressive sexuality embodied in the marriage. On the one
hand Gawain's offer to be Lunete's knight seems to be entirely free of sex —
which is to say, it is entirely composed of displaced sex. On the other hand the
notation of knights flirting with various ladies is entirely and directly erotic.
They both hint at a kind of provocation without end.[49] In *Le Chevalier au Lion*
desire is always mediated by a social arrangement meant to contain it, to which
it nevertheless always seems to stand in a transgressive or exorbitant relation.
The fundamental metaphor for this mediation of desire through social utility is
political marriage.[50]

Political Marriage

The marriage of Yvain and the Lady of Landuc is replayed in a set of variations
throughout the romance. In these variations, marriage as the officially happy
ending is anatomized and variously called into question in ways that continually reinstantiate the exorbitance of desire on the one side and the political fra-

gility of oaths and promises on the other. For example, the reconciliation scene that follows Yvain's victory over Count Alier on behalf of the Lady of Norison is composed of a long repetition of oaths, pledges, and promises of reparations to seal the alliance between the lady and the count. The fragility of peaceful resolution is underlined not only by the notations in the text of the long-standing violence of the powerful Count Alier's aggression against his less powerful neighbor but especially through the violence unleashed precisely because of the security Yvain inspires in the Lady of Norison's knights: they feel in his presence as if they were in a strong castle, "so that next to him they were as secure as if they were completely enclosed by a wall, high and thick, made of hard stone" [que lez lui sont ausi seür / con s'il fussent tuit clos a mur / haut et espés de pierre dur] (3257–59). The sense of security releases powerful aggressive urges in her knights and leads them to commit horrific violence and atrocities:

> The pursuit lasted a very long time until those who fled were exhausted, and their pursuers cut them down; they disemboweled all their horses. The living rolled on top of the dead as if they were wounding and killing each other. They abused each other very badly.
>
> > [La chace molt longuemant dure
> > tant que cil qui fuient estanchent
> > et cil qui chacent lor detranchent
> > toz lor chevax et esboelent.
> > Les vis desor les morz roelent
> > qui s'antr'afolent et ocïent
> > leidemant s'antre contralïent.]
> > (3260–66)

To contain this violence the answer would normally be a marriage arranged to seal the alliance between the two contending families—if not directly between the lady and the count, then at least between their relations. Yet because of his great prowess in subduing Count Alier, Yvain has become the cynosure of all eyes and the particular object of the lady's desire. All the people of the town desire Yvain as husband of their lady and lord of their land, a definition of political marriage:

And he won the heart of each man and woman so that, on account of the prowess that they saw in him, they all wished that he would take their lady and that the land would be in his rule.

> [et de cascun et de chascune
> a si les cuers que tuit voldroient,
> por la proesce qu'an lui voient
> que il eüst lor dame prise
> et fust la terre an sa justise.]
>
> (3246–50)

When Yvain refuses the lady's overtures, the episode ends inconclusively in anger and dismay rather than in reconciliation.

The ending of the Pasme Avanture is a mirror image of this episode: the terms are reversed but the lack of satisfactory closure is similar. Whereas the reconciliation between Count Alier and the Lady of Norison is based on giving pledges and repeatedly swearing oaths and agreements, the Pasme Avanture ends with the dissolution of oaths and agreements that were foolishly made to settle a private battle and have since become horrible traps. Yet the settlement almost comes to grief over Yvain's refusal to make a political marriage with the lord's daughter and have the wealth of his domain. Just as Yvain became an object of desire for the Lady of Norison and her people, the lord's daughter is presented by the narrator as already a supreme object of desire. Yet Yvain obviously wants no part of the settlement that could conclusively end the violence. He attempts to effect a reconciliation by giving an oath and pledge to return in the future and marry the daughter if he ever can—an oath that replicates the underlying situation that brought the Pasme Avanture into being in the first place. For the oath is a legal trick. Since, as Yvain knows, the time for his return will never come, the oath threatens to turn the future into a permanent deferral.

The inner/outer dichotomy and the fraught relation between desire and social being that political marriage would seem to reconcile are pushed into extreme tension in Yvain's departure from his wife: the narrator says that Yvain's body leaves but his heart stays behind—a tour de force of twenty-two lines playing on *cor* and *cuer* (2651–52). But the relation between body and heart is never transparent, and words are never fully adequate to the situation. The knight at the magic spring accuses Calogrenant of attempted murder since he attacked without words; Lunete accuses her lady of not keeping her word when she gets angry with her counsel; Yvain and his wife give each other one oath after another; and the promise that Yvain makes to return in a year is clearly made to be broken. Reconciliation would seem to be impossible.[51]

Lordship in a Broken World

Yvain becomes lord of her territory by marrying the Lady of Landuc, and his departure is as much a political disaster as it is a private crisis. Similarly, at the castle of Pasme Avanture, the victor over the demonic giants is promised both the land and a woman [Or seroiz nos / dameisiax, et sires de nos, / et nostre fille iert vostre dame / car nos la vos donrons a fame] (5693–96), and Yvain's refusal to remain there as lord places the land in a position of vulnerability. Political marriage promises to repair the broken world of *Le Chevalier au Lion,* in which the powerful are victimized by the more powerful. It promises to provide a place from which justice and peace may return to the world.

And the world of this romance is indeed broken. It is significant that the text passes over in silence the events of Yvain's tournament hopping with Gawain to present instead one situation after another of domination through violence,[52] narrated with an ever greater intensity of expression. These are situations in which Yvain's battles are motivated not for reputation but for determinate political ends. The landscape through which he travels is riddled with the violence of continual private war. Thus the atrocities that characterized Yvain's battle against Count Alier are reaccented and generalized in the encounter with the monstrous Harpin de la Montagne. That encounter is at once a nightmare and a realistic description of the geopolitics of private war. The combat between the giant and Yvain is described with particular emphasis on spilled blood and the torn body—description of the carnage is fleshy and done at length. Yvain cuts off a piece of Harpin's cheek, severs his shoulder, and pierces him to his liver, and the lion tears off pieces of the thigh from the giant, who screams in pain and fear. Eroticism is displaced throughout the episode into scenes of abjection: the torture and whipping of the imprisoned brothers is described in fascinated detail, and we have already discussed the giant's fantasy of sexually degrading their sister. The spectators do not gaze erotically at Yvain as in the Count Alier episode, but when the fight ends the whole town runs to gape at the huge and monstrous, wounded body. At the same time, the giant's depredations operate as a vehicle to display the mechanisms of ordinary siege warfare, which the text presents repeatedly by means of realistic notation.

Yvain on his arrival sees that the town is an impregnable fortress, strategically located and built to withstand attack:

> They went so far that they came close to a strong castle of a baron that was completely enclosed by a thick, strong, and high wall. The castle dreaded no war machine or catapult because it was extremely strong.

> [Sont tant alé qu'il vindrent pres
> d'un fort recet a un baron
> qui clos estoit tot an viron
> de mur espés et fort et haut.
> Li chastiax ne cremoit assaut
> de mangonel ne de perriere,
> qu'il estoit forz a grant meniere.]
> (3766–72)

Around the walls of this impregnable fortress, however, everything has been razed. As the baron explains, the giant has seized everything he wants in the vicinity of the castle [ja n'iert jorz que del mien ne praigne / tot ce que il an puet ateindre] (3852–53) and has burned the rest to the ground, a description that could have come directly from any number of chronicle accounts of, for example, William the Conqueror's northern campaigns.[53] With the countryside on which it is dependent for provisions devastated, the castle has become a prison rather than a fortress, and the inhabitants will die unless released. In the Pasme Avanture episode the castle is itself both a prison and a fortress that dominates the surrounding lands through terror. It collects tribute in the form of the young women embroidery workers, kept trapped in squalor while they make beautiful things for the lord's pleasure, and the castle itself terrorizes the countryside in the form of two demonic giants with whom travelers are forced to do battle.[54]

The king's court rested its legitimacy on its ability to relieve the pressure of constant private warfare. In the Harpin episode, Yvain immediately asks why, thus under attack by a powerful neighbor, the baron has not appealed for aid from the court of King Arthur. The answer reveals that the court is subject to the same play of domination and submission as the rest of the world. In a reference to the plot of Le Chevalier de la Charette, the baron explains that Gawain would be his natural protector, since he is the brother of his own wife and therefore uncle to his children, but he is away trying to rescue the queen, whom the king has foolishly entrusted to Kay's care. And he goes on: "He was a fool and she was careless to entrust herself to his escort. And I'm the one who suffers great pain and great loss from it." [Cil fu fos et cele musarde / qui an son conduit se fia / et je resui cil qui i a / trop grant domage et trop grant pert] (3919–23). Harpin's terrorizing of his neighbor is enabled precisely by the emergency in the distant court and by Gawain's absence on official court business. This is an emergency with effects in distant and unforeseen territories. No one is entirely in possession of his own adventure, and no adventure is complete in itself. Yvain will fight Harpin as much on Gawain's behalf as on his own.

The Ideology of Adventure

When Yvain inadvertently returns to the magic spring with the lion and laments his fate,[55] his lamentations are overheard by Lunete, who is imprisoned there in a chapel on his account. She has been accused of treason [Por ce ceanz sui an prison / qu'an m'apele de traïson] (3597–98) for advocating the marriage to Yvain. What Yvain learns is thus that his adventure does not at this point solely pertain to him and never has. Insofar as the adventure is Lunete's, the legal issue it raises hinges on a question of her intention. Did she counsel her lady to marry out of disloyalty or malice, or did she counsel with her lady's best interest at heart? Her answer goes right to the problem of external evidence for inner matters, yet another variation on the dichotomy between inner life and its outer manifestations that the romance is continually surfacing: [et je n'io consoil ne aïe / fors de moi seule qui disoie / c'onques vers ma dame n'avoie / traïson feite ne pansee] (3670–73). Lunete explains that there are only two men who would intervene to save her—that is, fight judicially to prove her innocence—Gawain and Yvain, Yvain because it is on his account that she has been accused of treason, Gawain because he has promised to serve her (3618–21). But Yvain is nowhere to be found, and Gawain is away trying to find the queen. That is, Gawain is caught up in the plot of the *Chevalier de la Charette.* This is the moment at which the text becomes an intertext and loses its appearance of independence, just as Yvain has lost the *propre* of his adventure. Even if the plot structurally centers on the wanderings and actions of an individual, no one's fate is his own exclusively, and everyone's fate is caught up in the affairs of the distant court.

The chivalric encounter—single combat between knights fighting first with lance on horseback and afterwards on foot with swords—is obviously modeled on the legal procedure of aristocratic trial by battle, the *iudicium dei*. At this moment when Yvain agrees to fight the next day on Lunete's behalf, Chrétien literalizes the metaphor and places Yvain in the situation of a real judicial combat. He does so again in the penultimate episode, the judicial combat between Yvain and Gawain over the inheritance dispute between the two sisters of La Noire Espine. The inclusion of these "real" judicial combats serves both to foreground and problematize the resemblance between all the chivalric encounters in the text and the legal form that is their model. The *iudicium dei* was the object of serious and sustained debate during the last half of the twelfth century,[56] and as the *Chevalier au Lion* interrogates the legality or efficacy of the procedure in one adventure after another, larger structures of significance are also brought into play and put in question. Not least of these is the ideology of adventure itself—that triumph in such an encounter or "success in the adventure" indicates the worth of the victor. This is in the first instance a generalization made from the *iudicium dei,* in which the meaning of the event is displaced most significantly from situation to character: rather than making manifest a question of right, the chivalric encounter makes manifest a judgment about the champion himself. Yet it is by no means clear by what scale of worth the champion or the event is to be measured in any given case. One sees this problem unequivocally in the famous Noauz scene of the *Chevalier de la Charette,* where Lancelot proves the depth of his love precisely by making a fool of himself in the tournament at the queen's command. Most usually, structural relations in Chrétien's plot put various scales of value into play at various times and in various instances. Since these can include scales of value as different from each other as general physical excellence (the *proesce* of epic praise) and technical legal right, it goes without saying that various ways of evaluating worth are almost inevitably in conflict with each other. For example, when Calogrenant narrates his battle at the magic spring, as I have argued, he displaces the significance from the question of what he has done to the land and town and presents it rather as a judgment on his own character. To put it another way, in seeing the chivalric encounter as an adventure he refuses to see it as a *iudicium dei.*

I have already noted the text's refusal to say anything about Yvain's year with Gawain going from tournament to tournament, the institution devoted directly to self-fashioning and the spread of reputation. In the encounters that the text does narrate, Yvain always fights as not quite himself: in the Harpin de la Montagne episode he is a substitute for Gawain, who, as we have already noted, is away trying to rescue the queen, and he is always the otherwise unknown Knight with the Lion. In his battle for Lunete he is both a substitute again for Gawain and also as it were for himself—as the Knight with the Lion he fights in place of Yvain. As opposed to Calogrenant in the prologue, the Knight with the Lion is not in search of occasions to demonstrate his prowess; he is pressed into service in one situation of emergency after another each in some way related to the *iudicium dei,* and the Lady of Landuc remains ignorant of any of them.[57]

The fight on behalf of the Lady of Norison is a reinscription of the fight at the magic spring, and it provides a classic instance of the *iudicium dei* assimilated completely to the chivalry topos. Here, however, the love provoked by the knight's prowess interferes with the process of reconciliation that was the purpose of the fight in the first place. As Yvain pursues Count Alier, the reader sees the action fully mediated through the perceptions of the spectators, first from the perspective of those fighting alongside Yvain, who grow braver by having him in their midst, and then from the perspective of the Lady of Norison and her companions, who watch from the tower of the castle.[58] As the description takes up the perspective of the lady in the tower, it begins by simply reporting what she sees. However, the text rapidly moves into free indirect discourse. Lines such as "But the courteous, the brave, the good Sir Yvain made them come to his mercy as a falcon does to a teal" [Mes li cortois, li preuz, li buens, / mes sire Yvains trestot ausi / les feisoit venir a merci / con fet li faucons les cerceles] (3188–91) draw their language from the content of the lady's consciousness. The perspective of the townspeople is couched in a long passage of direct discourse in the imperative (see how . . . ! and see how . . . !) that includes toward the end a comparison of Yvain to Roland. What the people thus see is not the emergence of legal right but the ever increasing splendor of the best knight. Consider for a moment in contrast the *iudicium dei* that ends the *Chanson de Roland.* The very ordinariness and small stature of Charlemagne's representative, Thierri, proclaims the justice of his victory over the giant Pinabel; the victory says nothing about the essential worthiness of Thierri but everything about the justice of his cause. Here in *Le Chevalier au Lion,* by the end of the battle Yvain has not only beaten Count Alier but conquered the hearts of all those who watch. This conquest is presented in a rhetorical ladder of literally growing splendor; what the combat brings to light is the ever brighter light that is Yvain:

And they say that the woman to whom he gave his love would be really fortunate. He is so powerful in arms and so recognizable over all others as a taper among little candles and the moon among the stars and the sun over the moon.

> [Et dïent que buer seroit nee
> cui il avroit s'amor donee,
> qui si est as armes puissanz
> et de sor toz reconoissanz
> si con cierges antre chandoiles
> et la lune antre les estoiles,
> et li solauz de sor la lune.]
>
> (3239–45)

Yvain is thus created in the imagination of those who see him as a fantasy object.[59] Those fighting with him want to become him, and those watching from the safety of the castle want to have him as both lord and lover (3246–50).[60] We have already noted the disastrous end of everyone's desire for Yvain: the knights fighting on his side commit outrageous atrocities; the Lady of Norison's pleasure in fantasy is turned to rage when she cannot in fact possess Yvain, who refuses to possess her as lover and lord.

If the battle against Count Alier is the classic instance of the chivalric encounter, Lunete's trial is at first a pure example of a successful *iudicium dei*. The *iudicium dei* is an intervention to bring the truth to light,[61] and indeed here, insofar as Lunete is vindicated, the procedure works just as it is designed to work. Yvain's answer to her accuser the seneschal, for example, mobilizes the full rhetoric of legal procedures meant to reveal a truth that would otherwise remain hidden from view (4426–42). He appeals to oaths sworn on peril of Lunete's soul and to the aid of God in demonstrating the truth of her words as a just reflection of her thought, that "she neither did nor said nor thought any treason toward her lady" [c'onques traïson vers sa dame / ne fist, ne dist, ne ne pansa] (4432–33). As the challenge continues, the narrator refers to Yvain as "he who knew the truth" [cil qui bien an set le voir] (4463). And of course Yvain is victorious against overwhelming odds. Yet just as the resolution of Count Alier's defeat needs to lie in the public world of peace and war and not in the privacy of eros, the real resolution of this episode does not lie entirely in Lunete's public vindication but rather in the secret of Yvain's identity and of his desire. This surplus of significance renders the episode incomplete in itself even if successful as a trial. When Yvain arrives at the trial, his whole desire is to see his lady, and when he sees her his psychic stress is narrated in complex figures of revelation and concealment (4338–51). To help Lunete, he has to rein in his heart, says the narrator, like one who, with great difficulty, pulls back his horse with a strong rein. In a parallel construction within the episode, similarly based on the distinction between outer appearance and inner truth, the lion, whom Yvain has forbidden to help, nevertheless comes to his rescue; the narrator says that the lion acts on what Yvain really wants, not on what he says. God and the right may be a unity, as the theory of the *iudicium dei* would have it, but here the *iudicium dei* is finally not a unity at all but a partial demonstration of a partial truth; Lunete's innocence is at stake in another way than what the trial has revealed, more is at stake than has seemed to be wagered, and Yvain and Lunete both know it.

In the second judicial combat in the text, the dispute over the inheritance of La Noire Espine, we witness both the *iudicium dei* and chivalric adventure in a state of total disarray.[62] The collapse of the affair is underlined in several ways, first, by the obvious injustice of the elder sister, who has claimed the whole inheritance for herself, an injustice apparent to everyone but one that the ordeal is ultimately unable to demonstrate. The text identifies her continuously as the "one who is wrong" and who is sure that she will prevail because she has managed to get the "best knight in the world" to be her champion.[63] That is, the older sister frames the judicial combat as a chivalric adventure. The younger sister, on the other hand, frames the event entirely in terms of the *iudicium dei:*

> May God and the right that I have, in which I have faith, aid him and protect from harm him who out of loyalty and love offered himself to my service. He does not know who I am, and I do not know who he is.

> [Dex et li droiz que je i ai,
> en cui je m'an fi, et fiai,
> en soit en aïde celui,
> e se lou deffende d'enui,
> qui par amors et par frainchise
> se poroffri de mon servise,
> si ne set il qui ge me sui,
> n'il ne me conoist, ne ge lui!]
> (5977–84)

As the older sister imagines it, the chivalric encounter and the *iudicium dei* are in direct contradiction. Since the combat reveals worth, then Gawain should win, because he is the best knight; if it revealed right, then Gawain would have to lose. When, on the other hand, the affair is introduced to Yvain, the *iudicium dei* and the chivalric encounter are spoken of as identical. Yvain is told: "If you can have the prize, you will have conquered and avenged the honor of the disinherited sister and increased your worthiness" [se le pris an poez avoir, / s'avroiz conquise et rachetee / l'enor a la desheritee / et creü vostre vaselage] (5076–79). That is, the judicial combat will simultaneously reveal Yvain's worth and the justice of the cause for which he fights. His answer also is based on the identity between chivalry and justice: "May God give me heart and grace, so that I, through this good adventure, can establish her rights." [or me doint Dex et cuer et grace / que je, par sa boene aventure, / puisse desresnier sa droiture] (5098–5100). When the judicial combat takes place, this kind of parallel between the *iudicium dei* and the chivalric encounter is decisively broken. The two knights, we remember, are closest companions, but each is unrecognizable to the other since Yvain fights as the otherwise unknown Knight with the Lion and Gawain, knowing he fights in a bad cause, has disguised his identity. Equal in prowess and ability, they fight inconclusively for a whole day. At nightfall they pause, and Yvain praises his opponent, asking for his name; as they make known their identities, they each, out of mutual love and chivalric honor, declare the other the victor and refuse to fight further. Thus chivalric honor and justice are entirely at odds.[64] As their respective scales of value are driven into direct conflict, other issues intervene, and the decision between the two sisters is reached by other means.

Besides definitively separating the chivalric encounter from the *iudicium dei,* the Noire Espine episode also pulls apart the constituent elements of chivalry. Eros and aggression are in continual contradiction throughout the episode, each as it were occupying the place of the other. Thus the sisters confront one another as enemies, whereas they should love, and at the center of the encounter between Yvain and Gawain the narrator embarks on a long disquisition on the miracle of Love and Hate inhabiting the same dwelling since the two knights, otherwise dearest friends and companions, want more than anything to kill each other. In this contradiction, the language of love—especially the repetition of the loaded term *par amors*—appears exclusively in the semantic context of the social bonds of mutual obligation and never in the context of erotic desire: friendship, in the quest of the young woman on behalf of the younger sister; family honor, in the younger sister's protestations of always loving her elder "autant com mon cuer" (5950); devotion to right, in the younger sister's appeal to Gawain—unbeknownst to her already pledged to the elder—to take up her cause "par amor et par proiere" (4760) and in the younger sister's characterization of Yvain as one who offered his service to her "par amors et par frainchise" (5981); companionship, in the devotion of Yvain and the Lion, "qu'il est a moi, et je a lui" (6461) and finally knightly honor in Yvain and Gawain's outpouring of love for one another.

The judicial combat at an absolute impasse, Arthur intervenes to settle the dispute. He almost resolves the issue by his verbal trickery—he extracts an unwilling confession from the elder sister by asking: "Where, he says, is the young woman who has virtually thrown her sister off her land and disinherited her by force and ill will?" [Ou est, fet il, la dameisele / qui sa seror a fors botée / de sa terre, et deseritée / par force et par male merci?] (6377–81). But when she protests that she merely answered, "je sui ci" in haste and protests the injustice of his taking her words literally, he settles the matter finally by the threat of state force: "It was apparent to him that she would not have given her sister anything, no matter what he might say, if there had been no force or threat" [s'est aparceüz molt bien / que ele ne l'en randist rien / por quan que dire li seüst / se force ou crieme n'i eüst] (6419–22).[65] The resolution that Arthur enforces hedges the question of partible inheritance; rather than giving the younger sister a share of the territory outright, he demands that the younger sister be immediately invested with what the elder has called "la part de mon heritage" (6429), and the text proceeds to note the relationships of dependency that follow with a striking degree of precision:

> Invest her with it immediately, said the king, and she will become your woman and hold it from you; love her as your woman, and she will love you as her lady and as her sister.

> > [—Revestez l'an tot or en droit,
> > fet li rois, et ele deveingne
> > vostre fame, et de vos la teingne;
> > si l'amez come vostre fame,
> > et ele vos come sa dame
> > et come sa seror germainne.]
> > (6432–37)

Here again the language of love is placed fully in the context of the ritual establishment of social dependency. The difference between the resolution of this episode and of all others in the romance is that this episode has never raised the question of an erotic relationship between the knight and the woman whose cause he champions. Yvain wins neither the land nor the younger sister. Whether either sister will be able to hold her land herself or will require protection against more powerful neighbors is left open; in the context of the rest of this romance, their future looks dubious.

Caught in the Game of Truth

Every episode in *Le Chevalier au Lion* is in the last analysis thus inconclusive. The romance itself achieves closure by a sudden shift in narrative premises, a laying bare of the device of chivalry that rather recapitulates the inconclusivity of the romance than resolves it.[66] Much as he has become an object of desire for others, Yvain's errance as the Knight with the Lion has not contributed in the least to the repair of his estrangement from his wife. In fact, strictly speaking she knows nothing of Yvain or of his deeds. She only knows that the Knight with the Lion, who fought on behalf of Lunete, is he who killed the giant Harpin. Rather than with the recovery of love, the romance ends as it began: with a journey to the magic spring for vengeance. Yvain does not woo the Lady of Landuc "par amors"; he besieges her domain using the magic spring as a weapon:[67] "so that by force and by compulsion it would befit them to make peace with him, or else he would never finish tormenting them with the spring" [que par force et par estovoir / li covanroit feire a lui pes / ou il ne fineroit ja mes / de la fontainne tormenter] (6512–15). The narrator describes the storm that Yvain causes in the language of siege warfare that the romance has often used. He devastates the surrounding forest and then so threatens the walls and tower of the fortified town that "they would rather be taken in Persia by the bravest among the Turks than be inside the walls" [Mialz volsist estre pris an Perse / li plus hardiz antre les Turs, / que leanz estre antre les murs] (6534–36). The inhabitants' wish to escape is vain; they are trapped within and curse their ancestors for founding the town in such a vulnerable place that "one man alone can invade us" [uns seus hom le puet envaïr] (6544). The Lady of Landuc is helpless to defend herself against the powerful onslaught. The fortified town has become a prison: "Indeed, they could never rest in that castle or dare to pass through the gates in the walls." [Ja mes voir ne reposerons / an cest chastel, ne n'oserons /

les murs ne la porte passer] (6551–53). Just as she is physically trapped in the town by the force of the siege, the Lady of Landuc is trapped by taking a series of oaths whose import she does not recognize. The conclusion thus gathers up the motifs developed in previous episodes, combining, for example, the siege warfare from the Harpin episode with the constrained oaths of the Pasme Avanture while all the while rewriting the initial encounter between Yvain and the Lady of Landuc, helpless without a man to withstand the threat posed by Arthur's threatened invasion. Just as the final episode recapitulates motifs developed throughout the romance, so too its language is a rich concentration of terms and phrases that have constantly been at play in the text. To take only one possible example of many, consider the oath that Lunete, "qui mot fu cortoise" (6620), has her lady swear:

> As you say it, I say it. By God and his saint, my heart will never fail to do all in my power. I will return to him the love and the grace that he used to have with his lady since I have the strength and power to do it.

> [Con tu l'as dit, et je le di
> que, si m'aïst Dex et li sainz,
> que ja mes cuers ne sera fainz
> que je tot mon pooir n'en face.
> L'amor li randrai et la grace
> que il sialt a sa dame avoir,
> puis que j'en ai force et pooir.]
>   (6642–48)

In this oath the language of love, the heart, force, and reciprocal obligation are all in play in complex ways whose full meaning lies outside the Lady of Landuc's awareness. For by this oath, "Lunete caught her in the game of truth, very courteously." [Au geu de la verté l'a prise / Lunete, molt cortoisemant] (6624–25).

And the reconciliation? Just as the Noire Espine episode ended by replacing the broken ties of family affection—the younger devoted to her sister "par amors" and loving her "autant com mon coeur"—with the socially dependent relation of homage and fealty, a relationship created under compulsion and guaranteed by force, so the passionate desire and joy in Yvain and the lady's first love gives way in the conclusion to the search for peace with each other.[68] In their

initial encounter, the language of homage, of judicial interrogation, and of confession all seemed provocations to an exorbitant desire that was their real meaning; this final scene is entirely disenchanted. The restoration of peace is given
in the same three registers—they swear allegiance to each other, the truth of
Yvain's identity is revealed, and he confesses his sin and crime. Yet the language
of reconciliation circles around another kind of affect entirely, the Lady of Landuc's undying grief and anger at a situation she is helpless to change. Not her joy:

> I would rather endure wind and storms all my life. If it were not such a
> base and shameful thing to perjure oneself, he would never find peace or
> accord with me, at any cost. I would have always wrapped it in my heart,
> like fire covered with ashes. But I do not wish to learn of this or to re-
> member it, since I have to be reconciled with him.

> [Mialz volsisse tote ma vie
> vanz et orages endurer,
> et s'il ne fust de parjurer
> trop leide chose et trop vilainne,
> ja mes a moi, por nule painne,
> pes ne acorde ne trovast
> Toz jorz mes el cors me covast,
> si con li feus cove an la cendre,
> ce don ge ne voel ore aprendre
> ne ne me chaut del recorder
> des qu'a lui m'estuet acorder.]
> (6756—66)

And as if to underline the arbitrariness and potential fragility of this reconciliation that is simultaneously a social trap, a willful surrender to political necessity,
and the best outcome that the Lady of Landuc could hope for, the narrator ends
with three assertions each more arbitrary than the previous and each a way of
forgetting the emotional cost of the final settlement: he asserts that Yvain is
now happier than he has ever been, that Lunete is entirely happy because she has
made a lasting peace between Yvain and her lady, and finally that this is the way
Chrétien ends his romance and if anyone says anything else they will be adding
lies. The romance ends here where the Lady of Landuc disappears into other
people's lives.

The World and the Text—Guigemar

The broken world of Chrétien's romance is framed by representations of violence in governance, from the *vilan*'s control of his beasts through force and fear to the strategic siege of the Lady of Landuc's domain. Yet there is throughout the text the suggestion of a possible redemption. In the experience of the unmeasurable joy of private fulfillment or in the mutual devotion figured in the companionship of Yvain and the Lion, in the devotion of Lunete to Yvain (who freely and kindly greeted her in Arthur's court when she was ignored by everyone else) and in his reliance on her, and in the unconditional love voiced in the words of the younger daughter of La Noire Espine, who loves her sister "more than her heart," there are glimpses of a possibility of a free and spontaneous love that stands over against the contradictory social reality and its constraints. But this possible redemption lies literally out of this world. In the absence of such freely given mutual devotion, one instead lives always in a state of its permanent deferral. Whether imaged as homage and fealty, regnal solidarity, or simply peace, one's destiny is pursued within a social bond that is enforced by the same fear and violence it is meant to contain and entered into by necessity.

The plotting of Yvain is like a love story. The young knight goes on a quest, finds his heart's desire, loses her through his unworthiness, seeks to repair the damage to his honor and reputation and to make himself worthy of love, and then recovers her. As we have seen, Chrétien complicates this schema immensely. In fact, the text uses the schema rather to represent a world in which such a story is impossible. In a similar way, Marie's *Guigemar* presents itself as if it were a story of exorbitant love and progressively reveals through a logic of substitution, repetition, and deferral that such a story is a dream version of an entirely different kind of social belonging. In the process, a story of desire becomes a pedagogy of desire that involves not only the hero of the story but its writer as well: to be wanted one needs to learn to want what the world offers for wanting.

After a brief prologue, which I will discuss later, Marie's *Guigemar* begins with a fifty-line presentation of the masculine, knightly world.[69] The presentation is fully normative, a quick resumé of the social imagination of the twelfth-century nobility—the family is represented as a patriarchal lineage dependent on a distant prince[70]—and is built of the code words that name, and by naming represent, the consciousness of the class out of which emerges the young Guigemar as its own exemplary representation and its reproduction. Marie does much with naming. Jean Flori has analyzed short descriptive passages from

Chaitivel, Lanval, Yonec, Deuz Amanz, and *Laüstic* that are all composed of variations on the same list—*beauté, pruesce, valur, largesce*—narrativized in the opening lines of *Guigemar.*[71] In rapid succession Guigemar is born, grows to young manhood, enters the service of a prince, is dubbed a knight receiving the armor that was "a sun talent" (48), and sets off on his period of errancy.[72] He is the picture of perfection except for the great exception: Guigemar will have nothing to do with love, for nature has erred in his creation and made him without desire [Mais il n'aveit de ceo talent] (64).

Guigemar's desire comes into being as a wound simultaneously self-inflicted and inflicted by what seems to be an absolute Other. For out hunting, as is his wont [talent li prist d'aler chacier] (76), Guigemar shoots a marvelous androgynous doe/stag.[73] The shot is mortal, but the arrow has uncannily rebounded from the beast to seriously wound Guigemar in the thigh, like the wound of Adonis, a figure of castration, the mark of desire. The wounded beast groans, speaks prophecy, and peremptorily dismisses her slayer. In her speech, the doe/stag gives and promises Guigemar the supplement that nature has neglected to supply. What is given, and given in excess, is a non-thing—a deprivation, a lack, a space of longing that reveals self-sufficiency to be itself a radical insufficiency. And no sooner is this gift of self-revelation given than desire precipitates Guigemar back into the world of prowess, the masculine world of the fathers where the genealogical and feudal chains are always already linked and never to be escaped. They are not, most certainly, to be escaped in a place of private ecstasy locked in the love story that is simultaneously their origin, their result, and their representation. Just as the doe/stag is absolutely strange, it is also, as are all such uncanny appearances, absolutely familiar. In its androgyny the beast mirrors the self-sufficient Guigemar; to wound the beast is to wound oneself; and the beast speaks in a mirroring syntax. Its prophecy promises a love story, one in which Guigemar will become, like itself, a marvel and also absolutely ordinary. In this promise, Guigemar is set in permanent opposition to a figure that will always mirror him:

> May you never find a cure
> for that wound that you have in your thigh
> until a woman heals you
> one who will suffer, out of love for you
> pain and grief
> such as no woman ever suffered before.

And out of love for her, you'll suffer as much;
The affair will be a marvel
to lovers, past and present
and to those yet to come.
Now go away, leave me in peace!

[N'avras tu jamés garisun
De la plaie k' as en la quisse,
De s[i] ke cele te guarisse
Ki suffera pur tue amur
Issi grant peine e tel dolur
Ke unkes femme taunt ne suffri;
E tu ref[e]ras taunt pur li,
Dunt tut cil s'esmerveillerunt
Ki aiment e amé avrunt
U ki pois amerunt aprés.
Va t'en de ci! Lais m'aver pes!]

(113–122)

The speech also precipitates the hero into a labyrinth of signification and a world of writing. The *plaie* (wound) received here becomes in the course of the narrative a *plait* (plea) for love, which is of course what it always was, and finally a *pleit* (knot) in the lovers' clothing and in their lives.[74] Guigemar is transported to a tower by a magic ship, and he arrives as a storyteller, where he adds the story of Guigemar to the Ovidian tales, *fabliaux,* and courtly romances that envelop and imprison the lady—he gives his story as a supplement to one who is already a character in it—and his arrival transforms a prison into the appearance of paradise.

In putting into play a complex set of connections among storytelling, the world of prowess, and the world of love, the *lai* of *Guigemar* is similar to the *lai* of *Chaitivel. Chaitivel*'s plot is simple. A lady is loved by four knights, and not wanting to lose all in order to have one, the lady strings them all along in hope, until a day when they all compete in a tournament. In the event three of the knights die, and the fourth is castrated. The lady prepares a bed for the castrated knight and nurses him until one day she tells him that she is going to compose a *lai* about the adventure: "I will make a lai about you four / And I will call you The Four Sorrows." [De vus quatre ferai un lai, / E Quatre Dols vus numerai] (203–4). The knight renames the *lai,* declaring that his name is original and proper: "Whoever calls it The Four Sorrows / will change its proper name." [Ki Quatre Dols le numera / Sun propre nun li changera] (227–28). The discussion raises a host of questions. Whose story is it? The story of the lady, the story of *tuz quatre,* or the story of the knight who survives, who escapes from the inscription *tuz quatre* without escaping from the inscription *tuz?*—for she does lose *tuz* and still have *l'un.* Is it four sorrows or one sorrow? And finally, whose sorrow is it that the story commemorates? The knight maintains that he is the proper namer and his is the *propre nun* of the *lai* because the sorrow is his *propre.* His reasons, as we shall discuss in a moment, are remarkably similar in language to an important passage in *Guigemar* (531–34). He says:

> I often see you coming and going
> speaking to me morning and evening
> I have no joy of it
> neither kissing nor hugging
> nor any other good except talking.

> [Vei sovent venir e aler,
> Parler od mei matin e seir,
> Si n'en puis nule joie aveir
> Ne de baisier ne d'acoler
> ne d'autre bien fors de parler.]
> (218–22)

Finally, after much further discussion, the lady agrees, and in her voice they name the *lai* together: "By my faith, she says, this is fine with me / Let's call it *Le chaitivel*" [—Par fei, fet ele, ceo m'est bel / Or l'apelum *Le Chaitivel!*] (229–30). Not being able to make love, they name it, talk about it, and make a poem of it. But no matter how much pleasure they take in this talk, and no matter how much their own fates are implicated in the "proper" naming of the poem, the poem, its title, and its meaning are finally not their own. The name of the *lai* may be inseparable from its origin, but its origin is not entirely identifiable with the conversation between the knight and the lady within the text:

> I shall tell you the adventure
> its name, and the city

where it was born and what it's called
It is called *Le Chaitivel*
but there are many
who call it *The Four Sorrows.*

[L'aventure vus en dirai
E la cité vus numerai
U il fu nez e cum ot nun.
Le Chaitivel l'apelet hum,
E si [i] ad plusurs de ceus
Ki l'apelent *Les Quatre Deuls.*]

(4–8)

The name is also inseparable from the *lai*'s career as a social artifact, a text necessarily separate from its origin, and its meaning looks outward to this social career. In fact, the poem is always doubly named, each name acting as a supplement to the other, just as the poem acts as a supplement and substitute for the unobtainable but always desired love scene that brought the poem into being: "Sometimes they call it *Four Sorrows* / Each of the names serves it well / *Le Chaitivel* is the usual name." [*Quatre Dols* l'apelent alquant; / Chescuns des nuns bien i afiert, / Kar la matire le requiert; / *Le Chaitivel* ad nun en us] (234–37). The love scene in *Guigemar,* while enjoyed by the lovers as this love cannot be, is itself not free from a similar play of substitutions and supplements. Strikingly similar to Chaitivel's complaint, which I quoted above, is the narrative of the lovers' happiness

They lie together and talk
and often kiss and hug
Indeed, the rest that others
usually have in this situation
would be fitting for them.

[Ensemble gisent e parolent
E sovent baisent e acolent;
Bien lur covienge del surplus,
De ceo que li autre unt en us!]

(531–34)

Much as readers would like it to be, the *surplus* of this scene is not the unspeakable joy of the body that exceeds narration;[75] it is rather the same joy that others customarily experience, and therefore it is exactly what exceeds the enclosed world of the individual lovers. In *Guigemar* itself, a succession of wounds, pleas, and knots — of *plai(t)es* — gives rise to the appearance of an enclosed world, but the significance of that appearance must be played out in the world that encloses, the world of feudal dependency through which whatever is *propre* is constituted. So too, in *Chaitivel* the poem composed in the bedchamber enters the social world, where in its circulation it comes back to its origin point in the long history of the discourse of desire. It finds that its end consists in further repetition.

    Guigemar's structure, like that of all romance, is a continuous repetition. It presents itself in the first instance as an alternation constantly repeated between a public and male world of linear succession, politics, history, and knighthood opposed to an alternative private and female world of desire, pleasure, *joie,* and love. The plot device effecting the transition from the one world to the other is magic — an androgynous speaking beast, a ship without a crew. From this perspective only, the love scene is the central episode, a scene of consummate joy beyond the powers of narrative to represent, a dream come true. The scene is thus similar to that moment in *Yonec* where a knight of desire flies through a lady's window only because she desired it, and his arrival turns her prison into an enclosed paradise of *joie* beyond measure. This initial opposition, however, repeats on the level of structure the illusion of self-sufficiency already figured on the level of plot as Guigemar's lack of desire, his lack of a lack. In *Yonec,* too, self-sufficient joy, the presence of an ecstasy beyond the powers of representation, is similarly exposed as illusion when, on the level of plot, the resolutions of desire are played out in political assassination and the restoration of what purports to be legitimate, agnatic succession. In *Yonec* on the level of form the illusion is exposed already when what prompted the lady to imagine a miraculous rescue was precisely her recollection of such things happening in romances. *Yonec* too finds its origin not in the interior desire of its characters but in the discourse that inhabits them. In *Guigemar*'s structure of repetition, the repeated is not the movement from one world to the next, for there is finally only one world.[76] The repeated is always the movement of enclosure itself. And each new enclosure is always at the same moment an opening, just as Guigemar's moment of love opens him yet again to the wound of loss and separation that first enabled him to love. Each opening is simultaneously an enclosure and each enclosure an opening, a wound and a knot, the public and private constantly giving rise to each other in constant circulation to produce signification and endow the process with significance.

In the final scene of the poem the lady has escaped from her imprisonment in the tower by walking through the unlocked door. In *Yonec* too the knight of desire would have flown through the window for the first time much sooner had the lady only asked for it. She enters the magic ship, which brings her not immediately to Guigemar but to what is ultimately a substitute for him and a repetition of the world she thought she had walked out of. Meriaduc, a *seignur*, abducts her, appropriates her into his *familia,* and imprisons her in his tower. Thus the magic ship takes her nowhere. At war, Meriaduc summons his feudal retainers. This summons is a ruse. It is a pretext to get Guigemar, who, Meriaduc has heard, has a shirt knotted like the lady's belt, into his presence. Yet the summons is also a true summons, and the war is real enough. The language of the summons is technical, a repetition of fealty:

> He sent for knights and enlisted them
> knowing very well that Guigemar would come.
> He sent for him as a favor
> As a friend and companion
> not to fail him in this need
> but to come to help him.
>
> [Chevalers manda e retient;
> Bien seit que Guigemar i vient.
> Il li manda par guer[e]dun,
> Si cum ami e cumpainun,
> Que a cel busuin ne li failist
> [E] en s'aïe a lui venist.]

(747–52)

After the recognition and the *despleie,* Guigemar asks for his lady. The language is again technical, a *commendatio:*

> Lords, he said, now listen,
> Here I know my love
> Whom I thought to have lost.

I beg and beseech Meriaduc,
Give her to me, out of grace!
I will become his liege man
I will serve him two or three years
with one hundred knights or more

[Seignurs, fet il, ore escutez!
Une m'amie ai cuneüe
Que jeo quidoue aver perdue.
Merïaduc requer e pri
Rende la mei, sue merci!
Ses hummes liges devendrai,
Deus anz u treis li servirai,
Od cent chevalers u od plus]

(838—45)

Meriaduc refuses with a simple assertion of seigneurial right: "I found her; I'll keep her" [Jeo la trovai, si la tendrai] (851). Guigemar makes a formal, public *défi;* his own followers make him a formal public *affiance* [Chescun li afie sa fei] (860), and they join Meriaduc's enemy, besiege the castle, surround it, starve it, raze it, and kill the *seignur* locked within.

The lady locked in the tower; the *seignur* locked in the tower. The language is the same, for the issue is the same: not love but that with which love in this romance and in the *Chevalier au Lion* is always in a metonymic chain—alliance, *amitié,* the social dependence of which love is a major part. Hence the ceaseless alternation: love presents itself as at once the ground of the social world and its opposite. This scene of destruction in which Guigemar besieges a tower, kills a man, and abducts a lady is a full construction of the world of feudal dependence and its issue: Guigemar lacks what nature never supplies, what is always a supplement to nature—a place in the social, political world, the "second nature" of law and dependence, and the necessary desire for that world, such that he would inhabit it as it already inhabits him.

The World, the Text, and the Vernacular Poet——Marie

From a moment of love, *Guigemar* elaborates in narrative what *Chaitivel* presents as either a vain desire, a deadly sorrow, or a joke. In *Chaitivel* the lovers, who want to have all, wind up with nothing but a *surplus:* they have no pleasure but the pleasure of talking.[77] Yet their talk about a love poem brings the love poem into being and launches it into the social world that it represents. In *Guigemar* the *surplus* inhabits the very moment of love: what seems entirely private, entirely the *propre* of the lovers, is not entirely so, and it thus opens the narrative to the customary world. Such permeability between the world and the text brings us to Marie.

The prologues to the *Lais* and to *Guigemar* make a bid for Marie as a writer precisely by seeming to reject writing.[78] That is, they pose an alternative that, like the alternative posed in *Guigemar,* is made to be undone: the world of writing as it is represented in the prologue — composed of texts, history, genealogy, and latinity — is set against the world of oral performance — speech, memory, adventure, and the vernacular. The unspoken in this dichotomy is its structural core: the world of writing is socially fully male; the world of speech, female. This, then, is the same dichotomy that seems to form the structure of *Guigemar,* only here it is implicitly gendered and explicitly social. By way of rejecting the world of texts, Marie says that it rejects her. She says that had she chosen to undertake a great work of translation, there would have been no reputation for her among all the others (Prologue 31–32). She chooses instead the world of performance. Yet no sooner does she make that choice than the opposition between the two worlds is revealed as illusory: the prologue immediately mentions the sheer labor of writing — "To rhyme them and put them into words, I've often stayed awake" [Rimez en ai e fait dietié / Soventes fiez en ai veillie] (41–42) — and proceeds to dedicate a book to a patron. Similarly, in the prologue to *Guigemar,* Marie promises to tell a true story that she has heard "Selunc la lettre e l'escriture," and the translation of a "bone histoire" that she renounced in the prologue immediately returns as the inescapable task of rewriting that always inhabits writing. All choices turn out to be the choice to translate, to make a book out of what has already become writing. Marie's choice to be a writer thus undoes the very oppositions that seem both to impel her to write and to prevent her from doing so. Marie's texts, made from reminiscences of the stories women tell, invariably behave as she tells us the ancient texts behaved:

> The custom among the ancients —
> as Priscian testifies —
> was to speak quite obscurely
> in the books they composed

so that those who were to come after
and were to study them
might gloss the letter
and supply the surplus from their own wisdom.

[Custume fu as ancïens,
Ceo tes[ti]moine Precïens,
Es livres ke jadis feseient
Assez oscurement diseient
Pur ceus ki a venir esteient
E ki aprendre les deveient,
Ki peüssent gloser la lettre
E de leur sen le surplus mettre.]

(9—16)

The reader supplies the gloss that completes the text. What befits Guigemar and his lady is similarly to be supplied as a gloss by the modern reader. What enables the equivalence is the necessary place of desire in social inclusion. For writing is throughout the prologues represented as a set of relations of dependence and desire: dependence on the ancient Latin text, dependence on the modern gloss, dependence on the pleasure of the patron, dependence on the remembered story, dependence on the recognition of the audience. Seeking this dependence and accepting it creates a world of *joie,* but also a world of *losengiers* and *gangleurs, feluns,* and *traisun* in which the *joie* seems to be enclosed, hidden away, or from which it seems always to be excluded. This is the inescapable world of love, of writing, of society, of romance.

Chapter Four

FROM ROMANCE TO EPIC

The new genres of the twelfth century claim to tell the truth about the past in order to clarify present circumstances. Sometimes this effort is explicitly in the service of pragmatic needs: lives of abbots and bishops need to be compiled to provide a record of parochial or monastic property holdings, rights, and governance. Sometimes the effort claims to be more theoretical and disinterested, to "repair the broken series of time" (interruptam temporum seriem sarcire), as William of Malmesbury puts it, as he proposes to fill the gap between Bede's history and his own time with a continuous narrative.[1] Geoffrey of Monmouth, probably echoing Malmesbury deliberately, presents his "translation" of Walter's ancient British book as commemorative, undertaken to preserve the deeds of the ancient British kings—and especially those of Arthur—for historical memory.[2] The earliest twelfth-century writers of vernacular narrative—Gaimar, Wace, Benoît de St.-Maure, and the other writers of the *romans d'antiquité*—all claim their works to be true histories, most often basing the authority of their new work on the prior existence of an authoritative ancient text, or, as we find in the *Roman de Rou* and especially in the *Estoire des Engleis,* on their own expertise as compilers. Gaimar names himself five times in the prologue to the *Estoire des Engleis,* primarily to tell us how long his research took and how many books he took into account in order to make his history.[3] The manuscripts that transmit these works to us almost invariably arrange them to compose a thick past woven of several threads. In the case of the Anglo-Norman realm, these works attempt to draw unbroken lines between the present and the Roman, Celtic, Anglo-Saxon, and Norman pasts.

Chrétien and Marie similarly present their work as historical efforts to transmit the past to the present. Chrétien opens *Cligés,* for example, by making

virtually all the same truth claims that one can find in the first generation of vernacular historians—he will tell us about his hero's paternity, his lineage, and his
land; he is careful to note that at the time of his story England was called Britain;
and he is scrupulous in naming his source and its provenance, a written history
found in the library of St. Peter's in Beauvais:

> We find this history, which I want to tell and reproduce for you, written
> in one of the books in the library of St. Peter's in Beauvais. That the story
> was extracted from it testifies that the history is true, and this makes it
> more worthy of belief.

> [Ceste estoire trovons escrite,
> Que conter vos vuel et retraire,
> En un des livres de l'aumaire
> Mon seignor saint Pere a Biauvez
> De la fu li conte estrez
> Qui tesmoingne l'estoire a voire:
> Por ce fet ele mialz a croire.]
> $(18-24)^4$

Similarly, *Le Chevalier au Lion* opens with the conventional assertion that
the utility of history lies in its pedagogical function. Arthur's prowess, the narrator begins, teaches us to be brave and courtly [Artus, li boens rois de Bretaigne / la cui proesce nos enseigne / que nos soiens preu et cortois] (1–3), a
lesson all the more necessary because in our days love, which should make one
"et preu et large et enorable," has been debased to the point that

> now love is turned to fable, because those who do not feel it at all say
> that they love. But they lie, and those who have no right to boast about
> it make it a fable and a lie.

> [or est Amors tornee a fable
> por ce que cil qui rien n'en santent
> dïent qu'il aiment, mes il mantent,
> et cil fable et mançonge an font
> qui s'an vantent et droit n'i ont.]
>   (24–28)

Much of the irony in these lines arises from Chrétien's particular use of the sharp distinction between *estoire* and *fable* that characterizes historical prologues. Here the distinction serves, among other things, to claim the serious purpose of historical instruction for the manifestly fabulous love story Chrétien is about to narrate.[5]

Marie, as we saw in the previous chapter, makes the claims that vernacular historians make for themselves even as she says that she will not write history.[6] Not only does she draw attention to her industry and expertise as a writer in making the book of the *lais,* but the *lais* themselves are presented as having the same commemorative function that Latin history has. She places her own work within the chain of commemoration by remembering

> Those who first began them
> and sent them forth
> made them for remembrance
> of the adventures that they heard.
>
> [ke pur remambrance les firent
> des aventures k'il oïrent
> Cil ki primes les comencierent
> E ki avant les enveierent.]
> (Prol. 35–38)

At the beginning of *Guigemar,* where the collection as a whole seems to re-begin for the third time, Marie takes up even more directly the stance of the vernacular historian:

> The stories which I know are true
> From which the Bretons made the *Lais*
> I will narrate to you briefly.
> And at the head of this beginning,
> According the the letter and the text,
> I will show you an adventure
> That happened in Brittany
> In former times.
>
> [Les contes ke jo sai verrais,
> Dunt li Bretun unt fait les lais,

Vos conterai assez briefment.
El chief de cest comencement,
Sulunc la lettre et l'escriture,
Vos mosterai un aventure
Ki en Bretaigne la Menur
Avint al tens ancïennur.]
(*Guigemar* 19–26)

In this passage Marie testifies from her own expertise that the story is true and that she will transmit it accurately. It is especially true, she says, because it is written, and the transmission is reliable because it follows the letter of the original writing. Between the event and its final reproduction *en romanz* Marie places herself within the line of learned experts, *clercs lisants*—such as Wace, who never fails to title himself *Maistre*—who because of their command of texts are under the moral obligation to preserve and transmit the past.[7]

Both the writers of romance and the writers of history thus associate themselves continually with the community of literate clerics, and they name themselves to establish their place and the place of their work within that community.[8] It is, as Benoît and Marie both note, a community that itself is thick with history, a continuous chain of transmission of texts linked together by those who have the expertise to recopy them, gloss them, and translate them for the education of future readers who, as Marie also says, will gloss them in turn. When the writers name themselves to place themselves within this line of historical transmission, their proper names thus point both to a past and to a future: they point to an obligation to the past—to preserve the past from oblivion—and to an intention to make a new text for new readers out of the collected texts of the past. Thus Benoît de St.-Maure sees his translation as the latest but not necessarily last step in a process of textual transmission that begins in Troy, passes through Rome, and now rests in *romance,* a linguistic and textual chain that, in going from Greek to Latin and finally to Romance, doubles the westward movement of both imperial and salvation history.[9] In *Cligés* Chrétien gives the most direct statement of this theme of *translatio imperii et studii* outside the Carolingian political theory from which it is drawn,[10] and he does so precisely to make the textual transition from talking about the old book found in Beauvais to naming himself as the initiator of the new task, a new writing that is simultaneously rewriting: "Chrétien begins his story just as the book recounts to us." [Crestïens comance son conte, / Si con li livres nos reconte] (43–44).

Historical and romance writing are thus always texts that represent their own circulation as texts. They draw their authority from the prior texts that they recount, as Marie says, "selunc la lettre et l'ecriture," yet they are also the *propre* of the contemporary writer who names himself with a proper name and thus becomes himself an author whose name is a sign that authorizes his version as uniquely true, one that can be drawn on by future generations. Like material property, this authority can be left as a legacy. Thus Geoffrey of Monmouth designates his successor, Caradoc of Llanfaron, endowing him with the authority of election while forbidding both William of Malmesbury and Henry of Huntingdon to write about the British kings because, not having Walter's British book, they lack the authoritative source that would make them authorities.[11] Similarly, at the close of *Le Chevalier de la Charette*, the continuator Godefroi de Leigni names himself as the one who finished the romance but more significantly names Chrétien twice as consenting to his work.[12] The new work thus is always a continuation of the work of the past. At the same time, since it bears the signature of its author, it is also an original. As such, it can become part of a canon list such as the one Chrétien supplies at the beginning of *Cligés*:

> He who wrote of Erec and of Enide, and put the commandments of Ovid and *The Art of Love* into romance, and wrote *The Shoulder Bite*, and wrote about King Mark and Iseut the Blonde, and the transformation of the hoopoe, the swallow, and the nightingale, begins again a new story.

> [Cil qui fist d'Erec et d'Énide,
> Et les comandemanz d'Ovide
> Et l'art d'amors en romans mist,
> Et le mors de l'espaule fist,
> Del roi Marc et d'Ysalt la blonde
> Et de la hupe et de l'aronde
> Et del rossignol la muance,
> Un novel conte rancomance.]
> (1–8)

This list asserts that Chrétien's work participates as a contemporary representative in the historical textual community that goes back as far as Ovid. At the same time, Chrétien's name is the name of a set of texts, and the inclusion in that named set of "the new tale that he again begins" names the tale as his alone and marks it as a written original.

History and romance writing thus begin with an already existing world of texts upon which writers draw to make a new text. No sooner is the new text made than it takes its place in the already existing textual treasury. We have seen this continuous relation among texts already in circulation in the intertextual relationship between the *Chevalier au Lion* and the *Chevalier de la Charette* that we remarked in the previous chapter. We can see it most definitely in the construction of the great prose romances of the thirteenth century, in which the separate stories of the previous century become merely parts of a single narrative cycle. Finally, we can see this reentry of the new text into the web of previously existing texts in a quite concrete, material way. In most of the manuscripts in which they are preserved, individual works of vernacular historiography are arranged to form a continuous cycle of secular history. Thus several Anglo-Norman and Angevin manuscripts are constructed of texts sequentially arranged to recreate the historical sequence outlined by Geoffrey of Monmouth, running from Troy to the rise of Anglo-Saxon hegemony, and thence to contemporary times.[13] To thicken this continuous history the scribe of BN ffr. 1450 even inserts the five romances of Chrétien de Troyes into the text of Wace's *Brut* at exactly the moment when Arthur has achieved a temporary peace. Just as William of Malmesbury says that he has done in his *Historia regum,* this insertion acts to fill a temporal gap in the narrative record.[14] The truth claim made by the writers of these new texts is always inextricably linked to writing, whether grounded in the continual circulation and compilation of texts or in the work of the author, an expert who can sign his work as his own. Writing, expertise, and truth each imply the others.

Writers of chivalric romance and vernacular history may continually associate themselves with the world of learned clerics—the world of monastery and cathedral—but of course they are working primarily within court circles.[15] They thus use the textual character of their new work self-consciously and directly to declare its superiority over the traditional epic forms of courtly entertainment. Because their new works are written, they write, they are therefore artistically excellent, whereas the old were oral and lacking craft, and they claim that their written works tell the truth while the old necessarily lie. In his earliest romance, Chrétien, to cite a very familiar example, tells us that he will fashion "une molt bele conjointure" out of the story of Erec and that his version alone is true.[16] His version, he writes, is especially superior to the oral ac-

counts traditionally recited in courtly settings because those are usually "fragmented and corrupted" [depecier et corronpre] (21) by their reciters. In these
lines Chrétien makes the distinction between his "true history" [estoire] (23)[17]
and traditional courtly versions of the past precisely in the technical language
used by his contemporaries to characterize imperfect manuscripts. As Douglas
Kelly points out, a manuscript *depecié* is missing leaves; a manuscript *corrunpu*
contains material that does not properly belong to it.[18] Some twenty years after
the appearance of *Erec et Enide,* Nicolas of Senlis begins his translation of the
Pseudo-Turpin Chronicle (1202) by declaring that no rhymed tale can ever be true
precisely because it is based only on oral transmission rather than on a written
record: " I want to begin the history when the good emperor Charlemagne went
to Spain by the land conquered by the Saracens. Many people have heard this told
and chanted, but what these chanters and joglars chant and say is only lies. What
they say is entirely lies because they only know what they have themselves heard
said." (Voil commencer l'estoire si cum li bons enpereires Karlemaine en ala en
Espagnie par la terre conquere sore les Sarrazins. Maintes genz si en ont oi conter et chanter mes n'est si menconge non co qui'il en dient e chantent cil chan-
teor ne cil iogleor. Nus contes rimes n'est verais. Tot est mencongie co qu'il
en dient car il n'en sievent rienz fors quant par oir dire.)[19] Nicolas continues
in a manner remarkably similar to the opening of Chrétien's *Cligés.* He writes
that his patron searched all the libraries (totz les armaires) to find in writing "la
vraie ystoire" that he will now present in turn. Both the courtly romance and
historical narrative mark themselves as new, place themselves in this way *after*
the chanson de geste, and assert that they are therefore superior to the chanson
de geste both in their written artistry and in the truth derived from writing
that they alone purvey.

Modern reading of medieval epics tends to go along unreflectively with
this medieval account and treat the epic as an early and therefore unproblematic form. In a variety of ways most contemporary scholarship places the chanson de geste prior to romance and the writing of history, even though most of
the chansons were written between 1170 and 1250, simultaneous with romance
composition, and several were written much later.[20] This chronological fact
of composition was insisted upon by Curtius in 1944.[21] Nevertheless, modern
reading still generally treats the chansons as "early." Scholars of the nineteenth
and earlier twentieth centuries typically argued that existing versions of extant
epics were based directly on lost manuscripts. The presumed existence of these
lost manuscripts pushed the date of their composition back to the early eleventh

century at the latest. While "individualists" such as Joseph Bédier argued for an eleventh-century French origin of the chansons de geste, "traditionalists" saw these same lost manuscripts as witnessing the continuous oral transmission of heroic legends going back to Carolingian times. The debate was overtly politically inflected: to situate the medieval epics in the context of the eleventh-century pilgrimage route, as Bédier had done,[22] was to make them purely French; to argue for a Carolingian origin was to place their origin within Germanic culture.[23] Both sides of this debate were in agreement, however, in placing the medieval epic well before the rise of romance.

The old traditionalist argument, absent its celebration of German national origins, became the dominant scholarly framework for the study of the chanson de geste in the later twentieth century when it was given new life by the application of the Parry-Lord thesis of oral formulaic composition to the medieval epic. Oral formulaic theory relegates the medieval epic to tradition even more decisively than the early traditionalists ever dreamed. In its most influential form, the Parry-Lord thesis creates a strict binary opposition between orality and literacy; thus the orality of the epic places it on the far side of an epistemological divide. Indeed, in the work of several of Lord's followers, most significantly in the brilliant historical speculations of Eric Havelock, the two technologies are said to determine two radically different forms of consciousness.[24]

I will come back in a moment to the problem of transitional literacy; what I want to underline here is that insisting on its orality situates the epic both chronologically and epistemologically before the romance and sees it as a traditional form whose meaning, qua form, is both unproblematic and unchanging—which is, of course, exactly how tradition always represents itself. The romance, when looked at from the side of production, brings new matter and meaning to representation in a new medium—it is individual, dynamic, erotic, psychological, and female (the epic being therefore collective, static, aggressive, social, and male). And the romance occupies its literary place self-consciously: it is always aware of itself as a new, written form, signed by a contemporary. The romance can become part of a canon list, while an epic never can—as we find in the opening of Chrétien's *Cligés,* where the new work is authorized not as belonging to tradition but as being a new production signed by its contemporary author. Or the new work can be represented as distinctively modern, doing something that has never been done before—as we find it expressed in Marie's prologue to the *Lais.* The epic, in this perspective, is never self-conscious as a form but simply *there,* for tradition is always there. Being there, at hand—*vorhanden,* as Heidegger nostalgically writes[25]—is precisely what makes it tradition. And if the epic continues to exist long after the appearance of the romance, as it in fact does, its continuance is, from this same perspective, only the repetition and prolongation of something old and never the production of something new. The continuation of the epic into "the age of romance" is a mere perseveration into the new age of a form and of a world long since superseded. The epic is nostalgic, conservative, obsolete.

The assimilation of the chanson de geste to the Homeric epic as a genre and as a technology of poetic performance has been a fixture of literary theory since the romantic period. Thus Georg Lukács's Hegelian distinction between the unselfconscious epic (that answers the question about the meaning of life even before the question can be posed) and the self-conscious novel is the paradigm for the opposition between the "primitive" chanson de geste and the "self-conscious" chivalric romance. And just as the *Iliad* is the one true Greek epic for romantic theory, the *Odyssey* being already novelized and self-conscious, so the Middle Ages requires its one true epic as well, a place filled by the *Chanson de Roland,* which makes the rest of the chansons de geste late by comparison. Here, *late* functions in the sense of "belated," tampered with by *remanieurs,* editors, educated scribes, or other epigones who litter them with elements—women, love plots, quests—drawn from romance and foreign to the *real* epic such as we find it embodied in *Roland.*[26]

The very influential thesis of Erich Köhler serves similarly to contain the epic and limit its expressive possibilities by treating it as a primitive, unselfconscious form in comparison to the chivalric romance. His seminal contribution to the Heidelberg Colloquium of 1961[27] develops the traditionalist argument, but from the side of reception rather than production. Köhler argues that whereas the epic is addressed to "un public mêlé, composé de représentants des catégories les plus diverses de la société" (23), the romance clearly makes a selection and does not address the lower orders, appealing as we have it, for example, in the *Roman de Thèbes,* only to "clergie et chevalerie," whom Köhler identifies as the newly conscious "class de droit" signaled by Marc Bloch as a product of the "second feudal age." That is, the romance comes "later" because it is addressed to a later social formation, and it registers the new concerns of this group. As I will argue later in this chapter, this undeniable differentiation in address is less a sociological fact of reception than a textual property of the fiction. The unity of address in the epic is the negative image of the differentiation of "clergie et chevalerie" in the romance; both are ideological projections in which a newly conscious class identifies itself as the whole of the social world.

In this chapter I will propose that the Old French epic is a construction that comes into being in the long twelfth century precisely in the context of new pressures on high-status nobility caused by the new reach and efficiency of both Angevin and Capetian state government and the state's use of advanced methods of administration, control, and coercion.[28] These methods invariably involve writing. Far from being "primitive" or "originary," the medieval epic is a new representation of the same contemporary situation that simultaneously brings romance and historical chronicle into being, and the epic is intended to make an intervention in that situation.[29] The pressure on the high-status nobility registered by the epic is twofold: from above by administrative royal government and the increasing importance of the increasingly non-noble urban, literate, clerical elite that staffs its administration from the chancery to the royal court,[30] from below by the emergence of merchant capital. What the epic does in the face of this dual pressure is to represent the world as if it consisted solely of the nobility, as if the king were a member of the same nobility, and as if merchants and other *vilans* were outsiders, literally having no place in the nobility's closed world. They are thrust beyond the borders of the human, like Saracens when they are outsiders; although Saracens, unlike merchants, are sometimes not outsiders: in the *Charroi de Nîmes,* for example, the Saracen nobility make exactly the same jokes about the "disguised" merchants, Guillaume and his noble followers, as Guillaume and his nobles make about the real ones. Merchants and *vilans* thus occupy a political, not an ontological exteriority: merchants, after all, exist, as do *vilans;* but the text relegates them to a comic, monstrous, or hostile "outside" to the emotionally and politically serious nobility, whose destiny matters.

To see the epic in the way that I am proposing is neither to discount its formulaic content nor to revert to Bédier's romantic imagination. I am suggesting here that writing in the epic mode at this time is a serious and deliberate choice, signified not by formal and linguistic transparency but rather by a degree of textual self-consciousness no less extreme than what we find in romance. We need only admit its possibility to see it in all epic texts. The relationship between the undeniably written artifacts that are the epics as we possess them in manuscript and their obvious surface manifestations of the procedures of oral, spontaneous composition in performance has been obscured by the strict opposition in oral formulaic theory between literacy and orality.[31] Indeed, the Parry-Lord thesis is at a loss to say how the epics as we have them came to be written.[32] Recent work, including especially Jeff Opland's fieldwork on African spontaneous composition, has helped enormously in our understanding of transitional literacy because it needed to be able to account for the undeniable existence of poets who were both literate and able to compose spontaneously in oral performance. This work has especially contributed to our understanding of the social and political implications of the shift in the technology of poetic composition.[33] Most important for our considerations here, the move from oral to literate composition seems always to be necessitated by a change in the social or political circumstances that force the poet to take advantage of the new means of dissemination that writing makes available, either because his access to his immediate audience has been cut off or because the traditional performance space has been co-opted by a social formation that would render the poet complicit with a political order from which he would otherwise disassociate himself. In this way, the manuscript page becomes itself a new political space in which the poet can "perform" in the new medium of writing. David Manisi, whose work Opland studied extensively, was, for example, both a tribal *mbongi* (an oral bard universally recognized for his spontaneous poetic brilliance as a spokesman for the people) and a writer highly literate in both Xhosa and English. His performances were undoubtedly spontaneously composed, often reflecting events that took place immediately before he stood to chant a poem; his writing in Xhosa was at times influenced by the English poetic tradition in which he was educated, sometimes incorporating stanzaic forms that he had learned from reading the English romantic poets. Yet on the level of diction, he wrote in highly formulaic lines indistinguishable from transcriptions of his spontaneous oral compositions, and he wrote only in the traditional genres of Xhosa oral practice.[34] Barred from tribal meetings during the period of apartheid, Manisi turned to books and newspapers as a venue for poetic performance and in so doing transformed books and newspapers into the kind of political space that could accommodate the poetic voice. Just a bit later, some of his younger contemporaries began composing orally at meetings of the African National Congress and thus granted it the status of a tribe and its leaders the status of tribal chief.[35] We see here an extremely self-conscious remaking of a traditional practice to meet the exigencies of new circumstances that have brought about a crisis in the very tradition that is being remade. In the process, the traditional form itself ceased being something merely at hand and became, as it were, a new weapon voluntarily forged, taken up, and wielded against those who were seen as illegitimate claimants to power. The appeal to tradition is in this context the very opposite of a conservative gesture.

Whatever its prehistory, the medieval epic as we have it is a written artifact, aware of itself as such in a highly literate world. Indeed, the epics are as filled with texts—laws, charters, histories, letters—as any romance, and they often claim to be based on written texts.[36] Examples are legion, but three will suffice here to make my point: the Oxford *Roland* continually cites the *Geste Francor* as its source and guarantee of truth, the plot of the *Chanson d'Aspremont* hinges on the existence of a written charter, and Bertrand names himself, calls himself "uns gentis clers," and describes himself writing *Girart de Vienne* in Bar-sur-Aube after hearing the event reported by a pilgrim returning from St. James of Campostella. Unlike romance, whose claim to truth and excellence is always associated with writing, medieval epics, filled with references to writing as they are, nevertheless make their primary truth claim through their use of the traditional form itself, linking truth with the techniques of oral performance. The textuality of the medieval epic is thus a representation of orality in which the epic appears to be the voice of tradition speaking the past. In being challenged from above and below, traditional ruling elites mark their opposition to the new order by claiming for themselves the authority of tradition: legitimate authority is what has always been, and "new customs" are decried as overturning the accepted order of things. Thus it is said that, when challenged by King Edward I, during the *quo warranto* investigations, to produce a document verifying his legal right to his land, the Earl Warenne came to the king's court with a rusty sword and claimed his land by its right, saying that it was with this sword that his ancestor had fought at the side of William the Conqueror and procured the land that was the heritage of all his heirs.[37] That modern historians have cast doubt on the truth of the story as told in the chronicle of Walter of Guisborough demonstrates all the more clearly how tradition is always in the process of being composed.

Absolute Vengeance

Taken as a whole, the corpus of chansons de geste reveals the new conditions of governance in a contradictorily coherent fashion by both actively denying their existence and manifestly refusing to comply with their procedures. In the process the epic mode has become problematic in itself: in becoming a text, all the elements that previously characterized oral performance—the bodily presence of the epic singer; the primacy of visual and concrete action; an unquestioned structure of values shared by the teller, the audience, and the tale itself; and the immediacy of the teller to the audience—enter a state of emergency. To illustrate this problematization of the epic form and complication of tradition, I want first to look briefly at some key moments in *Raoul de Cambrai.*[38] Afterwards, I will return to the broader discussion of the implications of the invention of tradition in the chanson de geste.

Usually classed as an "epic of revolt" along with, for example, *Huon de Bordeaux, Girart de Roussillon,* or *Gormond et Isembard, Raoul de Cambrai* distinguishes itself from them sharply in the radical opposition to royal authority—indeed, the radical opposition to all kinds of authority—that it stages, in the absolute irreconcilability of the conflicts it enacts, and in the terrifying violence of its representation. The single surviving complete manuscript of *Raoul de Cambrai,* BN ffr. 2493, is a codicological curiosity: it is written by two scribes, the second of whom begins in the middle of a laisse and over several lines of erasure, and then continues to the end. This same second scribe also wrote the first folio, clearly replacing a damaged leaf. Textually, *Raoul de Cambrai* is marked by an unusual switch from mono-rhymed laisses to assonance around line 5374, about one thousand lines before the second scribe takes over. This switch in versification has led to much literary critical discussion and some very dubious literary critical judgments. William Calin, for example, in his still essential *Old French Epic of Revolt* (1962), discusses only the first 5,555 lines (usually referred to as *Raoul I,* the assonating section being called *Raoul II*) and discounts the rest of the text as the work of a lesser continuator or reviser.[39] And Calin continues to treat the text this way in all his later work.[40] Alexandre Leupin, on the other hand, takes the lack of correspondence between the break in versification and the change in scribes as philological evidence for the unity of the text.[41] In what follows, I treat the text as we have it in the manuscript without concern for its possible prehistory, or, to put it more accurately, I would suggest that the appearance of the text's prehistory is generated by the text that we have and is part of its ideological burden. Let me simply note in this connection that *Raoul II,* the section most traditional in its versification, is composed of the least conventionally epic material. I am thus suggesting here that *Raoul de Cambrai* is aware of both its ancestry as an epic and the way its meanings are dependent on its intertextual position in the contemporary array of generic possibilities. Its deployment of romance elements constitutes a deliberate rewriting of romance as epic.

The poem begins by immediately placing itself into the epic cycle both by its content and by a self-conscious reference to other poetic performances. Its opening performs its own orality in its typical address to its listeners, calling them to hear a new song better than the old songs they already know. It does not invite the audience to read a new *estoire*—although at strategic moments the text does mark itself as most definitely written and at others as not a song but as a representation of a song.[42] At the same time as it summons its audience to a performance, it claims to fill a gap in poetic tradition, just as the historians claim to be mending the tears in the seam of time:

> Hear a song of joy and celebration! Many of you have heard and other singers have sung you a new song, but they leave out the flower of the great baronial family, who has so much valor: that is Raoul—he held the fief of Cambrai—and he was called Taillefer on account of his fierceness.

> [Oiez chançon de joie et de baudor!
> Oït avés auquant et li plusor
> —chantet vos ont cill autre jogleors—
> chançon novelle, mais il laissent la flor,
> del grant barnaige qui tant ot de valor:
> c'est de Raoul—de Canbrai tint l'onour—
> Taillefer fu clamés par sa fierour.]
>
> (1–7)

The new song promises to be "la flor" among all the songs heard before because it is the song of Raoul Taillefer, himself "la flor del grant barnaige." And the presentation of Raoul Taillefer that follows is most notable in the way it brings together, in one single laisse, an iconic portrait of chivalric value composed of all the elements that will be in disarray for the rest of the poem. Like Guigemar, who is set directly into the world of feudal and familial alliance, Raoul Taillefer is placed into the social world just as the text is inserted into the epic tradition:

> This Raoul Taillefer of whom I speak was a very bold man, he had a brave heart. He served the emperor of France so well that the emperor fully

rewarded him: he invested him with the Cambrésis as his legal fief and a beautiful wife, you never saw one more beautiful. Everyone approved this, family and friends. They celebrated the wedding, as you can hear, in the court of the strong King Louis; and he lived so long that his hair was white, and when it pleased God, he left this world. The noble lady Alice of the fair face made such mourning, you never heard mourning so great. They buried the baron in the monastery of St. Gerí. To tell you the truth, Alice was pregnant by this baron that I have been telling you about.

> [Icis Raoul Taillefer dont je dis
> fu molt preudons, si ot le cuer hardi.
> L'enpereor de France tant servi
> que l'enpereres li a del tot merit:
> de Canbrisin an droit fié le vesti
> et mollier belle, ains plus belle ne vis.
> Tuit l'ostrierent et parent et ami;
> noces en firent tex con poés oïr
> dedens la cort au fort roi Loeys;
> puis vesqui tant qu'ill ot le poil flori
> et quant Dieu plot del ciecle departi.
> La jantil dame Aalais au cler vis
> tel duel en fait, si grans ne fu oïs;
> et li baron l'avoient cevelit
> si l'enterrent au mostier Saint Geri,
> De cel baron dont vos ai contet ci
> estoit ensainte, par verté lle vos di.]
> (19–35)

This passage presents the biography of Raoul Taillefer as a metonym for the entire society. His life in the text begins when his service as a warrior (coeur hardi et preudons) merits and receives the "full reward" of a fief and a wife from the "emperor of France"—as we later learn, she is in fact the emperor's sister. "Parent et ami," family and alliance, are drawn into the circle of value and affection, approving the exchange and present at the wedding in the presence of the king, and by implication so are we, the epic audience (the poem says "con poés oïr," although the celebration is not narrated beyond the line that makes us present, for the possibility of this sort of presence is enough to guarantee its

existence). Then without event, Raoul's life ends, he dies "quant Dieu plot
del ciecle departi," and his body, whole and intact, is buried in the church of
the local saint. But in a formal gesture that will be repeated later in the text to
nightmarish effect, this moment of finality is also a moment of continuation:
his wife grieves but is pregnant, or as the text later puts it, "The count is dead,
he will not recover, but the lady has an heir from him" [Mors est li quens, n'i a
nul recovrier / mais de lui a la dame un iretier] (69–70), and his name is contin-
ued as well: "From his father, Taillefer the Marquis, they gave the child the name
Raoul de Cambrésis" [tout por son pere Taillefer l[e Marchis] / mist non l'enfant
R[aoul] de Cam[bresis]] (82–83). In the epic system of exchange the polity is
continuous, whole, and triumphant over death: Raoul is replaced by another
Raoul, named for the land he is to inherit, de Cambrésis, "un iretier" whose
identity is conceived of as homologous to his relations to his land, his "parents,"
and his "amis." In genealogical continuity, family, alliance, and land continue intact into another embodiment. If, as Bakhtin puts it, the epic presents "an absolute past" as a locus of value, a past of "peak times and best times," then only
here in a past anterior to the rest of the text can we find epic writing in its epic
function, for this is the last moment of strictly epic writing in the text.[43] From
this point on, the social harmony that is its formal burden ceases.

A comparison of this opening narrative with another moment in the text of
self-conscious epic writing is instructive. When Raoul comes of age, the emperor dubs him [Nostre emp[er]eres a adobé l'enffant] (292) and, in another instance of exchange in which the text signals its own ancestry as an epic, gives
him arms that come right out of the epic tradition, a helmet that once belonged
to a Saracen killed by Roland and a sword made by the legendary Germanic
smith Weland (314–16). Raoul is the object of everyone's approval; his taking up
the life of his father is a sign of the continuance of social value, and in carrying
weapons from the heroic past he, too, in the process seems to be a summary of
historical continuity and imperial triumph: "The French say, 'What a fine boy!
The honor of his father will be well matched!'" [Dient François: "ci a molt bel
enfant! / L'onnor son pere ira bien chalengant"] (340–41). But the continuity
signified by the circulation of weapons and by the unbroken genealogy of paternity and land is already illusory. The true beginning of *Raoul de Cambrai* does
not happen in the unfolding continuity of its narrative line but rather in the discontinuity caused by a prior act of disinheritance, an unsuitable exchange of land
and of a woman, that has already fragmented all the elements of the social world
here presented as if they were still whole.

In brief, King Louis has already tried to marry his widowed sister to Gibouin of Le Mans (she refuses) and has invested Gibouin with the Cambrésis, thus effectively disinheriting Raoul from his patrimony. This dispossession is nicely signified by the ensuing space between his proper name, Raoul de Cambrésis, and its proper referent.[44] When Raoul demands his father's fief as a reward for service, the king proposes a delay and a substitute—Raoul can have the first fief that comes vacant by death, which in the event turns out to be the Vermandois, claimed by each of the four sons of the recently deceased count. The king's temporizing maneuver thus begins a permanent crisis of unsuitable exchange, an endless multiplication of disinheritance that instigates what the text names "the great war without end" [la grant guere qi onques ne prist fin] (98). From this moment, the elements of the social world are driven into ever greater contradiction, a fragmentation of the social body that has as its analogue and expression the horrific fragmentation of physical bodies—"tant pié, tant poing, tante teste colpee" is the repeated formula—in a state of interminable war. Raoul's epic *démesure,* rather than leading to an affirmation of the ties of dependence that connect baron to emperor and God (as classically imaged in the death of Roland), escalates into pure atrocity in the famous scene of the burning of the convent at Origny, an atrocity that finally breaks all ties of family, alliance, and lineage and that will repeat itself endlessly throughout the poem. What composes the poem is not the forging but the breaking of ties—severing bodies, severing souls from bodies, severing marriages—and, as the action unfolds, Raoul will be killed (la teste colpée) by Bernier, the illegitimate brother of the Vermandois heirs but connected to Raoul by all possible ties of dependence and fidelity.

In her computer-assisted lexical study of *Raoul de Cambrai,* Françoise Denis found the exceptional usage of "la main" among all the words employed in the poem to designate body parts. With the exception of "la main," the series of body parts enters the poem only in expressions of dismemberment, either in confirmatory oaths (e.g., "ains me lairoie toz les menbres c[olper]," 200) or in actual description of the results of combat (e.g., "he cut the fist off his left arm" [del bras senestre li a le poing tolu], 2684). "La main," in contrast, only appears in expressions of fidelity, where it designates unbroken loyalty, along with, as Denis puts it, its truly detachable counterpart, "the sword" [le glaive], which is given as its sign.[45] Denis is surely correct in proposing the binary opposition "la main intacte / le poing coupé" as a structural element of the poem. This opposition makes visible a notion of chivalric exchange, socially staged in the *inmixtio manuum* of homage, in which justice is conceptualized as recompense for service, the perpetuation of *fides* circulating in the material form of property and women throughout the class of knights.[46]

In *Raoul de Cambrai* this world of perfect exchange is a shadow world. In its representation of the past, the text is haunted by the contradictions of the present, a time, let us remember, of constant conflict over the control of the very land that is at stake in the text—the Vexin, Normandy, Artois, and above all the Vermandois. That conflict eventuated ultimately in the victory of Philip Augustus at the Battle of Bouvines, a military victory that was the reflex of a new political, economic, and social configuration.[47] Not the circulation of *fides* but rather the repetition of a deadly vengeance, absolute, unreconciliable, and interminable, is the content of the text. Like Roland, Raoul dies in the first third of the poem, but the act of vengeance that Raoul both enacts and provokes is ceaselessly repeated, a repetition of perpetual violence that marks the defeat of the social normativity that he is meant to represent. The ceaseless repetition writes that defeat by simultaneously soliciting and forestalling it in endless deferral.

Thus the marriage of Beatrix, the daughter of Raoul's uncle Guerri le Sor, to Bernier, dispossessed heir to the Vermandois and Raoul's killer, should promise to bring an end to war by unifying the families of the Cambrésis and the Vermandois. In the kind of moment that romance writing endlessly explores, the text presents the happy satisfaction of their long and intense desire for each other[48] in metaphoric language simultaneously personal and political: "The one kissed the other through good fortune, because through them the great war was ended" [L'un baise l'autre par bone desstinee, / car par aus fu la grant guere finee] (5567–68). The end to "the great war" refers in conventional love language to the consummation of their desire while at the same time it literally marks the resolution of the political struggle in the peace accord created by their marriage. In Marie's *Guigemar,* the same expression similarly refers at once to the cessation of local conflict and to the happiness of sexual fulfillment: "The lord sheltered them and he was very happy and glad about Guigemar and his aid: he knew well that the war was over." [Li sires les ad herbergiez, / Ki mut en fu joius e liez / De Guigemar e de s'aïe: / Bien seit que la guere est finie!] (865–68). In *Guigemar* these words both represent and create the social harmony of Guigemar's rightful possession of the lady whom he loves and who loves him and his rightful position in the social order. At this same moment in *Raoul de Cambrai* the wish is made absolute: it expresses the hope of ultimate reconciliation, the great war brought to a conclusion once for all by "bone desstinee." Time, how-

ever, does not stop, and the hope is immediately dashed in the very next line
that continues the sentence, the narrative, and the war: "until the day that it was
renewed, that Gautier restarted it with a sword" [desc' a un jor qe fu renou-
velee / qe Gautelés la reprist a l'espee] (5569–70). The wished-for end becomes
rather the occasion for a further repetition of vengeance. The crisis in *Raoul* is
permanent and inescapable. In the enamorment that leads to their marriage,
desire is represented as provoked by displays of aggression, a fundamental conceptual strategy of romance to contain heroic violence that we examined in
the previous chapter. Beatrix describes her enamorment by using a variation
of the chivalry topos — the women fall in love while watching the men prove
their worthiness in combat. Here the topos is not visual but rendered precisely
in an epic mode, for Beatrix falls in love not by watching Bernier in action but
by listening to what amounts to an epic praise poem, recited in the aristocratic
great hall:

> If I love you, I must not be blamed, because I heard your great renown
> when my father was in his flagstone hall; every one of his household
> knights used to say that whomever you struck with your smooth lance
> never remained in his gilded saddle.

> > [se je vos aim, n'en doi estre blasmee,
> > car de vos ert si grans la renoumee,
> > qant mes pere ert en sa sale pavee
> > trestuit disoient a maisnie privee
> > cui vos ferié de la lance plenee
> > ne remanoit en la cele doree.]
> > (5572–77)

But in this interiorization in which aggression is fulfilled in love, the nightmarish landscape of the poem is also reenacted, not overcome but preserved:
"I have been so desirous for you that I would rather be burned or dismembered
than ever be married to anyone but you" [De vos avoir estoie entalentee; /
miex vossisse estre ou arce ou desmenbree / d'autre de vos fuse ja mariee]
(5578–80). Burning and dismemberment, the metaphoric language for the beginning of chivalric love, is simultaneously its opposite and its literal end. For
this scene is doubled not only by the burning of Origny, the great dislocation
that began Bernier's heroic career and thus made him a worthy object of desire,

but also by the end of the poem, where the same landscape is narrated in a literal nightmare. Riding home from a penitential pilgrimage, Guerri le Sor and
Bernier, Beatrix's father and husband, pass Origny, and Bernier sighs deeply in
memory of Raoul. Pressed to say why he sighed, Bernier with great reluctance
tells Guerri the story that Guerri has known all along. Hearing of the event—
an analogue to the epic recital of a traditional story—an event that he already
knows and in which he himself played a great part, Guerri grieves, and his grief
turns to an obsessive, implacable inward rage. Later in the journey, the two men
stop to water their horses. While the horses drink:

> He put his hand on his stirrup strap, and very prettily he released the
> stirrup, struck Bernier on the head with it, he broke his head, and tore
> the flesh; the brains fell out in that place and Count Bernier fell down
> into the water.

> [ill a sa main a son estrivier mis
> tout bellement son estrier despendi,
> parmi le chief Bernecon en feri,
> le tes li brise e la char li ronpi
> enmi la place la cervelle en chaï
> Li cuens Berniers dedens l'aigue chaï.]
> (8229–34)

Far away at this very same moment Beatrix dreams

> that I saw my lord return: Guerri my father attacked him fiercely and
> struck him down to earth in front of me, he tore the two eyes from his
> body and he took out my left eye. Then I saw this hall and the palace fall.

> [que je veoie mon singnor revenir:
> Guerris mes peres l'ot forment envait
> que devant moi a terre l'abati,
> fors de son cors les deus iex li toli
> et moi meisme le senestre toli
> puis vis ces sales et ces palais chair.]
> (8286–91)

The murder and prophetic dream are each in their own way and taken together literally nightmarish parodies of romance reconciliation, where the inner life stands as a sign and realization of social value. Bernier's brains spill out of his head as his body falls; in the dream his eyes are taken from his body as the building falls around him. These passages also function as parodies of epic presence, as we have it also, for example, in the curious *mise en abyme* where the text narrates its own origin in the future, puts itself into circulation, and becomes a historical fact:

> Bertolai says that he will make a song, no singer will ever chant such a one . . . he makes a song about it — you will never hear a better one, and it has since been heard in many palaces — about Guerri the Red and the lady Alice and about Raoul who was the liege lord of Cambrai.

> [Bertolai dist qe chançon en fera,
> jamais jougleres tele ne chantera.
>
> . . . .
>
> chançon en fist — n'oreis milor ja mais,
> puis a esté oïe en maint palais —
> del sor G[ueri] et de dame A[alais]
> et de R[aoul] — siens fu liges Cambrais.]
>   (2263–64, 2269–72)

Here blindness in the dream reverses the fundamental claim of epic presence — to narrate so vividly to the listening audience that they seem to be seeing the action unfolding around them. And let us underline that this vividness is itself staged within the poem as a stimulus to further violence: Guerri is moved to action precisely by hearing the story, which he already knows, narrated yet again. And in the dream, the death of the hero is rendered as the blinding of the witness (moi mesme li senestre toli) and by the collapse of the house around the spectator. The vengeance in *Raoul de Cambrai* is thus absolute, irreconcilable, and interminable, and the epic, rather than representing a valorized past of peak times and best times, stages its own anxiety over the meaning, value, and possession of the past, a past that continually rises up into the present to be reenacted in yet another act of murderous vengeance.

King and Lord

The motivating episode of *Raoul de Cambrai* is the disinheriting of the young Raoul, a politically obtuse attempt by the king to guarantee the future prosperity of his sister, Raoul's widowed mother, by arranging an unsuitable political marriage. While earlier scholars cited this disinheritance as an archaism, Pauline Matarasso identified it as a sign of the text's reflection of the political situation of the late twelfth century[49]—namely "baronial resentment at the successful imposition of royal authority," as Sarah Kay puts it.[50] Throughout *Raoul de Cambrai* the king is a fantasy figure, at once weak to the point of powerlessness and all-powerful and irresistible. Intimately related to this contradictory portrait of the king is the poem's concern with a discrepancy between law and justice, and so too, as Kay writes, is the poem's "translation of this discrepancy into issues of marriage and inheritance which were central and notorious aspects of Philippe-Auguste's policy."[51] This translation onto issues of marriage and inheritance, we need to add, conceptualizes justice entirely in the language of *fides* and thus casts land tenure as a sign of personal connections between men, freely entered into. Yet the language of the feudal order is inadequate to represent fully the social and political realities that have provoked the very attempt to contain reality in feudal terminology.

In *Raoul de Cambrai* the feudal order operates as a discourse signifying its opposite: a realm with a sovereign and an administration to which the aristocratic elite are subject on grounds other than marriage and land tenure. That is to say, the feudal language is used to represent a realm with a code of law, a set of social practices, and above all a type of sovereignty that all together have different structural bases from the network of alliances and obligations that the feudal language encodes as if that network of family, alliance, and land were the sole reality of the social world. This lack of correspondence between the form of representation and the social relations that demand representation is the mark of a desire. The historical imperative to turn to the world, to record and remember the past and thus to claim it for the present as its ground of value, is haunted by the disavowed wish to abolish that same past, a hopeless wish to rewrite present reality. The desire for history is here entangled with the wish to change the world by rewriting it in fantasy. And the epic impulse to make the past present, by remembering it and by articulating it in speech, is thus written in *Raoul de Cambrai* as the evocation of absence and the solicitation of death.

In its use of feudal language to represent the totality of the realm, *Raoul de Cambrai,* as I said a moment ago, creates the king as a fantasy figure, simultaneously impotent and all-powerful, the same fantasy figure that we can find in the earliest chansons de geste, such as the poems of the Guillaume cycle, as well as in other later epics. It is apparent, as well, in the contradictory portrayal of Charlemagne in the Oxford *Roland,* where he is at once an embodiment of transcendent sovereignty, at times described in the manner of early Christian imperial iconography, and powerless in the face of the familial rivalries of his court. The contradiction that inhabits these representations of royalty does not lie simply in an indecision on the part of the traditional nobility about whether it would be better to have a weak or a strong king. It lies rather in a fundamental contradiction within the conceptualization of sovereignty itself: on the one hand the king is *sui generis,* a sacral figure, and on the other hand he is a lord like other lords, *primus,* to be sure, but *inter pares.*[52] Briefly, is the king part of the realm, a power, however superior in strength, in essence like any other power in the realm, or is he a singularity, a power comparable to no other and therefore transcendent to the realm that he holds?

The pressure of the state-making designs of the Capetians and Angevins on the high-status nobility brings with it a continuous preoccupation with the grounds of authority and the reason to obey the sovereign. Resistance to and compliance with the king continually foreground the nature of sovereignty and the structure of dependence. Whether the king is strong or weak is never really at issue; the sovereign question of the epic is whether the king is a power among powers within his realm or is rather a singularity who transcends the realm that he "holds" and whose compliance he therefore deserves unconditionally. When we turn to the realm of medieval political theory, the picture is as complex and contradictory as it is in political practice. Some forms of post-Gregorian Reform political theory think the king as a thoroughgoing correspondence to the realm in fictions of the king's body as the body politic.[53] Law-centered kingship and the debates about whether the king's pleasure is the origin of the law or whether the king is a creature of the law—that is, whether the king is transcendent to the law or whether the law is transcendent to the king[54]—seem in the light of these arguments to be efforts to force the king back into the realm, to make him not a secular embodiment of sacred power but precisely a governor accountable along with his administration for the welfare of his people (and this can well mean the population as an aggregate, not a particular elite slice).[55] When the "traditional" form of the epic forces the king back into his realm precisely by "feudalizing" the realm, it attempts to put the king into the position of any other lord, even if first among them in a legible hierarchy of status and property. There is a fine example of this effort in a twelfth-century Latin life of Girart, Count of Roussillon, and its thirteenth-century French translation. The Latin sentence is a simple notation of time—during the reign of Philip I when Humbert was abbot of the monastery of Pothières— but it makes this notation by blending regnal and governmental terminologies used to refer to multiple sovereignties. The terminology is drawn directly from classical political rhetoric: "For at that time when Pope Alexander ruled the apostolic seat, and Philip the son of Henry the outstanding king held the reins of France, Humbert of blessed memory, as already said, was governing the coenobitic community." (Sane eo tempore quo Alexander papa apostolicam gerebat sedem, Philippusque, Henrici regis incliti filius, Francie tenebat habenas, gubernante quoque bone memorie Humberto jam dicti cenobii culmen.) In a series of learned and conventional metonymies and metaphors meant to be seen through—that is, meant to be read as recognizable metonymies and metaphors—classical figures of governance are arranged in a logical series: Pope Alexander directs the apostolic seat, Philip holds the reins of France, and Humbert of blessed memory governs a coenobitic community.[56] The French translation shifts the metaphor directly and surprisingly into a feudal register and in so doing isolates the king from the ecclesiastical figures: "In that time when Pope Alexander governed the faith of the apostle, and Philip son of King Henry held the seigneurie of France, and Humbert, of blessed memory, governed the dignity of the said abbey" (Quar en cel temps que l'apostoles Alixandres governoit la foy d'apostole, et Philippes filz dou roy Henri tenoit la seignorie de France, et Humberz, jadis de bone memoire governoit la dignité de la dite abbaïe).[57] Instead of holding the metaphoric reins of governance, Philip now has literal tenure over the seigneurie of France, a shift that transforms the territory of France into material property even as it turns the king into the seigneur who holds it. The ecclesiastical officials, on the other hand each govern an abstraction ("the faith" and "the dignity") and thus belong to an entirely different order of power. Since the king is in practice in a position whose power does differ from the power of any other powerful lord—and the emergence of effective means of royal administration makes this difference all the more apparent—the feudal vocabulary is always exceeded by the situation it attempts to control, and the contradiction within the epic representation of the king as a seigneur remains unresolved. It surfaces in the formal inconclusivity of the epic, which we will discuss later, in fictions of interminable conflict, and in extreme textual self-consciousness even in the face of the desire to appear simply traditional. The epic is thus always looking over its shoulder, as it were, at romance and history, taking up the same subject matters while challenging their self-authorization: in the name of tradition the epic brings into sharp relief the new conditions of social power.

How Am I to Love a Felon King?

For the rest of this chapter I will consider the relationship between the king and his nobles as the question is taken up in some of the many texts that narrate the life of Girart, Lord of Roussillon.[58] Like *Raoul de Cambrai,* where the breakdown of the relationship between the sovereign and a powerful lord is the beginning of a more general crisis, these texts, written between 1150 and 1180, continuously explore the place of the great lord in the realm, the set of relations that connect the king, the lord, and the realm together or pull them apart into irreconcilable opposition. In so doing, they revisit the same issues that occupied us in the previous chapter—lordship, political marriage, and erotic desire. These are not romance elements, extrinsic to the real being of the epic, but matters as proper to the chanson de geste as to the romance.

The *Chanson de Girart de Roussillon,* for example, begins when Charles breaks an agreement carefully worked out by his court in which he is to marry the elder of two sisters and Girart, the Lord of Roussillon, the younger, whom Girart loves. Charles suddenly demands the younger sister designated for Girart; Girart reluctantly agrees to marry the rejected sister but in return demands that the king give to him and his lineage his "own fief as an allod without homage" [E quel reis le m'otreit e mon lignage / Lo mien fiu en alue senz omenage] (laisse 34), an absolute declaration of the great lord's independence displaced onto property and made in legal language. Charles grants Girart's conditions while secretly scheming to take back Roussillon. That the emperor is in the wrong from beginning to end raises all the crucial questions regarding Charles's sovereignty, his territorial rights, and his connection to the nobility that serves him and on which he needs to rely. By what are his barons bound to him? And by what is he bound? In what ways is he connected to the realm that he rules, and to the rules by which it is to be ruled? These questions are dramatically addressed in the atmosphere of war and crisis that Charles's actions provoke. For example, the council scenes after the first battle over Roussillon, which Girart has won, turn on questions of just war and on the obligations of Charles's men to participate further in an unjust war—the barons maintain that the king is wrong because he seized Roussillon unprovoked and won it only by a ruse, not by force of war; moreover, he was the aggressor and Girart fought back in self-defense. These arguments cover virtually all the topics in the medieval discourse of the just war.[59]

In this context the king raises the issue of sovereignty directly by asking his barons whether they think he and Girart are equal. The king may think this is a rhetorical question; no matter what the king thinks, the difficulty posed by the possibility of both a positive and a negative answer haunts the text as a whole: "Lords, are Girart and I equal? I will go in a ship across the sea, or live seven years as a hermit in the woods before you set me up as a footstool." [Segnor, eu e Girarz em dunt egau? / Abanz en passerie ca mar o nau, / O serie set anz ermite en gau, / Que vos ja me metez en escabau!] (laisse 113).[60] The debate proceeds to circle around the question of the relation of service to property. Thierry, who has been one of Charles's most unfailing supporters to this point, accuses the king of absolute injustice in his refusal to submit to the law (laisse 115). Charles's closest counselors say that he made them felons when he contradicted their word by not living up to the marriage agreement that they made in his name, and they in turn accuse him of felony because of his refusal to take their counsel. They do not, however, dissolve their ties to him, nor do they fail to continue in his service, for which they expect reward even while declaring that the war he is pursuing is absolutely unwarranted and unjust. The question of equality is thus never quite answered, while the breach between law and justice is insisted upon. From one perspective the king is judged as a fellow noble: subject to their advice and consent as well as their reproach, he is constrained by the same agreements that constrain them. As a ruler he is thus also a creature of agreement and law. On the other hand, he continues to demand and receive their absolute support; his superiority to Girart is not simply a matter of his possessing a greater practical power of coercion.

Whereas *Girart de Roussillon* begins from the assumption of Girart's dependence on Charles and then sees his growing independence as a mounting crisis, the *Chanson d'Aspremont*,[61] which similarly represents Girart d'Eufrate's independence entirely in the feudal register, begins from Girart's absolute independence and then examines ways of integrating him and the territory that he holds into the realm. In a military emergency brought about by a Saracen takeover of

Calabria, the Emperor Charles calls all the noble lords of his realm together for aid. He does not, however summon to his court Girart d'Eufrate, called Lord of Burgundy, the Auverne, Gascony, Gévaudin and Cosence. Since Girart has never done homage and has received neither fief nor rent from Charlemagne, the king says that he has no grounds on which to demand his service. Charlemagne finally decides to send Archbishop Turpin to get Girart's aid against the Saracens. He is to do this by arguing that serving Charles is the way to save Christianity. Girart refuses Turpin in no uncertain terms, and when Turpin threatens him, in the name of the pope, with excommunication, Girart throws a knife at him and declares that he is dependent on God alone and on no earthly being for his property and power (1124–43). This declaration opens a debate about the grounds for compliance with the king's demand, a debate that remains unresolved throughout the poem even though certain temporary accommodations are reached from time to time.

After Turpin leaves without success, Emmeline, Girart's wife, talks him into serving the king. She begins her argument with a statement that grounds royal sovereignty in the strongest possible way in a transcendental register: the king, she says, holds power unconditionally over all. His power is a function of divine law: "The king of France is powerful over all: God commands it in law and in Scripture." [Li rois de France est sor tols poëstis: / Dex le comande en lois et en escris] (1440–41). In this light, fighting for the king is equivalent to serving God, and Emmeline thus argues that the battle will be itself a penitential pilgrimage and will provide Girart an opportunity to save his soul. To drive the point home she lists Girart's offenses, a catalog containing virtually all the usual denunciations of noble arrogance, conventional since the time of the Peace of God: Girart, she says, has raided churches, burned convents, preyed on widows and orphans, killed his rivals and prostituted their daughters.[62] Girart agrees to join Charles but without assenting to the terms of Emmeline's argument. The text ultimately represents Girart's integration into the king's realm as a purely secular and opportunistic event, and it does so by repeatedly dramatized acts of homage done by Girart himself and his heirs. In spite of these repeated rituals of dependence, Girart remains always a figure of opposition. Thus, when he finally agrees to help Charles, Girart first invests each of his sons and nephews with his territories, and together the Burgundians head for Aspremont. When the king rides up with his troops, the French and Burgundians fight, not recognizing each other and thinking that each is part of the Saracen force. We will return later to the significance of this kind of confusion between

Saracens and Christians. For now, I only want to consider Charles and Girart's mutual recognition; it is simultaneously a reconciliation and a ruse by which Girart is trapped into Charles's service. Seeing Charlemagne, Girart approaches him. As they exchange the kiss of peace Charlemagne's hat falls off:

> Girart bends down to pick it up. He bows and hands it back to Charles. That day, Turpin was standing in front of Charles. He remembered when Girart his cousin threw the sharp knife at him down at Vienne in the marble palace, that time when he went as a messenger for Pepin's son, how he would have killed him if he could. He took pen and ink and parchment, wrote the charter, translated it from Romance into Latin— that Girart went down on the road in front of Charles and that he bowed, that he handed back his sable hat. Charles has this man's homage at last; it was fitting that Girart submit to him. Thus people say, "Whoever has a felon for a neighbor often has a bad morning."

> [Girars s'abasse, si l'en a redrecié
> Parfont l'encline, a Karlon le rendié.
> Devant Karlon s'estut le jor Turpin,
> Qant li ramenbre de Girart son cosin,
> Ki li jeta son cotel acerin
> Dedens Vïane sus el palais marbrin
> Qant el mesage ala le fil Pepin,
> Se il peüst, dont l'eüsst trait a fin,
> Il a pris penne et enke et parcemin,
> Escrist le cartre del romans en latin,
> Si con Girars descendi el cemin,
> Encontre Karle et con li fist enclin,
> Con li rendi son capel sebelin.
> Celui homage ot Karles en la fin;
> Girars covint qu'il fust a lui aclin.
> Por ce dist on: "Qui a felon voisin
> Par maintes fois en a malvais matin."]
> (4147–63)

In this passage, Turpin belongs simultaneously to two worlds. On the one hand, he enacts a clear version of epic vengeance: witnessing the event, he calls to mind the insult done to him earlier in Gerart's castle, an insult here staged as both personal and familial (it was done by "Girart son cosin"), and he acts instantly to avenge it. Yet this act of epic vengeance is done not with the sword but with the pen and is performed by the learned clerk in court service. Its outcome is to make Girart the king's man. The charter transforms the chivalric return of the king's hat by his status equal into the ritual of homage, and once he is thus bound Girart becomes inescapably subject to the power of the king. Just as the epic typically lingers over the equipment of the warrior knight, here it dwells for several lines on Turpin's even more powerful weapons, not forgetting to note his linguistic expertise—with pen, ink, and parchment the clerk translates the epic presence of the vernacular into the authoritative Latin with which he intends to bind Girart forever.

In thus becoming subject to the king, Girart is put exactly where the Saracen emperor Agolant tried to put Charlemagne in the motivating event of the poem. In that scene, too, oral language and the ritual gestures of feudal nobility are entangled with the administrative power of writing. Having invaded Calabria, Agolant sends a messenger to Aix to demand that Charlemagne submit to his rule. As he rides into the court, Balan the messenger is described as an ideal knight, fully commanding in his physical presence. He is extremely attractive, physically strong, and beautifully dressed—"You could scarcely find a man so outstanding" [Poi trovissiés home si ensegnié] (215)—and he delivers a personal challenge (he has vowed, he says, to kill a Frank before his return) before proceeding to identify himself as a spokesman for Agolant. These notations of Balan's attractive appearance function here as one of the principal topics of the exordium of a forensic oration, the argument drawn from the person of the speaker.[63] He begins his official business by grounding its truth in a second sort of ritual witness. In a parodic version of the *iudicium dei,* Balan says that he will fight any champion the court should choose to prove that the words he brings as a messenger are true, and he then orally proclaims the emperor's message: just as the earth is divided into three, Asia, Africa, and Europe, and just as the Saracen emperor Agolant holds the best, it is right, says Balan, that the lesser two submit to the greater. In language identical to Girart's submission to Charles— [Girars covint qu'il fust a lui aclin] (4161)—Agolant demands that Charlemagne's lands be subject to his greater power—[Les dos devoient a la tierce acliner] (251). Moreover, Agolant claims the land by right of inheritance; as Alexander's descendant he claims all his land as "son iretage" (460). Slightly later in the text the terms of Charles's submission are laid out in explicitly feudal terms. Balan

says that Charles is to commend himself to Agolant, become his man, and receive back his land in fief: "I will take you to the land of Aspremont. You will
join your hands, become his man and receive the land as his gift." [Conduirai vos
el tertre d'Aspremon. / Joigniés vos mains, si devenrés ses hom / Et recevés
la tiere de son don] (475–77). The truth of Balan's oral message is not only guaranteed by his visual authority, heroic boasts, and ritual challenges but authorized even more definitively by a document, a letter or charter ("le brief" and
"la cartre" are used interchangeably throughout the scene) from Agolant himself that Balan presents to Charles. And just as Turpin belongs both to the heroic world of family vengeance and to the courtly world of literate functionaries
when he writes the charter binding Girart, so here a comic contrast between
Turpin and the Abbot Fromer marks the passage of clerical literacy from the
monastery to the court. When Charles hands the letter immediately to the
Abbot Fromer to read, the abbot panics:

> He breaks the seal; he begins to think; he kept silent for a long time; he
> begins to sigh from the bottom of his heart; he began to weep from both
> his eyes; his fingers relax, he lets the letter go.

> [Cil fraint le cire, si comence a penser;
> Une grant piece comença a garder;
> Del cuer del ventre comence a sospirer,
> D'ansdeus les iolx comença a plorer;
> Lasque les dois, si lait le brief aler.]
> (280–84)

Turpin retrieves the letter and reads it, but not before taunting the abbot
over his kind of literacy; the abbot is able to recite his hours, and his Latin is suffi-
cient for reading a saint's life, but letters such as this require a *clerc lisant* who really knows how to read: "Go, sir Abbot, and chant your matins. You would read
the life of St. Omer better. I, who really know how to read, will read this." [Alés,
sire abes, vos matines canter. / Miols lirriés la vie Saint Omer; / Mais jel lirai
quil sarai deviser] (294–96). As Turpin mocks the abbot for being barely literate,
able to read a saint's life but unable to read the parchment sent to the emperor,
writing has escaped the confines of church and is in circulation in practical use
in the secular world. It has become the property of a class of experts, educated within clerical circles but not operating in clerical circles, and like Turpin

valuable in court not so much as spiritual counselors but as secular advisors. And when the abbot tries to associate Turpin directly with himself and bring Turpin back into the strict ecclesiastical fold, saying that kings and princes need ecclesiastical counselors such as themselves only for matters within their own proper expertise (son mestier)—to keep princes from sinning—the irrelevance of his argument to Turpin's real role at court marks the transformation as irrevocable.

The structural parallel between Girart's submission to Charles and Charles's submission to Agolant is neutralized in the text by casting the struggle between Agolant and Charles not only as a fight for territorial control but as the kind of world-historical battle for Truth that we find in the Oxford *Roland*, in which Charles's renunciation of Christianity would be horrifically unthinkable. Indeed, the continuous summoning of the Saracen threat that runs throughout so many chansons de geste can be read as a means of arresting the flux of transitory alliance. All battles represent the final battle, and lines such as "Listen, lord, to what Agolant claims, he would destroy Christianity and all Christians" [Oiés, segnor, dont Agolans tençone / Crestïenté destruit et despersone] (333–34) are obviously meant to be bone-chilling. Nevertheless, the instability of judgment that continues to hover over Girart's relation to Charles similarly threatens the impermeability of the border and the clarity of allegiance that the difference between Saracen and Christian is intended to create. Thus in the *Chanson d'Aspremont* the Burgundians and the French each take the other for Saracens; and in the *Prise d'Arles* the intermingled bodies of dead Saracens and Christians lying outside the walls of Arles after a horrific battle cannot be distinguished one from the other and are separated only by a divine miracle.[64] Charles certainly needs Girart's military aid, but does it profit Girart to recognize Charles as both lord and king, and if so, on what grounds? Or by entering his service is he simply caught in Charles's administrative trap? Does Girart need to serve Charles in order to serve God, or can he serve God directly without the intermediary of service to the emperor?

All the reconciliation scenes in the text are rendered in the language of homage, fealty, and investiture, in which the various orders of power—ecclesiastical, familial, and personal—seem to be integrated into the realm whose head is the sovereign emperor. In these scenes integration into the king's realm is interchangeable with becoming Christian and accepting the power of the church hierarchy. For example, after Charles's victory at Aspremont, a victory in which Girart played a decisive role, Charles installs Girart as Lord of Reggio. In the palace, Girart finds Agolant's very beautiful widow, along with twelve other Saracen queens and twenty young girls. He puts them all under his personal protection and has them baptized by the pope. On becoming Christian, the widow of Agolant is renamed Clarence. Girart commends Emmeline's brother, Florent, to Charles, who dubs him and puts him in possession of Hungary, Florent's father being dead and Hungary, his fief, having reverted to Charles. Also at Girart's request, Charles gives Florent Clarence to marry. Girart, meanwhile, gives the other women, each with her own realm, to Charles. The commendation and dubbing are followed by Florent's homage to Charles, who then invests him with his heritage and presents him with his wife:

> He takes him in homage with no obstacle, afterwards he swears fealty and he ties on the sword of the realm. And the queen rises and stands. The king gives her to him by the right hand and Florent kisses and embraces her.

> [Prist en l'omage sans nule trestornee
> Après li a sa fëelte juree
> Et del roiaume li a çainte l'espee.
> Et la roïne est en estant levee:
> Par le poing destre li a li rois donee
> Et Florens l'a baisie et acolee.]
> (11141–46)

Thus agnatic lineage (as Florent takes possession of his heritage), cognatic alliance (in the political marriage of Florent to the ward of his brother-in-law), and feudal dependence (in Florent's homage and fealty to Charles and in Charles's gift to his own dependent Girart) all serve here to increase both the power of the sovereign and the territory of the realm, and they together create the structure of regnal solidarity. The secular ritual is immediately validated by the church: on the next day there is a coronation ceremony in which the pope blesses the marriage and crowns Florent with the rich crown that Agolant had brought from Africa while Charles again grants him his heritage. These rituals of integration and reward are accompanied by a set of repeated laisses in which Girart, with Charles's permission, gives his new son-in-law advice: "I want to instruct this young man a little / to whom you have given a realm and a wife" [cest demoisel vuel un poi ensegnier / Cui vos donrés et roiame et mollier]

(11178−79). The advice begins as a catalog detailing the principles of chivalric honor for a great lord: don't listen to flatterers, honor the church, do not despise poor knights but reward them, grant mercy to widows and orphans, lines in fact that reverse Emmeline's earlier catalog of Girart's vices. As Girart continues, the advice gradually shades away from a concern with chivalric behavior to focus rather on ways of maintaining individual political autonomy. This movement begins with the advice never to make a bishop out of the son of a shepherd [Ne fai evesque de fil a ton pastor] (11214) but rather to choose the son of a king, duke, or count, or even a poor knight and "If he has two of them, then take the younger; let the elder have the heritage" [S'il en a deus, si en prent le menor; /A iretage li laisse le gragnor] (11219). From this sort of pragmatic counsel to follow the customary patterns of aristocratic inheritance, Girart's speech proceeds to focus more and more on how to make oneself supreme in one's land through securing control of all administrative structures and especially of the church. Thus Girart says that in his own land he has seven archbishops and fifty-four bishops, all descended from the highest lineages. Moreover, not a one of them has ever ordained a priest without first clearing the choice with Girart, and the priest may not be ordained until witnesses have sworn before Girart that he is born of a legal marriage between a noble woman and a free man [Si con il sont tuit enserementé / De jentil feme, de franc ome engenré / Qui sont ensanle leument espossé] (11321−23). Then only after he has proved himself to be chaste will he be allowed to touch the Eucharist [li sains cors] (11325). The whole argument for keeping the church an aristocratic preserve is made simultaneously pragmatically [Ne faire mie de ton serf ton segnor] (11223) and in terms of the awesome presence of the Eucharist—it is never to be put into the hands of a non-noble not worthy by birth to touch it [Jo ne vuel mie ne ne l'ai esgardé / Que il soit ja, fils de vilain livré] (11306−07). The unique might of the Eucharist finally serves as an efficacious sign and guarantee of Girart's absolute individuality and freedom from the constraints of any earthly power. The Eucharist is absolute, and thus, says Girart, so is his own power in his own land, since it is authorized directly by God and derives only from God. After detailing how to staff his own church, Girart suddenly separates himself first from any dependence whatsoever on the ecclesiastical hierarchy—

> "I have my clerks so wise and well taught in the credo that I don't need
> or want the pope for authority, not for baptism or Christianity. When
> I was in my prosperity, I held nothing from anyone except God."

["Jo ai mes clers tant sages et fondé
Ja de creance ne de l'autorité
Ne por baptesme ne por crestïenté
N'ierrt l'apostoles requis ne demandé.
Qanque jo ai en ma prosperité.
Ne tenrai jo de nul ne mais de Dé."]

(11333–38)

—and then from any sort of dependence on Charles:

"Ah! Charles, lord, I won't conceal this from you. In this necessity I have
been beneath you; in the battle I made an avowal to you, and I called you
lord with my mouth. I must not be reproved in your great court: What
I did, I did for love of God. I am not your man, nor have I sworn fealty
to you, nor will I as long as I'm alive."

["A! Karles, sire, ja ne vos iert celé:
En cest besoing avons desus esté;
En la batalle vos trais a avoé
Et de ma boce fustes sire clamé.
Ne me doit estre en grant cort reprové:
Qanque j'ai fait en fis par amor Dé.
Ne sui vostre om ne li vostre juré
Ne ne serai ja jor de mon aé."]

(11339–46)

He calls for his horse and rides off, and the poem suddenly ends exactly
where it began, with all the questions of dependence unresolved. In this final
declaration, Girart again draws his own political authority directly from God;
service to the emperor, and more importantly, obedience to any authority, is
in Girart's formulation rendered as entirely prudential, a temporary alliance
determined by the immediate conditions of the balance of power. If the emperor, as Emmeline put it, is made sovereign by God, then so too in his own
realm is Girart. Earlier in the poem, in fact, Charles opens this same question,
but from the secular side, regarding the status equivalence of lords and kings.
Upon seeing Girart fighting valiantly at Aspremont, Charles suddenly asks why
Girart isn't a king. In his answer, Girart says that although he has neither the sta-

tus nor the power of king, he holds any lands that are his in peace: "'Lord Girart, why are you not a king?' The duke responds, 'It is not given to me that I am worth so much or have the power: But I hold whatever I have to hold in peace.'" [Sire Girars, por qoi ne fustes roi? / Respont li dus: N'est pas remés en moi / Je ne val tant ne n'en ai le pouoir: / Mais em pais tieng ce que je tenir doi] (7155–58). Thus, while denying himself both the status and power, Girart places himself directly in the position of a king. For in this answer his land has become not his property but his realm, and if he can guarantee peace to the land that he holds, then he is a king in his own realm with no need for dependence on a distant sovereign, a claim that is enforced by his exit from Charles's service at the end of the poem.

Like the *Chanson d'Aspremont,* the conclusion of *Girart de Vienne* hovers continuously over the excess of signification caused by representing royal administration in terms drawn from feudal ritual. For the poem is almost a pure ideological mask. It uses the traditional form of the epic and the traditional content of the conflict between a lord and his vassal to represent a new regime: the territorial state in which the king is not merely a feudal lord. It uses the economy of the gift, as well, to represent the town that instead of being a fortified encampment has become an economic entity differentiated from the country on which it is dependent, and dependent as well on active foreign trade and on the free coming and going of merchants. The wealth and status of the town's rulers and thus of Girart is thus a double dependency—on the monarch for preferment and on the viability of merchant trade. Charles, for example, presents the most absolute version of his sovereignty in language that will in the next century become technical and legal:

> And God, says Charles, who has all in his governance, the glorious Father who is born of Mary, I have conquered the seigneurie of seven kings; through power and through chivalry I have put them all in my governance. All serve and commend themselves to me; they each hold their property from me.

> > [Et Deus, dit Charles, qui tot as en baillie,
> > glorïeus Pere qui naquis de Marie
> > de .vii. rois ai conquis la seignorie;
> > par pooesté et par chevalerie
> > les ai toz mis en la moie baillie.

Trestuit me servent et font ma comendie,
si tient chascun de moi sa menentie.]
(6175–81)[65]

    Seignorie, poosté, chevalerie, baillie—Charles's imperial victory is stated here as pure feudal allegiance in which all kings hold what has been their own land (la seignorie) directly from the emperor, to whom they have handed their possessions in order to receive them back.[66] The emperor is simultaneously lord and sovereign, the land simultaneously territory subject to royal justice and personal possession. The reconciliation scene between Girart and Charles stretches over many lines. Repeated several times in the text, where each repetition is continuously reaccentuated, it enacts the same duality in which the king is simultaneously nothing other than lord and always more than lord. On hearing that Charles, who has been engaged in protracted siege warfare against Girart and whom Girart has steadily resisted throughout the poem, has become separated from his companions while out hunting in the vicinity of Vienne, Aymeri counsels his immediate assassination. Girart responds with a declaration of Charles's transcendent lordship, expressed again in the language of land tenure and the gift: "'May it never please God,' Girart answered him, 'that the king of France ever be shamed by me! I will be his man, if he have mercy on me, and from him I will hold my land and my country.'" [—Ne place Deu," Girart li respondi, / "que rois de France soit ja par moi honniz! / Ses hom serai s'il a de moi merci, / de lui tendrai ma terre et mon païs"] (6414–17). There follows a scene of general homage and fealty. Charles offers Girart one-third of his revenue: Girart refuses, saying that Hernaut is his older brother and is to be preferred. Hernaut does homage [lors s'agenoille Hernaut devant le roi, / ses hom devint loiaument sanz belloi] (6451–52), Girart does the same, and then Milon of Puglia pledges fealty [Mille de Puille li replevi sa foi] (6454), as does Oliver. Aymeri stands aside but finally yields only after expressing great resistance. He describes seeing the others caught in a trap like birds [quant ge mon pere et mes oncles ci voi, / qui si sont pris come oiselet au broi] (6463–64). As in the *Chanson d'Aspremont,* becoming the emperor's man is at once the sole path to one's own fulfillment and a trap:[67] Charles makes Aymeri his own warrior along with Oliver and Roland [et Olivier et vos me serviroiz, / et mon neveu dant Rollant seroiz trois, / et m'oriflanbe en estor porteroiz] (6474–76). Aymeri agrees, Girart commands him to kneel, Charles lifts him up, and they are all at peace.

The aristocratic reconciliation in the fields is reaccented when they all arrive in the streets of Vienne and run into Guibourc, Girart's wife, walking with
Aude on their way back from the Church of St. Maurice.[68] In the reaccentuation
of this scene, there is a general reconciliation between the claims of sovereignty,
feudalité, and family alliance. Guibourc speaks to Girart:

> Say, duke, where was this king found? Make sure, by God, that there is
> no cruelty, and don't do anything beyond your rank. But immediately
> present yourself at his feet and give him Vienne as a heritage.

> > [Dites, frans dus, ou fu cist rois trovez?
> > Gardex, por Deu, qu'il n'i ait cruauté,
> > ne li faciez riens nule outre son gré.
> > Mes a son pié molt tost vos presantez,
> > si li randez Vïenne en herité.]
> > $$(6546-50)$$

The emphasis now falls directly on land transfer; Guibourc wants Girart to kneel
before the king and give him Vienne "en herité"—the implication being that the
king will give it right back to Girart in fief. Girart answers:

> Lady, he says, you have spoken wrongly. Since this morning I have done
> his will. I became his man and his vassal. I did homage and fealty and so
> did all my brothers whom you see here.

> > [Dame, fet il, a tart avez parlé:
> > des hui matin ai fet sa volenté
> > devenuz sui ses hom et ses chasez,
> > si li ai fet homaje et feüté,
> > et tuit mi frere que vos ici veez.]
> > $$(6551-55)$$

Homage, fealty, and property transfer together become the full equivalent of
Girart's entry into the king's service. In the next part of their conversation,
family will mean not only all the brothers but the whole lineage, which Guibourc
imagines as being raised in status by hosting, serving, and honoring the king for
the one night. We are suddenly on very different grounds; the king on progress

through his *regnum* will hold his court within the territory ruled in his name by
his noble hosts, and his noble hosts will be the recipients of great honor on his
account:

> "God," says the lady, "you will be honored! Whoever can be a host for
> one night and serve and honor him in Vienne, his whole lineage will be
> raised up." Says Girart: "Lady, you have ample time to do your service."

> ["Deus!" dit la dame, "Vos soiez aorez!
> Qui une nuit le porroit osteler,
> et en Vïenne servir et ennorer,
> toz ses lingnajes en seroit alevez."
> Dit Girart: "Dame, bon loisir en avez
> de fere son servise."]
>
> (6556–61)

The scene of celebration inside Vienne is entirely courtly. Charles is presented hieratically, surrounded by the brothers; Oliver serves from a golden
cup, and Aymeri waits on all his elders. Across from Charles sit Guibourc and
Aude. Charles asks Girart for Aude so that he can give her to his nephew Roland. What was before a mutually agreed-on family arrangement between Oliver
and Roland to enter into alliance with each other, an alliance signified and sealed
by Oliver's transfer of Aude to Roland, is now rewritten as an integration of
the two young warriors and their families into the realm: the transfer of Aude
places Girart's whole lineage into the *poosté* of the king and is therefore homologous with the transfer of Vienne. The fantasy enacted in this scene is that all
social structures to which one can declare allegiance—personal, familial, feudal, political—that have been in conflict throughout the poem are subsumed
within the single entity of the realm; the reconciliation is performed in the
transfer of Aude from the family of Girart to the family of Charles: "Says Girart:
'Lord, all at your command; we can do everything at your desire.' In front of
everyone he gave his glove; Charles the king thanked him hugely." [Dist Girart:
"Sire, tot a vostre comant; / fere en poez tot a vostre talant" / Par devant toz
l'en a doné le gant / Charles li rois l'en mercie forment] (6641–44).

Everything that transpired at the banquet is formally ratified the next day
when Charles holds court in Vienne. This time Charles asks Hernaut for Aude,
and by this shift from Girart to Aude's older uncle the transfer becomes a mat-

ter of personal lineage rather than regnal solidarity: not only do Charles and Hernaut speak of uniting their lineages (with Hernaut's family raised in status by the alliance with a family of royal blood), but Charles projects the familial alliance into the future, imagining "the great good" that will come of Roland and Aude having an heir:

> "After this is done, our lineages will never be separated. And if God, through his mercy, gives them the issue of an heir, a great good could come from this." Hernaut answers, "Lord, thank you; my niece could marry no higher than in your lineage."

> > ["Jamés nul jor, puis pu'il en ert sessi,
> > nostre lingnaje ne seront departi.
> > Et se Deus done, qui onques ne menti,
> > c'un oir en isse, par la seue merci,
> > encor porroit grant bien venir de li."
> > Hernaut respont: "Sire, vostre merci;
> > plus haut ne puet ma niece avoir mari
> > que en vostre lingnaje."]

> > > (6814–21)

No sooner does Charles hand her to Roland (in front of witnesses, for the scene is ceremonial) and no sooner is the day set for the *noçoier* than a messenger arrives to announce that pagans have invaded Bordeaux. Moreover, they have named May 1 as the day they will continue up the Gironde past Orleans to Bourges, which they claim as their own by heritage [ce on dit et conté / qu'ele fu leur jadis en herité] (6856–57). Hearing this, Charles prays for counsel to God and asks counsel from his men. The elements composing the prayer and request are simultaneously feudal while again also transforming Charles into a figure who transcends all earthly alliances and agreements. He is the earthly king who holds all his power from God, the "true king" of all, and thus the whole realm is subject to his direction:

> "And God," says Charles, "true king of majesty who wished, by your goodness, that I hold crown and royalty, advise me, through your pity, how I can destroy the pride of this people who have criminally entered my realm. Advise me, my knights, since you are my men and my vassals.

You have been in my service for a long time, all for love of me, that is the truth. You have served me willingly and rightly on account of the large fiefs that I have given you; now serve again the majesty of God and conquer for his love."

> [—"Et Deus!" dit Charles, "Voir rois de majesté
> qui ce vosites, par la vostre bonté
> que ge tenisse coronne et roiauté,
> conseilliez moi par la vostre pité
> c'aie l'orgueil de cele gent maté,
> qui a tel tort sont en mon resne entré.
> Conseilliez moi, mi chevalier menbré,
> si com vos estes mi home et mi chasé:
> ici avez une grant piece esté
> tout por m'amor, ce est la verité;
> servi m'avez volentiers et de gré
> por les granz fiez que ge vos ai doné;
> or reservez por Deu de majesté,
> et por s'amor conquerre!"]
>
> (6859—72)

These courtly celebrations are followed immediately by a depiction of the town newly able to regain its old prosperity. While the poem begins by treating merchants as figures of comedy and contempt, as is common throughout many of the chansons de geste, it is nevertheless filled with constant references to economic prosperity, and it generally uses monetary value as its ultimate measure of worth. Similarly, the conspicuous wealth and status of Vienne and of its rulers are remarked by everyone who enters the town, and the town's entire dependence on merchants for necessary possessions and for luxury is constantly displayed. Thus Oliver, in desperate need of armor and weapons, gets them from the Jewish merchant Joachim, who provides him with the famous sword Halteclere and valuable armor. These pieces of equipment come into the poem with their histories intact—Joachim has bought them after much changing of hands. And whereas the king's gift of weapons to Raoul de Cambrai serves to insert him into the epic tradition in precisely the epic manner, here it is merchant trade that directly links the present to the past—weapons used by Hector and Aeneas at Troy become objects of exchange value that end up after much buying and selling in the contemporary merchant's stock. This commodity trading has an interesting textual analogue: in a demonstration of the chanson writer's self-conscious positioning of his text vis-à-vis romance and history, the history of the arms given to Oliver is lifted directly from the *Roman d'Eneas.*[69]

Just as commodity trading links the present to the past in historical continuity, and thus is the real vehicle of tradition, the first result of the peace is the arrival of merchants in Vienne:

> Then the merchants began to arrive, who carried their goods for sale; from morning at daybreak until the evening when it was twilight, they did not finish coming and going so that the city was entirely filled. They lodged outside the town in the fields and they set up their tents and pavilions. The barons and peers and clerks and priests and tonsured monks all had great joy because of the peace that was sworn.

> [Lors comencierent marcheant a errer,
> qui les avoirs ont a vendre aporté;
> des le matin, que il fu ajorné,
> de si au soir, qui il fu avespré,
> ne finent il de venir ne d'aler,
> que tote en ful enplie la cité.
> Defors la vile se logent enz es prez,
> et ont lor tres et paveillons fermez.
> Grant joie moinent li baron et li per,
> et clerc et prestre et moine coronné,
> de la pes qu'est juree.]

(6780–90)

The arrival links the whole population—carefully catalogued as barons, peers, clerks, priests, and monks—together in joy and renewed prosperity after the privations of the long siege. Thus for the town to be rich and its lord to be victorious, it must be doubly dependent, on the favor of the distant ruler and on commodity trading. This double dependence is epitomized in the fiction of an underground tunnel "built long ago by the pagans," that links the town to the world around it. By making the walled town permeable to the outside world for trade and supplies, this secret, underground passage is the guarantee of the city's strategic invulnerability. The inhabitants of Vienne can stay walled up during the very longest siege precisely because the tunnel allows them to bring in food from the countryside and to bring in goods from "foreign lands." Thus, in order to be able to be closed up in the city, the city must have an opening:[70]

> Indeed, says Girart, in all my life, you would not have taken our thoroughly closed-up city, because here I could go hunting and take my pigs and fine antlered stags, and bring in my goods from foreign lands. These make Vienne rich and richly endowed.

> ["Voir," dit Gerart, "en trestot voz aez
> n'eüsiez prises noz mestres fermetez,
> car par ici seu ge chacier aler,
> prendre mes pors et mes cras cers ramez,
> d'estrange terres mes avoirs amener,
> dont en Vienne fesoie largetez,
> et estïens richement conreez.]
>
> (6520—26)

In brief, the texts that we have been examining are all marked by the strongly contradictory desire to represent the noble lord as entirely an independent being, a king in his own realm, while simultaneously trying to explain the nature and significance of his entire dependence on the power of the king. Girart thus becomes represented as a lord who can stand as a ruler only if he is also not a ruler (the king is the ruler), who can keep his land only if it is no longer his (the language of allod and fief is endemic to the chansons), who achieves personal power only by being the surrogate for the power of an other, and who is nothing outside the chain of feudal dependence, while to be inside is to be trapped into perpetual servitude. Indeed, the beginning of *Girart de Vienne* is a classic *enfances* narrative in multiple genres (quest, romance, fabliaux) in which Girart desperately tries to find a place in the court. When he finally gets a place, his services are stolen. Susan Reynolds has argued that "feudalism" comes into existence in the discourse of the lawyers of the thirteenth century, advisors to kings and lords whose specialized knowledge had become invaluable for negotiating the limits of power and obligation.[71] In the chansons de geste we have seen a representation of the social formation, which will not come to technical expression until the thirteenth century, already in existence; if the language is not legally exact, it nevertheless continually creates a legal nexus among alliances between lineages, the formation and continuity of personal dependencies, and the transfer of property and women, and it is thus entirely preoccupied with the matter of inheritance. Yet the discourse that unites lineage, inheritance, and property transfer finally also serves to represent an entirely different structure of power. It serves to create the figure of the king in his realm to whom all are subject. Charles's daydream about the great good that will issue from Roland and Aude's heir is nothing short of a dream of sovereign power. Feudal society is the realm's shadow.

Epic Desire

In their working through this set of contradictions, powerfully erotic affective relations, including especially heterosexual desire, become important tools to think with. Thus the discourse of eros comes into being precisely at the same time as the governmental transformations of which it is a part.[72] In the passage quoted a moment ago, for example, Charles demands counsel in the name of love (tout por m'amor, ce est la verité). Similar is the description of Charles's final reconciliation with Girart, where their relation is described in the highly charged language of the love lyric: "Indeed we have experienced God's mercy; now we have that for which we waited so long, Girart and I are friends and lovers; the war is over." [La merci Deu, bien nos est avenu: / ore avons ce c'avons tant atendu, / moi et Girart somes ami et dru, / s'est remesse la guerre] (6724–27). Chivalric romance abolishes the state by collapsing it into the personal affective tie between the king and his courtier/knight while simultaneously displacing that tie onto the knight and his lady. The chansons de geste in their turn are filled with erotic episodes that can be called romance intrusions only if we think that the chansons are "primitive," coming from an age before the "invention" of erotic love in the lyric and in romance. Far from being intrusive, these erotic episodes form the thematic and conceptual core of the epic, for it is their peculiar burden to probe the inner workings of desire and the pleasure of being possessed by an other. One could multiply examples indefinitely, for on the level of language the discourse of *amitie*, of *drurerie*, of *amors* is everywhere to be found. On the level of plot, the drivenness of erotic longing and the joy of consummated love are structural elements as fundamental to the chanson de geste as they are to romance.

In *Girart de Vienne,* for example, the love plot involving Roland and Aude is fully overdetermined, finally serving to condense the thematic totality of the poem. It begins in the pure desire for the unobtainable, a *coup de foudre,* when Roland (Charles's nephew, in the midst of desperate combat against Oliver, who is fighting for Girart) sees Oliver's sister and is overcome with such desire that he leaves the battle, seizes Aude, and tries to carry her off. Yet in many ways the love between Roland and Aude is a displacement of Roland and Oliver's already developed chivalric emulation of each other, and it serves as the emotional counterpart to their continual longing to measure themselves against the other, a longing that will end in their famous companionship. Both these longings are always potentially disruptive: Roland especially is subject to continual suspicion that he has betrayed Charles out of desire for Oliver's sister. Finally, as we have seen, the love plot becomes the scene of multiple masculine reconciliations, first in a private agreement between Oliver and Roland and then as both the sign and vehicle of Girart and Charles's final reconciliation. Again here the formal inconclusiveness of the epic itself is doubled by the inconclusiveness of the marriage arrangements. As the text itself makes clear, Roland and Aude will never marry because Roland will die first in the Pyrenees. They will have produced no heir. Just as the question of Girart's real place in the realm remains open, the poem concludes with the marriage that promises to settle everything, a marriage that will never happen.

The conceptual power for the epic of the discourse of enamorment is perhaps most clearly exemplified throughout *Girart de Roussillon,* which is simultaneously always a love story and always a piece of political theory about the nature of sovereignty and territoriality. In the midst of the barons' most serious argument with Charles over his desire for the sister who was supposed to have married Girart, and as the negotiations threaten to break into open rebellion, the words of Charles's baron Fouque collocate all the principles that are invoked by the nobility to tie together the community of the realm and the king:

"Lord," said Fouque then, "we will go.
We will not bring a plea, nor law, nor love from here
And we will announce what we have here
We will return to Girart the count,
We will tell it in his plenary court."

["Segner," co dist dans Folche, "er non irem.
Plait ne drei ne amor n'en porterem,
E co que cai auem nonscierem
A dun(c) Girart au conte ou retrairem,
En sa plenire cort ou conterem."]

(laisse 129)[73]

The terminology here, "plea — law — love," is central to the legal discourse of "feudal society"; and it is of course central to the private discourse of romantic love. For *fides* is precisely the place where the distinction between the erotic and the political, or the public world of political alliance and the private realm of desire, needs to be made most sharply, and it is the very place where that distinction falls apart. *Fides* creates a public contract that is absolutely dependent on an interior state that the ritual of homage and the words of fealty both represent and substitute for, while the gestures and words also provide a perfect cover for the absence of intention in the performance of the act. In the Oxford *Roland* Charles asks his barons how to deal with Marsile's offer to become his man and hold his land in fief. Marsile says that he is willing to put his hands together for Charles, give hostages to guarantee the agreement, and rule Spain as Charles's surrogate, yet, says Charles, "I don't know what is in his heart" (jo ne sai quels en est sis curages).[74] In the *Chanson d'Aspremont,* as we have seen, Turpin immediately writes the charter when Girart picks up Charles's hat and hands it to him — it is a written witness of his act of submission that turns out not to have ever been an act of submission but rather a ruse. Like the incest taboo for the distinction between nature and culture, *fides* is thus a scandal for public and private difference. In *Girart de Roussillon,* the king's supremacy is simultaneously always unquestioned as absolute while constantly being called into question as undeserving of love.

Girart de Roussillon begins in the unruliness of desire when Charles breaks the carefully arranged diplomatic agreement that Girart negotiated with the emperor of Constantinople in which Charles will marry the older daughter and Girart the younger. Girart brings the two daughters back to Charles, and Charles immediately demands the younger, with whom he has suddenly fallen in love. She continues to love Girart, who loves her in return, and this doubling of the Tristan plot constantly threatens to undo any possible political settlement between Girart and Charles. Yet the resolution of the conflict between Girart and

Charles, a conflict that threatens to be interminable, is effected precisely by the love of Charles's wife for Girart. This is another version of formal inconclusivity: the text ultimately sidesteps the permanent crisis by a leap out of history—that is, the crisis is resolved in the fantasy of another existence that operates by different rules. Once Girart loses everything—on account of traditional epic *démesure,* because he wrongly refuses to make any kind of peace with the king in the conflict that follows multiple assassinations—he wanders to foreign, wild places and becomes a charcoal merchant, acting as a middleman between the charcoal makers in the forest and the townspeople who buy the coal from him; Berthe, his wife, becomes an in-demand couturier, working in a little house outside the town. And after the great reconciliation with the king, effected by the undying love of Charles's wife for Girart, they become founders of La Madeleine at Vézelay and retire from the world. Thus the text ends in hagiography, a realm of countervalues where the political world, become unthinkable, is abolished in the absolute. The chanson de geste expropriates the narrative of the Carolingian past from monarchical authority and claims it along with the whole realm of the sacred for a radical interrogation of the claims of authority. And it does this precisely by writing in a traditional form. In this way epic composition uses the past—we should better say, it creates the past—as a contemporary self-representation in an effort to recuperate the power of a class becoming conscious of itself as such at the very moment of its own transformation, a transformation that appears to be an entry into permanent crisis. This is its historiographical impulse.

EPILOGUE

Sovereignty and Governmentality

I have been suggesting that the medieval epic emerges as a form of resistance to the increasing ability of royal administration to govern, the collateral bureaucratization and routinization of royal sovereignty, the new deployments of writing for purposes of administration and social control, and the emergence of a class of literate and numerate intellectuals who possessed the requisite knowledge and skills for administrative control.[1] Susan Reynolds has persuasively argued that the consequent political play of coercion and resistances demanded ever finer distinctions, definitions, and arguments within the realm of increasingly technical and specialized law. Thus, as Reynolds presents it, "feudalism" is the creation of the professionalization of law and the growth of a class of specialists in what is essentially a form of esoteric knowledge who act as royal functionaries and also as advisors to high-status members of the realm. Reynolds indeed shows that the very idea of a premodern feudal society consisting of a hierarchy that is simultaneously a hierarchy of property holdings and of office or status comes into being as a technical discourse precisely in the context of the spread of royal administration. It is a creation first of the increasingly professionalized law and professional lawyers of the thirteenth century and then of the historiography of the seventeenth and eighteenth centuries. The master narrative in which "feudal society" "preexists" the modern state (and thus possesses an entirely different *mentalité*) is haunted by a deeply racist and powerfully imperial ghost in the machine of historiography that creates the idea of "the primitive." Much of the conventional story of the development of the medieval state is based on the idea of the succession from the Germanic war band united by pure ties of personal affection — because they were too primitive to think abstractly — to a regime of lords and vassals whose primitive personal ties have become ritualized and wedded to a particular property form.[2] As the "not yet modern" feudal world coalesces into the "modern state," these concrete and personal ties give way to the more abstract, modern ties of nationalism and patriotism that form the basis of "regnal solidarity" and national identity, until finally the state is itself governmentalized to the point that we refer to it simply as "the government." At this point subjects have become citizens with legal identities.[3] So goes the story.

Reynolds sees the professional legal discourse of the thirteenth century as a new political space opened by the growing reach and rationalization of state administration and the resistance to it. This is a political space, I am arguing, already opened in the discourses of twelfth-century narrative representation—in historiography, epic, and romance.[4] In this new political space the principal weapon of those most affected by the imperial designs of royalty is the appeal to tradition—since tradition alone underwrites the claim that what the king demands, having never been demanded before, is therefore illegitimate. Thus governmental innovation creates at the same time and in the same political space the wholesale reliance on historical memory, or rather it creates the construction of history as a specifically political tool. Tradition is the name of this tool as a locus of resistance. John of Salisbury, for example, places the utility of history in as direct a way as possible in the service of political action:

> For, as the pagan says, "The lives of others are our teachers"; and whoever knows nothing of the past hastens blindly into the future. Besides, the records of the chronicles are valuable for establishing or abolishing customs, for strengthening or destroying privileges; and nothing, after knowledge of the grace and law of God, teaches the living more surely and soundly than knowledge of the deeds of the departed.

> [Nam, ut ait ethnicus, *aliena uita nobis magistra est,* et qui ignarus est preteritorum, quasi cecus in futurorum prorumpit euentus. Valet etiam noticia cronicorum ad statuendas uel euacuandas prescriptiones et priuilegia roboranda uel infirmanda; nichilque post gratiam et legem Dei uiuentes rectius et ualidius instruit quam si gesta cognouerint decessorum.][5]

The traditional form of the epic represents tradition by "feudalizing" the realm: what we find in the epic is not in fact an archaic or old form of a feudal polity prolonged into new circumstances but rather an anachronistic representation of contemporary society tendentiously and willfully feudalized. The epic's narrative of the past is a political weapon constructed out of the present need of those who are in the process of being dispossessed. Like the romance, the epic is a dream of another world placed into a past that has never been, but one with a real stake in the making of a future reality.

In his 1978–79 lectures at the Collège de France on governmental rationality and biopolitics, Michel Foucault began his discussion of "the governmentalization of the state" by looking at the question of royal sovereignty in Machiavelli's *Prince*. Foucault was especially interested in a group of texts by sixteenth-century anti-Machiavellians because they forcefully remind us that governance need not be identical to sovereignty and indeed takes place in a great variety of situations. Those who write on the art of government, says Foucault, "constantly recall that one speaks also of 'governing' a household, souls, children, a province, a convent, a religious order, a family." And he continues:

> These points of simple vocabulary actually have important political implications. Machiavelli's prince, at least as these authors interpret him, is by definition unique in his principality and occupies a position of externality and transcendence. We have seen, however, that practices of government are, on the one hand, multifarious and concern many kinds of people: the head of a family, the superior of a convent, the teacher or tutor of a child or pupil; so that there are several forms of government among which the prince's relation to his state is only one particular mode; while, on the other hand, all these other kinds of government are internal to the state or society. It is within the state that the father will rule the family, the superior the convent, etc. Thus we find at once a plurality of forms of government and their immanence to the state: the multiplicity and immanence of these activities distinguishes them radically from the transcendent singularity of Machiavelli's Prince.[6]

Foucault poses the problem with great perspicacity but gets the history wrong. If Machiavelli's *Prince* is a compendium of late medieval political practice—as I would insist it most assuredly is—then it is no surprise that the problem of sovereignty as it is manifest in the operation and structure of medieval political practice should come to light in an early modern theoretical debate between the Machiavellians and the anti-Machiavellians.[7] Foucault takes the early modern theorists at their word and analyzes this theoretical debate as if it entirely concerned sixteenth-century affairs, rather than being at the heart of the medieval practice that was the basis of Machiavelli's political formation. It is only caricatural notions of medieval society that led Foucault to wall off medieval political life from modern social processes, placing it on the far side of an epistemological and practical divide from modernity.

Here one must be a better Foucauldian than Foucault, for the historical error leads to a theoretical problem with more than academic consequences. To understand the crisis in postmodern sovereignty (and make the kind of practical intervention in contemporary affairs that governmentality theorists want to make)[8] one needs especially to understand governmentalities that transcend the state, or at least those whose boundaries cross state borders: I have in mind of course multinational corporations, but also various postmodern ideological forms of what Foucault would have been the first to call knowledge/power— fashion, popular culture, electronic communication, organized religious fundamentalisms, and international networks using terror among other political weapons and functioning without state sponsorship. These have no epistemological or institutional boundary reducible to a political border. With regard to the medieval state there are a wealth of similar institutional, epistemological, and practical structures whose history and function might teach us much about our own contemporary institutional life: the superior rules the convent both within the state and without the state (I mean the ambiguity); orders such as the Templars are disciplinary, militant, and transnational, as are geopolitical entities like the conjoint Diocese of Arras-Cambrai, a governmental entity that crosses lines of both national identity and state sovereignty as well as two linguistic frontiers. Our collective task as medievalists is to understand the regime of knowledge—in the twelfth-century case, this means the apparatus of pedagogy, literacy, state bureaucracy, record keeping, and surveying (Domesday Book, etc.) and the appearance of new professions and professional elites, including lawyers, professional courtiers and diplomats like Thomas Becket, Jordan Fantosme, and John of Salisbury, and historians like William of Malmesbury—and to understand this regime in its historical specificity but not in isolation from later and other historical formations. Understanding these similarities and differences involves among other things attending to techniques, social space, the professional status of the functionaries, and the kinds of political spaces that are accordingly opened for social complicity or political resistance—and not least, it seems to me, attending to the significances of changes in formal representational practices that this book has been concerned with. Representational practices, too, are real actors in the social world.

NOTES

INTRODUCTION

1. The list of works that discuss the simultaneous appearance of contemporary chronicles and romance is extremely long. Among those who have suggested some kind of affinity between them, see especially Bernard Guenée, *Histoire et culture historique dans l'occident médiéval,* Collection historique (Paris: Aubier Montaigne, 1980), 77–128; Robert Marichal, "Naissance du roman," in *Entretiens sur la renaissance du 12ᵉ siècle,* ed. Maurice de Gandillac and Edouard Jeauneau (Paris: Mouton, 1968), 449–92; Eugene Vance, "Semiotics and Power: Relics, Icons, and the *Voyage de Charlemagne à Jérusalem et à Constantinople,*" in *The New Medievalism,* ed. Marina S. Brownlee, Kevin Brownlee, and Stephen G. Nichols (Baltimore: Johns Hopkins University Press, 1991), 226; Michel Zink, "Une mutation de la conscience littéraire: Le langage romanesque à travers des exemples français du XIIᵉ siècle," *Cahiers de Civilisation Médiévale (Xᵉ–XIIᵉ Siècles)* 24 (1981): 3–27.

2. The best discussion of the material entanglements of romance with historiography is to be found in the introduction to Richard Trachsler, *Clôtures du cycle arthurien: Étude et textes* (Geneva: Droz, 1996), 5–7. Among other things, Trachsler notes the difficulty of determining, from the side of their contemporary reception, the border between the two genres: "Il n'est pas facile de distinguer, pour les premiers textes en langue vernaculaire, ceux qui seraient actuellement perçus comme des 'romans' de ceux que nous appellerions aujourd'hui des 'chroniques.' Notamment dans le milieu anglo-normand du XIIᵉ siècle, les mêmes auteurs écrivent indifféremment et tour à tour des 'chroniques' et des 'romans' destinés sans aucun doute au même public" (5). Trachsler propose que la formal resemblance between the two genres arises from the vernacular romance writer's basing his practice on that of the historiographer and having a similar narrative goal: "faire le témoignage les plus authentiques, qui seront rassemblés et arrangés de façon à ce qu'il en ressorte une œuvre nouvelle, cohérente et, à sa manière, 'vraie,' 'ornée' et 'belle.'" To which he adds: "À cette similitude dans la manière de procéder, s'ajoute celle de la matière, car elle aussi est dans une très large mesure commune à l'ecrivain de roman et à l'auteur de chronique. Tous deux s'adressent à un public noble et désireux d'en savoir plus long sur l'histoire familiale, nationale ou universelle. Tous deux, en conséquence, rappellent les *res gestae,* les événements saillants, les hauts

faits du passé. Chroniqueurs et poètes puisent donc leurs matériaux dans le même réservoir de savoir véhiculé par une tradition identique" (6). Perhaps the most important recent theoretical discussion of the deep intimacy between history and fiction is Paul Ricoeur, *Time and Narrative,* vol. 3 (Chicago: University of Chicago Press, 1984).

3. Charles Tilly, *Coercion, Capital, and European States, AD 990–1992,* rev. ed., Studies in Social Discontinuity (Cambridge, MA: Blackwell, 1992); this book is in many ways intended as a corrective to his earlier but still very valuable *Formation of National States in Western Europe* (Princeton: Princeton University Press, 1975); see also Charles Tilly and Willem Pieter Blockmans, *Cities and the Rise of States in Europe,* A.D. *1000 to 1800* (Boulder, CO: Westview Press, 1994), and Wayne Ph Te Brake, *Shaping History: Ordinary People in European Politics, 1500–1700* (Berkeley: University of California Press, 1998), 178–83.

4. Tilly and Blockmans, *Cities,* 4.

5. Ibid., 7.

6. See also Immanuel Maurice Wallerstein, *The Modern World-System: Capitalist Agriculture and the Origins of the European World-Economy in the Sixteenth Century,* Studies in Social Discontinuity (New York: Academic Press, 1976).

7. Among the many studies that have touched on the place of writing in governance, see especially John W. Baldwin, *The Government of Philip Augustus: Foundations of French Royal Power in the Middle Ages* (Berkeley: University of California Press, 1986); Robert Bartlett, *England under the Norman and Angevin Kings, 1075–1225,* New Oxford History of England (Oxford: Clarendon Press, 2000); Michael T. Clanchy, *From Memory to Written Record: England, 1066–1307* (Cambridge, MA: Harvard University Press, 1979); Brian Stock, *The Implications of Literacy: Written Language and Models of Interpretation in the Eleventh and Twelfth Centuries* (Princeton: Princeton University Press, 1983); Joseph Reese Strayer, *Medieval Statecraft and the Perspectives of History* (Princeton: Princeton University Press, 1971), and *On the Medieval Origins of the Modern State* (Princeton: Princeton University Press, 1970).

8. In his presidential address to the Medieval Academy of America, Lester Little remarked on how "unabashedly teleological" the master narrative of European civilization still is and how "out of kilter" that teleology has become with what we actually know, largely thanks to the past three decades of study especially in religious history and women's history. Little notes further that "religious history and women's history, for all their differences, share an important characteristic: they are not constructed of events. It is for this reason above all others — including ideology — that they do not fit comfortably, if at all, into the master narrative," for the master narrative is evenemential. See Lester K. Little, "Cypress Beams, Kufic Script, and Cut Stone: Rebuilding the Master Narrative of European History," *Speculum* 79 (2004): 909–28, quotation at 917.

9. Michel Foucault, "Truth and Power," in *Power/Knowledge: Selected Interviews and Other Writings, 1972–1977,* ed. Colin Gordon (New York: Pantheon, 1980), 121.

10. See the important polemical review of governmentality theory, Derek Kerr, "Beheading the King and Enthroning the Market: A Critique of Foucauldian Governmentality," *Science and Society* 63 (1999): 173–202.

11. For a compelling recent discussion of statehood in the context of nonstate actors, see Anne-Marie Slaughter, *A New World Order* (Princeton: Princeton University Press, 2004).

12. Homi K. Bhabha, "Dissemination: Time, Narrative, and the Margins of the Modern Nation," in *The Location of Culture* (New York: Routledge, 1994). A fine example is the students' recital in the lycées of colonial Indochina, "Nos ancêtres sont les Gaulois," a practice no less absurd when performed inside the Hexagon in 1950.

13. The key study is Benedict R. O'G. Anderson, *Imagined Communities: Reflections on the Origin and Spread of Nationalism,* rev. and extended ed. (New York: Verso, 1991). For a thorough discussion of the place of memory in the construction of the nation, see Hue-Tam Ho Tai, "Remembered Realms: Pierre Nora and French National Memory," *American Historical Review* 106 (2001): 906–22.

14. Robert Bartlett, *The Making of Europe: Conquest, Colonization, and Cultural Change, 950–1350* (Princeton: Princeton University Press, 1993), 24–59.

15 The fluidity of the border before the fifteenth century and the various kinds of political negotiations to which this fluidity continually gave rise are well treated in the case of France by Bernard Guenée. See Bernard Guenée, "Des limites féodales aux frontières politiques," in *Les lieux de mémoire,* 3 vols. in 8 parts, ed. Pierre Nora et al. (Paris: Gallimard, 1984–), 2.2.11–33, esp. 14–18.

16. Sometimes these margins were formerly centers. Thus the imperial and Capetian border during the eleventh century was the center of Carolingian imperial hegemony during the ninth.

17. See Nancy F. Partner, "Making up Lost Time: Writing on the Writing of History," *Speculum* 61 (1986): 90–117; Nancy F. Partner, *Serious Entertainments: The Writing of History in Twelfth-Century England* (Chicago: University of Chicago Press, 1977).

18. R. W. Southern, *The Making of the Middle Ages* (New Haven: Yale University Press, 1953), 219–57.

19. For a similar conclusion, see Sarah Kay, *The Chansons de Geste in the Age of Romance: Political Fictions* (Oxford: Clarendon Press, 1995).

CHAPTER ONE.   Sacred Authority and Secular Power: The Bishops of Cambrai

1. For a brief biography of Gerard, see Heinrich Sproemberg, "Gerhard I., Bischof von Cambrai (1012–1061)," in *Mittelalter und demokratische Geschichtsschreibung,* ed. Manfred Unger (Berlin: Akademie Verlag, 1971), 103–18.

2. All references to the *Deeds of the Bishops of Cambrai* are from V. C. L. C. Beth-mann, *Gesta pontificum Cameracensium,* Monumenta Germaniae historica, Scriptores rerum Germanicarum 7 (1846; reprint, Kraus, 1963). References are to book, section, and line number and will be made parenthetically in the text. Translations are my own. In the manuscripts, the first book of the chronicle is rubricated *Liber primus de gestis episcopo-rum,* and this has given modern scholars the name for the whole, *Gesta episcoporum Cam-eracensium.* The second and third books each are rubricated separately: *secundus de monas-teriis quae infra episcopium constant* and *liber tercius de rebus gestis Gerardi episcopi* (Bethmann, *Gesta pontificum Cameracensium,* 393 n. 1).

3. R. W. Southern, *Western Society and the Church in the Middle Ages,* Pelican History of the Church (Harmondsworth: Penguin Books, 1970), 214. For the topography and early history of Cambrai, the researches of two nineteenth-century local scholars, Andre le Glay and Eugène Bouly, are still useful. See Andre Joseph Ghislain Le Glay, *Cameracum Christianum: Ou, histoire ecclésiastique du diocèse de Cambrai. Extraite du Gallia Christiana et d'autres ouvrages, avec des additions considérables et une continuation jusqu'à nos jours, publiée sous les auspices de S.E. Mgr. Le Cardial Archévêque de Cambrai* (Lille: L. Lefort, 1849); André Joseph Ghislain Le Glay, *Glossaire topographique de l'ancien Cambrésis: Suivi d'un receuil de chartes et diplômes pour servir à la topographie et à l'histoire de cette province* (Cambrai: F. Delinge, 1849); and Eugène Bouly, *Dictionnaire historique de la ville de Cambrai: Des ab-bayes, des chateaux-forts et des antiquités de Cambrésis* (1854; reprint, Brussels: Editions culture et civilisation, 1979). For modern studies, see Louis Trenard, ed., *Histoire de Cambrai,* His-toire des Villes du Nord/Pas-de-Calais 2 (Lille: Presses Universitaires de Lille, 1982), and its excellent bibliography; Henri Platelle, "Cambrai et le Cambrésis au XVᵉ siècle," *Revue du Nord* 58 (1976): 349–82; Michel Rouche, "Topographie historique de Cambrai durant le haut Moyen Âge, Vᵉ–Xᵉ siècles," *Revue du Nord* 58 (1976): 339–47. For the relations be-tween ecclesiastical and secular sovereignty in both the Empire and Capetian France, see Olivier Guyotjeannin, *Episcopus et comes: Affirmation et déclin de la seigneurie épiscopale au nord du royaume de France (Beauvais-Noyon, Xᵉ–début XIIIᵉ siècle),* Memoires et documents publiés par la Société de l'École des chartes (Geneva: Librairie Droz, 1987).

4. In 1001, for example, the Emperor Otto III gives to Cambrai the right to es-tablish a market at Cateau-Cambrésis, to coin money there, to hold exchange there, to have the ban, and to institute officers there for public affairs. This diploma also gives to the merchants at Cateau the same rights that "the merchants at Cambrai" enjoy, and it subjects any merchant there who breaks the peace to the same sanctions as are visited against the merchants of Cambrai. The diploma is quoted in Fernand Vercauteren, *Étude sur les civitates de la Belgique Seconde: Contribution à l'histoire urbaine du nord de la France de la fin du XIᵉ siècle,* Académie royale de Belgique, Classe des lettres et des sciences morales et politiques, Memoires 33 (Brussels: Palais des Académies, 1934), 228. Vercauteren ar-gues that this diploma implies that by the end of the tenth century the merchants at Cambrai are numerous enough to demand such special notice.

5. See Michel Parisse, "L'évêque d'empire au XIe siècle: L'exemple Lorrain," *Cahiers de Civilisation Médiévale (X^e–XIIe Siècles)* 27 (1984): 95–105.

6. In Hincmar of Reims's ninth-century life of St. Remi, St. Remi not only baptizes Clovis but anoints and crowns him king of the Franks. In 1026, Henry I was crowned and anointed in Reims by the bishop in obvious reminiscence of the story of Clovis and also of the subsequent crowning in Reims of Louis the Pious. From that time on, Reims was the place of Capetian consecration. In turn, the king of France was the holder of the temporalities of Reims, and he invested the bishop, whom he essentially appointed even though the bishop was officially elected by the clergy. See Jacques Le Goff, "Reims, ville du sacre," in *Les lieux de mémoire,* 3 vols. in 8 parts, ed. Pierre Nora et al. (Paris: Gallimard, 1984–), 2.1.103–5.

7. Heinrich Sproemberg, "Die Gründung des Bistums Arras im Jahre 1094," in Unger, *Mittelalter,* 119–54.

8. "Sub eodem tempore erat vir quidam Johannes nomine, potens tam in Camera-censium quam Vermandensium genere, qui majordomatu ceteris prestabat in urbe sub pontificati auctoritate" (1.93.36–40). In the next sentence he is referred to as "praedic-tus castellanus."

9. See Vercauteren, *Étude sur les civitates,* 422–23.

10. See Jean-François Lemarignier, *Le gouvernement royal aux premiers temps capétiens (987–1108)* (Paris: Picard, 1965), 69–70. The literature on the so-called "mutation féo-dale" is immense and thoroughly polemical. See, among others, Eric Bournazel and Jean-Pierre Poly, *Féodalités,* Histoire générale des systèmes politiques (Paris: Presses Universi-taires de France, 1998); Jean-Pierre Poly and Eric Bournazel, *The Feudal Transformation: 900–1200,* trans. Caroline Higgitt, Europe Past and Present Series (New York: Holmes and Meier, 1991); Jean-Pierre Poly and Eric Bournazel, *La mutation féodale: X^e–XIIe siècles,* Nouvelle Clio 16 (Paris: Presses Universitaires de France, 1980); for a strong critique of Poly and Bournazel, see Dominique Barthélemy, *Chevaliers et miracles: La violence et le sacré dans la société féodale* (Paris: Colin, 2004), *La mutation de l'an mil, a-t-elle eu lieu? Servage et chevalerie dans la France des Xe et XIe siècles* (Paris: Fayard, 1997), *La société dans le comté de Vendôme: De l'an mil au XIVe siècle* (Paris: Fayard, 1993), *Les deux âges de la seigneurie banale: Pouvoir et société dans la terre des sires de Coucy, milieu XIe–milieu XIIIe siècle* (Paris: Publications de la Sorbonne, 1984), and *L'ordre seigneurial: XI–XIIe siècles,* Nouvelle histoire de la France médiévale 3 (Paris: Seuil, 1990); see also the important review essay by Thomas Bisson, "The Feudal Revolution," *Past and Present* 142 (1994): 6–42.

11. Vercauteren, *Étude sur les civitates,* 423.

12. Dominique Barthélemy, *L'an mil et la paix de dieu: La France chrétienne et féodale, 980–1060* (Paris: Fayard, 1999), 450.

13. Georges Duby, *The Three Orders: Feudal Society Imagined,* trans. Arthur Gold-hammer (Chicago: University of Chicago Press, 1982), 24. Indeed, the *Gesta episcoporum* provides a very early witness of the ritual of homage in this setting. Count Otto swears

his oath to God, St. Mary, and the bishop "in the hands of the bishop." [Promisit Otto comes Deo sanctaeque Mariae et episcopo Gerardo in manu sua] (3.46.38).

14. For dating and composition, see Erik van Mingroot, "Kritisch Onderzoek Omtrent de Datering van de *Gesta episcoporum Cameracensium*," *Revue Belge de Philologie et d'Histoire* 53 (1975): 281–332. Very strong evidence for the 1036 updating by the original writer is brought forward in David C. Van Meter, "The Peace of Amiens-Corbie and Gerard of Cambrai's Oration on the Three Functional Orders: The Date, the Context, the Rhetoric," *Revue Belge de Philologie et d'Histoire* 74 (1996): 633–57. Duby, *Three Orders,* 21, seriously overstates the reorganization caused by the final rewriting.

15. See *BHL.*

16. See Baudouin de Gaiffier, *Études critiques d'hagiographie et d'iconologie,* Subsidia Hagiographica 43 (Brussels: Société des Bollandistes, 1967), 503.

17. For an extended critique of Duby's treatment of the Peace of God and especially of his reading of the significance of Gerard's opposition, see Barthélemy, *L'an mil.* For the Peace of God and Truce of God, see the very useful collection by Thomas Head and Richard Allen Landes, eds., *The Peace of God: Social Violence and Religious Response in France around the Year 1000* (Ithaca: Cornell University Press, 1992). See also Georges Duby, *L'an mil* (Paris: Gallimard, 1980), 210–18. For the idea of the orders of society, see also Giles Constable, *Three Studies in Medieval Religious and Social Thought: The Interpretation of Mary and Martha, the Ideal of the Imitation of Christ, the Orders of Society* (Cambridge: Cambridge University Press, 1995).

18. See the following classic studies: George Boas, *Primitivism and Related Ideas in the Middle Ages* (Baltimore: Johns Hopkins University Press, 1997); Arthur O. Lovejoy and George Boas, *Primitivism and Related Ideas in Antiquity* (New York: Octagon Books, 1965); and especially Erwin Panofsky, *Studies in Iconology: Humanistic Themes in the Art of the Renaissance* (New York: Harper and Row, 1962), 33–68.

19. The whole argument is made in Lactantius, *Institutiones,* in PL 6:666B–671A (Paris: Garnier, 1887).

20. Michel Sot, *Gesta episcoporum, gesta abbatum,* Typologie des sources du Moyen Âge occidental 37 (Turnhout: Brepols, 1981), argues that bishops' lives as a genre are relatively free of miracle stories because they are concerned with contemporary affairs. I argue rather that the particular deployment of miracles stories is due to the particular struggle with competing authorities that brings the eleventh-century bishops' lives into being in the first place, a struggle in which the lives as a genre intend to make an intervention. It is no accident that the earliest of these texts, the *Deeds of the Bishops of Cambrai* and the *Deeds of the Bishops of Liège,* are composed in intimately connected dioceses that all experience similar conflicts among competing authorities.

21. 1.33.23. For the date, see Bethmann's marginal note in *Gesta pontificum Cameracensium.*

22. For discussion of romanesque manuscript painting, see Meyer Schapiro's still unsurpassed 1939 essay "From Mozarabic to Romanesque in Silos," in *Romanesque Art* (New York: Braziller, 1977), 28–102.

23. Monika Otter, *Inventiones: Fiction and Referentiality in Twelfth-Century English Historical Writing* (Chapel Hill: University of North Carolina Press, 1996).

24. C. Stephen Jaeger, *The Origins of Courtliness: Civilizing Trends and the Formation of Courtly Ideals, 923–1210* (Philadelphia: University of Pennsylvania Press, 1985), has discussed the figure of the prince-bishop in connection with the growth of the courtly ideal. For a good description of the obligations of an imperial prince-bishop, see Michel Parisse, "Les hommes et le pouvoir dans la Lorraine de l'an mil," in *Religion et culture autour de l'an mil: Royaume capétien et Lotharingie; Actes du Colloque Hugues Capet 987–1987, La France de l'An Mil, Auxerre, 26 et 27 juin, Metz, 11 et 12 sept. 1987,* ed. Dominique Iogna-Prat and J. C. Picard (Paris: Picard, 1990), 264.

25. Miri Rubin has pointed similarly to the receding of the miraculous in the face of the routinization of power. See Miri Rubin, *Corpus Christi: The Eucharist in Late Medieval Culture* (New York: Cambridge University Press, 1991), 13.

26. See Jo Ann McNamara, "Women and Power through the Family Revisited," in *Gendering the Master Narrative: Women and Power in the Middle Ages,* ed. Mary C. Erler and Maryanne Kowaleski (Ithaca: Cornell University Press, 2003), 22. In the *Acta synodi Attrebatensis,* by the same writer as the *Gesta episcoporum,* the division between cleric and layman with regard to sexual conduct is sharply articulated: "Indeed, just as between secular and clerical men there is a particular distinction of order, so even in their intercourse a particular kind of distinction ought to be preserved. For once he has left the service of the world and is counted in the ranks of the Lord, without violating the military belt of his profession, a cleric cannot deliver himself up again to the conjugal couch. But for secular men, who are not bound by any yoke of ecclesiastical discipline, neither evangelical nor apostolic law forbids legitimate marriage, provided that they know that sexual pleasure ought always to be subject to their control, and they also understand that there are definite occasions for sex, when they ought to join and when they ought to abstain from their wives." [Porro sicut inter saeculares et ecclesiasticos viros quaedam ordinis discretio est, ita et conversatio eorum quadam discretionis ratione servanda est. Nam vir ecclesiasticus, postquam relicta saeculi militia in sortem domini computatur, non potest, salvo professionis suae cingulo, coniugali toro se iterum mancipare. At viris saecularibus, qui nulli ecclesiastici regiminis iugo sunt obnoxii, nec evangelica, nec apostolica decreta legitima praeiudicant connubia, si tamen sciunt omni tempore sibi debere esse subiectam coniugii voluptatem, et si discernunt certa concubitus tempora, quando coeundum, et quando ab uxoribus sit abstinendum.] *Acta synodi Attrebatensis,* in PL 142:1299D–1300A (Paris: Garnier, 1887). Translations are my own.

27. *Acta synodi Attrebatensis*, 1294B: "For the head designates the ruling of the mind; and just as the body is ruled by the mind, so the Church, which is the body of Christ, is ruled by the bishop." (Caput enim principale mentis designat; et sicut mente corpus regitur, ita per episcopos Ecclesia, quae est corpus Christi, regitur.) As we shall see, in the argument of the *Gesta episcoporum* all of secular society is subsumed in the Church.

28. The classic study is Ernst Hartwig Kantorowicz, *The King's Two Bodies: A Study in Mediaeval Political Theology* (Princeton: Princeton University Press, 1957).

29. Rubin, *Corpus Christi,* 14.

30. "No one should be precipitately removed from the body and blood of the Son of God through whose mystery the true life is lived, since a man is dead when excommunicated justly, even though he be alive." Harriet Pratt Lattin, ed., *The Letters of Gerbert, with His Papal Privileges as Sylvester II,* Records of Civilization, Sources and Studies 60 (New York: Columbia University Press, 1961), 273, letter 12.

31. Ibid., 275—76, letter 14.

32. Ibid., 367, letter 263.

33. Robert Boenig, *Saint and Hero: Andreas and Medieval Doctrine* (Lewisburg, PA: Bucknell University Press, 1991); Jean de Montclos, *Lanfranc et Bérenger, la controverse eucharistique du XIe siècle* (Leuven: Spicilegium Sacrum Lovaniense, 1971); Kenneth Hein, *Eucharist and Excommunication: A Study in Early Christian Doctrine and Discipline,* European University Papers Series 23, Theology 19 (Bern: Peter Lang, 1973); Gary Macy, *The Theologies of the Eucharist in the Early Scholastic Period* (Oxford: Clarendon Press, 1984); Charles E. Sheedy, *The Eucharistic Controversy of the Eleventh Century against the Background of Pre-Scholastic Theology* (Washington, DC: Catholic University Press, 1947); C. R. Shrader, "The False Attribution of an Eucharistic Text to Gerbert of Aurillac," *Medieval Studies* 35 (1973): 178—204.

34. Cf. *Acta synodi Attrebatensis,* 1294C: "For a secular man does not have the power to fulfill the office of a priest, since he neither holds his office nor knows his duty, and he cannot teach what he has not learned." (Non enim valebit saecularis homo sacerdotii magisterium implere, cuius nec officium tenuit, nec disciplinam cognovit, sed neque docere potest quod non didicit.)

35. The Gregorian miracles, including the story of the appearance of a finger in the wine, the bleeding host, and the priest Plegild who sees angels dividing the body of a baby while he divides the bread, were included by Paschasius Hradbertus in the earliest treatise on the Eucharist. See Radbertus Paschasius and Paulus Beda, *De corpore et sanguine Domini: Cum appendice epistola ad Fredugardum,* CCSL, Continuatio Mediaevalis 16 (Turnholt: Brepols, 1969). These miracles are universally cited in eucharistic discussion throughout the Middle Ages. That these miracles are adduced in the *Acts of the Synod of Arras* makes their omission in the *Gesta episcoporum* all the more strikingly deliberate.

36. For example, *subtolarium* in 3.20 for "shoe." The Francophone writer is probably thinking "soulier."

37. Compare the continual association in theological literature between the composition of the host, of the church building, and of the community that assembles there. For one example among many, see Master Simon, *De sacramentis:* "Sicut vero unus panis ex multis granis fit . . . sic misticum Christi corpus, id est Ecclesia, ex multis personis velut granis collecta," 27–28, quoted in Rubin, *Corpus Christi,* 23. Master Simon wrote in the Lower Rhineland ca. 1145, but, as Rubin points out, he employed traditional terms that had been in circulation at least a century earlier.

38. In 1.48 we find the first instance of a bishop excommunicating a layman. A man "negotiis militaribus deditus" despoils the possessions of St. Mary in Arras and after having been warned several times is excommunicated by the bishop. He contemns the curse, but suddenly his viscera take fire and he dies. He is buried near the public road outside the town. For three years there is neither rain nor mist in the field where he is buried, and nothing grows there. The bishop in a vision sees the horrible torments being inflicted on the knight; "moved by this wretched fate," he has "a slave who belonged to the knight as customary property" (unum servum qui ei habendis usibus inhaeserat) perform the penance on behalf of his lord and gives the slave his freedom for so doing. "Afterwards truly the land was seen to bring forth grass" (Postea vero tullus visa est herbidare) ends the story.

39. Ademar of Chabannes, *Ademari Cabannensis chronicon,* ed. P. Bourgain and Richard Allen Landes, CCSL, Continuatio Mediaevalis 129 (Turnhout: Brepols, 1999), 3.25.42–45): "Often Alduin, on account of the depredations of the warriors and the devastation of the paupers, put into practice a new observance, namely that the churches and monasteries cease the divine service and the holy sacrifice, and the populace, like pagans, cease from divine praises, and he considered this observance excommunication." [Sepe idem Alduinus, pro rapina militum et devastatione pauperum, novam observantiam constituit, scilicet ecclesias et monasteria cessare a divino cultu et sancto sacrificio, et populum quasi paganum a divinis laudibus cessare, et hanc observantiam excommunionem censebat.] My translation.

40. Richard Allen Landes, *Relics, Apocalypse, and the Deceits of History: Ademar of Chabannes, 989–1034,* Harvard Historical Studies 117 (Cambridge, MA: Harvard University Press, 1995), 36. Landes notes as well the connection of this sort of use of the interdict with the practice of humiliation of relics, which also dates from this period. See also Patrick Geary, "Humiliation of Saints," in *Saints and Their Cults,* ed. Stephen Wilson (Cambridge: Cambridge University Press, 1983).

41. For a discussion of the dating and composition of the *Acta Synodi,* see Erik van Mingroot, "Acta Synodi Attrebatensis (1025): Problèmes de critique de provenance," *Studia Gratiana (Mélanges G. Fransen)* 19–20 (1976): 201–29. Mingroot has conclusively identified the recipient as Roger I, bishop of Chalon-sur-Marne, rather than Reginard of Liège.

42. Although it is in the form of a letter, the text is actually a little treatise, called a *libellus* by the writer (1270B), deploying a great display of learning, including citations

of the fathers of the church and lengthy passages of biblical exegesis, to "refute the poison of their errors."

43. The following are especially clear examples: "Once Christ suffered, once he died; yet daily he suffers in the church for us, daily he dies for us, when, as he commands, the memory of his most holy passion is performed, and the salvation of his body and the mystery of his blood are renewed through the ministry of the priest" [Semel namque Christus passus, semel mortuus, quotidie in Ecclesia nobis patitur, quotidie nobis moritur, dum, ipso jubente, sacrosanctae passionis eius memoria agitur, et per sacerdotum ministerium salutaria corporis eius et sanguinis mysteria renovantur] (1281 B); "For just as our Lord and Redeemer in these sanctifying mysteries taught by these things that he especially prepared or that his ministers especially consecrated, so also he chose the place in which they would be sacrificed, that is to say, in the holy church, which is especially called the house of God, since there is no place outside the Catholic Church for true sacrifices." [Sicut enim Dominus et Redemptor noster in his sanctificandis mysteriis, quibus ex rebus conficerentur specialiter, quibusve ministris consecrarentur, instituit, ita et quo in loco specialiter sacrificarentur, elegit, id est in ecclesia sancta quae domus Dei specialiter appellatur, quia veri sacrificii extra catholicam Ecclesiam non est locus] (1284C–D).

44. 1287B–C.

45. The quoted line of Ps. 67 would surely evoke the whole, which begins, "Exsurgat Deus et dissipentur inimici eius / et fugiant qui oderunt eum a facie eius" and ends with a vision of all secular powers submitting to God in Jerusalem. In the psalm the dynamic that I have discussed in the punitive miracles is also traced: the envisioned unity is achieved by a catalog of violent exclusions from the community. I quote from the *Psalterium Gallicanum* in *Biblia sacra iuxta vulgatam versionem,* 2nd ed. (Stuttgart: Württembergische Bibelanstalt, 1975).

46. See Mary Carruthers, *The Craft of Thought: Meditation, Rhetoric, and the Making of Images, 400–1200,* Cambridge Studies in Medieval Literature (Cambridge: Cambridge University Press, 1998), and Mary Carruthers, *The Book of Memory: A Study of Memory in Medieval Culture,* Cambridge Studies in Medieval Literature 10 (New York: Cambridge University Press, 1990).

47. Carruthers, *Craft of Thought,* 120.

48. In the *Acta synodi Attrebatensis,* Gerard answers the heretics' iconoclasm by developing, through concrete examples, the Gregorian proposition that images are the Bible of the illiterate. He thus provides instruction in how to make just such a contemplative chain from the image of the crucified Christ:

Indeed, simple and illiterate people in church, since they cannot look through the Scriptures, contemplate this through the outlines of a certain picture, that is,

Christ in his humility, how he wished to suffer and die for us. When they venerate this image, Christ ascending on the cross, Christ suffering on the cross, and
dying on the cross, they adore Christ alone and not the work of the hands of men.
For the wooden stock is not adored, but by means of that visible image the interior
mind of a man is aroused, in which the suffering and death of Christ, undergone
for us, is inscribed as it were on the parchment of the heart, so that each one recognizes in himself how much he owes to his Redeemer.

[Simpliciores quippe in ecclesia et illiterati, quod per Scripturas non possunt intueri,
hoc per quaedam picturae liniamenta contemplantur, id est, Christum in ea humili-
tate, qua pro nobis pati et mori voluit. Dum hanc speciem venerantur, Chistum
in cruce ascendentem, Christum in cruce passum, in cruce morientem, Christum
solum, non opus manuum hominum adorant. Non enim truncus ligneus adoratur,
sed per illam visibilem imaginem mens interior hominis excitatur, in qua Christi
passio et mors pro nobis suscepta tanquam in membrana cordis inscribitur, ut in se
unusquisque recognoscat quanta suo Redemptori debeat.] (1306D)

It is worth noting in passing that Gerard does not use this contemplative exercise to
emphasize the *gloria passionis* but rather to evoke in affective terms "how much each of
us owes the Redeemer for his suffering," a kind of devotion that will occupy a central
place in lay spirituality in the next centuries.

    49. Ibid., 1307C.

    50. Ibid.

    51. See Marie-Dominique Chenu, "The Symbolist Mentality," in *Nature, Man, and
Society in the Twelfth Century,* ed. Jerome Taylor and Lester K. Little (Chicago: University of Chicago Press, 1968), 99–145; Gabrielle M. Spiegel, "History as Enlightenment:
Suger and the *Mos Anagogicus,*" in *The Past as Text: The Theory and Practice of Medieval Historiography* (Baltimore: Johns Hopkins University Press, 1997), 163–77. Duby noticed
this reference to Pseudo-Dionysius and compared it to the similar reference in Adal-
beron of Laon's poem to King Robert, which seems to depend on this very text, and
wondered whether a copy of the *Ecclesiastical and Celestial Hierarchies* existed in Cambrai. If the writer did not have actual access to the Pseudo-Dionysian texts, he certainly
understood their purport and implications for his historical project. See Duby, *Three
Orders,* 34 and 49. See also Duby, *L'an mil,* 82–100.

    52. *BHL,* no. 861. There is no modern edition. I quote from Fulbert of Chartres,
Vita S. Autberti Cameracensis et Atrebatensis episcopi, in *Acta sanctorum Belgii selecta,* 4 vols.,
ed. Joseph Ghesquière (Brussels: Lemaire, 1785), 3:529–65. References will be to pages
in this edition and will be given parenthetically within the text. Translations are my
own. There is a badly truncated text among the works of Fulbert of Chartres in PL 141
(Paris: Garnier, 1880).

53. Thomas Head, *Hagiography and the Cult of the Saints: The Diocese of Orleans, 800–1200* (Cambridge: Cambridge University Press, 1990), 81–90; Landes, *Relics, Apocalypse,* 55–56; de Gaiffier, *Études critiques,* 425–27.

54. Landes, *Relics, Apocalypse,* 56 n. 24.

55. No less an authority than Baudouin de Gaiffier dismisses this attribution out of hand, but he presents no argument for the dismissal, always simply referring to the author of the life as "Canon Fulbert of Cambrai." This seems unlikely. See de Gaiffier, *Études critiques,* 458, for one example among many.

56. The manuscript tradition of the *Vita Autberti* clearly illustrates practices of devotional reading. The *Vita Autberti* appears generally in manuscripts designed as lectionaries, containing the lives of saints arranged according to the calendar of feasts. Among the lives in these manuscripts one finds texts read widely throughout Europe, but more importantly one finds lives of saints pertaining specifically to the locality in which the manuscript was produced. Thus Brussels 7808 from the Church of St. Waldetrude at Mons contains the *Vita Autberti* along with the lives of Sts. Vaast, Aldegund, Waldetrude, and Amand—each associated either in life or in death with Mons. All of the extant manuscripts that contain the *Vita Autberti* belonged to altars specifically dedicated to the saint, or to monasteries whose history included one of the saint's significant deeds. When the text was read publicly, it was thus at a site made holy originally by the presence of the saint or at a site significantly involved with the saint's presence in life.

57. For descriptions of the manuscripts of the *Vita Autberti,* see Bollandists, *Catalogus codicum hagiographicorum Bibliothecae Regiae Bruxellensis,* pt. 1, vol. 2 (Brussels: Polleunis, Ceuterick, and de Smet, 1889), and Bollandists, *Catalogus codicum hagiographicorum latinorum antiquiorum saeculo XVI qui asservantur in Bibliotheca Nationali Parisiensi,* 3 vols. (Brussels: Polleunis, Ceuterick, and de Smet, 1889–93).

58. MS 7808, from Mons, contains no prologue and only chapters 1 and 2 under the rubric "Vita Autberti episcopi et confessoris." Significantly, the life in this form ends with the event most pertinent to the owners of the manuscript, Aubert's veiling of St. Waldetrude and her founding of the community at Mons. See Bollandists, *Catalogus codicum . . . Bruxellensis,* pt. 1, 2:130. Brussels MS 9120, a large collection of lives and passions organized calendrically, contains chapters 1 through 3 under the same rubric, "Vita Autberti episcopi et confessoris," and then presents chapter 4 under the rubric "Translatio S. Autberti episcopi," as if it were an independent text in a different genre—or to put it more correctly, it thus makes what is in other places a fourth chapter into an independent text in a different genre and thus draws special attention to the circumstances of his *translatio.* Ibid., 276.

59. Brussels 21002, which belonged to the altar of St. Aubert in the Church of Mary Magdalene in Brussels, contains first the *Vita Autberti* and then, under the rubric "In elevatione S. Autberti et de ejus miraculis," an account of five miracles performed after his death by the very relics that are present at the altar. Ibid., 431.

60. The epitome occupies 1.18–20.

61. Baudouin de Gaiffier, *Études critiques,* 457–58.

62. Alcuin, *Vita Vedastis,* in *Passiones vitaeque sanctorum aevi Merovingici et antiquiorum aliquot,* ed. Bruno Krusch and W. Levison, Monumenta Germaniae historica, Scriptorum rerum Merovingicarum 3–7, ed. Bruno Krusch (1896–; reprint, Hannover: Hahn, 1977), 3:414–27.

63. Leon van der Essen, *Étude critique et littéraire sur les vitae des saints mérovingiens de l'ancienne Belgique* (Leuven: Bureaux du Recueil, 1907), 275–76.

64. *BHL,* no. 4696. *Vita S. Landelini Abbatis ex antiquis mss. codicibus,* in *Acta sanctorum Belgii selecta,* 4:458–62. Translations are my own

65. See the discussions of rhetorical *enargeia* throughout Carruthers, *Book of Memory* and *Craft of Thought.*

66. In the *Vita Autberti* this episode is filled with reality effects that locate the action definitively in the world of the eleventh-century nobility; the whole story of Landelin's vision of hell and his return to spiritual direction is nevertheless a calque on a story about John the Evangelist attributed to Clement of Alexandria and reported at length by Eusebius of Caesarea in the *Historia ecclesiastica.* See Eusebius of Caesarea, *History of the Church,* trans. G. A. Williamson (Harmondsworth: Penguin Books, 1965), 3.3. Fulbert makes the comparison explicit: "In the matter of the present example who would not think Aubert to be like the Apostle John, since John made a healthy provider of the church out of a thief, and Aubert similarly made from a thief and impious robber a priest of the Lord?" [In praesentis autem exempli negotio quis non simillem Apostolo Johanni arbitretur Autbertum, dum ille ex latrone tutum ecclesiae provisorem, iste ex aeque latrone et ex impio raptore verum facit Domini sacerdotem?] (546). In this story Aubert thus occupies the position both of Jesus (as redeemer) and of John, his biographer.

67. On the ideal vision of towns unified under archbishops as a historiographical weapon against the movement for monastic independence on the one hand and "fracturing urban competitions" on the other, see Felice Lifshitz, *The Norman Conquest of Pious Neustria: Historiographic Discourse and Saintly Relics, 684–1090* (Toronto, Ontario: Pontifical Institute of Mediaeval Studies, 1995), 184. See also Giles Constable, *The Reformation of the Twelfth Century* (Cambridge: Cambridge University Press, 1998); H. E. J. Cowdrey, *The Cluniacs and the Gregorian Reform* (Oxford: Clarendon Press, 1970), esp. 23–32. Cowdrey notes that in the Council of Chelles (993–94) the French bishops took a hard line in favor of their conciliar authority against a papal grant of monastic immunity to Fleury. In letters 7 and 8 (numbered 17 and 16 respectively in PL 141) Fulbert of Chartres writes entirely on the side of the bishops' position at Chelles. In letter 7 he advises the bishop of Orleans to persist in his demand for canonical obedience from the abbot of Fleury, and in letter 8 he reminds the abbot of Fleury to reread the third degree of humility in Benedict's Rule, on obedience to one's superior, and threatens him

with excommunication. See *The Letters and Poems of Fulbert of Chartres,* ed. Frederick Behrends (Oxford: Clarendon Press, 1976), 116–20 and lxx–lxxiii.

68. "Whether I shall turn out to be the hero of my own life, or whether that station will be held by anybody else, these pages must show," begins the first chapter of *David Copperfield.* The novel is one of the clearest demonstrations that one becomes the hero of one's own life as much by a rhetorical strategy as by moral action.

69. *Vita S. Waldetrudis ex vetustis codicibus mss.,* in *Acta sanctorum Belgii selecta,* 4:440–48.

70. Universally attributed to Cicero during the Middle Ages, the *Rhetorica ad Herennium* was among the most important school texts throughout Europe. I quote from [Cicero], *Rhetorica ad Herennium,* ed. Harry Caplan, trans. Harry Caplan, Loeb Classical Library (Cambridge, MA: Harvard University Press, 1964). The *narratio* is discussed at 1.8.12–1.9.2.

71. For a discussion of various senses of the miraculous, see Caroline Walker Bynum, "Wonder," *American Historical Review* 102 (1997): 1–26.

72. Michel de Certeau, *The Writing of History,* trans. Tom Conley (New York: Columbia University Press, 1988), 277.

73. I quote from the translation by Dom Gerard Sitwell of Odo of Cluny, "Life of St. Gerald of Aurillac," in *St. Odo of Cluny,* ed. Dom Gerard Sitwell (London: Sheed and Ward, 1958). References are by page number. In some few places I have silently corrected the translation.

74. Text and translation are from Rodolphus Glaber, "Vita Domni Willelmi Abbatis," in *Rodulfus Glaber opera,* ed. Neithard Bulst, John France, and Paul Reynolds, Oxford Medieval Texts (Oxford: Clarendon Press, 1989). References are by page number.

75. Ibid., 292–96.

76. This narrative is a perfect example of the ideal of death that Philippe Ariès has demonstrated to be widespread in the eleventh and twelfth centuries. See Philippe Ariès, *Images de l'homme devant la mort* (Paris: Seuil, 1983) and *L'homme devant la mort* (Paris: Éditions du Seuil, 1977).

77. "Principium sumitur aut ab nostra, aut ab eius de quo loquemur, aut ab eorum qui audient persona, aut ab re. Ab nostra, si laudabimus: aut officio facere, quod causa necessitudinis intercedat; aut studio, quod eiusmodi virtute sit ut omnes commemorare debeant velle; aut quod rectum sit ex aliorum laude ostendere qualis ipsius animus sit." [Cicero], *Rhetorica ad Herennium,* 3.6.11.

78. The succession narrative is closely modeled on a passage in Alcuin's *Life of St Vaast,* a text that Fulbert knows well and uses as a source for the third part of the *Vita Autberti.* Here it is greatly expanded and quite altered by rhetorical variation. Alcuin begins by a simple opposition between the one and the many. "Where once," he writes, "the darkness of the world was illuminated by the incarnate Jesus as if by a single sun, after his departure the many learned saints, Vaast among them, have lit up the world

like the stars in the night sky." See Alcuin, *Vita Vedastis,* 3:414–27. In Fulbert's version the simile of the sun and stars is suppressed, only to reemerge in a metaphor of spiritual illumination, and the passage from Christ to his successors is given a strong temporal direction that emphasizes the process of succession from generation to generation. Aubert in this text is a singularity in his generation, not simply one of many holy men.

79. For the image of Dagobert as a legitimizing tool for Carolingian and Capetian rulers, see Lifshitz, *Norman Conquest,* 69; Laurent Theis, "Dagobert, St-Denis, et la royauté française au Moyen Âge," in *Le métier d'historien au Moyen Âge: Études sur l'historiographie médiévale,* ed. Bernard Guenée (Paris: Université de Paris I Panthéon-Sorbonne, Centre de recherches sur l'histoire de l'occident médiévale, 1977), 19–30.

80. In an early article that should not be neglected, Morton Bloomfield discussed the replacement of typology by this kind of allegorical reading in advanced intellectual circles of the High Middle Ages. See Morton W. Bloomfield, "Symbolism in Medieval Literature." *Modern Philology* 56 (1958): 73–81. See also the very important article by F. Lotter, "Methodisches zur Gewinnung historischer Erkenntnisse aus hagiographischen Quellen," *Historische Zeitschrift* 229 (1979): 298–356, esp. 315–16, for a discussion of typology in bishops' vitas.

81. Felice Lifshitz notes "the values of the Lotharingian and Cluniac reformers, who wished to emphasize virtuous living not miraculous power as the mark of holiness, a holiness which was to be demonstrated through descriptions of realistic and mundane activities." Lifshitz, *Norman Conquest,* 168–69. Cf. Lotter, "Methodisches zur Gewinnung Historischer Erkenntnisse," 319. I have been arguing that this is not simply a matter of the reformers' values; the fact that Cluniac reformers and their opponents share the same perspective demonstrates that the values themselves are coordinate with a real struggle for sovereignty in which they are both engaged.

82. See Mary Carruthers, "The Poet as Master Builder: Composition and Locational Memory in the Middle Ages," *New Literary History* 24 (1993): 881–904; Carolyn M. Carty, "The Role of Gonzo's Dream in the Building of Cluny III," *Gesta* 27 (1988): 113–23. Carruthers ("Poet," 890) notes that Ezekiel's temple vision gains a privileged authority by the connection to Paul, who in 1 Cor. 3:10–17 compares himself to a "wise master builder."

CHAPTER TWO.   Narrating the English Nation after 1066

Part of this chapter appeared in slightly different form as "The Trouble with Harold: The Ideological Context of the Vita Haroldi," *New Medieval Literatures* 2 (1998): 181–204.

1. For England, Robert W. Hanning, *The Vision of History in Early Britain* (New York: Columbia University Press, 1966), is foundational; for Italy, see Kenneth Baxter

Wolf, *Making History: The Normans and Their Historians in Eleventh-Century Italy* (Philadelphia: University of Pennsylvania Press, 1995).

2. Erich Auerbach was extremely aware of the debt of his own work to Hegel and German romanticism as well as to Vico. In the "Epilegomena to Mimesis," in *Mimesis: The Representation of Reality in Western Literature,* 50th Anniversary ed., trans. Willard R. Trask (Princeton: Princeton University Press, 2003), he writes that *Mimesis* would be "conceivable in no other tradition than in that of German romanticism and Hegel. It would never have been written without the influences that I experienced in my youth in Germany" (571). See also the brilliant analysis of the work of Auerbach and its reception in America in Paul Bové, *Intellectuals in Power: A Genealogy of Critical Humanism* (New York: Columbia University Press, 1986). For the importance of Vico, see Erich Auerbach, "Giovambattista Vico e l'idea della filologia," *Convivium* 4 (1956): 394–403; Edward W. Said, *Beginnings: Intention and Method* (New York: Columbia University Press, 1985).

3. The classic studies of the modern national state as an imaginary construction are Anderson, *Imagined Communities,* and Bhabha, "Dissemination."

4. The process is by no means over. The Medieval Academy of America Annual Meeting, Spring 2000, Austin, TX, devoted a session to examining whether Middle English is a creole. The answer was a definite no—in fact, the answer was a no in thunder—and emotions ran very much higher than one would ever expect to find in response to a panel presentation using quantitative historical linguistic methodology.

5. It is still so asserted in Sigmund Freud, *Civilization and Its Discontents,* Standard ed., trans. James Strachey (New York: W. W. Norton, 1989).

6. See Edward W. Said, *Culture and Imperialism* (New York: Vintage Books, 1994), for the way that late-nineteenth- and early-twentieth-century documents of culture speak empire. For medievalism and its imperial entanglements, see Jeffrey Jerome Cohen, *The Postcolonial Middle Ages* (New York: St. Martin's Press, 2000), and Allen J. Frantzen, *Desire for Origins: New Language, Old English, and Teaching the Tradition* (New Brunswick: Rutgers University Press, 1990).

7. John M. Ganim, "Medievalism and Orientalism at the World's Fairs," *Studia Anglica Posnaniensia* 38 (2002): 179–90, and "Native Studies: Orientalism and Medievalism," in Cohen, *Postcolonial Middle Ages,* 123–34.

8. Clare Simmons, *Reversing the Conquest: History and Myth in Nineteenth-Century British Literature* (New Brunswick: Rutgers University Press, 1990).

9. In this light it is no accident that the Subaltern Studies Group found a very powerful conceptual model for the study of colonial and postcolonial social and ideological formations in the work of the Annales historians. See the important study of this relationship by Bruce W. Holsinger, "Medieval Studies, Postcolonial Studies, and the Genealogies of Critique," *Speculum* 77 (2002): 1195–1228.

10. Felix Liebermann, *Die Gesetze der Angelsachsen* (Halle: Max Niemeyer, 1903–11), 2:292–93. Liebermann quotes copiously from Anglo-Norman collections, many of

which purport to be of Anglo-Saxon origin although they were not written until the reign of Henry I or later.

11. Cf. David J. Bernstein, *The Mystery of the Bayeux Tapestry* (Chicago: University of Chicago Press, 1986), 152–59.

12. "Heroldus etiam ipse in primo militum congressu occcubuit uulneribus letaliter confossus." William of Jumièges, *The Gesta Normannorum ducum of William of Jumièges, Orderic Vitalis, and Robert of Torigni,* ed. Elisabeth M. C. Van Houts, Oxford Medieval Texts (New York: Oxford University Press, 1992), 168.

13. See *The Anglo-Saxon Chronicle,* ed. Dorothy Whitelock, David C. Douglas, and Susie Tucker (London: Eyre and Spottiswoode, 1961), 143; Florence of Worcester, *Chronicon ex chronicis,* ed. Benjamin Thorpe, English Historical Society Publications 13 (London: Bentley, Wilson, and Fley, 1848), 1:227 ("heu, ipsemet cedidit crepusculi tempore").

14. Guillaume de Poitiers, *Histoire de Guillaume le Conquérant,* ed. Raymonde Foreville (Paris: Société d'Édition "Les Belles Lettres," 1952), xxi. All quotations are from this text. Translations are my own. I cite parenthetically by book and section number. I have also consulted William of Poitiers, *The Gesta Guillelmi of William of Poitiers,* ed. and trans. R. H. C. Davis and Marjorie Chibnall, Oxford Medieval Texts (New York: Clarendon Press, 1998).

15. "Jam inclinato die haud dubie intellexit exercitus Anglorum se stare contra Normannos diutius non valere. Noverunt se diminutos interitu multarum legionum; regem ipsum et fratres ejus, regnique primates nonnullos occubuisse; quotquot reliqui sunt prope viribus exhaustos; subsidium quod expectent nullum relictum" (2.23).

16. "Gens equidem illa natura semper in ferrum prompta fuit, descendens ab antiqua Saxonum origine ferocissimorum hominum" (2.24).

17. "Sic victoria consummata, ad aream belli regressus, reperit stragem, quam non absque miseratione conspexit, tametsi factam in impios; tametsi tyrannum occidere sit pulchrum, fama gloriosum, beneficio gratum. Late solum operuit sordidatus in cruore flos Anglicae nobilitatis atque juventutis" (2.25).

18. "Propius regem fratres ejus duo reperti sunt. Ipse carens omni decore, quibusdam signis, nequaquam facie, recognitus est, et incastra ducis delatus qui tumulandum eum Guillelmo agnomine Maletto concessit, non matri pro corpore dilectae prolis auri par pondus offerenti. Scivit enim non decere tali commercio aurum accipi. Aestimavit indignum fore ad matris libitum sepeliri, cujus ob nimiam cupiditatem insepulti remanerent innumerabiles. Dictum est illudendo, oportere situm esse custodem littoris et pelagi, quae cum armis ante vesanus insedit" (2.25).

19. Guy of Amiens, *Carmen de Hastingae proelio,* ed. Catherine Morton and Hope Muntz (Oxford: Clarendon Press, 1972), xv–xxx. All quotations are from this edition. I cite parenthetically in the text by page number. Translations are my own.

20. For the suggestion that Harold's burial "savours of age-old magic" and Viking burial rites, see ibid., xliii–xliv. For Capetian claims of sacred kingship, Marc Bloch, *Les*

rois thaumaturges: Étude sur le caractère surnaturel attribué à la puissance royale particulièrement en France et en Angleterre, Publications de la Faculté des lettres de l'Université de Strasbourg 19 (Strasbourg: Librairie Istra, 1924), 79–88, is still indispensable. See also Geoffrey Koziol, "England, France, and the Problem of Sacrality in Twelfth-Century Ritual," in *Cultures of Power,* ed. Thomas Bisson (Philadelphia: University of Pennsylvania Press, 1995), 124–48.

21. For a good summary of the grounds on which William rested his claim to the English throne, see Guillaume de Poitiers, *Histoire de Guillaume le Conquérant,* xvi.

22. Eadmer, *Historia novorum in Anglia,* ed. Martin Rule, Rolls Series 81 (London: Longman, 1884), 8–9. My translation. One finds the language of divine judgment similarly used by Ralph of Coggeshalle, writing in England at the end of the twelfth century: "Anno ab incarnatione Domini MLXVI. Willelmus dux Normannorum, contracto a partibus transmarinis innumerabili exercitu, in Angliam applicuit apud Hastinghes, ac justo Dei judicio die Sancti Calixti Papae, regem Haraldum, qui imperium Angliae injuste usurpaverat, regno simul ac vita privavit." Ralph of Coggeshall, *Radulphi de Coggeshall chronicon Anglicanum, de expugnatione terrae sanctae libellus, Thomas Agnellus de morte et sepultura Henrici regis Angliae junioris, gesta Fulconis Filii Warini, excerpta ex otiis imperialibus Gervasii Tileburiensis,* ed. Joseph Stevenson, Rolls Series 66 (London: Longman, 1875), 1.

23. William of Malmesbury's *Gesta regum Anglorum* is written by 1125. As we shall see in a moment, the Waltham tradition is already formed by then, and William has access to it.

24. *The Waltham Chronicle: An Account of the Discovery of Our Holy Cross at Montacute and Its Conveyance to Waltham,* ed. Leslie Watkiss and Marjorie Chibnall, Oxford Medieval Texts (Oxford: Clarendon Press, 1994).

25. The college of secular canons at Waltham was replaced in 1177 by an abbey of Augustinian canons as part of Henry's penitence for the murder of Thomas Becket; William de Mandeville, whom the chronicler addresses, died in 1189. See ibid., xxxiii.

26. Ibid., 46.

27. If this is a reference to William's vow to found Battle Abbey, as seems likely, it is the only contemporary reference to the vow outside the so-called *Chronicle of Battle Abbey.* See *Chronicle of Battle Abbey,* ed. Eleanor Searle, Oxford Medieval Texts (Oxford: Clarendon Press, 1980), 36.

28. *Waltham Chronicle,* 54.

29. Ibid., 56.

30. William of Malmesbury, *Gesta regum Anglorum,* ed. and trans. R. A. B. Mynors, Rodney M. Thomson, and Michael Winterbottom, vol. 1 (Oxford: Clarendon Press, 1998), 3.243–45. There is a convenient reprint of the nineteenth-century translation, William of Malmesbury, *A History of the Norman Kings,* trans. Joseph Stevenson (Lampeter: Llanerch Press, 1991). Henry of Huntingdon's version of Harold's death, written

about 1135, is closest to the Bayeux tapestry, including his notice of Halley's comet: "Meanwhile the whole shower of arrows fell around King Harold, and he himself fell, struck in the eye. A multitude of soldiers broke through and killed the wounded king. . . . So the change was accomplished, by the right hand of the Most High, that a huge comet had signified at the beginning of that same year. And thus it is said, 'In the year one thousand sixty-six / The lands of the English sensed the flames of a comet.'" [Interea totus imber sagittariorum cecidit circa regem Haraldum, et ipse in oculo ictus corruit. Irrumpens autem multitudo equitum, regem uulneratum interfecit. . . . Sic facta est mutatio dextere excelsi. Quam cometa ingens in exordio eiusdem anni designauerat. Unde dictum est: "Anno milleno sexageno quoque seno / Anglorum mete flammas sensere comete."] Henry Archdeacon of Huntingdon, *Historia Anglorum, the History of the English People,* ed. and trans. Diana Greenway, Oxford Medieval Texts (Oxford: Clarendon Press, 1996), 6.30. My translation. Henry says nothing further about Harold's body or his burial. In a strange encyclopedic dream vision, written in Latin elegiacs in the last years of the eleventh century and addressed to the Countess Adela, Baudri of Bourgueil describes a tapestry containing a depiction of the battle of Hastings. There too Harold is killed by an arrow as a manifestation of divine justice:

> Many dying went unbidden to the lower kingdom
> And a thousand speeded their fate by their own hand.
> Neither side was without injury in victory.
> The dry ground flowed with the blood of the slain.
> Finally, lest the presages of heaven were vain,
> The propitious gods favored the Normans.
> By chance a lethal arrow pierced Harold.
> He ended the war, he indeed was the cause.
> He circled his impure head with royal gold.
> He himself offended the scepter with his perjured hand.
> The English crowd grew frightened; God himself increased their fear
> And the whole legion quickly gave way to flight.

> [Multus abit moriens iniussus ad infera regna
> Fataque mille suis accelerant manibus
> Indemnis neutri caedet victoria parti
> Arrida caesorum gleba cruere fluit.
> Tandem ne coeli praesagia vana fuissent
> Normannis deitas propitiata favet.
> Perforat Hairaldum casu letalis aundo
> Is belli finis, is quoque causa fuit
> Is caput impurum regali cinxerat auro
> Sceptraque periura laeserat ipse manu.

Anglica turba pavet, auget deus ipse pavorem
Inque fugam legio tanta repente labat.]

Baudri of Bourgueil, "Vadis ut insolites videas, mea cartula, fastes," poem 196 in Baudri of Bourgueil, *Les oeuvres poétiques de Baudri de Bourgueil (1046–1130),* ed. Phyllis Abrahams (Paris: Champion, 1926), lines 457–68. Abrahams supplies a full presentation of arguments for and against associating this ecphrastic tapestry with the Bayeux tapestry.

31. The contemporary title of Guibert of Nogent's crusade narrative *Gesta dei per Francos* shows a similar sense of transcendental historical agency, though one that was fast coming under severe challenge in law and philosophy.

32. I use the text and translation of Walter de Gray Birch, *Vita Haroldi: The Romance of the Life of Harold, King of England* (London: Elliot Stock, 1885). For a list of the contents of Harley 3776, see his introduction, vii–ix. There is an available translation, closely based on that of Birch, in Michael Swanton, ed., *Three Lives of the Last Englishmen,* Garland Library of Medieval Literature 10 (New York: Garland, 1984). Unfortunately, Swanton's version is extremely unreliable.

33. Aelred of Rievaulx, *Vita Edwardi regis et confessoris,* in PL 195:738–39 (Paris: Garnier, 1885).

34. Ibid., cols. 773–74.

35. Ibid., col. 766.

36. Ibid., col. 773.

37. Ibid., col. 774.

38. Christopher Gill and T. P. Wiseman, *Lies and Fiction in the Ancient World* (Austin: University of Texas Press, 1993); T. P. Wiseman, *Clio's Cosmetics: Three Studies in Greco-Roman Literature* (Totowa, NJ: Rowman and Littlefield, 1979), and *Historiography and Imagination: Eight Essays on Roman Culture,* Exeter Studies in History 33 (Exeter: University of Exeter Press, 1994); A. J. Woodman, *Rhetoric in Classical Historiography: Four Studies* (London: Croom Helm, 1988).

39. Wace, *Le Roman de Rou,* ed. A. J. Holden, Société des anciens textes francais (Paris: Picard, 1970), lines 8173–74. All further citations are given parenthetically by line number in the text. My translations.

40. The far-reaching developments in legal administration during the reign of Henry II and the emergence of the sphere of law as a growing point of intellectual inquiry have been much studied. See Frank Barlow, *The Feudal Kingdom of England, 1042–1216* (New York: Longman, 1988), 306–20; Richard Mortimer, *Angevin England, 1154–1258* (Cambridge, MA: Blackwell, 1996), 51–76.

41. The process by which the Norman rulers of England found English ancestors for themselves and otherwise asserted the legitimacy of their being in England has begun to attract long overdue scholarly attention, as has the converse possibility, the self-identification of prosperous Englishmen with Norman elites. See S. J. Ridyard,

"Condigna Veneratio: Post-Conquest Attitudes to the Saints of the Anglo-Saxons," in *Anglo-Norman Studies IX: Proceedings of the Battle Conference, 1986,* ed. R. Allen Brown (Woodbridge: Boydell Press, 1987); David Townsend, "Anglo-Latin Hagiography and the Norman Transition," *Exemplaria* 3 (1991):385–433; Frank Barlow, "The Effects of the Norman Conquest," in *The Norman Conquest: Its Setting and Impact. A Book Commemorating the Ninth Centenary of the Battle of Hastings* (London: Eyre and Spottiswoode, 1966); Ralph V. Turner, "Changing Perceptions of the New Administrative Class in Anglo-Norman and Angevin England: The Curiales and Their Conservative Critics," *Journal of British Studies* 29 (1990): 93–117, and *Men Raised from the Dust: Administrative Service and Upward Mobility in Angevin England* (Philadelphia: University of Pennsylvania Press, 1988).

42. Several codifications of law, all purporting to be of venerable date, are composed during the reign of Henry II. One of the most important of these texts is titled *Leges Edwardi confessoris.* See Liebermann, *Gesetze der Angelsachsen.*

43. Giraldus Cambrensis, *Itinerarium Cambriae,* in *Giraldus Cambrensis opera omnia,* ed. James F. Dimock, Rolls Series 21.6 (London: Longman, 1868), 140. The translation is from Gerald of Wales, *The Journey through Wales; the Description of Wales,* trans. Lewis Thorpe (Harmondsworth: Penguin Books, 1978), 198–99.

44. "Vidimus hic quod in oculis nostris novum apparuit, caseos scilicet cervinos." Giraldus Cambrensis, *Itinerarium,* 141.

45. "[Rusticos] prodigiorum novitate stupescens, et tam deformes biformis naturae formas abhorrens, baculo quem manu gestabat . . . cunctos interemit." Ibid.

46. de Certeau, *Writing of History,* 270. See also Head, *Hagiography;* Thomas Heffernan, *Sacred Biography: Saints and Their Biographers in the Middle Ages* (Oxford: Oxford University Press, 1988); Stephen Wilson, "Cult of Saints in the Churches of Central Paris," in *Saints and Their Cults,* ed. Stephen Wilson (Cambridge: Cambridge University Press, 1983), 233–60.

47. *Vita Haroldi,* 142. All citations to the text and translation of the *Vita Haroldi* are given parenthetically in the text. In a few places I have silently altered Birch's translation.

48. I want to thank Sandra Pierson Prior for first pointing out the resemblance between the *Vita* and the vulgate cycle and Christopher Baswell for reminding me that the *Vita Haroldi* was written in the same milieu and at the same time as the vulgate romances were being translated from the vernacular into Latin.

49. See Tsvetan Todorov, "The Quest of Narrative," in *Poetics of Prose* (Ithaca: Cornell University Press, 1977). See also Jean Rychner, *Formes et structures de la prose française médiévale: L'articulation des phrases narratives dans "La Mort Artu"* (Geneva: Droz, 1970).

50. Sulpicius Severus, *Vita S. Martini,* ed. Jacques Fontaine, Sources chrétiennes 133 (Paris: Éditions du Cerf, 1967), 250–54.

51. The text is from *Liber monasterii de Hyda,* ed. Edward Edwards, Rolls Series 45 (London: Longmans, 1866), 294. My translations.

52. *Impono* has a complex range of references, most of which are negative. Operative here is its sense of providing finality as in bringing an end to hope, putting the final stroke on a painting, or bringing an end to war. See Charleton T. Lewis and Charles Short, *A Latin Dictionary* (Oxford: Oxford University Press, 1969), s.v. impono II. A.

53. The great nineteenth-century historian of the Conquest Edward Freeman, for example, even as he asserts it as temporary, deplores the transfer of England from one dominion to the next on October 14, 1066: "[I]t is from the memorable day of Saint Calixtus that we may fairly date the overthrow, what we know to have been only the imperfect and temporary overthrow, of our ancient and free Teutonic England. In the eyes of men of the next generation that day was the fatal day of England, the day of the overthrow of our dear country, the day of her handing over to foreign lords . . . till it was a shame to be called an Englishman, and the men of England were no more a people." Edward Augustus Freeman, *The History of the Norman Conquest of England, Its Causes and Its Results,* 2nd ed., 6 vols. (Oxford: Clarendon Press, 1875), 3:503.

54. Christopher Hill, "The Norman Yoke," in *Puritanism and Revolution* (London: Secker and Warburg, 1958), 57.

55. One of the principal strategies of minimizing the historical impact of the Conquest is to insist upon 1066 as the very *last* time that sovereign England would be conquered. The devotion to the English past as a repository of value for the English present has been, of course, a primary impetus to insular medieval scholarship, sometimes indeed of the highest order. J. R. R. Tolkien, for example, is popularly reported to have been "pained" by the Norman Conquest "as if it had happened to him personally in his own lifetime." See Anthony Lane, "The Hobbit Habit," *New Yorker* 77, no. 39 (2001): 98–105. And such devotion is by no means a particular possession of the political right, as Furnivall's career amply attests. Whether supportive of a right- or left-wing commitment, it is nevertheless a historical illusion.

56. William of Malmesbury, *Gesta regum Anglorum,* 3.254.3.

57. The essential study is William E. Kapelle, *The Norman Conquest of the North: The Region and Its Transformation, 1000–1135* (Chapel Hill: University of North Carolina Press, 1979). Among the huge number of studies, see especially Barlow, "Effects of the Norman Conquest" and *Feudal Kingdom of England*; Marjorie Chibnall, *The Debate on the Norman Conquest* (Manchester: Manchester University Press, 1999); Michael T. Clanchy, *England and Its Rulers: Foreign Lordship and National Identity, 1066–1272* (Totowa, NJ: Rowman and Littlefield, 1983); Brian Golding, *Conquest and Colonisation: The Normans in Britain, 1066–1100,* British History in Perspective (New York: St. Martin's Press, 1994); John Hudson, *Land, Law, and Lordship in Anglo-Norman England* (Oxford: Clarendon Press, 1994); Ted Johnson-South, "The Norman Conquest of Durham: Norman Historians and the Anglo Saxon Community of St. Cuthbert," *Haskins Society Journal* 4 (1992): 85–95; David Walker, *The Normans in Britain,* Historical Association Studies (Oxford: Blackwell, 1995); Ann Williams, *The English and the Norman Conquest* (Woodbridge: Boy-

dell Press, 1995). Some recent literary studies have begun to trouble the master narrative considerably. While their focus is considerably outside the chronological limits of my study, two have significant theoretical convergences with my own project: Patricia Clare Ingham, *Sovereign Fantasies: Arthurian Romance and the Making of Britain* (Philadelphia: University of Pennsylvania Press, 2001), and Geraldine Heng, *The Empire of Magic: Medieval Romance and the Politics of Cultural Fantasy* (New York: Columbia University Press, 2003).

58. By no means unique in this regard is David Douglas, who, while denying that anything resembling "modern national feeling" exists in the eleventh century, nevertheless writes page after page in which the agents of all the action and their objects are territorial states. It is no accident that his chief analytical tool in this regard is balance-of-power analysis, the dominant method of the mid-twentieth-century American foreign policy establishment. David C. Douglas, *The Norman Achievement* (Berkeley: University of California Press, 1969), 10–11, 49, and throughout. A very important attempt to understand the precise contours of Norman territorial administration in its own historical specificity and without recourse to a narrative of the rise of England is John Le Patourel, *The Norman Empire* (Oxford: Clarendon Press, 1976).

59. For the importance of the Bamburgh house, see Kapelle, *Norman Conquest,* 24–26, 44–50, and throughout. See also Robin Fleming, *Kings and Lords in Conquest England* (Cambridge: Cambridge University Press, 1991).

60. See *Anglo-Saxon Chronicle.* For the conspiracy, 1075 E: "Earl Roger was there and Earl Waltheof and bishops and abbots, and there they plotted to expel the king from the realm of England." D: "Earl Roger was there and Earl Waltheof and bishops and abbots, and there they plotted to drive their royal lord out of his kingdom" (156–57). For the punishment, 1076 E: "And Earl Waltheof was beheaded at Winchester; and his body was taken to Crowland." D: "And in this year Earl Waltheof was beheaded at Winchester on St. Petronella's Day [31 May]; and his body was taken to Crowland, and he is buried there" (158).

61. The exception is Henry of Huntingdon, whose narrative of the conspiracy of 1074 is centered entirely on the fate of Ralph of Gael. For Waltheof, Henry translates a single sentence of the *Peterborough Chronicle* almost verbatim: "Sed Walthef consulem decollari fecit apud Winceastre, et sepultus est apud Crulande." Henry Archdeacon of Huntingdon, *Historia Anglorum,* 308–9.

62. See the introduction to *Le roman de Waldef (cod. Bodmer 168),* ed. A. J. Holden (Cologne: Fondation Martin Bodmer, 1984).

63. *Chroniques anglo-normandes, recueil d'extraits et d'écrits relatifs à l'histoire de Normandie et d'Angleterre pendant les XIe et XIIe siècles,* vol. 2, ed. Francisque Michel (Rouen: Edouard Frere, 1836), contains the *Gesta antecessorum comitis Waldevi, Vita et passio Waldevi Comitis, de Juditha uxore Waldevi comitis, miracula sanctus Waldevi* from a manuscript dating from the end of the twelfth or beginning of the thirteenth century, Douai 801.

64. N. Denholm Young, "An Early Thirteenth Century Anglo-Norman MS," *Bodleian Quarterly Record* 6 (1932): 225–30.

65. For the text, see *Le roman de Waldef.* For a serious reevaluation of this important, neglected poem, see Rosalind Field, "Romance as History, History as Romance," in *Romance in Medieval England,* ed. Maldwyn Mills, Jennifer Fellows, and Carol M. Meale (Cambridge: D. S. Brewer, 1991), 163–73, and "Waldef and the Matter of/with England," in *Medieval Insular Romance: Translation and Innovation,* ed. Judith Weiss, Jennifer Fellows, and Morgan Dickson (Cambridge: D. S. Brewer, 2000), 25–39.

66. The *Pseudo-Ingulph Chronicle* is a pastiche constructed primarily out of material found in earlier writings. Its account of Earl Waltheof adds nothing to the reports of Ordericus Vitalis, who spent five weeks at Crowland. David Roffe, "The Historia Croylandensis: A Plea for Reassessment," *English Historical Review* 110 (1995): 93–108, has argued for its historical utility in documenting material preserved in the oral traditions of Crowland Abbey.

67. Text is from Florence of Worcester, *Chronicon ex chronicis;* translations are from Florence of Worcester, *A History of the Kings of England,* ed. and trans. Joseph Stevenson (Lampeters: Llanerch Enterprises, 1988). I cite parenthetically by page numbers.

68. "Qui mox ut potuit, Landfrancum Dorubernensem archiepiscopum adiit, poenitentiamque ab eo pro facto licet non sponte sacramento accepit ejusque consilio regem Willelmum in Normannia degentem petiit, eique rem ex ordine gestam pandens, illius misericordiae ultro se dedit" (10).

69. Translation is Simeon of Durham, *The Historical Works of Simeon of Durham,* ed. and trans. Joseph Stevenson, Church Historians of England, Pre-Reformation Series 3:2 (1855; reprint, Lampeter: Llanarch Press, 1987). I cite the 1987 reprint by page number. The text is Simeon of Durham, *Symeonis Monachi opera omnia,* ed. Thomas Arnold, Rolls Series 75:2 (London: Longman, 1882).

70. For a brilliant discussion of the creation of strategic family alliances among the Normans, see Eleanor Searle, *Predatory Kinship and the Creation of Norman Power, 840–1066* (Berkeley: University of California Press, 1988).

71. Simeon of Durham, *Historical Works,* 142–45.

72. Ibid., 144. In pre-Conquest England, *earl*—a title introduced by Cnut—was not a territorial honor but a family status designator. Some twenty-five families during the reign of Edward the Confessor had rights to the title, and it was borne by all the sons even while the father was alive. In Latin writing before the Conquest this term was almost universally translated as *dux.* In his rationalization of English administration, William introduced the Norman practice of territorializing honors. From the time of the Conquest on, Latin writers reserve *dux* for William alone and translate *earl* as *comes,* registering the change from family status to territorial lord. It is this very practice—the territorialization of the countship—that creates English identity by associating the English with the territory as its native inhabitant and therefore its "natural" ruler, while

the Normans become almost by definition newcomers, invaders, settlers, and usurpers. That is, Norman territorialization is inseparable from the value of the ethnic terms. See C. P. Lewis, "The Early Earls of Norman England," *Anglo-Norman Studies* 13 (1991): 207–22.

73. Ethnic identities were subject to constant negotiation throughout the Anglo-Norman regnum, as we shall discuss in what follows. See George Garnett, "Franci et Angli: The Legal Distinction between Peoples after the Conquest," *Anglo-Norman Studies* 8 (1986): 108–37; Ian Short, "Tam Angli Quam Franci: Self-Definition in Anglo-Norman England," *Anglo-Norman Studies* 18 (1996): 153–75.

74. See Kapelle, *Norman Conquest,* 136.

75. William of Malmesbury, *Gesta regum Anglorum.* Citations are by volume, section, and line number. Translations are my own.

76. Text is William of Malmesbury, *De gestis pontificum Anglorum,* ed. N. E. S. A. Hamilton, Rolls Series 52 (1870; reprint, Wiesbaden, Kraus, 1964). Translations are my own. All quotations are from the Crowland section, book 4, section 182.

77. In a much discussed passage at the beginning of the third book of the *Gesta regum Anglorum,* William reports his own mixed ethnicity with the metaphor of a hybrid body—the blood, he says, of both the Normans and the English flows in his veins—claiming that his own hybridity allows him to judge William the Conqueror dispassionately. See Robert M. Stein, "Making History English: Cultural Identity and Historical Explanation in William of Malmesbury and Laȝamon's *Brut,*" in *Text and Territory: Geographical Imagination in the European Middle Ages,* ed. Sealy Gilles and Sylvia Tomasch (Philadelphia: University of Pennsylvania Press, 1998), 97–115.

78. Lewis and Short, *A Latin Dictionary,* s.v. compaginatum.

79. Text and facing page translation from Ordericus Vitalis, *The Ecclesiastical History of Orderic Vitalis,* 6 vols., ed. and trans. Marjorie Chibnall, Oxford Medieval Texts (Oxford: Clarendon Press, 1969). All information about the text and the chronology of its writing is from this edition. I have frequently altered Chibnall's very graceful translation to make it correspond more literally to the Latin original. I cite by volume and page number to the Latin text.

80. Orderic constantly conceptualizes the situation in terms of foreigner and native. For one example among hundreds, "So when the Normans had become over-wealthy on the spoils garnered by others, they arrogantly abused their authority and mercilessly slaughtered the native people like the scourge of God smiting them for their sins." [Adeptis itaque nimiis opibus quas alii aggregarant; Normanni furentes immoderate tumebant, et indigenas diuino uerbere pro reatibus suis percussos impie mactabant] (2.268).

81. "Et tanti comitis corpus pro posse suo gratanter honorauerunt, et Vitali Angligenae uersibus heroicis epitaphium eius edere iusserunt" (2.350).

82. The execution scene is at 2.322.

83. The Crowland material is narrated in 2.324−50. The oppression of native English by foreign invaders is a constant theme. For example, "Later England was much troubled by various storms of war, and the native English kings who ruled the country were supplanted by the barbarous rulers Inguar and Halfdene and Guthrum and the other tyrants coming from Denmark and Norway" [Variis bellorum tempestatibus Anglia postmodum perturbata, et barbaris sub ducibus Inguar et Halfdene ac Gudrun aliisque tirannis superuenientibus a Dacia uel Norregania, Angligenarum regum qui naturaliter Angliae praefuerant mutatione facta] (2.340), or "Not long afterwards the same abbot [Wulfketel], who was an Englishman hated by the Normans, was accused by his enemies, deposed by Lanfranc, and sent to the monastery of Glastonbury" [Post non multum temporis praefatus abbas quoniam Angligena erat et Normannis exosus ab emulis accusatus est et a Lanfranco archiepiscopo depositus et Glestoniae claustro deputatus est] (2.344).

CHAPTER THREE. "Dreaming of Other Worlds": Romance as Reality Fiction

Part of this chapter was originally published, in a much earlier form, as "Desire, Social Reproduction, and Marie's *Guigemar*," in *In Quest of Marie de France, a Twelfth Century Poet,* ed. Chantal A. Maréchal (Lewiston, NY: Mellen, 1992), 280−94.

1. I have been concerned with some examples of hagiographical motives in historical writing. Felice Lifshitz has similarly drawn attention to the thoroughly historiographical impulse of hagiography. See Felice Lifshitz, "Beyond Positivism and Genre: 'Hagiographical' Texts as Historical Narrative," *Viator* 25 (1994): 95−113, *Norman Conquest,* and "The Politics of Historiography: The Memory of Bishops in Eleventh-Century Rouen," *History and Memory* 10 (1998): 118−37. See also Paul Fouracre, "Merovingian History and Merovingian Hagiography," *Past and Present* 127 (1990): 3−38; Elisabeth M. C. Van Houts, "Historiography and Hagiography at St. Wandrille: The 'Inventio et Miracula Sancti Vulframni,'" *Anglo-Norman Studies* 12 (1989): 233−51. That drawing a border between intimately related genres, in this case history and hagiography, is as impossible as it is essential for their analysis is nicely discussed in Jacques Derrida's important essay "The Law of Genre," under the rubric "The law of genre is the law of contamination." See Jacques Derrida, "The Law of Genre," in *Acts of Literature,* ed. Derek Attridge (New York: Routledge, 1992), 221−52.

2. Robert Hanning's foundational *Vision of History in Early Britain* discusses Geoffrey's work as a fictional critique of the practices of his historian contemporaries, especially of William of Malmesbury. I will argue that Geoffrey's fiction making is an attempt from within the protocols of historical writing to seize the territory that lies outside the historian's ken.

3. The text is in *Chronicles of the Reigns of Stephen, Henry II., and Richard I. Edited from Manuscripts by Richard Howlett. Published by the Authority of the Lords Commissioners of Her Majesty's Treasury, under the Direction of the Master of the Rolls,* ed. Richard Howlett, Rolls Series 82 (London: Longman, 1884). Translations are my own. For William of Newburgh true history is identical to Bede's historiography. Kellie Robertson has analyzed Geoffrey's wholesale severing of British history from its dependence on a Roman antecedent and thus from Bede. See Kellie Robertson, "Geoffrey of Monmouth and the Translation of Insular Historiography," *Arthuriana* 8, no. 4 (1998): 42–57.

4. Alphonse Dupront's discussion of the historiography of the First Crusade places its spirituality firmly on the side of hagiography as I have drawn the line here: "tout événement profane est transcendé au niveau d'une sortie de l'histoire, c'est-à-dire d'une entrée de plain-pied dans l'éternel, dans la Présence, cette présence que magnifie, postule la guerre sainte, cette guerre qui doit être la dernière des guerres, après quoi ils seront 'un.'" Alphonse Dupront, *Du sacré: Croisades et pèlerinages, images et langages,* Bibliothèque des histoires (Paris: Gallimard, 1987), 256.

5. In this wedding of romance and hagiography as the borders of history, it is interesting to consider Reto Bezzola's observation that octosyllabic couplets, virtually the definitive form of courtly romance composition, were first used "pendant la première moitié du 12ᵉ siècle, à la cour d'Angleterre pour la poésie hagiographique (*Le Voyage de saint Brendan* de Beneeit) et didactique (Lapidataires, Bestiaires)." Reto Radoulf Bezzola, *Les origines et la formation de la littérature courtoise en occident (500–1200),* 5 vols. (Paris: H. Champion, 1960), 3.1:150.

6. See chap. 4 of *The Poetics* (1448b), where Aristotle counters his teacher Plato's extreme suspicion of simulacra by appealing to a primary meaning of *mimesis,* making models, including dolls, miniatures, and anatomical drawings, in order to learn the properties of the things they represent. For Aristotle such representational activity is a natural part of human cognition, and therefore the pleasure in mimesis is always cognitive. For a translation that makes this complicated section clear, see Aristotle, *Poetics,* trans. Gerald F. Else (Ann Arbor: University of Michigan Press, 1967).

7. That *romanz* in its earliest appearances always evokes the fact of translation, and that the romance text therefore draws its authority from its avowed dependence on a Latin original, has been persuasively argued by Peter Damian-Grint. See Peter Damian-Grint, "*Estoire* as Word and Genre: Meaning and Literary Usage in the Twelfth Century," *Medium Aevum* 66 (1997): 189–206, and *The New Historians of the Twelfth-Century Renaissance: Inventing Vernacular Authority* (Woodbridge: Boydell Press, 1999). Certainly by the time of Chrétien de Troyes, however, *romanz* refers to an independent text in a recognizable form, and as such its textual authority is based on the compositional expertise of the writer. Beginning in the lyric tradition, this shift to vernacular originality is signaled by the employment of the technical language of rhetorical *inventio*—*trobar* and its other romance cognates—to indicate both authorial expertise and textual

authority. The same terminology appears in a thirteenth-century praise of Chrétien: "Por ce que mors est Crestïens / de Troies, cil qui tant ot pris / de trover, ai hardement pris / de mot a mot meitre en escrit." See Huon de Méri, *Tornoiemenz Antecrit* (lines 1235–38), quoted in Chrétien de Troyes, *Le Chevalier au Lion ou Le roman d'Yvain,* ed. and trans. David Hult, Lettres gothiques (Paris: Le Livre de Poche, 1994), 11.

8. Text is Geoffrey of Monmouth, *The Historia regum Britannie of Geoffrey of Monmouth I: Bern Burgerbibliothek, MS. 568,* ed. Neil Wright (Cambridge: D. S. Brewer, 1985). Translations are my own. I cite by page number to this edition.

9. The identification of *imperium* with *ecclesium* is a well-known part of Carolingian political theory from as early as the writings of Alcuin. See Y. Congar, *L'ecclésiologie du haut Moyen Âge de Saint Grégoire le Grand à la désunion entre Byzance et Rome* (Paris: Edition du Cerf, 1968), 270. Dominique Boutet points out the long life of this identification in such thirteenth-century chansons de geste as *Fierabras,* in Arthurian literature, and above all in representations of the crusade: "La croisade est la vocation extérieure de cet empire, comme on le voit dans les chansons de geste du Cycle du roi et du Cycle de Guillaume, parce que sa vocation unique est de rendre l'*orbis christianus* coextensif à l'ensemble du monde habité." Dominique Boutet, *Formes littéraires et conscience historique aux origines de la littérature française (1100–1250)* (Paris: Presses Universitaires de France, 1999), 49.

10. For the history and extent of the legal maxim *rex est imperator in regno suo,* see Kantorowicz, *King's Two Bodies,* 51 n. 20 and the bibliography cited there. See also Robert M. Stein, "Signs and Things: The *Vita Heinrici IV. Imperatoris* and the Crisis of Interpretation in Twelfth Century History," *Traditio* 43 (1987): 105–19.

11. See Robert W. Hanning, *The Individual in Twelfth-Century Romance* (New Haven: Yale University Press, 1977), 55, where Hanning discusses this scene.

12. Arthur's address begins, "Consocii, inquit, prosperitatis et aduersitatis, quorum probitates hactenus et in dandis consiliis et in miliciis agendis expertus sum" (113). Aeneas's famous lines "O socii, neque enim ignari sumus ante malorum, / o passi graviora, dabit deus his quoque finem. / vos et Scyllaeam rabiem penitusque sonantes / accestis scopulos, vos et Cyclopea saxa /experti" (Aen. 1. 198–202) are here not quoted verbatim; rather, their gist is refigured while they are also signaled by verbal echoes. On the rhetorical dignity of this practice, and the fact that it is as recognizable an allusion as verbatim quotation, see Carruthers, *Book of Memory.* Amaury Chauou also points to the various devices of Arthurian legitimation in this scene, especially his conquests, which put him on a par with Alexander and Charlemagne, and his Trojan genealogy. Chauou sees this glorification of Arthur as simply and unproblematically Angevin propaganda. See Amaury Chauou, *L'idéologie Plantagenêt: Royauté arthurienne et monarchie politique dans l'espace Plantagenêt (XIIe–XIIIe siècles)* (Rennes: Presses Universitaires de Rennes, 2001), esp. 43–49.

13. Geoffrey's medieval translators unequivocally understand the significance of this narrative of ethnic difference. Wace and especially Lawman develop Geoffrey's cata-

log with rhetoric drawn from descriptions of monstrous races in the "wonders of the East" tradition. In this regard, it is no accident that the narrative of Arthur's conquest of Gaul begins with stories of his encounter with two fantastic creatures, simultaneously figures of extreme difference and psychic doubles, the Giant of Mont St. Michel and the giant with the cloak of beards. Jeffrey Jerome Cohen has discussed these figures thoroughly in their manifold relations with the representation of the psychic space of imperial conquest. See Jeffrey Jerome Cohen, *Of Giants: Sex, Monsters, and the Middle Ages* (Minneapolis: University of Minnesota Press, 1999), 36—55.

14. This is the moment at which Geoffrey names himself and says he will say nothing further about the situation: "Nec hoc quidem, consul auguste, Galfridus Monemutensis tacebit" (129).

15. The last sentence, definitively indicating Arthur's death, is lacking in many manuscripts, including all the manuscripts of the First Variant. The messianic fantasy of Arthur's eventual return is proclaimed and contested throughout the twelfth and thirteenth centuries in various ways: in a manuscript of the first variant with Welsh interests, the *Vera historia de morte Arturi* is interpolated at this point; on the other hand, the "discovery" of Arthur's remains at Glastonbury in 1190 may well have been a way to counter rising British resistance to Angevin central control. See Erich Köhler, *Ideal und Wirklichkeit in der höfischen Epik: Studien zur Form der frühen Artus- und Graldichtung,* Beihefte zur Zeitschrift für Romanische Philologie 97 (Tübingen: Max Niemeyer, 1956); I cite from the French translation, *L'aventure chevaleresque: Idéal et réalité dans le roman courtois: Études sur la forme des plus anciens poèmes d'Arthur et du graal* (Paris: Gallimard, 1974), 68. See also Michelle R. Warren, *History on the Edge: Excalibur and the Borders of Britain, 1100—1300* (Minneapolis: University of Minnesota Press, 2000), 60—82, and Chauou, *L'idéologie Plantagenêt.*

16. Later Arthurian narratives, such as the Old French *Mort Artu,* will attempt to effect a rapprochement between sacred history and secular processes and in so doing will emphasize the incest motif by displacing it onto Arthur himself: Modred is the son born of the incest committed in ignorance by Arthur and his sister. The destruction of the Arthurian world in those narratives is treated as a fatality, a sign and result of the fallen condition of the world and the inevitability of sin.

17. For Bede's revision of the Gildas tradition of British historiography, see Hanning, *Vision of History.*

18. When the British first settle: "Patriam donante duce sorciuntur. Agros incipiunt colere, domos aedificare, ita ut in breui tempore terram ab euo inhabitatam censeres" (13). The Saxons: "At Saxones sapientius agentes, pacem et concordiam inter se habentes, agros colentes, ciuitates et opida aedificantes et sic abiecto dominio Britonum, iam toti Loegriae imperauerant duce Adelstano qui primus inter eos diadema portauit" (147).

19. Geoffrey of Monmouth, *The Historia regum Britannie of Geoffrey of Monmouth II: The First Variant Version, a Critical Edition,* ed. Neil Wright (Cambridge: D. S. Brewer, 1988), 192.

20. That there is no such prophetic utterance earlier in the text is irrelevant to its function in this passage.

21. See Stein, "Making History English," 113–14.

22. Text is from Wace, *Roman de Brut: Text and Translation,* ed. and trans. Judith Weiss (Exeter: University of Exeter Press, 1999). Translations are my own. I cite by line number.

23. Durham Cathedral Library C.iv.27 (I) and Lincoln Cathedral Library 104. Ibid., xxvii.

24. The importance of Virgil in Geoffrey's historiographical design has frequently been remarked. See among others Hanning, *Vision of History,* and Francis Ingledew, "The Book of Troy and the Genealogical Construction of History: The Case of Geoffrey of Monmouth's *Historia regum Britanniae," Speculum* 69 (1994): 65–704.

25. Valerie I. J. Flint, "The Historia regum Britanniae of Geoffrey of Monmouth: Parody and Its Purpose. A Suggestion," *Speculum: A Journal of Medieval Studies* 54, no. 3 (1979): 447–68.

26. The dating of the *Historia regum* is by no means certain. Based on Geoffrey's recycling of dedications, the consensus dating for the first recension is 1136, which places the actual conception and writing of the project before the outcome of the war over the royal succession after the death of Henry I was even foreseeable.

27. "All die vielen Schlösser und Burgen, Kämpfe und Abenteuer der höfischen Romane, insbesondere der bretonischen, sind Märchenland, denn sie erscheinen vor uns jedesmal wie aus dem Boden gewachsen; ihr geographisches Verhältnis zur bekannten Erde, ihre soziologischen und wirtschaftlichen Grundlagen bleiben unaufgeklärt; selbst ihre moralische oder symbolische Bedeutung ist nur selten mit einiger Sicherheit zu ermitteln." Erich Auerbach, *Mimesis: Dargestellte Wirklichkeit in der Abendländischen Literatur* (Bern: A. Francke, 1946), 128. The translation is Auerbach, *Mimesis: Representation of Reality,* 130.

28. For Hegel, this moment of representation is due to the antithetical relationship between medieval society and the state, an antithesis that will be overcome with Enlightenment; for Auerbach it represents a crisis of consciousness in the aristocratic class provoked by the late medieval pacification of Europe. The reasoning is different, but the master narrative is identical. In the "Epilogomena to Mimesis," Auerbach says that his own work cannot be understood outside the tradition of the early romantics and Hegel (571). This relation has been only rarely taken into account in American appreciations of *Mimesis.* Even contemporary medievalists concerned with the social dimensions of texts tend to read chivalric romances as *Bildungsromanen.* Donald Maddox, to take one example among many, although reading the romances of Chrétien as thoroughly engaged with social and legal customs, nevertheless sees Yvain's series of adventures as marking his "moral growth" from "self-serving objectives" to altruism. See Donald Maddox, *The Arthurian Romances of Chrétien de Troyes: Once and Future Fictions,* Cambridge Studies in Medieval Literature 12 (New York: Cambridge University Press,

1991). The quotations are at 69. See also Grace M. Armstrong, "Questions of Inheritance: Le Chevalier au Lion and La Queste del Saint Graal," *Yale French Studies* 95 (1999): 171–92, esp. 160, for a similar tendency.

29. See Köhler, *Ideal und Wirklichkeit*. See also the essays collected in Georges Duby, *The Chivalrous Society,* trans. Cynthia Postan (Berkeley: University of California Press, 1980); Georges Duby, *Hommes et structures du Moyen-Age* (Paris: Flammarion, 1988).

30. Auerbach, *Mimesis: The Representation of Reality,* 135.

31. From a point of view somewhat different from mine, Emmanuelle Baumgartner similarly notes the multiple descriptions of the magic spring as something that distinguishes Chrétien's compositional method from the literary practice of any of his sources. "Il est enfin symptomatique qu'aucune de ces descriptions n'est exhaustive. De l'une à l'autre s'ajoutent ou se perdent ou se modifient des éléments du décor: ajouts, absences, déplacements qui sont autant de points de vue différents et complémentaires sur le lieu évoqué." See Emmanuèle Baumgartner, "La fontaine au pin," in *Le Chevalier au Lion: Approches d'un chef-d'oeuvre,* ed. Jean Dufournet (Paris: Champion, 1988), 36. I would add that these additions, absences, and displacements not only serve to deepen the significance of the place described and to characterize the point of view from which the place is perceived but also function thematically in the development of the significance of the text as a whole.

32. All quotations are from Chrétien de Troyes, *Le Chevalier au Lion (Yvain),* ed. Mario Roques, Les classiques français du Moyen Âge (Paris: Champion, 1971), and will be identified by line numbers parenthetically in the text. Translations are my own. I have also consulted with great profit Chrétien de Troyes, *Le Chevalier au Lion* (Hult ed.); Chrétien de Troyes, *Yvain (Le Chevalier au Lion),* ed. Wendelin Foerster with introduction, notes, and glossary by T. B. W. Reid (Manchester: Manchester University Press, 1942), and the excellent English translation by David Staines in Chrétien de Troyes, *The Complete Romances of Chrétien de Troyes,* trans. David Staines (Bloomington: Indiana University Press, 1993). The joy is redoubled even in the diction when Calogrenant hears the birds: "De lor joie me resjoï" (470).

33. Stephen Knight has discussed this adventure in the context of private war. Knight ultimately reads the poem, however, in full agreement with romantic medievalism. He sees it as expressive of an unresolvable conflict between individuality and the demands of the collective, a conflict between *proesce* and *courtoisie.* Throughout his reading, Knight relies on a rather statically conceived "ideological context" that the poem seems for him simply to reflect while resolving unhappy parts of it in fantasy. See Stephen Knight, *Arthurian Literature and Society* (New York: St. Martin's Press, 1983), esp. 87–88.

34. That the forest belongs to culture as much as if not more than to nature is signaled immediately in lines such as Calogrenant's description of the basin as "made of finer gold than would be for sale at any fair" [del plus fin or qui fust a vandre / encor onques en nule foire] (420–21). Moreover, as Emmanuelle Baumgartner explains, *fontaine*

in the twelfth and thirteenth centuries typically refers to a controlled spring. The narrative details are also typical of the visual iconography in the manuscripts: a mounting stone on one side, a stone or brick curb on the other, and even the nearby chapel are all expectable elements that point to domestic use. See Emmanuèle Baumgartner, *Chrétien de Troyes: Yvain, Lancelot, la charrette et le lion,* Études littéraires (Paris: Presses Universitaires de France, 1992), 52.

35. There is a nice instance of this dependence of town, forest, and countryside in the Noire Espine episode. The elder sister refuses to divide her land with the younger: "Lord, God confound me if ever I divide with her a castle, village, plowland, wood, field, or any other thing" [Sire, Dex me confonde / se ja de ma terre li part / chastel, ne vile, ne essart, / ne bois, ne plain, ne autre chose] (4785–89).

36. Cf. Marie-Louise Ollier, "The Author in the Text: The Prologues of Chrétien de Troyes," *Yale French Studies* 51 (1974): 30. "Chrétien's originality consists in making a romance, that is, a significant whole, invested with meaning at every level of its structure."

37. When the king appears just after Calogrenant has finished telling the court his story, the text lets us know that the queen tells him the whole thing word for word [tot mot a mot], and adds that she was a good storyteller [que bien et bel conter li sot] (660). The circulation of stories, constantly remarked in romance texts, is an external manifestation of the internal repetition that characterizes romance plotting: one writes the story over again because meaning is never exhausted in a single instance.

38. I am indebted to H. Marshall Leicester's brilliant reading of the *Lais* of Marie de France for this view of the characters in romance as conscious users of romance conventions. See H. Marshall Leicester Jr., "The Voice of the Hind: The Emergence of Feminine Discontent in the *Lais* of Marie de France," in *Reading Medieval Culture: Essays in Honor of Robert W. Hanning,* ed. Robert M. Stein and Sandra Pierson Prior (Notre Dame: University of Notre Dame Press, 2005), 132–69.

39. Brigitte Cazelles's reading of Chrétien's *Conte du Graal* proceeds from this very dynamic. She sees the adventure plot of that romance as structured by the conflict between the claims of lineage, affiliation, and local allegiance on the one hand and the claims of the sovereign monarchy on the other. See Brigitte Cazelles, *The Unholy Grail: A Social Reading of Chrétien de Troyes's "Conte du Graal"* (Stanford: Stanford University Press, 1996).

40. David Hult notes that in two manuscripts the seneschal of the lady's court refers to her having been married to Esclados for less than six years, while in the same manuscripts Calogrenant specifies that his adventure took place seven years before (in other manuscripts the numbers vary between six and ten). Hult continues: "Simple inconséquence de la transmission ou peut-être désir de faire savoir que ce ne fut pas Esclados qui avait jeté Calogrenant de son cheval, *mais son prédécesseur?* [Hult's emphasis]." If so, then this is yet another example of the continual play of substitutions, replace-

ments, and variations that structures the romance. See Chrétien de Troyes, *Le Chevalier au Lion* (Hult ed.), 14.

41. Bloch quotes Glanvil: "Duo autem sunt genera homicidii. Unum est quod dicitur murdrem, quod nullo vidente, nullo sciente clam perpetratur." See R. Howard Bloch, *Medieval French Literature and the Law* (Berkeley: University of California Press, 1977), 34–35, n. 57.

42. As David Hult explains, of the ten manuscripts that contain this passage only three provide the Lady of Landuc with a name, Laudine, and she is named only in the one line that narrates her marriage to Yvain: "Par la main d'un suen chapelain / prise a la dame de Landuc [prise a Laudine de Landuc] / l'andemain, qui fu fille au duc / Laududez, dom an note un lai" (2151–55). Hult contrasts this single possible naming with the multiple naming of her confidante, Lunete, and notes further that whether the name, obviously calqued on that of her father, Laududez or Laudunez, is original to Chrétien or is the invention of an ingenious scribe, it functions as an eponym, placing her "au système patriarcal de succession agnatique et de seigneurie mâle." The lady is thus depersonalized even by her proper name, the emphasis falling on her role and her domain. In this depersonalization she is like every other woman in a ruling position in this romance, since none of them are named. Let us note, too, that we are told here that her father is the subject of a *Lai,* yet another example of the continual textual circulation noted in the romance. See Chrétien de Troyes, *Le Chevalier au Lion* (Hult ed.), 14 and the notes and variants on 182–83.

43. The comparison to wounds made by weapons is made explicitly again at line 1373.

44. For homage and fealty, 1974–76 (Mes sire Yvains maintenant joint / ses mains, si s'est a genolz mis / et dit, come verais amis); confessional language begins on 1993 (et, se je pooie amander / la mort don j'ai vers vos mesfet, / je l'amanderoie sanz plet), and continues through the lady's absolution, 2014 (toz torz et toz mesfez vos quit); for judicial interrogation, see esp. 1997–2013, involving the question of whether in killing her husband Yvain intended or did any harm to the lady directly.

45. The intense turn to the consideration of intention and motive in both ethical philosophy and law in the period has been much discussed. See Peter Abelard, *Peter Abelard's Ethics,* ed. and trans. D. E. Luscombe, Oxford Medieval Texts (Oxford: Clarendon Press, 1971). See also Christopher Nugent Lawrence Brooke, *The Twelfth Century Renaissance* (New York: Harcourt Brace and World, 1970), 25–50; Hanning, *Individual in Twelfth-Century Romance,* 244–46; Colin Morris, *The Discovery of the Individual, 1050–1200* (New York: Harper and Row, 1973). On the importance of intent in judicial interrogations, see R. H. Bloch, *Law,* 28–41.

46. She needs a champion not simply in terms dictated by the mechanism of adventure (pour water, the storm happens, then a knight appears) but prudentially:

Arthur will conquer her land if she can't withstand him [et li rois vient a si grant ost / qu'il seisira tot, sanz desfansse] (1439–40).

47. Compare also lines 2115–16. In "The Lady Lunete: Literary Conventions of Counsel and the Criticism of Counsel in Chrétien's *Yvain* and Hartmann's *Iwein*," *Neophilologus* 85 (2001): 335–54, J. M. Sullivan notes that this scene is the only instance of public deliberation in the romance, other counsel scenes being private and individual. I think it no accident that this one is entirely manipulated, a justificatory ritual designed to legitimize what is ultimately a transgressive act.

48. Jeffrey Jerome Cohen discusses the giant as a figure of what Jacques Lacan called *extimité:* an absolute Other who is yet entirely familiar. Harpin's fantasies are ultimately no more perverse than the combination of sex and violence in Yvain and the Lady of Landuc's union. See Cohen, *Of Giants,* 93–94, 178–80, and, for Harpin in particular, 77–78.

49. We will find virtually the same list of verbs (lines 2249–53) that describe the flirtation—*acoler, baisier, parler, veoir*—in two of Marie de France's *Lais, Chaitivel* and *Guigemar,* in each case connected to sex: in *Guigemar* they describe foreplay; in *Chaitivel* they describe nothing but foreplay in a lament by a castrated knight for his inability to do anything else. For a discussion of these passages, see below.

50. The tensions surrounding aristocratic marriage in the late twelfth century have been investigated in Georges Duby, *The Knight, the Lady and the Priest: The Making of Modern Marriage in Medieval France,* trans. Barbara Bray (Chicago: University of Chicago Press, 1993), and *Love and Marriage in the Middle Ages,* trans. Jane Dunnett (Chicago: University of Chicago Press, 1994); John W. Baldwin, *The Language of Sex: Five Voices from Northern France around 1200* (Chicago: University of Chicago Press, 1994).

51. Like so much else in this romance, the opposition between an outer appearance and an inner location of truth is already shadowed in the first few lines of the prologue in an entirely different register. Calogrenant agrees to tell his shameful story only on the condition that he will have the listeners' hearts as well as their ears: "Cuers et oroilles m'aportez, / car parole est tote perdue / s'ele n'est de cuer entandue" (150–52); a few lines later this same condition is coupled with a truth claim for the narrative: "Et qui or me voldra entandre, / cuer et oroilles me doit randre, / car ne vuel pas parler de songe, / ne de fable, ne de mançonge" (169–72). The last line is a direct reference to Wace's famous passage in the *Roman de Brut* about Arthurian storytelling: "Ne tut mençunge, ne tut veir, / Ne tut folie ne tut saveir / Tant unt li cunteür cunté / E lli fableür fablé / Pur lur cuntes enbeleter, / Que tut unt fait fable sembler" (9793–98).

52. In his presidential address to the Medieval Academy of America, Thomas Bisson argued that during the Middle Ages lordship was experienced for the most part in the form of direct, personal domination. See Thomas Bisson, "Medieval Lordship," *Speculum* 70 (1995): 743–59.

53. Perceval's adventures in the town Beaurepaire sketch the same geopolitics. The land around the town is waste—the result, if only by implication, of protracted siege warfare—and the town itself is devoid of production. The maiden who rules has been being propositioned by Clamadeu, a powerful local lord. Perceval fights Clamadeu's seneschal and beats him in single combat. The next day Clamadeu himself arrives with large forces, but their plans for victory by isolating the town are defeated when merchants on a barge arrive at the riverside entrance to the town and provision it with enough food and drink to withstand a siege. In freeing the town from what is essentially private war, Perceval acts as an agent of Arthur, to whom he sends the defeated Clamadeu and his seneschal. Thus the figure of Arthur—even though distant—is the ultimate guarantor of peace and justice in what is more and more figured as his realm. Chrétien de Troyes, *Complete Romances,* 363–72.

54. Jean Subrenat points to the resemblance between the scheme of the Pasme Avanture and the tribute that King Mark of Cornwall was forced to pay to Ireland. See Jean Subrenat, "Pourquoi Yvain et son lion ont-ils affronté les fils de Netun?" in Dufournet, *Le Chevalier au Lion,* 183. *Le Chevalier au Lion* is filled with such reminiscences of Tristan. Matilda Bruckner signals the parallel between Tristan's and Yvain's madness; David Hult similarly finds Tristan "délicatement tissé à travers [les] éléments du roman." See Matilda Tomaryn Bruckner, *Shaping Romance: Interpretation, Truth, and Closure in Twelfth-Century French Fictions,* Middle Ages Series (Philadelphia: University of Pennsylvania Press, 1993), 92, and Chrétien de Troyes, *Le Chevalier au Lion* (Hult ed.), 16.

55. Moved by the lamentations and believing wrongly that Yvain has died of despair, the lion tries to kill himself. These variations on Pyramus and Thisbe present the problem of desire and the difficulty of judging appearances yet once more, this time, of course, as farce.

56. Ross G. Arthur, "The Judicium Dei in the Yvain of Chrétien de Troyes," *Romance Notes* 28, no. 1 (1987): 3–4. See also R. H. Bloch, *Law,* 13–62, esp. 18–24.

57. When Lunete counsels the Lady of Landuc to go in search of the Knight with the Lion he is referred to simply as the knight who beat the seneschal and who killed the giant. That is, the Lady of Landuc only knows what she has seen and what exactly she had been told.

58. The text repeats verbs of seeing no fewer than fourteen times in the eighty-five lines that describe the contest (3164–3249), moving from third-person indicative to the imperative in direct discourse, and ends in verbs of saying that directly represent the spectators' praise for what they point out to each other.

59. The process by which Yvain becomes a fantasy object is laid bare by the scene of enamorment in which Yvain, possessed of the ring of invisibility, watches the Lady of Landuc reading her Psalter in intense grief for her husband. Her being visible to him alone as he desires her has the structure of a screen memory in which being watched

substitutes for watching: Yvain's desire for the Lady of Landuc is a displaced wish to be the object of her desire.

60. The whole scene continuously underlines the fact that the townspeople are both men and women; expressions like *tuit et tote, chascun et chascune, d'ome ne de fame, des chevaliers et de la dame*—abound all the way through the episode.

61. Yvain gives the *iudicium dei* its classic formulation as he takes up Lunete's cause: "Et qui le voir dire an voldroit / Dex se retint de vers le droit, / et Dex et droiz a un s'an tienent" (4437–39).

62. This may actually be the third judicial combat. The introduction of the episode employs a legal metaphor that assimilates the death of the Lord of la Noire Espine to a judicial combat: "But meanwhile it happened that the Lord of la Noire Espine had a suit with Death" [Mes dedanz ce fu avenu / que a la mort ot plet tenu / li sires de la Noire Espine] (4697–99). Although the episode is introduced as a digression while Yvain and the lion are being cured of wounds suffered in their combat for Lunete, it in many ways recapitulates the most significant thematic material of the text as a whole.

63. There are many instances of her identification as the one in the wrong. Typical is this passage: "La dameisele qui tort a, / vers sa seror, trop desapert, / veant toz, l'a a cort offert / que par lui desresnier voldroit / la querele ou ele n'a droit" (5878–82). The elder sister's rush to Arthur's court to secure the best knight before her younger sister can get there is an obvious reminiscence of Yvain's initial rush to the magic spring ahead of the court.

64. See especially lines 6335–49, where Gawain says that he deserves to lose both because of Yvain's prowess and because he knows he is on the wrong side. Yvain forcibly contradicts him, saying that in the battle it is rather he who is "oltrez et recreanz sanz faille." The argument ends in magnificent ineffectuality: "—mes ge.—Mes ge, fet cil et cil" (6351).

65. For a discussion of this episode, see Armstrong, "Questions of Inheritance," 184.

66. The extremely thorough article on the conclusion of *Yvain* by Fredric L. Cheyette and Howell Chickering, "Love, Anger, and Peace: Social Practice and Poetic Play in the Ending of *Yvain*," *Speculum* 80 (2005): 75–117, appeared just as this book was being readied for the press. Their method of reading the ending in the context of documentary evidence for procedures of conflict resolution among twelfth-century elites accords very nicely with my reading here. Their final contention that Chrétien's contemporary readers would not have "found tension in the final scene between the characters' presumed states of mind and the rapid happy ending" (77) seems to me extremely unlikely in view of Chrétien's very complex play with the vocabulary and gestures of conflict resolution that the authors of the article themselves bring forward. That the thematic inconclusivity is nevertheless aesthetically satisfying, as they aver, is beyond question. Aesthetic closure is, however, a substitute for the thematic closure that remains permanently deferred.

67. The language of Yvain's final return to the spring is directly reminiscent of Yvain's first departure alone, ahead of the court: "et panse qu'il se partiroit / toz seus de cort, et si iroit / a sa fontainne guerroier" (6507–9).

68. Cf. Hanning, *Individual in Twelfth-Century Romance,* 121. Lunete's revelation of the Knight with the Lion's identity as lord and husband rather than as lover, "c'est mes sire Yvains, vostre epos" (6748), is a structural analogue to the power relations created by Arthur to solve the inheritance of La Noire Espine. In each case, an individual, subjective state is replaced by a social reconciliation among contending people.

69. All quotations are from Marie de France, *Les Lais de Marie de France,* ed. Jean Rychner, Les classiques français du Moyen Âge (Paris: Champion, 1983), and cited by line number parenthetically in the text; translations are from *The Lais of Marie de France,* trans. Robert. W. Hanning and Joan M. Ferrante (Grand Rapids, MI: Baker Books, 1995). In some very few cases I have silently altered their translation.

70. The change in the organization of the European medieval aristocratic family from a loose amalgam of relationships to a patriarchal lineage, the spread downward of this practice from the royal family of the Carolingian era to the lesser nobility of the late twelfth century, and the geographic dispersion of this mode of thinking about kinship have been much studied since the foundational work of Karl Schmid, "Zur Problematik von Familie, Sippe und Geschlecht; Haus und Dynastie beim mittelalterlichen Adel," *Zeitschrift für die Geschichte des Oberrheins* 105 (1957): 1–62 ; for French- and Provençal-speaking areas, several papers of Georges Duby, notably "Structure de parenté et noblesse, France du Nord, XIᵉ–XIIᵉ siècles" and "Remarques sur la littérature généalogique en France aux XIᵉ et XIIᵉ siècles," both originally from 1967, and his "Lignages, noblesse et chevalerie au XIIᵉ siècle dans la région maconnaise: une révision," from 1973, all reprinted in Duby, *Hommes et structures du Moyen-Âge* and available in English in Duby, *Chivalrous Society,* have prompted much work with implications for fiction. See especially Gabrielle M. Spiegel, "Genealogy: Form and Function in Medieval Historical Narrative," *History and Theory* 22 (1983): 43–53, reprinted in Gabrielle M. Spiegel, *The Past as Text: The Theory and Practice of Medieval Historiography* (Baltimore: Johns Hopkins University Press, 1997), 99–110; and R. Howard Bloch, *Etymologies and Genealogies: A Literary Anthropology of the French Middle Ages* (Chicago: University of Chicago Press, 1983). See also Thomas Bisson, "Nobility and Family in Medieval France: A Review Essay," *French Historical Studies* 16 (1990): 597–613.

71. Jean Flori, "Aristocratie et valeurs 'chevaleresques' dans la seconde moitié du XIIᵉ siècle: L'exemple des Lais de Marie de France," *Le Moyen Age: Revue d'Histoire et de Philologie* 96 (1990): 43–44.

72. Flori's remarks on *Yonec* (462–66), the four-line narration of the boy's growing up and his dubbing, underline both Marie's use of normative naming and the oddness of her compressed narration. "Relation laconique! Aucune description d'une quelconque cérémonie. Aucune mention de la personnalité des adoubeurs. Pas de fête

signalée. Cette sobriété contraste avec les descriptions si amples, si redondantes, que l'on trouve fréquemment dans les œuvres de la seconde moitié et plus encore de la fin du siècle." Ibid., 50.

73. See also Leicester, "Voice of the Hind," 132–39.

74. This instance of punning (*adnominatio* for the rhetoricians) is signaled by Robert Hanning as the structural core of *Guigemar*. See Robert W. Hanning, "'I Shal Finde It in a Maner Glose': Versions of Textual Harassment in Medieval Literature," in *Medieval Texts and Contemporary Readers,* ed. Laurie A. Finke and Martin B. Shichtman (Ithaca: Cornell University Press, 1987), 35 and n. 15.

75. Many have wanted to see this silence as an expression of joy. R. Howard Bloch, for example, explains these lines: "An excess that cannot be said, the presence of the body is excluded from the text." See R. Howard Bloch, "New Philology and Old French," *Speculum* 65 (1990):38–58, esp. 54. Robert Hanning connects the use of *surplus* in this passage to a variety of other twelfth-century instances of erotic pleasure. See Hanning, "'I Shal Finde It,'" 35 and n. 16.

76. In his introduction to the *Lais,* Rychner remarks on Marie's general underplaying or even outright suppression of the marvelous and otherworldly motifs of the Celtic materials with which she works and her inclusion of material from what he calls "courtly experience." All of Rychner's illustrations are of a specifically political or legal nature, e.g., the trial scene in Lanval. See Marie de France, *Les Lais de Marie de France,* xvii–xviii. Chrétien too invariably underplays or disenchants magical elements. Thus the associations of the Lady of Landuc with the fountain do not finally make her a fée; and Lunete's ring of invisibility, and the ring that the lady gives to Yvain on his departure, a ring that she says will serve him as "escuz et haubers" (2612), bring us back to the ordinary world. In *Le Chevalier de la Charette,* Lancelot's magic ring, able to break the spells of all enchantments, is useless because he is imprisoned by normal means in an ordinary prison, "mes il voit bien a son apel / et a la pierre de l'anel / qui'l n'i a point d'anchantemant, / et set trestot certainnemant / qu'il sont anclos et anserré" (2351–55). I quote from Chrétien de Troyes, *Le Chevalier de la Charette,* ed. Mario Roques, Les classiques français du Moyen Age (Paris: Champion, 1970). For a discussion of disenchanted magic, see among others Baumgartner, *Chrétien de Troyes,* 70. In the introduction to his edition of *Le Chevalier de la Charrette,* Charles Mela puts the psychological identity between the Other World and ordinary life very precisely: "Lancelot, mystérieux et masqué, dépossédé de lui-même et de son nom, s'engage sur les chemins de ce monde qui n'est Autre que faute d'être reconnu le même, à moins qu'il ne faille plutôt penser que le même n'existe jamais que comme Autre, et les aventures surgissent du dehors comme la fantasmagorie de ce qu'il emporte au plus intime de soi." See Chrétien de Troyes, *Le Chevalier de la Charette,* ed. and trans. Charles Mela, Lettres gothiques (Paris: Le Livre de Poche, 1992), 18. For both Marie and Chrétien, magic serves in the end always to guarantee the normality of the disenchanted world.

77. The antithesis between having pleasure and talking about it is ubiquitous in the lyric tradition: that is, it is ubiquitous in the literary form that represents pleasure by talking about it. Rather than multiply examples, I mention only the end of Guillaume IX's "Ab la dolchor del temps novel": "Qu'eu sai de paraulas com van / Ab u beu sermon que s'espel, / Que tal se van d'amor gaban, / Nos n'avem la pessa e.l coutel." Guillaume IX, *Les chansons de Guillaume IX,* ed. Alfred Jeanroy, Les classiques français du Moyen Âge (Paris: Champion, 1967), 27–30.

78. The prologues have been much discussed. Still essential is Leo Spitzer, "The Prologue of the Lais of Marie de France and Medieval Poetics," *Modern Philology* 41 (1943–44): 96–102. See, among others, Jean-Claude Delclos, "Encore le prologue des lais de Marie de France," *Le Moyen Âge* 90 (1984): 223–32; M. J. Donovan, "Priscian and the Obscurity of the Ancients," *Speculum* 36 (1961): 75–80; Alfred Foulet and Karl D. Uitti, "The Prologue to the Lais of Marie de France: A Reconsideration," *Romance Philology* 35 (1981): 242–49; Eva Rosenn, "The Sexual and Textual Politics of Marie's Poetics," in *In Quest of Marie de France, a Twelfth-Century Poet,* ed. Chantal A. Maréchal (Lewiston, NY: Mellen, 1992); Pavel Skarup, "Les prologues qui précèdent le Lai de Guigemar," *Revue Romane* 16 (1981): 166–75.

CHAPTER FOUR.   From Romance to Epic

1. William of Malmesbury, *Gesta regum* 1.prol.4.

2. Geoffrey of Monmouth, *Historia regum* 1. See also Wace, *Le Roman de Rou,* 2.1–10.

3. On this point, see Damian-Grint, *New Historians,* 85–142; on Gaimar, 98–99.

4. Chrétien de Troyes, *Cligés,* ed. Alexandre Micha, Les classiques français du Moyen Âge (Paris: Champion, 1970). I cite by line number. Translations are my own.

5. For historical prologues and the pedagogical function of history, see Bernard Guenée, *Histoire et culture historique* and *Politique et histoire au Moyen Âge: Recueil d'articles sur l'histoire politique et l'historiographie médiévale (1956–1981),* Publications de la Sorbonne, Série Réimpressions 2 (Paris: Publications de la Sorbonne, 1981); Benoît Lacroix, *L'historien au Moyen Âge,* Conférence Albert-le-Grand for 1966 (Paris: Librairie J. Vrin, 1971); Marie Schulz, *Die Lehre von der historischen Methode bei den Geschichtschreibern des Mittelalters (VI.–XIII. Jahrhundert)* (Berlin: W. Rotschild, 1909).

6. Marie's complex relation to historiographical writing, particularly her cutting loose her *Lais* from the historical framework established by Geoffrey of Monmouth, is discussed at length by Linda Georgianna in the book she coauthored with Katherine O'Brien O'Keeffe, *The Literary Cultures of Early England* (Oxford: Oxford University Press, forthcoming). I am extremely grateful to the authors for letting me consult this work in draft.

7. The openings of the *Roman de Troie,* the *Roman de Thebes,* and Wace's *Brut* all make a similar claim by similar means. These have been studied extensively by Peter Damian-Grint. See Peter Damian-Grint, *New Historians* and "Translation as *Enarratio* and Hermeneutic Theory in Twelfth-Century Vernacular Learned Literature," *Neophilologus* 83 (1999): 349–67.

8. They also name the community. See Ian Short, "Gaimar's Epilogue and Geoffrey of Monmouth's *Liber vetustissimus,*" *Speculum* 69 (1994): 323–43.

9. See the prologue to the *Roman de Troie,* lines 1–144. There is a convenient edition of generous extracts, Benoît de Sainte-Maure, *Le roman de Troie,* ed. and trans. Emmanuèle Baumgartner and Françoise Vielliard, Lettres gothiques (Paris: Livre de Poche, 1998).

10. Chrétien de Troyes, *Cligés,* 25–42. For the topos, see Ernst Robert Curtius, *European Literature and the Latin Middle Ages,* Bollingen Series 36 (New York: Pantheon Books, 1953), 29–30, 383–85. Kellie Robertson notes that in making the Britons direct descendants of the Trojans, Geoffrey of Monmouth manages to delegitimize Roman authority, eliminating it entirely from the *translatio imperii;* this leap is matched by Geoffrey's claim that his work translates Walter of Oxford's British book—a book, that is to say, written in a vernacular more prestigious and more ancient than Latin, since it derives directly from its Trojan ancestor, "a kind of crooked Greek." In thus reconfiguring the *translatio imperii et studii,* Robertson argues, Geoffrey "resists the tacit Anglo-Latin alliance that was Bede's legacy and that had governed the writing of history on the island since the ninth century." See Robertson, "Geoffrey of Monmouth," esp. 42–43.

11. Geoffrey of Monmouth, *Historia regum,* 147. Damian-Grint, *New Historians,* discusses some vernacular passages of authority as similarly authorizing gestures.

12. Godefroi names himself at line 7102; he names Chrétien at 7105 and 7107.

13. BN ffr 1450, for example, concatenates the *Roman de Troie, Eneas,* Wace's *Brut,* and the *Dolopathos* (The Romance of the Seven Sages). All of the existing manuscripts of Gaimar's *Estoire des Engleis* place it after Wace's *Brut,* thus forming a continuous history of insular sovereignty, and in two instances Gaimar's history is followed by Jordan Fantosme's chronicle, which brings the narrative up to date. For descriptions of the manuscripts, see Wace, *Roman de Brut,* xxvii–xxix, and Jordan Fantosme, *Jordan Fantosme's Chronicle,* ed. R. C. Johnston (Oxford: Clarendon Press, 1981), xliv–li. For the general significance of these kinds of concatenations, see the important essay "The Influence of the Concepts of *Ordinatio* and *Compilatio* on the Development of the Book," in Malcolm B. Parkes, *Scribes, Scripts and Readers: Studies in the Communication, Presentation and Dissemination of Medieval Texts* (London: Hambledon Press, 1991), 35–71.

14. See David F. Hult, "Author/Narrator/Speaker: The Voice of Authority in Chrétien's Charrete," in *Discourses of Authority in Medieval and Renaissance Literature,* ed. Kevin Brownlee and Walter Stephens (Hanover, NH: University Presses of New England, 1989), 267 n. 3. The relations of romance writing to Wace's silence regarding this

period of peace have been suggestively explored by Ad Putter, "Finding Time for Romance: Mediaeval Arthurian Literary History," *Medium Aevum* 63 (1994): 1–16, who at 5–6 also discusses the insertion into BN 1450.

15. Gerald A. Bond, *The Loving Subject: Desire, Eloquence and Power in Romanesque France* (Philadelphia: University of Pennsylvania Press, 1995), from a perspective very different from mine, similarly connects the interest in "an elite, secular, and private self" with "the hybrid subculture which had developed from the increased employment of clerics" in secular households.

16. Chrétien de Troyes, *Erec et Enide,* ed. Mario Roques, Les classiques français du Moyen Âge (Paris: Champion, 1973).

17. For the precise meaning of *estoire,* see Damian-Grint, *"Estoire* as Word."

18. Douglas Kelly, *The Art of Medieval French Romance* (Madison: University of Wisconsin Press, 1992), 125–29.

19. B. N. ffr. 124, fol. 1r, quoted in Gabrielle M. Spiegel, *Romancing the Past* (Berkeley: University of California Press, 1993), 55.

20. Even the most significant contemporary exception to the assumption that epic is the earlier form, Sarah Kay's brilliant book, *The Chansons de Geste in the Age of Romance,* by its very title signifies the romance as proper to its age, the chanson de geste becoming thereby a chronological interloper.

21. Ernst Robert Curtius, "Über die Altfranzösische Epik," *Zeitschrift für Romanische Philologie* 64 (1944): 233–320.

22. Joseph Bédier, *Les légendes épiques: Recherches sur la formation des chansons de geste,* 3rd. ed., rev. and corrected (Paris: Champion, 1926), was written between 1908 and 1913. In arguing for the pilgrimage routes around the time of the First Crusade as the moment of origin of the chansons de geste, Bédier not only rescues the chansons from their dependence on German sources but also frees them from any connection with Provençal language and culture. Even if they were composed on southern soil, Bédier imagines them to be the product of French jongleurs following in the company of northern French pilgrims along the route to St. James of Campostella. The epics become thus purely French. See esp. 1:434–36. On the colonial inflected history of the symbol of the Hexagon as the proper border of the French nation and the elevation of "La France profonde" as the truth of its national character, see Eugen Weber, "L'hexagone," in *Les lieux de mémoire,* ed. Pierre Nora et al. (Paris: Gallimard, 1986), 2.2:96–116.

23. For a good summary of the dispute over the origin of the chanson de geste, see Michel Zink, "Commentary," in *Girart de Roussillon, ou, l'épopée de Bourgogne,* ed. Roger-Henri Guerrand et al. (Paris: Philippe Lebaud, 1990), 13–22.

24. For the Parry-Lord thesis of oral formulaic performance/composition very few medievalists have read beyond Lord's wonderful report of Parry's conclusions in Albert Bates Lord, *The Singer of Tales* (Cambridge, MA: Harvard University Press, 1960), but see also Milman Parry and Adam Parry, *The Making of Homeric Verse: The Collected*

Papers of Milman Parry (New York: Oxford University Press, 1987); for a persuasive and nuanced application to medieval epic literature, see John Miles Foley, *The Theory of Oral Composition: History and Methodology* (Bloomington: Indiana University Press, 1988), and *Traditional Oral Epic: The Odyssey, Beowulf, and the Serbo-Croatian Return Song* (Berkeley: University of California Press, 1990); for the chanson de geste in particular, see Joseph J. Duggan, *The Song of Roland; Formulaic Style and Poetic Craft* (Berkeley: University of California Press, 1973) and *Oral Literature: Seven Essays* (New York: Barnes and Noble Books, 1975). Eric Havelock's most radical presentation of the opposition between the oral and literate mentality is *Preface to Plato* (Cambridge, MA: Harvard University Press, 1963), but see as well *The Literate Revolution in Greece and Its Cultural Consequences* (Princeton: Princeton University Press, 1982). Although very late in his career Lord began to consider the possibility of transitional literacy, the oral-literate divide remains basically unbridgeable even in Lord's last works. See Albert Bates Lord, *Epic Singers and Oral Tradition* (Ithaca: Cornell University Press, 1991); Albert Bates Lord and Mary Louise Lord, *The Singer Resumes the Tale* (Ithaca: Cornell University Press, 1995). While the Parry-Lord thesis has defined the field of Old French epic studies, some have still not adopted it. See, for example, William Calin, "L'épopée dite vivante: Réflexions sur le prétendu caractère oral des chansons de geste," *Olifant* 8 (1981): 227–37, and "Littérature médiévale et hypothèse orale: Une divergence de méthode et de philosophie," *Olifant* 8 (1981): 256–85.

25. See Meyer Schapiro's brilliant 1968 essay "The Still Life as a Personal Object: A Note on Heidegger and Van Gogh," in *Theory and Philosophy of Art: Style, Artist, and Society* (New York: Braziller, 1994), 135–42.

26. For the distinction, see György Lukács, *Die Theorie des Romans: Ein geschichts-philosophischer Versuch über die Formen der grossen Epik,* 2nd ed. (Neuwied am Rhein: Luchterhand, 1963), especially the first two chapters. On the romantic quest for the real medieval epic, see Andrew Taylor, "Was There a Song of Roland?" *Speculum* 76 (2001): 28–65. R. Howard Bloch is fond of quoting Adorno to the effect that each culture gets one and only one true epic, *Roland* being the medieval equivalent to the *Iliad*; I have never been able to find the source for the quote, I doubt that it is from Adorno, but the sentiment is a commonplace of romantic criticism.

27. Erich Köhler, "Quelques observations d'ordre historico-sociologique sur les rapports entre la chanson de geste et le roman courtois," in *Chanson de Geste und höfischer Roman: Heidelberger Kolloquium 30 Januar 1961,* ed. Hans Robert Jauss (Heidelberg: Carl Winter Universitätsverlag, 1963). See also Köhler, *Ideal und Wirklichkeit,* which connects the genesis of romance to the particular sociological situation of the lesser nobility in the Angevin realm. Among the most fruitful applications of Köhler's thesis to English material is Susan Crane, *Insular Romance: Politics, Faith, and Culture in Anglo-Norman and Middle English Literature* (Berkeley: University of California Press, 1986).

28. The bibliography for the emergence of the new administrative state in the late twelfth century is vast. Most important for me have been Baldwin, *Government of Philip Augustus*; Clanchy, *From Memory to Written Record* and *England and Its Rulers*; Bartlett, *England,* esp. chap. 3; Judith A. Green, *The Aristocracy of Norman England* (Cambridge: Cambridge University Press, 1997), and *The Government of England under Henry I* (Cambridge: Cambridge University Press, 1989); Mortimer, *Angevin England,* esp. pt. 1.

29. Sarah Kay, *Chansons de Geste,* also starts from the proposition that romance and epic have a dialectical relation to each other. While both her method of investigation, surveying a very large number of epics and indicating places in romances that treat similar material, and her emphases differ from mine, our final conclusions are in many ways convergent.

30. See Robert F. Berkhofer, *Day of Reckoning: Power and Accountability in Medieval France* (Philadelphia: University of Pennsylvania Press, 2004), and Turner, *Men Raised from the Dust.*

31. Joseph Duggan's very valuable lexical study of the Oxford *Roland* assumes the absolute irreconcilability of oral and literate composition so that, for Duggan, a high incidence of formulaic expression in a text demonstrates conclusively that the text was composed orally in performance. See Duggan, *Song of Roland.* R. Howard Bloch is similarly able to refer to the "oral formulaic composition" of the *Chanson de Roland* as the reason why the poem shows "no attempt to look behind appearances to find a rival reality" since formulas are "a communal form of language that implies that the world is what it seems to be." R. Howard Bloch, *The Anonymous Marie de France* (Chicago: University of Chicago Press, 2003), 22. In discussions of form, the assumption of a strict opposition between epic and romance composition has obscured not only the great variety of matter but also the variety of metrical procedures used by vernacular poets and has drawn a hard line where there is often a very fluid border. The Alexander Romances, for example, use twelve-syllable lines and assonating laisses; Wace experimented with a variety of metrical forms, some characteristic of epic, others, such as octosyllabic couplets, that have long been regarded as signifying romance; and Jordan Fantosme wrote a verse chronicle in epic measures while claiming truth-telling intentions using all the modern, "postepic" procedures.

32. Parry's pre–World War II fieldwork in Bosnia was hampered by the difficulties of transcription experienced by the very able shorthand clerks and court reporters hired to take down performances: the continuous performances of the poets taxed the abilities of the secretaries; if the poets slowed down to the secretaries' pace, they stumbled in their performances. Critical discussions among the first generation of scholars who tried to apply oral formulaic theory to what used to be called "primary epic" tend to be embarrassing in their attempt to negotiate the difference between the oral source and the fixed, written text that we read in the manuscript. See, for one example

among many, Cedric Hubbell Whitman, *Homer and the Heroic Tradition* (Cambridge, MA: Harvard University Press, 1958).

33. For the African material, see Jeff Opland, "The Early Career of D. L. P. Yali-Manisi, Thembu Imbongi," *Research in African Literatures* 33 (2002): 1–26, and "Imbongi Nezibongo: The Xhosa Tribal Poet and the Contemporary Poetic Tradition," *PMLA* 90 (1975): 185–208; Richard Priebe and Jeff Opland, "Xhosa Tribal Poetry," *PMLA* 91 (1976): 119–20. For work on medieval literacy that has significantly widened the concept of literacy and complicated the sense of an oral-literate divide, see Clanchy, *From Memory to Written Record*; Brian Stock, *After Augustine: The Meditative Reader and the Text* (Philadelphia: University of Pennsylvania Press, 2001), *Implications of Literacy,* and *Listening for the Text: On the Uses of the Past* (Baltimore: Johns Hopkins University Press, 1990); Franz H. Bäuml, "Varieties and Consequences of Medieval Literacy and Illiteracy," *Speculum* 55 (1980): 237–65, Rosamond McKitterick, *Books, Scribes, and Learning in the Frankish Kingdoms, 6th–9th Centuries* (Aldershot: Variorum, 1994), *Carolingian Culture: Emulation and Innovation* (New York: Cambridge University Press, 1994) *The Carolingians and the Written Word* (New York: Cambridge University Press, 1989), and *The Uses of Literacy in Early Medieval Europe* (New York: Cambridge University Press, 1990); Katherine O'Brien O'Keeffe, *Visible Song: Transitional Literacy in Old English Verse* (Cambridge: Cambridge University Press, 1990). From his earliest work, Walter Ong has insisted on the very slow and very uneven movement from orality to literacy as a dominant cultural fact, and his concept of "oral residue" severely complicates any attempt to attribute a thoroughly transformed consciousness to literacy. See Walter J. Ong, *Interfaces of the Word: Studies in the Evolution of Consciousness and Culture* (Ithaca: Cornell University Press, 1977), "Oral Residue in Tudor Prose Style," *PMLA* 80 (1965): 145–54, *Orality and Literacy: The Technologizing of the Word* (London: Methuen, 1982), and *Ramus: Method, and the Decay of Dialogue. From the Art of Discourse to the Art of Reason* (Cambridge, MA: Harvard University Press, 1958).

34. At a lecture demonstration by David Manisi and Jeff Opland, Columbia University, February 18, 1988, I had the opportunity to ask Manisi to describe the difference that he experienced between oral performance and writing. He answered, "I perform in joy but write in pain," and went on to describe his worrying over the proper word when he wrote and his constant revision—a process familiar to all writers—and the degree of self-consciousness and self-doubt that the process of writing always made him feel. In contrast, his oral compositions, he said, just happened. Nevertheless, the final products of each process were indistinguishable from each other on the page. For a discussion of Manisi's occasional amalgamation of European stanzaic forms with Xhosa oral diction, see Opland, "Early Career," 13.

35. Opland discusses and translates Manisi's poem about Nelson Mandela, written on his return from an ANC meeting in 1954 at which Mandela made a brief appearance. Opland says this is the earliest recorded poem about Mandela. Ibid., 20.

36. Discussions of medieval ideas of authorship and the emergence of vernacular literacy have been hampered by conceiving of literature strictly as what used to be called "belles lettres" and isolating it from nonliterary uses of literacy. This practice is only now coming under scrutiny. For some very suggestive recent work that explores ways of ending this isolation, see the papers gathered in Michel Zimmermann, *Auctor et auctoritas: Invention et conformisme dans l'écriture médiévale: Actes du colloque tenu à l'Université de Versailles-Saint-Quentin-en-Yvelines, 14–16 juin 1999,* Mémoires et documents de l'Ecole des chartes, 59 (Paris: École des chartes, 2001). See also Jocelyn Wogan-Browne, *Saints' Lives and Women's Literary Culture: Virginity and Its Authorizations, c. 1150–1300* (Oxford: Oxford University Press, 2001).

37. The story appears in one version of the *Chronicle of Walter of Guisborough,* quoted in Clanchy, *From Memory to Written Record,* 36.

38. The date of composition of *Raoul de Cambrai* is very difficult to determine precisely. The consensus opinion places it sometime during the reign of Philip Augustus (1180–1223), and since the character of Raoul is widely referred to around the turn of the thirteenth century, the text as we have it was probably already in circulation before 1200. See *Raoul de Cambrai,* ed. Sarah Kay (Oxford: Oxford University Press, 1992), lxxii–lxxiii. All quotations are from this edition and will be identified by line numbers parenthetically in the text. Translations are my own, although I have often been helped by Kay's excellent translations.

39. William C. Calin, *The Old French Epic of Revolt: Raoul de Cambrai, Renaud de Montauban, Gormond et Isembard* (Geneva: Librairie Droz, 1962).

40. See, for example, William Calin, "Un univers en decomposition: Raoul de Cambrai," *Olifant* 1 (1974): 3–9.

41. Alexandre Leupin, "Raoul de Cambrai: The Illegitimacy of Writing," in *The New Medievalism,* ed. Kevin Brownlee, Marina S. Brownlee, and Stephen Nichols (Baltimore: Johns Hopkins University Press, 1991), 148–49. The 1980s saw a flurry of very interesting critical writing on *Raoul de Cambrai.* See especially Françoise Denis, *Barons et chevaliers dans Raoul de Cambrai: Autopsie d'un phénomène de glissement* (New York: Peter Lang, 1989); Thelma S. Fenster, "The Son's Mother: Aalais and Marsent in Raoul de Cambrai," *Olifant* 12 (1987): 77–93; Sarah Kay, "Raoul de Cambrai or Raoul Sans Terre?" *Neuphilologische Mitteilungen* 84 (1983): 311–17; Ronald G. Koss, "Raoul de Cambrai and Inheritance Disputes in Feudal Society," *Olifant* 13 (1988): 97–110.

42. E.g., "ce conte li escris" (95); "tex en est la chançons" (1862).

43. M. M. Bakhtin, "Epic and Novel," in *The Dialogic Imagination: Four Essays,* ed. Michael Holquist, trans. Caryl Emerson and Michael Holquist (Austin: University of Texas Press, 1981), 14–18.

44. Kay, "Raoul de Cambrai," following Pauline Matarasso, *Recherches historiques et littéraires sur Raoul de Cambrai* (Paris: Nizet, 1962), has discussed the relations between the control of Cambrai and of the Cambrésis as it is represented in the poem. The

intriguing resemblance between the secular conflicts in the poem and the continuous struggle, which I discussed in my first chapter, between the bishops of Cambrai and the secular lords of both Cambrai and the Cambrésis that eventuated in the complete control of the whole territory by the urban prince-bishop has gone unnoticed in the critical literature. One of the burdens of *Raoul de Cambrai* is the thorough secularization of territorial power: the ecclesiastical realm exists only as an alternative society—a world of outsiders, monks and nuns who enter the poem only as pure victims of the struggle for power among secular lords—and never as landholders, abbots and bishops who are themselves great princes of the realm.

45. Denis, *Barons et chevaliers,* 162–74, 192, 254.

46. For homage as a social ritual, see Jacques Le Goff, "The Symbolic Ritual of Vassalage," in *Time, Work, and Culture in the Middle Ages,* trans. Arthur Goldhammer (Chicago: University of Chicago Press, 1980), 237–87.

47. In addition to Baldwin, *Government of Philip Augustus,* see Georges Duby, *Le dimanche de Bouvines: 27 Juillet 1214,* Trente journées qui ont fait la France 5 (Paris: Gallimard, 1973). For the political importance of the Vermandois marriage settlement to Philip Augustus, see Spiegel, *Romancing the Past,* 11–54.

48. The enamorment begins at 5380; the narrative primarily takes up the point of view of Beatrix, who gazes desirously at Bernier and fantasizes about him in lines such as "anyone who could hold him totally naked under the sheet would find him worth more than anything alive" [qi le tenroit tot nu soz sa cortine, / miex li valroit qe nule rien qi vive] (5411–12).

49. Matarasso, *Recherches historiques,* 90, 125.

50. *Raoul de Cambrai,* lxvi.

51. Ibid.

52. For a powerful discussion of the theoretical contradictions within the idea of the sovereign, see Giorgio Agamben, *Homo Sacer: Sovereign Power and Bare Life,* trans. Daniel Heller-Roazen (Stanford: Stanford University Press, 1998); Cf. Chaou, *L'idéologie Plantagenêt,* 144, who notes this contradiction with regard to portrayals of Arthur as sometimes suzerain and sometimes a companion of the Round Table: "On sent bien ici toutes les implications possibles d'un système de représentation qui privilégie tantôt le roi, tantôt la société chevaleresque comme centre du pouvoir: il n'est pas admissible, du point de vue féodal laïc, qu'un roi demeure étranger à la société chevaleresque, et qu'il n'y occupe pas la première place; mais il n'est pas non plus possible de considérer que son seul office de roi suffise à faire entrer de plain-pied dans l'ordre chevaleresque, que mépris des exigences morales qui définissent l'idéal chevaleresque. La fonction royale, qui marque son grand retour sur le devant de la scène, est donc au centre d'une intense réflexion après une longe éclipse depuis les Carolingiens." Whether royalty was ever at a conceptual eclipse is surely debatable, but Chaou's basic point, that the function of royalty is at the center of intense theoretical activity, is surely correct for this period.

53. For one example among many, see John of Salisbury, *Policraticus* 5.2 for the exposition of the organic metaphors and 6.24 for his reading of the famous parable of the body's head, members, and stomach. John of Salisbury, *Policraticus: Of the Frivolities of Courtiers and the Footprints of Philosophers,* ed. Cary J. Nederman (Cambridge: Cambridge University Press, 1990).

54. This is a persistent debate whose terms are constantly subject to redefinition. What J. C. Holt calls "one of the most celebrated absolutist tags from the Institutes of Justinian"—*quod principi placuit, legis habet vigorem*—is used by English jurists of the twelfth century to justify everything from the supreme power of the king to the force of unwritten common law. James Clarke Holt, *Magna Carta,* 2nd ed. (New York: Cambridge University Press, 1992), 86–89. It reappears in the report of the deposition of Richard II in 1399, where it is cited as one of Richard's more tyrannical claims: "Item: the same king did not wish to preserve or protect the just laws and customs of his realm but according to the judgment of his will he did whatever occurred to his desire, and whenever the laws of his realm were explained and declared to him by judges and others of his council, so that according to those laws he might show justice to his petitioners, he said expressly, with an austere and impudent expression, that his laws were in his mouth, and sometimes in his heart, and that he alone could change or establish the laws of his realm. And seduced by this opinion he did not permit many of his lieges to do justice, but rather compelled them to cease from the prosecution of common law." [ITEM, idem Rex nolens justas Leges et Consuetudines Regni sui servare seu protegere, set secundum sue arbitrium Voluntatis facere quicquid desideriis ejus occurrerit, quandoque et frequentius quando sibi expositi et declarati fuerant Leges Regni sui per Justicios et alios de Consilio suo et secundum Leges illas petentibus justiciam exhiberet; dixit expresse, vultu austero et protervo, quod Leges sue erant in ore suo, et aliquotiens in pectore suo: Et quod ipse solus posset mutare et condere Leges Regni sui. Et opinione illa seductus, quam pluribus de ligeis suis Justiciam fieri non permisit, set per minas et terrores quamplures a prosecutione communis Justicie cessare coegit.] Great Britain, Parliament, Richard Blyke, and John Strachey, *Rotuli parliamentorum; ut et petitiones, et placita in parliamento* (London, 1767), 3:419, sec. 33. My translation.

55. The literature on sacral and law-centered kingship is vast. See Kantorowicz, *King's Two Bodies.* For bibliography, see Stein, "Signs and Things." Sovereign governance, conceptualized as concern with the welfare of the realm as a whole, is not an exclusively modern political idea. While the form of the late-twentieth-century welfare state certainly differs from anything that one can find in earlier periods, the notion of governance as the provision of the conditions for a peaceful and prosperous life for all members of the realm can frequently be found in medieval political discourse. To cite only one typical example, the imperial Roncaglia decrees of 1158 contain the following: "It is fitting to imperial skill to care for the state and find favorable conditions for the

subjects so that the wealth of the realm may endure uncorrupted and the status of individuals be preserved continually without harm." [Imperialem decet sollertiam ita rei publicae curam gerere et subiectorum commoda investigare, ut regni utilitas incorrupta persistat et singulorum status iugiter servetur illesus.] *Monumenta Germaniae historica, Const.* 1.247, quoted in Holt, *Magna Carta,* 87.

56. In classical usage, teneo habenas is frequently used in contexts of governance (ranging from governing the state to controlling one's urges) but the metaphor of putting a brake on something is always quite apparent. For example, in book 1 of the Aeneid (and thus universally known to the point of memorization by anyone who went to school in the twelfth century) it is said that Jove to Aeolus "[ventis] regem dedit qui foedere certo / Et premere et laxas sciret dare iussus habena." *Thesaurus linguae Latinae,* 2nd ed. (Lipsiae: Teubner, 1990). s.v. habena, cites an early Christian inscription: "Deus cali terraeque Petro conmisit habenas"—that quotes Matt 16:19 but substitutes habenas for the scriptural claves.

57. The texts are edited in Paul Meyer, "La Légende de Girart de Roussillon," *Romania* 7 (1878): 161–235. The quotation is on 222–23. Translations are my own.

58. The reference in the subtitle is to *La chanson de Girart de Roussillon,* ed. and trans. Micheline de Combarieu Du Gres and Gerard Gouiran, Lettres gothiques (Paris: Livre de Poche, 1993), laisse 178. All further citations will be by laisse. Translations are my own.

59. For the development of the medieval theory of the just war, see James Turner Johnson, *Ideology, Reason, and the Limitation of War: Religious and Secular Concepts, 1200–1740* (Princeton: Princeton University Press, 1975), *Just War Tradition and the Restraint of War: A Moral and Historical Inquiry* (Princeton: Princeton University Press, 1981), and *The Quest for Peace: Three Moral Traditions in Western Cultural History* (Princeton: Princeton University Press, 1987); Frederick H. Russell, *The Just War in the Middle Ages* (New York: Cambridge University Press, 1975).

60. The metaphor is from Ps. 110.

61. For dating between 1185–90, see Kay, *Chansons de Geste,* 242; Bertrand de Bar-sur-Aube, *Girart de Vienne,* ed. Wolfgang van Emden (Paris: Société des anciens textes français, 1977), xxxiv. I cite by line number from *La chanson d'Aspremont,* ed. Louis Brandin, 2 vols., Les classiques français de Moyen Âge (Paris: Champion, 1923). Translations are my own.

62. These accusations are made in laisses 81–85, using the resources of composition in laisses similaires while at the same time being rich in variation. The accusations in laisse 83 are typical:

> Says Emmeline: "Girart, noble sir, do you remember how you served God? Was not Duke Alon killed by you? And did you not prostitute his two daughters? You were never happy or joyful except when you wounded or shamed people. You amend nothing, you only get worse."

[Dist Enmeline: "Gerars, frans paleïs,

Car te remenbre con tu as Deu servis.

Ne fu par toi li dus Alons ocis?

Et ses dos filles a putage mesis.

Tu ne fus onques ne liés ne resbaudis

Se n'eüs gens afolés et honis.

N'amendes rien, ainz empires tos dis."]

(1475–81)

63. [Cicero], *Rhetorica ad Herennium*; the *principium ab nostra persona* is at 3.6.11.

64. The *Prise d'Arles* no longer exists. Before 1150 the *Prise* was epitomized by a Cleric of Ratisbonne in the *Kaiserchronik,* in *Monumenta Germaniae Historica Deutsche Chroniken T. 1 Der Kaiserchronik,* ed. Eduard Schroeder (Hannover: Hahn, 1892), 14.885–14.908.

65. The text is Bertrand de Bar-sur-Aube, *Girart de Vienne*. I cite by line numbers. Translations are my own.

66. Van Emden glosses *menentie* as "propriété, domaine." Frédéric Godefroy, *Lexique de l'ancien français,* ed. J. Bonnard and Am Salmon (Paris: Champion, 2000), s.v. manantie, supplies the technical definition: "droit de l'habitant de la commune ou possession en général." Similarly, the meaning of *commendie* ranges from being under someone's domination in general to the fee paid to a seigneur for his protection. See A. J. Greimas, ed., *Dictionnaire de l'ancien français* (Paris: Larousse, 1995). s.v. commander; Godefroy, *Lexique,* s.v. commandie.

67. On homage as a trap, cf. Meyer Schapiro's reading of the story of Theophilus in his 1939 essay "The Sculptures of Souillac," in Schapiro, *Romanesque Art,* 118–19.

68. The name of Girart's wife here is another example of the textual self-consciousness of the epic, since the name is drawn from the cycle of Guillaume d'Orange and serves to associate this text directly with the earlier epic. Similarly, *Girart de Vienne* ends by announcing its continuation in the Chanson of Aymeri of Narbonne, thus placing itself as prequel into both the Roland and the Guillaume cycle.

69. Bertrand de Bar-sur-Aube, *Girart de Vienne,* 329 and Van Emden's note to line 4942.

70. The underground tunnel is, of course, a two-way street. In the *Prise d'Orange* there is also a tunnel, but it renders the city extremely vulnerable—permeability is good for the invaders, not the inhabitants. It is used first by the Saracens to capture William, who has walled himself up in what is described as a palace but also seems like a fortified town—there are walls, moats, and a drawbridge—and is used again by William's messenger to escape from confinement and then to lead an invading army in to definitively capture the city. In the *Prise d'Orange* the tunnel seems to suggest that no town is invulnerable, no matter how well fortified and prepared. See *La prise d'Orange: Chanson de geste de la fin du XIIᵉ siècle,* 4th ed., ed. Claude Régnier, Bibliothèque française et romane, Série B, Editions critiques de textes 5 (Paris: Klincksieck, 1972).

71. Susan Reynolds, *Fiefs and Vassals: The Medieval Evidence Reinterpreted* (Oxford: Clarendon Press, 1996), 65–74.

72. Raymonde Foreville has called attention to the important place of the concept of love in the discourse concerning the place of the archbishop of Canterbury within royal government that develops from Lanfranc to Becket. The circle of intellectuals around the bishops, which of course includes such figures as Anselm among the bishops themselves, includes as well John of Salisbury, decisive in conceptualizing royal government. Anselm's metaphysical speculations regarding the relation between God and man are homologous with the political problem of the relation between the king and his realm. Foreville puts it nicely: "La preuve dialectique contenue dans le *Monologion* ne porte pas seulement sur l'objet de la croyance—Dieu—mais sur le mode d'adhésion à cet objet, c'est-à-dire la foi impliquant l'amour. Mais le *quaero vultum tuum* du *Proslogion* ne serait d'aucune efficacité s'il n'était grâce d'adhésion à Dieu autant que grâce d'illumination. 'Pourquoi, Seignor, mon âme ne te voit-elle pas, si elle t'a trouvé? N'a-t-elle pas trouvé celui dont elle a reconnu qu'il était la Lumière et la Vérité?'" Raymonde Foreville, "Naissance d'une conscience politique dans l'Angleterre du 12ᵉ siècle," in *Entretiens sur la Renaissance du 12ᵉ siècle,* ed. Maurice de Gandillac and Edouard Jeauneau (Paris: Mouton, 1968), 191.

73. The same language is repeated by Girart: "Bien sabei, dist Girarz, fei qe vos dei, / Plait ne dreit nen aurie, n'amor del rei" (laisse 138).

74. *La chanson de Roland,* 2nd ed., ed. and trans. Ian Short, Lettres gothiques (Paris: Livre de Poche, 1990), line 191.

EPILOGUE.   Sovereignty and Governmentality

1. Holt, *Magna Carta,* 23–49, contains an excellent comparative account of the impact of these related changes in governance on the feudal nobility throughout much of Europe.

2. Reynolds, *Fiefs and Vassals,* 3–14.

3. For a powerful critique of this historiographical fiction in the postmodern era, see Mahmood Mamdani, *Citizen and Subject: Contemporary Africa and the Legacy of Late Colonialism,* Princeton Studies in Culture/Power/History (Princeton: Princeton University Press, 1996), and *When Victims Become Killers: Colonialism, Nativism, and the Genocide in Rwanda* (Princeton: Princeton University Press, 2001).

4. From this perspective, Elizabeth A. R. Brown's "tyrannical construct" turns out to be a construction not of the nineteenth but of the twelfth century. See Elizabeth A. R. Brown, "The Tyranny of a Construct: Feudalism and the Historians of Medieval Europe," *American Historical Review* 79 (1974): 1063–88.

5. John of Salisbury, *The Historia pontificalis of John of Salisbury,* ed. and trans. Marjorie Chibnall, Nelson's Medieval Texts (London: Thomas Nelson and Sons, 1956), 3–4. I want to thank my former student Professor Geoffrey Rector for first drawing my attention to this remarkable passage.

6. Michel Foucault, "Governmentality," in *The Foucault Effect: Studies in Governmentality,* ed. Graham Burchell, Colin Gordon, and Peter Miller (Chicago: University of Chicago Press, 1991), 90–91.

7. It is one of the tenets of reception theory that contradictions within a text will most often be revealed in critical debates about the content of a text. See among others, Wolfgang Iser, *The Act of Reading: A Theory of Aesthetic Response* (Baltimore: Johns Hopkins University Press, 1978), and *Prospecting: From Reader Response to Literary Anthropology* (Baltimore: Johns Hopkins University Press, 1989); Hans Robert Jauss, *Toward an Aesthetic of Reception,* Theory and History of Literature 2 (Minneapolis: University of Minnesota Press, 1982).

8. See Partha Chatterjee, "Civil Society and the Forms of Governmental Power: Extensions to Mamdani's Arguments," *Political Power and Social Theory* 12 (1998): 253–58; Mitchell Dean, *Governmentality: Power and Rule in Modern Society* (Thousand Oaks, CA: Sage Publications, 1999); U. Kalpagam, "Colonial Governmentality and the Public Sphere in India, I," *Journal of Historical Sociology* 14 (2001): 418–40, and "Colonial Governmentality and the Public Sphere in India, II," *Journal of Historical Sociology* 15 (2002): 35–58; Dorte Salskov-Iversen, Hans Krause Hansen, and Sven Bislev, "Governmentality, Globalization, and Local Practice: Transformations of a Hegemonic Discourse," *Alternatives* 25 (2000): 183–222.

WORKS CITED

PRIMARY SOURCES

Abelard, Peter. *Peter Abelard's Ethics*. Edited and translated by D. E. Luscombe. Oxford Medieval Texts. Oxford: Clarendon Press, 1971.

Acta synodi Attrebatensis. PL 142:1269B–1312D. Paris: Garnier, 1887.

Ademar of Chabannes. *Ademari Cabannensis chronicon*. Edited by P. Bourgain and Richard Allen Landes. CCSL, Continuatio Mediaevalis 129. Turnhout: Brepols, 1999.

Aelred of Rievaulx. *Vita Edwardi regis et confessoris*. PL 195. Paris: Garnier, 1885.

Alcuin. *Vita Vedastis*. In *Passiones vitaeque sanctorum aevi Merovingici et antiquiorum aliquot*, edited by Bruno Krusch and W. Levison, Monumenta Germaniae historica, Scriptorum rerum Merovingicarum 3:414–27. Hannover: Hahn, 1896–. Reprint, 1977.

The Anglo-Saxon Chronicle. Edited by Dorothy Whitelock, David C. Douglas, and Susie Tucker. London: Eyre and Spottiswoode, 1961.

Aristotle. *Poetics*. Translated by Gerald F. Else. Ann Arbor: University of Michigan Press, 1967.

Baudri of Bourgueil. *Les oeuvres poétiques de Baudri de Bourgueil (1046–1130)*. Edited by Phyllis Abrahams. Paris: Champion, 1926.

Benoît de Sainte-Maure. *Le Roman de Troie*. Edited and translated by Emmanuèle Baumgartner and Françoise Vielliard. Lettres gothiques. Paris: Livre de Poche, 1998.

Bertrand de Bar-sur-Aube. *Girart de Vienne*. Edited by Wolfgang van Emden. Paris: Société des anciens textes français, 1977.

Biblia Sacra iuxta vulgatam versionem. 2nd ed. Stuttgart: Württembergische Bibelanstalt, 1975.

Chrétien de Troyes. *Cligés*. Edited by Alexandre Micha. Les classiques français du Moyen Âge. Paris: Champion, 1970.

———. *The Complete Romances of Chrétien de Troyes*. Translated by David Staines. Bloomington: Indiana University Press, 1993.

———. *Erec et Enide*. Edited by Mario Roques. Les classiques français du Moyen Âge. Paris: Champion, 1973.

————. *Le Chevalier au Lion ou Le roman d'Yvain*. Edited and translated by David Hult. Lettres gothiques. Paris: Le Livre de Poche, 1994.

————. *Le Chevalier au Lion (Yvain)*. Edited by Mario Roques. Les classiques français du Moyen Âge. Paris: Champion, 1971.

————. *Le Chevalier de la Charette*. Edited and translated by Charles Mela. Lettres gothiques. Paris: Le Livre de Poche, 1992.

————. *Le Chevalier de la Charette*. Edited by Mario Roques. Les classiques français du Moyen Âge. Paris: Champion, 1970.

————. *Yvain (Le Chevalier au Lion)*. Edited by Wendelin Foerster, with introduction, notes, and glossary by T. B. W. Reid. Manchester: Manchester University Press, 1942.

Chronicle of Battle Abbey. Edited by Eleanor Searle. Oxford Medieval Texts. Oxford: Clarendon Press, 1980.

Chronicles of the Reigns of Stephen, Henry II, and Richard I. Edited from Manuscripts by Richard Howlett. Published by the Authority of the Lords Commissioners of Her Majesty's Treasury, under the Direction of the Master of the Rolls. Edited by Richard Howlett. Rolls Series 82. London: Longman, 1884.

Chroniques Anglo-Normande, Recueil d'extraits et d'écrits relatifs à l'histoire de Normandie et d'Angleterre pendant les XIe et XIIe siècles. Vol. 2. Edited by Francisque Michel. Rouen: Edouard Frere, 1836.

[Cicero]. *Rhetorica ad Herennium*. Edited and translated by Harry Caplan. Loeb Classical Library. Cambridge, MA: Harvard University Press, 1964.

Eadmer. *Historia novorum in Anglia*. Edited by Martin Rule. Rolls Series 81. London: Longman, 1884.

Eusebius of Caesarea. *History of the Church*. Translated by G. A. Williamson. Harmondsworth: Penguin Books, 1965.

Florence of Worcester. *Chronicon ex chronicis*. Edited by Benjamin Thorpe. English Historical Society Publications 13. London: Bentley, Wilson, and Fley, 1848.

————. *A History of the Kings of England*. Edited and translated by Joseph Stevenson. Lampeter: Llanerch Enterprises, 1988.

Fulbert of Chartres. *The Letters and Poems of Fulbert of Chartres*. Edited by Frederick Behrends. Oxford: Clarendon Press, 1976.

————. *Vita S. Autberti Cameracensis et Atrebatensis episcopi*. In *Acta sanctorum Belgii selecta*, 4 vols., edited by Joseph Ghesquière, 3:529–65. Brussels: Lemaire, 1785.

Fulbert [of Chartres]. *Opera omnia*. PL 141. Paris: Garnier, 1880.

Geoffrey of Monmouth. *The Historia regum Britannie of Geoffrey of Monmouth I: Bern Burgerbibliothek, MS. 568*. Edited by Neil Wright. Cambridge: D. S. Brewer, 1985.

————. *The Historia regum Britannie of Geoffrey of Monmouth II: The First Variant Version, a Critical Edition*. Edited by Neil Wright. Cambridge: D. S. Brewer, 1988.

Gerald of Wales [Giraldus Cambrensis]. *Itinerarium Cambriae.* Edited by James F. Dimock. Vol. 6 of *Giraldi Cambrensis opera omnia,* edited by J. S. Brewer. Rolls Series 21. London: Longman, 1868.

————. *The Journey through Wales; the Description of Wales.* Translated by Lewis Thorpe. Harmondsworth: Penguin Books, 1978.

Gesta pontificum Cameracensium. In Monumenta Germaniae historica, Scriptores 7. Edited by V. C. L. C. Bethmann. Hannover, 1846. Reprint, Kraus, 1963.

Great Britain, Parliament, Richard Blyke, and John Strachey. *Rotuli parliamentorum; ut et petitiones, et placita in parliamento.* London, 1767.

Guillaume de Poitiers [William of Poitiers]. *The Gesta Guillelmi of William of Poitiers.* Edited and translated by R. H. C. Davis and Marjorie Chibnall. Oxford Medieval Texts. Oxford: Clarendon Press, 1998.

————. *Histoire de Guillaume le Conquérant.* Edited by Raymonde Foreville. Paris: Société d'édition "Les Belles Lettres," 1952.

Guillaume IX. *Les chansons de Guillaume IX.* Edited by Alfred Jeanroy. Les classiques français du Moyen Âge. Paris: Champion, 1967.

Guy of Amiens. *Carmen de Hastingae proelio.* Edited by Catherine Morton and Hope Muntz. Oxford: Clarendon Press, 1972.

Henry Archdeacon of Huntingdon. *Historia Anglorum, The History of the English People.* Edited and translated by Diana Greenway. Oxford Medieval Texts. Oxford: Clarendon Press, 1996.

John of Salisbury. *The Historia pontificalis of John of Salisbury.* Edited and translated by Marjorie Chibnall. Nelson's Medieval Texts. London: Thomas Nelson and Sons, 1956.

————. *Policraticus: Of the Frivolities of Courtiers and the Footprints of Philosophers.* Edited by Cary J. Nederman. Cambridge: Cambridge University Press, 1990.

Jordan Fantosme. *Jordan Fantosme's Chronicle.* Edited by R. C. Johnston. Oxford: Clarendon Press, 1981.

Kaiserchronik. In *Monumenta Germaniae historica, Deutsche Chroniken T. 1 Der Kaiserchronik.* Edited by Eduard Schroeder. Hannover: Hahn, 1892.

La chanson d'Aspremont. 2 vols. Edited by Louis Brandin. Les classiques français de Moyen Âge. Paris: Champion, 1923.

La chanson de Girart de Roussillon. Edited and translated by Micheline de Combarieu Du Grès and Gérard Gouiran. Lettres gothiques. Paris: Livre de Poche, 1993.

La chanson de Roland. 2nd ed. Edited and translated by Ian Short. Lettres gothiques. Paris: Livre de Poche, 1990.

La prise d'Orange: Chanson de geste de la fin du XIIe siècle. 4th ed. Edited by Claude Régnier. Bibliothèque française et romane, Série B, Editions critiques de textes 5. Paris: Klincksieck, 1972.

Lactantius. *Institutiones*. PL 6. Paris: Garnier, 1887.

Lattin, Harriet Pratt. *The Letters of Gerbert, with His Papal Privileges as Sylvester II*. Records of Civilization, Sources and Studies 60. New York: Columbia University Press, 1961.

Le Roman de Waldef (Cod. Bodmer 168). Edited by A. J. Holden. Cologne: Fondation Martin Bodmer, 1984.

Liber monasterii de Hyda. Edited by Edward Edwards. Rolls Series 45. London: Longmans, 1866.

Marie de France. *The Lais of Marie de France*. Translated by Robert W. Hanning and Joan M. Ferrante. Grand Rapids, MI: Baker Books, 1995.

———. *Les Lais de Marie de France*. Edited by Jean Rychner. Les classiques français du Moyen Âge. Paris: Champion, 1983.

Meyer, Paul. "La Légende de Girart de Roussillon." *Romania* 7 (1878): 161–235.

Odo of Cluny. *Life of St. Gerald of Aurillac*. In *St. Odo of Cluny*, edited and translated by Dom Gerard Sitwell, 89–180. London: Sheed and Ward, 1958.

Ordericus Vitalis. *The Ecclesiastical History of Orderic Vitalis*. 6 vols. Edited and translated by Marjorie Chibnall. Oxford Medieval Texts. Oxford: Clarendon Press, 1969.

Paschasius Radbertus and Paulus Beda. *De corpore et sanguine Domini: Cum appendice epistola ad Fredugardum*. CCSL, Continuatio Mediaevalis 16. Turnholt: Brepols, 1969.

Ralph of Coggeshall. *Radulphi de Coggeshall chronicon Anglicanum, de expugnatione terrae sanctae libellus, Thomas Agnellus de morte et sepultura Henrici regis Angliae junioris, gesta Fulconis Filii Warini, excerpta ex otiis imperialibus Gervasii Tileburiensis*. Edited by Joseph Stevenson. Rolls Series 66. London: Longman, 1875.

Raoul de Cambrai. Edited and translated by Sarah Kay. Oxford: Oxford University Press, 1992.

Rodolphus Glaber. "Vita Domni Willelmi abbatis." In *Rodulfus Glaber opera*, edited by Neithard Bulst, John France, and Paul Reynolds, Oxford Medieval Texts, 254–59. Oxford: Clarendon Press, 1989.

Simeon of Durham. *The Historical Works of Simeon of Durham*. Edited and translated by Joseph Stevenson. Church Historians of England. Pre-Reformation Series 3:2. London: Seeleys, 1855. Reprint, Lampeter: Llanarch Press, 1987.

———. *Symeonis Monachi opera omnia*. Edited by Thomas Arnold. Rolls Series 75:2. London: Longman, 1882.

Sulpicius Severus. *Vita S. Martini*. Edited by Jacques Fontaine. Sources chrétiennes 133. Paris: Éditions du Cerf, 1967.

Vita Haroldi: The Romance of the Life of Harold, King of England. Edited and translated by Walter de Gray Birch. London: Elliot Stock, 1885.

Vita S. Landelini abbatis. In *Acta sanctorum Belgii selecta*, edited by Joseph Ghesquière, 4:458–62. Brussels: Lemaire, 1785.

Vita S. Waldetrudis ex vetustis codicibus mss. In *Acta sanctorum Belgii selecta,* edited by Joseph Ghesquière, 4:440–48. Brussels: Lemaire, 1785.

Wace. *Le roman de Rou.* Edited by A. J. Holden. Société des anciens textes français. Paris: Picard, 1970.

―――. *Roman de Brut: Text and Translation.* Edited and translated by Judith Weiss. Exeter: University of Exeter Press, 1999.

The Waltham Chronicle: An Account of the Discovery of Our Holy Cross at Montacute and Its Conveyance to Waltham. Edited by Leslie Watkiss and Marjorie Chibnall. Oxford Medieval Texts. Oxford: Clarendon Press, 1994.

William of Jumièges. *The Gesta Normannorum ducum of William of Jumièges, Orderic Vitalis, and Robert of Torigni.* Edited by Elisabeth M. C. Van Houts. Oxford Medieval Texts. New York: Oxford University Press, 1992.

William of Malmesbury. *De gestis pontificum Anglorum.* Edited by N. E. S. A. Hamilton. Rolls Series 52. London: Longman, 1870. Reprint, Wiesbaden: Kraus, 1964.

―――. *Gesta regum Anglorum.* 2 vols. Edited and translated by R. A. B. Mynors, Rodney M. Thomson, and Michael Winterbottom. Vol. 1: Text. Oxford: Clarendon Press, 1998.

―――. *A History of the Norman Kings.* Translated by Joseph Stevenson. Lampeter, Dyfed: Llanerch Press, 1991.

SECONDARY SOURCES

Agamben, Giorgio. *Homo Sacer: Sovereign Power and Bare Life.* Translated by Daniel Heller-Roazen. Stanford: Stanford University Press. 1998

Anderson, Benedict R. O'G. *Imagined Communities: Reflections on the Origin and Spread of Nationalism.* Rev. and extended ed. London: Verso, 1991.

Ariès, Philippe. *Images de l'homme devant la mort.* Paris: Seuil, 1983.

―――. *L'homme devant la mort.* Paris: Éditions du Seuil, 1977.

Armstrong, Grace M. "Questions of Inheritance: *Le Chevalier au Lion* and *La Queste del Saint Graal.*" *Yale French Studies* 95 (1999): 171–92.

Arthur, Ross G. "The Judicium Dei in the *Yvain* of Chrétien de Troyes." *Romance Notes* 28, no. 1 (1987): 3–12.

Auerbach, Erich. "Epilegomena to Mimesis." In *Mimesis: The Representation of Reality in Western Literature,* 50th Anniversary ed., translated by Willard R. Trask, 559–74. Princeton: Princeton University Press, 2003.

―――. "Giovambattista Vico e l'idea della filologia." *Convivium* 4 (1956): 394–403.

―――. *Mimesis: Dargestellte Wirklichkeit in der Abendländischen Literatur.* Bern: A. Francke, 1946.

————. *Mimesis: The Representation of Reality in Western Literature*. 50th Anniversary ed. Translated by Willard R. Trask. Princeton: Princeton University Press, 2003.

Bakhtin, M. M. *The Dialogic Imagination: Four Essays*. Edited by Michael Holquist. Translated by Caryl Emerson and Michael Holquist. Austin: University of Texas Press, 1981.

Baldwin, John W. *The Government of Philip Augustus: Foundations of French Royal Power in the Middle Ages*. Berkeley: University of California Press, 1986.

————. *The Language of Sex: Five Voices from Northern France around 1200*. Chicago: University of Chicago Press, 1994.

Barlow, Frank. "The Effects of the Norman Conquest." In *The Norman Conquest: Its Setting and Impact. A Book Commemorating the Ninth Centenary of the Battle of Hastings*, edited by Dorothy Whitelock, 125–61. London: Eyre and Spottiswoode, 1966.

————. *The Feudal Kingdom of England, 1042–1216*. New York: Longman, 1988.

Barthélemy, Dominique. *Chevaliers et miracles: La violence et le sacré dans la société féodale*. Paris: Colin, 2004.

————. *La mutation de l'an mil, a-t-elle eu lieu? Servage et chevalerie dans la France des Xᵉ et XIᵉ siècles*. Paris: Fayard, 1997.

————. *L'an mil et la paix de dieu: La France chrétienne et féodale, 980–1060*. Paris: Fayard, 1999.

————. *La société dans le comté de Vendôme: De l'an mil au XIVᵉ siècle*. Paris: Fayard, 1993.

————. *Les deux âges de la seigneurie banale: Pouvoir et société dans la terre des sires de Coucy, milieu XIᵉ–milieu XIIIᵉ siècle*. Paris: Publications de la Sorbonne, 1984.

————. *L'ordre seigneurial: XI–XIIᵉ siècles*. Nouvelle histoire de la France médiévale 3. Paris: Seuil, 1990.

Bartlett, Robert. *England under the Norman and Angevin Kings, 1075–1225*. New Oxford History of England. Oxford: Clarendon Press, 2000.

————. *The Making of Europe: Conquest, Colonization, and Cultural Change, 950–1350*. Princeton: Princeton University Press, 1993.

Baumgartner, Emmanuèle. *Chrétien de Troyes: Yvain, Lancelot, la charrette et le lion*. Études littéraires. Paris: Presses Universitaires de France, 1992.

————. "La fontaine au pin." In *Le Chevalier au Lion: Approches d'un chef-d'oeuvre*, edited by Jean Dufournet, 31–46. Paris: Champion, 1988.

Bäuml, Franz H. "Varieties and Consequences of Medieval Literacy and Illiteracy." *Speculum* 55 (1980): 237–65.

Bédier, Joseph. *Les légendes épiques: Recherches sur la formation des chansons de geste*. 3rd ed., rev. and corrected. Paris: Champion, 1926.

Benjamin, Walter. *Ursprung des deutschen Trauerspiels*. Edited by Rolf Tiedemann. Wissenschaftliche Sonderaugabe. Frankfurt a/M: Suhrkamp, 1963.

Berkhofer, Robert F. *Day of Reckoning: Power and Accountability in Medieval France*. Philadelphia: University of Pennsylvania Press, 2004.

Bernstein, David J. *The Mystery of the Bayeux Tapestry.* Chicago: University of Chicago Press, 1986.

Bezzola, Reto Raduolf. *Les origines et la formation de la littérature courtoise en occident (500–1200).* 5 vols. Paris: Champion, 1960.

Bhabha, Homi K. "Dissemination: Time, Narrative, and the Margins of the Modern Nation." In *The Location of Culture,* 139–70. New York: Routledge, 1994.

Bisson, Thomas. "The Feudal Revolution." *Past and Present* 142 (1994): 6–42.

———. "Medieval Lordship." *Speculum* 70 (1995): 743–59.

———. "Nobility and Family in Medieval France: A Review Essay." *French Historical Studies* 16 (1990): 597–613.

Bloch, Marc. *Les rois thaumaturges: Étude sur le caractère surnaturel attribué à la puissance royale particulièrement en France et en Angleterre.* Publications de la Faculté des lettres de L'université de Strasbourg 19. Strasbourg: Librairie Istra, 1924.

Bloch, R. Howard. *The Anonymous Marie de France.* Chicago: University of Chicago Press, 2003.

———. *Etymologies and Genealogies: A Literary Anthropology of the French Middle Ages.* Chicago: University of Chicago Press, 1983.

———. *Medieval French Literature and the Law.* Berkeley: University of California Press, 1977.

———. "New Philology and Old French." *Speculum* 65 (1990): 38–58.

Bloomfield, Morton W. "Symbolism in Medieval Literature." *Modern Philology* 56 (1958): 73–81.

Boas, George. *Primitivism and Related Ideas in the Middle Ages.* Baltimore: Johns Hopkins University Press, 1997.

Boenig, Robert. *Saint and Hero: Andreas and Medieval Doctrine.* Lewisburg, PA: Bucknell University Press, 1991.

Bollandists. *Bibliotheca hagiographica latina antiquae et mediae aetatis.* Subsidia Hagiographica 6. Brussels: Société des Bollandistes, 1949.

———. *Bibliotheca hagiographica latina antiquae et mediae aetatis: Novum supplementum.* Edited by H. Fros. Subsidia Hagiographica 70. Brussels: Société des Bollandistes, 1986.

———. *Catalogus codicum hagiographicorum Bibliothecae Regiae Bruxellensis.* Pt. 1, vol. 2. Brussels: Polleunis, Ceuterick, and de Smet, 1889.

———. *Catalogus codicum hagiographicorum latinorum antiquiorum saeculo XVI qui asservantur in Bibliotheca Nationali Parisiensi.* 3 vols. Brussels: Polleunis, Ceuterick, and de Smet, 1889–93.

Bond, Gerald A. *The Loving Subject: Desire, Eloquence and Power in Romanesque France.* Philadelphia: University of Pennsylvania Press, 1995.

Bouly, Eugène. *Dictionnaire historique de la ville de Cambrai: Des abbayes, des chateaux-forts et des anitquités de Cambrésis.* Brussels: Editions Culture et Civilisation, 1854. Reprint, 1979.

Bournazel, Eric, and Jean-Pierre Poly. *Féodalités. Histoire générale des systémes politiques*. Paris: Presses Universitaires de France, 1998.

Boutet, Dominique. *Formes littéraires et conscience historique aux origines de la littérature française (1100–1250)*. Paris: Presses Universitaires de France, 1999.

Bové, Paul. *Intellectuals in Power: A Genealogy of Critical Humanism*. New York: Columbia University Press, 1986.

Brooke, Christopher Nugent Lawrence. *The Twelfth Century Renaissance*. New York: Harcourt Brace and World, 1970.

Brown, Elizabeth A. R. "The Tyranny of a Construct: Feudalism and the Historians of Medieval Europe." *American Historical Review* 79 (1974): 1063–88.

Bruckner, Matilda Tomaryn. *Shaping Romance: Interpretation, Truth, and Closure in Twelfth-Century French Fictions*. Middle Ages Series. Philadelphia: University of Pennsylvania Press, 1993.

Bynum, Caroline Walker. "Wonder." *American Historical Review* 102 (1997): 1–26.

Calin, William. "L'épopée dite vivante: Réflexions sur le prétendu caractère oral des chansons de geste." *Olifant* 8 (1981): 227–37.

———. "Littérature médiévale et hypothèse orale: Une divergence de méthode et de philosophie." *Olifant* 8 (1981): 256–85.

———. *The Old French Epic of Revolt: Raoul de Cambrai, Renaud de Montauban, Gormond et Isembard*. Geneva: Librairie Droz, 1962.

———. "Un univers en decomposition: Raoul de Cambrai." *Olifant* 1 (1974): 3–9.

Carruthers, Mary. *The Book of Memory: A Study of Memory in Medieval Culture*. Cambridge Studies in Medieval Literature 10. New York: Cambridge University Press, 1990.

———. *The Craft of Thought: Meditation, Rhetoric, and the Making of Images, 400–1200*. Cambridge Studies in Medieval Literature. New York: Cambridge University Press, 1998.

———. "The Poet as Master Builder: Composition and Locational Memory in the Middle Ages." *New Literary History* 24 (1993): 881–904.

Carty, Carolyn M. "The Role of Gonzo's Dream in the Building of Cluny III." *Gesta* 27 (1988): 113–23.

Cazelles, Brigitte. *The Unholy Grail: A Social Reading of Chrétien de Troyes's "Conte du Graal."* Stanford: Stanford University Press, 1996.

Chatterjee, Partha. "Civil Society and the Forms of Governmental Power: Extensions to Mamdani's Arguments." *Political Power and Social Theory* 12 (1998): 253–58.

Chauou, Amaury. *L'idéologie Plantagenêt: Royauté arthurienne et monarchie politique dans l'espace Plantagenêt (XIIᵉ–XIIIᵉ siècles)*. Rennes: Presses Universitaires de Rennes, 2001.

Chenu, Marie-Dominique. "The Symbolist Mentality." In *Nature, Man, and Society in the Twelfth Century*, edited by Jerome Taylor and Lester K. Little, 99–145. Chicago: University of Chicago Press, 1968.

Cheyette, Fredric, and Howell Chickering. "Love, Anger, and Peace: Social Practice and Poetic Play in the Ending of *Yvain*." *Speculum* 80 (2005): 75–117.

Chibnall, Marjorie. *The Debate on the Norman Conquest*. Manchester: Manchester University Press, 1999.

Clanchy, Michael T. *England and Its Rulers: Foreign Lordship and National Identity, 1066–1272*. Totowa, NJ: Rowman and Littlefield, 1983.

————. *From Memory to Written Record: England, 1066–1307*. Cambridge, MA: Harvard University Press, 1979.

Cohen, Jeffrey Jerome. *Of Giants: Sex, Monsters, and the Middle Ages*. Minneapolis: University of Minnesota Press, 1999.

————. *The Postcolonial Middle Ages*. New York: St. Martin's Press, 2000.

Congar, Y. *L'ecclésiologie du haut Moyen Âge de Saint Grégoire le Grand à la désunion entre Byzance et Rome*. Paris: Edition du Cerf, 1968.

Constable, Giles. *The Reformation of the Twelfth Century*. Cambridge: Cambridge University Press, 1998.

————. *Three Studies in Medieval Religious and Social Thought: The Interpretation of Mary and Martha, the Ideal of the Imitation of Christ, the Orders of Society*. Cambridge: Cambridge University Press, 1995.

Cowdrey, H. E. J. *The Cluniacs and the Gregorian Reform*. Oxford: Clarendon Press, 1970.

Crane, Susan. *Insular Romance: Politics, Faith, and Culture in Anglo-Norman and Middle English Literature*. Berkeley: University of California Press, 1986.

Curtius, Ernst Robert. *European Literature and the Latin Middle Ages*. Bollingen Series 36. New York: Pantheon Books, 1953.

————. "Über die Altfranzösische Epik." *Zeitschrift für Romanische Philologie* 64 (1944): 233–320.

Damian-Grint, Peter. "*Estoire* as Word and Genre: Meaning and Literary Usage in the Twelfth Century." *Medium Aevum* 66 (1997): 189–206.

————. *The New Historians of the Twelfth-Century Renaissance: Inventing Vernacular Authority*. Woodbridge: Boydell Press, 1999.

————. "Translation as *Enarratio* and Hermeneutic Theory in Twelfth-Century Vernacular Learned Literature." *Neophilologus* 83 (1999): 349–67.

de Certeau, Michel. *The Writing of History*. Translated by Tom Conley. New York: Columbia University Press, 1988.

de Gaiffier, Baudouin. *Études critiques d'hagiographie et d'iconologie*. Subsidia Hagiographica 43. Brussels: Société des Bollandistes, 1967.

de Montclos, Jean. *Lanfranc et Bérenger: La controverse eucharistique du XIᵉ siècle*. Leuven: Spicilegium Sacrum Lovaniense, 1971.

Dean, Mitchell. *Governmentality: Power and Rule in Modern Society*. Thousand Oaks, CA: Sage Publications, 1999.

Delclos, Jean-Claude. "Encore le prologue des Lais de Marie de France." *Le Moyen Âge* 90 (1984): 223–32.

Denis, Françoise. *Barons et chevaliers dans Raoul de Cambrai: Autopsie d'un phénomène de glissement.* New York: Peter Lang, 1989.

Derrida, Jacques. "The Law of Genre." In *Acts of Literature,* edited by Derek Attridge, 221–52. New York: Routledge, 1992.

Donovan, M. J. "Priscian and the Obscurity of the Ancients." *Speculum* 36 (1961): 75–80.

Douglas, David C. *The Norman Achievement.* Berkeley: University of California Press, 1969.

Duby, Georges. *The Chivalrous Society.* Translated by Cynthia Postan. Berkeley: University of California Press, 1980.

———. *Hommes et structures du Moyen Âge.* Paris: Flammarion, 1988.

———. *The Knight, the Lady and the Priest: The Making of Modern Marriage in Medieval France.* Translated by Barbara Bray. Chicago: University of Chicago Press, 1993.

———. *L'an mil.* Paris: Gallimard, 1980.

———. *Le dimanche de Bouvines; 27 juillet 1214.* Trente journées qui ont fait la France 5. Paris: Gallimard, 1973.

———. *Love and Marriage in the Middle Ages.* Translated by Jane Dunnett. Chicago: University of Chicago Press, 1994.

———. *The Three Orders: Feudal Society Imagined.* Translated by Arthur Goldhammer. Chicago: University of Chicago Press, 1982.

Duggan, Joseph J. *Oral Literature: Seven Essays.* New York: Barnes and Noble Books, 1975.

———. *The Song of Roland: Formulaic Style and Poetic Craft.* Berkeley: University of California Press, 1973.

Dupront, Alphonse. *Du sacré: Croisades et pèlerinages, images et langages.* Bibliothèque des histoires. Paris: Gallimard, 1987.

Fenster, Thelma S. "The Son's Mother: Aalais and Marsent in Raoul de Cambrai." *Olifant* 12 (1987): 77–93.

Field, Rosalind. "Romance as History, History as Romance." In *Romance in Medieval England,* edited by Maldwyn Mills, Jennifer Fellows and Carol M. Meale, 163–73. Cambridge: D. S. Brewer, 1991.

———. "Waldef and the Matter of/with England." In *Medieval Insular Romance: Translation and Innovation,* edited by Judith Weiss, Jennifer Fellows, and Morgan Dickson, 25–40. Cambridge: D. S. Brewer, 2000.

Fleming, Robin. *Kings and Lords in Conquest England.* Cambridge: Cambridge University Press, 1991.

Flint, Valerie I. J. "The Historia regum Britanniae of Geoffrey of Monmouth: Parody and Its Purpose. A Suggestion." *Speculum* 54, no. 3 (1979): 447–68.

Flori, Jean. "Aristocratie et valeurs 'chevaleresques' dans la seconde moitié du XIIe siècle: L'exemple des Lais de Marie de France." *Le Moyen Âge: Revue d'Histoire et de Philologie* 96 (1990): 35–65.

Foley, John Miles. *The Theory of Oral Composition: History and Methodology.* Bloomington: Indiana University Press, 1988.

———. *Traditional Oral Epic: The Odyssey, Beowulf, and the Serbo-Croatian Return Song.* Berkeley: University of California Press, 1990.

Foreville, Raymonde. "Naissance d'une conscience politique dans l'Angleterre du 12ᵉ siècle." In *Entretiens sur la Renaissance du 12ᵉ siècle,* edited by Maurice de Gandillac and Edouard Jeauneau, 179–201. Paris: Mouton, 1968.

Foucault, Michel. "Governmentality." In *The Foucault Effect: Studies in Governmentality,* edited by Graham Burchell, Colin Gordon, and Peter Miller, 87–104. Chicago: University of Chicago Press, 1991.

———. "Truth and Power." In *Power/Knowledge: Selected Interviews and Other Writings, 1972–1977,* edited by Colin Gordon, 109–33. New York: Pantheon, 1980.

Foulet, Alfred, and Karl D. Uitti. "The Prologue to the Lais of Marie de France: A Reconsideration." *Romance Philology* 35 (1981): 242–49.

Fouracre, Paul. "Merovingian History and Merovingian Hagiography." *Past and Present* 127 (1990): 3–38.

Frantzen, Allen J. *Desire for Origins: New Language, Old English, and Teaching the Tradition.* New Brunswick: Rutgers University Press, 1990.

Freeman, Edward Augustus. *The History of the Norman Conquest of England, Its Causes and Its Results.* 2nd ed. 6 vols. Oxford: Clarendon Press, 1875.

Freud, Sigmund. *Civilization and Its Discontents.* Standard ed. Translated by James Strachey. New York: W. W. Norton, 1989.

Ganim, John M. "Medievalism and Orientalism at the World's Fairs." *Studia Anglica Posnaniensia* 38 (2002): 179–90.

———. "Native Studies: Orientalism and Medievalism." In *The Postcolonial Middle Ages,* edited by Jeffrey Jerome Cohen, 123–34. New York: St. Martin's Press, 2000.

Garnett, George. "Franci et Angli: The Legal Distinction between Peoples after the Conquest." *Anglo-Norman Studies* 8 (1986): 108–37.

Geary, Patrick. "Humiliation of Saints." In *Saints and Their Cults,* edited by Stephen Wilson, 123–40. Cambridge: Cambridge University Press, 1983.

Georgianna, L. M., and Katherine O'Brien O'Keeffe. *The Literary Cultures of Early England.* Oxford: Oxford University Press, forthcoming.

Gill, Christopher, and T. P. Wiseman. *Lies and Fiction in the Ancient World.* Austin: University of Texas Press, 1993.

Golding, Brian. *Conquest and Colonisation: The Normans in Britain, 1066–1100.* British History in Perspective. New York: St. Martin's Press, 1994.

Green, Judith A. *The Aristocracy of Norman England.* Cambridge: Cambridge University Press, 1997.

———. *The Government of England under Henry I.* Cambridge: Cambridge University Press, 1989.

Guenée, Bernard. "Des limites féodales aux frontières politiques." In *Les lieux de mémoire,* 3 vols. in 8 parts, edited by Pierre Nora et al., 2.2.11–33. Paris: Gallimard, 1984–.

———. *Histoire et culture historique dans l'occident médiéval.* Collection historique. Paris: Aubier Montaigne, 1980.

———. *Politique et histoire au Moyen Âge: Recueil d'articles sur l'histoire politique et l'historiographie médiévale (1956–1981).* Publications de la Sorbonne. Serie Reimpressions 2. Paris: Publications de la Sorbonne, 1981.

Guyotjeannin, Olivier. *Episcopus et comes: Affirmation et déclin de la seigneurie épiscopale au nord du royaume de France (Beauvais-Noyon, X^e–début XIIIe siècle).* Memoires et documents publiés par la Société de l'École des chartes. Geneva: Librairie Droz, 1987.

Hanning, Robert W. "'I Shal Finde It in a Maner Glose': Versions of Textual Harassment in Medieval Literature." In *Medieval Texts and Contemporary Readers,* edited by Laurie A. Finke and Martin B. Shichtman. Ithaca: Cornell University Press, 1987.

———. *The Individual in Twelfth-Century Romance.* New Haven: Yale University Press, 1977.

———. *The Vision of History in Early Britain.* New York: Columbia University Press, 1966.

Havelock, Eric Alfred. *The Literate Revolution in Greece and Its Cultural Consequences.* Princeton: Princeton University Press, 1982.

———. *Preface to Plato.* Cambridge, MA: Harvard University Press, 1963.

Head, Thomas. *Hagiography and the Cult of the Saints: The Diocese of Orleans, 800–1200.* Cambridge: Cambridge University Press, 1990.

Head, Thomas, and Richard Allen Landes. *The Peace of God: Social Violence and Religious Response in France around the Year 1000.* Ithaca: Cornell University Press, 1992.

Heffernan, Thomas. *Sacred Biography: Saints and Their Biographers in the Middle Ages.* Oxford: Oxford University Press, 1988.

Hein, Kenneth. *Eucharist and Excommunication: A Study in Early Christian Doctrine and Discipline.* European University Papers Series 23, Theology 19. Bern: Peter Lang, 1973.

Heng, Geraldine. *Empire of Magic: Medieval Romance and the Politics of Cultural Fantasy.* New York: Columbia University Press, 2003.

Hill, Christopher. "The Norman Yoke." In *Puritanism and Revolution.* London: Secker and Warburg, 1958.

Holsinger, Bruce W. "Medieval Studies, Postcolonial Studies, and the Genealogies of Critique." *Speculum* 77 (2002): 1195–1228.

Holt, James Clarke. *Magna Carta.* 2nd ed. New York: Cambridge University Press, 1992.

Hudson, John. *Land, Law, and Lordship in Anglo-Norman England.* Oxford: Clarendon Press, 1994.

Hult, David F. "Author/Narrator/Speaker: The Voice of Authority in Chrétien's Charrete." In *Discourses of Authority in Medieval and Renaissance Literature,* edited by Kevin

Brownlee and Walter Stephens, 76–96. Hanover, NH: University Presses of New England, 1989.

Ingham, Patricia Clare. *Sovereign Fantasies: Arthurian Romance and the Making of Britain.* Philadelphia: University of Pennsylvania Press, 2001.

Ingledew, Francis. "The Book of Troy and the Genealogical Construction of History: The Case of Geoffrey of Monmouth's Historia regum Britanniae." *Speculum* 69 (1994): 665–704.

Iser, Wolfgang. *The Act of Reading: A Theory of Aesthetic Response.* Baltimore: Johns Hopkins University Press, 1978.

———. *Prospecting: From Reader Response to Literary Anthropology.* Baltimore: Johns Hopkins University Press, 1989.

Jaeger, C. Stephen. *The Origins of Courtliness: Civilizing Trends and the Formation of Courtly Ideals, 923–1210.* Philadelphia: University of Pennsylvania Press, 1985.

Jauss, Hans Robert. *Toward an Aesthetic of Reception.* Theory and History of Literature 2. Minneapolis: University of Minnesota Press, 1982.

Johnson, James Turner. *Ideology, Reason, and the Limitation of War: Religious and Secular Concepts, 1200–1740.* Princeton: Princeton University Press, 1975.

———. *Just War Tradition and the Restraint of War: A Moral and Historical Inquiry.* Princeton: Princeton University Press, 1981.

———. *The Quest for Peace: Three Moral Traditions in Western Cultural History.* Princeton: Princeton University Press, 1987.

Johnson-South, Ted. "The Norman Conquest of Durham: Norman Historians and the Anglo Saxon Community of St. Cuthbert." *Haskins Society Journal* 4 (1992): 85–95.

Kalpagam, U. "Colonial Governmentality and the Public Sphere in India, I." *Journal of Historical Sociology* 14 (2001): 418–40.

———. "Colonial Governmentality and the Public Sphere in India, II." *Journal of Historical Sociology* 15 (2002): 35–58.

Kantorowicz, Ernst Hartwig. *The King's Two Bodies: A Study in Mediaeval Political Theology.* Princeton: Princeton University Press, 1957.

Kapelle, William E. *The Norman Conquest of the North: The Region and Its Transformation, 1000–1135.* Chapel Hill: University of North Carolina Press, 1979.

Kay, Sarah. *The Chansons de Geste in the Age of Romance: Political Fictions.* Oxford: Clarendon Press, 1995.

———. "Raoul de Cambrai or Raoul sans Terre?" *Neuphilologische Mitteilungen* 84 (1983): 311–17.

Kelly, Douglas. *The Art of Medieval French Romance.* Madison: University of Wisconsin Press, 1992.

Kerr, Derek. "Beheading the King and Enthroning the Market: A Critique of Foucauldian Governmentality." *Science and Society* 63 (1999): 173–202.

Knight, Stephen. *Arthurian Literature and Society.* New York: St. Martin's Press, 1983.

Köhler, Erich. *Ideal und Wirklichkeit in der höfischen Epik: Studien zur Form der frühen Artus-und Graldichtung.* Beihefte zur Zeitschrift für Romanische Philologie 97. Tübingen: Max Niemeyer, 1956.

———. *L'aventure chevaleresque: Idéal et réalité dans le roman courtois: Études sur la forme des plus anciens poémes d'Arthur et du Graal.* Paris: Gallimard, 1974.

———. "Quelques observations d'ordre historico-sociologique sur les rapports entre la chanson de geste et le roman courtois." In *Chanson de Geste und höfischer Roman: Heidelberger Kolloquium 30 Januar 1961,* edited by Hans Robert Jauss. Heidelberg: Carl Winter Universitätsverlag, 1963.

Koss, Ronald G. "Raoul de Cambrai and Inheritance Disputes in Feudal Society." *Olifant* 13 (1988): 97–110.

Koziol, Geoffrey. "England, France, and the Problem of Sacrality in Twelfth-Century Ritual." In *Cultures of Power,* edited by Thomas Bisson, 124–48. Philadelphia: University of Pennsylvania Press, 1995.

Lacroix, Benoît. *L'historien au Moyen Âge.* Conférence Albert-le-Grand for 1966. Paris: Librairie J. Vrin, 1971.

Landes, Richard Allen. *Relics, Apocalypse, and the Deceits of History: Ademar of Chabannes, 989–1034.* Cambridge, MA: Harvard University Press, 1995.

Lane, Anthony. "The Hobbit Habit." *New Yorker* 77, no. 39 (2001): 98–105.

Le Glay, Andre Joseph Ghislain. *Cameracum Christianum: Ou, histoire ecclésiastique du diocèse de Cambrai. Extraite du Gallia Christiana et d'autres ouvrages, avec des additions considérable et une continuation jusqu'à nos jours, publiée sous les auspices de S.E. Mgr. Le Cardial Archévêque de Cambrai.* Lille: L. Lefort, 1849.

———. *Glossaire topographique de l'ancien Cambrésis: Suivi d'un receuil de chartes et diplômes pour servir à la topographie et à l'histoire de cette province.* Cambrai: F. Delinge, 1849.

Le Goff, Jacques. "Reims, ville du sacre." In *Les lieux de mémoire,* 3 vols. in 8 parts, edited by Pierre Nora et al., 2.1.103–5. Paris: Gallimard, 1984–.

———. "The Symbolic Ritual of Vassalage." In *Time, Work, and Culture in the Middle Ages,* translated by Arthur Goldhammer, 237–87. Chicago: University of Chicago Press, 1980.

Le Patourel, John. *The Norman Empire.* Oxford: Clarendon Press, 1976.

Leicester, H. Marshall, Jr. "The Voice of the Hind: The Emergence of Feminine Discontent in the *Lais* of Marie de France." In *Reading Medieval Culture: Essays in Honor of Robert W. Hanning,* edited by Robert M. Stein and Sandra Pierson Prior, 132–69. Notre Dame: University of Notre Dame Press, 2005.

Lemarignier, Jean-François. *Le gouvernement royal aux premiers temps capétiens (987–1108).* Paris: Picard, 1965.

Leupin, Alexandre. "Raoul de Cambrai: The Illegitimacy of Writing." In *The New Medievalism,* edited by Kevin Brownlee, Marina S. Brownlee, and Stephen Nichols, 131–54. Baltimore: Johns Hopkins University Press, 1991.

Lewis, C. P. "The Early Earls of Norman England." *Anglo-Norman Studies* 13 (1991): 207–22.

Liebermann, Felix. *Die Gesetze der Angelsachsen*. Halle: Max Niemeyer, 1903–11.

Lifshitz, Felice. "Beyond Positivism and Genre: 'Hagiographical' Texts as Historical Narrative." *Viator* 25 (1994): 95–113.

————. *The Norman Conquest of Pious Neustria: Historiographic Discourse and Saintly Relics, 684–1090*. Toronto: Pontifical Institute of Mediaeval Studies, 1995.

————. "The Politics of Historiography: The Memory of Bishops in Eleventh-Century Rouen." *History and Memory* 10 (1998): 118–37.

Little, Lester K. "Cypress Beams, Kufic Script, and Cut Stone: Rebuilding the Master Narrative of European History." *Speculum* 79 (2004): 909–28.

Lord, Albert Bates. *Epic Singers and Oral Tradition*. Ithaca: Cornell University Press, 1991.

————. *The Singer of Tales*. Cambridge, MA: Harvard University Press, 1960.

Lord, Albert Bates, and Mary Louise Lord. *The Singer Resumes the Tale*. Ithaca: Cornell University Press, 1995.

Lotter, F. "Methodisches zur Gewinnung historischer Erkenntnisse aus hagiographischen Quellen." *Historische Zeitschrift* 229 (1979): 298–356.

Lovejoy, Arthur O., and George Boas. *Primitivism and Related Ideas in Antiquity*. New York: Octagon Books, 1965.

Lukács, György. *Die Theorie des Romans: Ein geschichtsphilosophischer Versuch über die Formen der grossen Epik*. 2nd ed. Neuwied am Rhein: Luchterhand, 1963.

Macy, Gary. *The Theologies of the Eucharist in the Early Scholastic Period*. Oxford: Clarendon Press, 1984.

Maddox, Donald. *The Arthurian Romances of Chrétien de Troyes: Once and Future Fictions*. Cambridge Studies in Medieval Literature 12. New York: Cambridge University Press, 1991.

Mamdani, Mahmood. *Citizen and Subject: Contemporary Africa and the Legacy of Late Colonialism*. Princeton: Princeton University Press, 1996.

————. *When Victims Become Killers: Colonialism, Nativism, and the Genocide in Rwanda*. Princeton: Princeton University Press, 2001.

Marichal, Robert. "Naissance du roman." In *Entretiens sur la renaissance du 12ᵉ siècle,* edited by Maurice de Gandillac and Edouard Jeauneau, 449–82. Paris: Mouton, 1968.

Matarasso, Pauline. *Recherches historiques et littéraires sur Raoul de Cambrai*. Paris: Nizet, 1962.

McKitterick, Rosamond. *Books, Scribes, and Learning in the Frankish Kingdoms, Sixth–Ninth Centuries*. Aldershot: Variorum, 1994.

————. *Carolingian Culture: Emulation and Innovation*. New York: Cambridge University Press, 1994.

————. *The Carolingians and the Written Word*. New York: Cambridge University Press, 1989.

————. *The Uses of Literacy in Early Medieval Europe.* New York: Cambridge University Press, 1990.

McNamara, Jo Ann. "Women and Power through the Family Revisited." In *Gendering the Master Narrative: Women and Power in the Middle Ages,* edited by Mary C. Erler and Maryanne Kowaleski, 17–30. Ithaca: Cornell University Press, 2003.

Mingroot, Erik van. "Acta Synodi Attrebatensis (1025): Problèmes de critique de provenance." *Studia Gratiana (Mélanges G. Fransen)* 19–20 (1976): 201–29.

————. "Kritisch Onderzoek Omtrent de Datering van de *Gesta episcoporum Cameracensium.*" *Revue Belge de Philologie et d'Histoire* 53 (1975): 281–332.

Morris, Colin. *The Discovery of the Individual, 1050–1200.* New York: Harper and Row, 1973.

Mortimer, Richard. *Angevin England, 1154–1258.* Cambridge, MA: Blackwell, 1996.

O'Brien O'Keeffe, Katherine. *Visible Song: Transitional Literacy in Old English Verse.* Cambridge: Cambridge University Press, 1990.

Ollier, Marie-Louise. "The Author in the Text: The Prologues of Chrétien de Troyes." *Yale French Studies* 51 (1974): 26–41.

Ong, Walter J. *Interfaces of the Word: Studies in the Evolution of Consciousness and Culture.* Ithaca: Cornell University Press, 1977.

————. "Oral Residue in Tudor Prose Style." *PMLA* 80 (1965): 145–54.

————. *Orality and Literacy: The Technologizing of the Word.* London: Methuen, 1982.

————. *Ramus: Method, and the Decay of Dialogue. From the Art of Discourse to the Art of Reason.* Cambridge, MA: Harvard University Press, 1958.

Opland, Jeff. "The Early Career of D. L. P. Yali-Manisi, Thembu Imbongi." *Research in African Literatures* 33 (2002): 1–26.

————. "Imbongi Nezibongo: The Xhosa Tribal Poet and the Contemporary Poetic Tradition." *PMLA* 90 (1975): 185–208.

Otter, Monika. *Inventiones: Fiction and Referentiality in Twelfth-Century English Historical Writing.* Chapel Hill: University of North Carolina Press, 1996.

Panofsky, Erwin. *Studies in Iconology: Humanistic Themes in the Art of the Renaissance.* New York: Harper and Row, 1962.

Parisse, Michel. "Les hommes et le pouvoir dans la Lorraine de l'an mil." In *Religion et culture autour de l'an mil: Royaume capétien et Lotharingie; Actes du Colloque Hugues Capet, 987–1987, La France de l'An Mil, Auxerre, 26 et 27 juin, Metz, 11 et 12 sept. 1987,* edited by Dominique Iogna-Prat and J.-C. Picard, 259–66. Paris: Picard, 1990.

————. "L'évêque d'empire au XIᵉ siècle: L'exemple Lorrain." *Cahiers de Civilisation Médiévale (Xᵉ–XIIᵉ Siècles)* 27 (1984): 95–105.

Parkes, Malcolm B. "The Influence of the Concepts of *Ordinatio* and *Compilatio* on the Development of the Book." In *Scribes, Scripts and Readers: Studies in the Communication, Presentation and Dissemination of Medieval Texts,* 35–70. London: Hambledon Press, 1991.

Parry, Milman, and Adam Parry. *The Making of Homeric Verse: The Collected Papers of Milman Parry*. New York: Oxford University Press, 1987.

Partner, Nancy F. "Making up Lost Time: Writing on the Writing of History." *Speculum* 61 (1986): 90–117.

———. *Serious Entertainments: The Writing of History in Twelfth-Century England*. Chicago: University of Chicago Press, 1977.

Platelle, Henri. "Cambrai et le Cambrésis au XVᵉ siècle." *Revue du Nord* 58 (1976): 349–82.

Poly, Jean-Pierre, and Eric Bournazel. *The Feudal Transformation: 900–1200*. Translated by Caroline Higgitt. Europe Past and Present Series. New York: Holmes and Meier, 1991.

———. *La mutation féodale: Xᵉ–XIIᵉ siècles*. Nouvelle Clio 16. Paris: Presses Universitaires de France, 1980.

Priebe, Richard, and Jeff Opland. "Xhosa Tribal Poetry." *PMLA* 91 (1976): 119–20.

Putter, Ad. "Finding Time for Romance: Mediaeval Arthurian Literary History." *Medium Aevum* 63 (1994): 1–16.

Reynolds, Susan. *Fiefs and Vassals: The Medieval Evidence Reinterpreted*. Oxford: Clarendon Press, 1996.

Ricoeur, Paul. *Time and Narrative*. Vol. 3. Chicago: University of Chicago Press, 1984.

Ridyard, S. J. "Condigna Veneratio: Post-Conquest Attitudes to the Saints of the Anglo-Saxons." In *Anglo-Norman Studies IX: Proceedings of the Battle Conference, 1986*, edited by R. Allen Brown, 179–206. Woodbridge: Boydell Press, 1987.

Robertson, Kellie. "Geoffrey of Monmouth and the Translation of Insular Historiography." *Arthuriana* 8, no. 4 (1998): 42–57.

Roffe, David. "The Historia Croylandensis: A Plea for Reassessment." *English Historical Review* 110 (1995): 93–108.

Rosenn, Eva. "The Sexual and Textual Politics of Marie's Poetics." In *In Quest of Marie de France, a Twelfth-Century Poet*, edited by Chantal A. Maréchal, 225–42. Lewiston, NY: Mellen, 1992.

Rouche, Michel. "Topographie historique de Cambrai durant le haut Moyen Âge, Vᵉ–Xᵉ siècles." *Revue du Nord* 58 (1976): 339–47.

Rubin, Miri. *Corpus Christi: The Eucharist in Late Medieval Culture*. New York: Cambridge University Press, 1991.

Russell, Frederick H. *The Just War in the Middle Ages*. New York: Cambridge University Press, 1975.

Rychner, Jean. *Formes et structures de la prose française médiévale: L'articulation des phrases narratives dans "La mort Artu."* Geneva: Droz, 1970.

Said, Edward W. *Beginnings: Intention and Method*. New York: Columbia University Press, 1985.

———. *Culture and Imperialism*. New York: Vintage Books, 1994.

Salskov-Iversen, Dorte, Hans Krause Hansen, and Sven Bislev. "Governmentality, Globalization, and Local Practice: Transformations of a Hegemonic Discourse." *Alternatives* 25 (2000): 183–222.

Schapiro, Meyer. "From Mozarabic to Romanesque in Silos." In *Romanesque Art,* 28–102. New York: Braziller, 1977.

———. "The Sculptures of Souillac." In *Romanesque Art,* 102–30. New York: Braziller, 1977.

———. "The Still Life as a Personal Object: A Note on Heidegger and Van Gogh." In *Theory and Philosophy of Art: Style, Artist, and Society,* 135–42. New York: Braziller, 1994.

Schmid, Karl. "Zur Problematik von Familie, Sippe und Geschlecht; Haus und Dynastie beim mittelalterlichen Adel." *Zeitschrift für die Geschichte des Oberrheins* 105 (1957): 1–62.

Schulz, Marie. *Die Lehre von der historischen Methode bei den Geschichtschreibern des Mittelalters (VI.–XIII. Jahrhundert).* Berlin: W. Rotschild, 1909.

Searle, Eleanor. *Predatory Kinship and the Creation of Norman Power, 840–1066.* Berkeley: University of California Press, 1988.

Sheedy, Charles E. *The Eucharistic Controversy of the Eleventh Century against the Background of Pre-Scholastic Theology.* Washington, DC: Catholic University Press, 1947.

Short, Ian. "Gaimar's Epilogue and Geoffrey of Monmouth's *Liber vetustissimus.*" *Speculum* 69 (1994): 323–43.

———. "Tam Angli Quam Franci: Self-Definition in Anglo-Norman England." *Anglo-Norman Studies* 18 (1996): 153–75.

Shrader, C. R. "The False Attribution of an Eucharistic Text to Gerbert of Aurillac." *Medieval Studies* 35 (1973): 178–204.

Simmons, Clare. *Reversing the Conquest: History and Myth in Nineteenth-Century British Literature.* New Brunswick: Rutgers University Press, 1990.

Skarup, Pavel. "Les prologues qui précèdent le lai de Guigemar." *Revue Romane* 16 (1981): 166–75.

Slaughter, Anne-Marie. *A New World Order.* Princeton: Princeton University Press, 2004.

Sot, Michel. *Gesta episcoporum, gesta abbatum.* Typologie des sources du Moyen Âge occidental 37. Turnhout: Brepols, 1981.

Southern, R. W. *The Making of the Middle Ages.* New Haven: Yale University Press, 1953.

———. *Western Society and the Church in the Middle Ages.* Pelican History of the Church. Harmondsworth: Penguin Books, 1970.

Spiegel, Gabrielle M. "Genealogy: Form and Function in Medieval Historical Narrative." *History and Theory* 22 (1983): 43–53.

———. "History as Enlightenment: Suger and the *Mos Anagogicus.*" In *The Past as Text: The Theory and Practice of Medieval Historiography,* 163–77. Baltimore: Johns Hopkins University Press, 1997.

————. *The Past as Text: The Theory and Practice of Medieval Historiography.* Baltimore: Johns Hopkins University Press, 1997.

————. *Romancing the Past.* Berkeley: University of California Press, 1993.

Spitzer, Leo. "The Prologue of the Lais of Marie de France and Medieval Poetics." *Modern Philology* 41 (1943–44): 96–102.

Sproemberg, Heinrich. "Die Gründung des Bistums Arras im Jahre 1094." In *Mittelalter und demokratische Geschichtsschreibung,* edited by Manfred Unger, 119–54. Berlin: Akademie Verlag, 1971.

————. "Gerhard I., Bischof von Cambrai (1012–1061)." In *Mittelalter und demokratische Geschichtsschreibung,* edited by Manfred Unger, 103–18. Berlin: Akademie Verlag, 1971.

Stein, Robert M. "Making History English: Cultural Identity and Historical Explanation in William of Malmesbury and La3amon's *Brut*." In *Text and Territory: Geographical Imagination in the European Middle Ages,* edited by Sealy Gilles and Sylvia Tomasch, 97–115. Philadelphia: University of Pennsylvania Press, 1998.

————. "Signs and Things: The *Vita Heinrici IV. Imperatoris* and the Crisis of Interpretation in Twelfth Century History." *Traditio* 43 (1987): 105–19.

Stock, Brian. *After Augustine: The Meditative Reader and the Text.* Philadelphia: University of Pennsylvania Press, 2001.

————. *The Implications of Literacy: Written Language and Models of Interpretation in the Eleventh and Twelfth Centuries.* Princeton: Princeton University Press, 1983.

————. *Listening for the Text: On the Uses of the Past.* Baltimore: Johns Hopkins University Press, 1990.

Strayer, Joseph Reese. *Medieval Statecraft and the Perspectives of History.* Princeton: Princeton University Press, 1971.

————. *On the Medieval Origins of the Modern State.* Princeton: Princeton University Press, 1970.

Subrenat, Jean. "Pourquoi Yvain et son lion ont-ils affronté les fils de Netun?" In *Le Chevalier au Lion: Approches d'un chef-d'oeuvre,* edited by Jean Dufournet, 173–93. Paris: Champion, 1988.

Sullivan, J. M. "The Lady Lunete: Literary Conventions of Counsel and the Criticism of Counsel in Chrétien's Yvain and Hartmann's Iwein." *Neophilologus* 85 (2001): 335–54.

Swanton, Michael, ed. *Three Lives of the Last Englishmen.* Garland Library of Medieval Literature 10. New York: Garland, 1984.

Tai, Hue-Tam Ho. "Remembered Realms: Pierre Nora and French National Memory." *American Historical Review* 105 (2001): 906–22.

Taylor, Andrew. "Was There a Song of Roland?" *Speculum* 76 (2001): 28–65.

Te Brake, Wayne Ph. *Shaping History: Ordinary People in European Politics, 1500–1700.* Berkeley: University of California Press, 1998.

Theis, Laurent. "Dagobert, St-Denis, et la royauté française au Moyen Âge." In *Le métier d'historien au Moyen Âge: Études sur l'historiographie médiévale,* edited by Bernard Guenée, 19–30. Paris: Université de Paris I Panthéon-Sorbonne, Centre de recherches sur l'histoire de l'Occident médiévale, 1977.

Tilly, Charles. *Coercion, Capital, and European States, AD 990–1992.* Rev. ed. Studies in Social Discontinuity. Cambridge, MA: Blackwell, 1992.

——. *Formation of National States in Western Europe.* Princeton: Princeton University Press, 1975.

Tilly, Charles, and Willem Pieter Blockmans. *Cities and the Rise of States in Europe, A.D. 1000 to 1800.* Boulder, CO: Westview Press, 1994.

Todorov, Tsvetan. "The Quest of Narrative." In *Poetics of Prose.* Ithaca: Cornell University Press, 1977.

Townsend, David. "Anglo-Latin Hagiography and the Norman Transition." *Exemplaria* 3 (1991): 385–433.

Trachsler, Richard. *Clôtures du cycle arthurien: Étude et textes.* Geneva: Droz, 1996.

Trenard, Louis, ed. *Histoire de Cambrai.* Histoire des Villes du Nord/Pas-de-Calais 2. Lille: Presses Universitaires de Lille, 1982.

Turner, Ralph V. "Changing Perceptions of the New Administrative Class in Anglo-Norman and Angevin England: The Curiales and Their Conservative Critics." *Journal of British Studies* 29 (1990): 93–117.

——. *Men Raised from the Dust: Administrative Service and Upward Mobility in Angevin England.* Philadelphia: University of Pennsylvania Press, 1988.

van der Essen, Leon. *Étude critique et littéraire sur les vitae des saints mérovingiens de l'ancienne Belgique.* Leuven: Bureaux du Recueil, 1907.

Van Houts, Elisabeth M. C. "Historiography and Hagiography at St. Wandrille: The 'Inventio et Miracula Sancti Vulframni.'" *Anglo-Norman Studies* 12 (1989): 233–51.

Van Meter, David C. "The Peace of Amiens-Corbie and Gerard of Cambrai's Oration on the Three Functional Orders: The Date, the Context, the Rhetoric." *Revue Belge de Philologie et d'Histoire* 74 (1996): 633–57.

Vance, Eugene. "Semiotics and Power: Relics, Icons, and the *Voyage de Charlemagne à Jérusalem et à Constantinople.*" In *The New Medievalism,* edited by Marina S. Brownlee, Kevin Brownlee, and Stephen G. Nichols. Baltimore: Johns Hopkins University Press, 1991.

Vercauteren, Fernand. *Étude sur les civitates de la Belgique Seconde: Contribution à l'histoire urbaine du nord de la France de la fin du XIe siècle.* Académie royale de Belgique, Classe des lettres et des science morales et politiques, Memoires 33. Brussels: Palais des Académies, 1934.

Walker, David. *The Normans in Britain.* Historical Association Studies. Oxford: Blackwell, 1995.

Wallerstein, Immanuel Maurice. *The Modern World-System: Capitalist Agriculture and the Origins of the European World-Economy in the Sixteenth Century.* Studies in Social Discontinuity. New York: Academic Press, 1976.

Warren, Michelle R. *History on the Edge: Excalibur and the Borders of Britain, 1100–1300.* Minneapolis: University of Minnesota Press, 2000.

Weber, Eugen. "L'hexagone." In *Les lieux de mémoire,* 3 vols. in 8 parts, edited by Pierre Nora et al., 2.2.96–116. Paris: Gallimard, 1984–.

Whitman, Cedric Hubbell. *Homer and the Heroic Tradition.* Cambridge, MA: Harvard University Press, 1958.

Williams, Ann. *The English and the Norman Conquest.* Woodbridge: Boydell Press, 1995.

Wilson, Stephen. "Cult of Saints in the Churches of Central Paris." In *Saints and Their Cults,* edited by Stephen Wilson, 233–60. Cambridge: Cambridge University Press, 1983.

Wiseman, T. P. *Clio's Cosmetics: Three Studies in Greco-Roman Literature.* Totowa, NJ: Rowman and Littlefield, 1979.

———. *Historiography and Imagination: Eight Essays on Roman Culture.* Exeter Studies in History 33. Exeter: University of Exeter Press, 1994.

Wogan-Browne, Jocelyn. *Saints' Lives and Women's Literary Culture: Virginity and Its Authorizations, c. 1150–1300.* Oxford: Oxford University Press, 2001.

Wolf, Kenneth Baxter. *Making History: The Normans and Their Historians in Eleventh-Century Italy.* Philadelphia: University of Pennsylvania Press, 1995.

Woodman, A. J. *Rhetoric in Classical Historiography: Four Studies.* London: Croom Helm, 1988.

Young, N. Denholm. "An Early Thirteenth Century Anglo-Norman MS." *Bodleian Quarterly Record* 6 (1932): 225–30.

Zimmermann, Michel. *Auctor et auctoritas: Invention et conformisme dans l'écriture médiévale: Actes du Colloque tenu à l'Université de Versailles-Saint-Quentin-en-Yvelines, 14–16 juin 1999.* Mémoires et documents de l'Ecole des chartes 59. Paris: Ecole des chartes, 2001.

Zink, Michel. "Commentary." In *Girart de Roussillon, ou, l'épopée de Bourgogne,* edited by Roger-Henri Guerrand, Marcel Thomas, Michel Zink, and Jean Wauquelin, 13–180. Paris: Philippe Lebaud, 1990.

———. "Une mutation de la conscience littéraire: Le langage romanesque à travers des exemples français du XIIe siècle." *Cahiers de Civilisation Médiévale (X^e–XIIe Siècles)* 24 (1981): 3–27.

INDEX

Acta synodi Attrebatensis, 32
  on sexual conduct of clerics and laymen,
    217n26
Adhemar of Chabannes, 29
adventure
  as essential element of romance, 125–26
  ideology of, in *Le Chevalier au Lion,* 141–48
Aelred of Rievaulx, 73–75
African spontaneous composition, 171
Alcuin, 224n78
  as source of *Vita Autberti,* 37, 59
amour courtois, 109–10
amplificatio
  and memorability, 40
  in *Vita Autberti,* 31–32, 39–40
Arras, Diocese of, 15
Ars Amatoria (Ovid), 124
Auerbach, Erich
  "Epilogomena to Mimesis," 240n28
  on *Le Chevalier au Lion,* 126–27
  on romance, 125

Bakhtin, M. M., 176
  on effect of new modes of literary
    expression, 1
Baldwin IV, Count of Flanders, 23
  and castellan of Cambrai, 15–16
Bartlett, Robert, 5
Baudouin de Gaiffier, 37
Baumgartner, Emmanuelle, 241n31
Bayeux tapestry, 66

Bédier, Joseph, 168
Benoît de St.-Maure
  claim to truth, 161
  on community of literate clerics, 164
Berengar of Tours, 27
Bhabha, Homi, 5
bishops. *See also* prince-bishop of Cambrai
  and regulation of secular life, 26–27
  Michel Sot on lives of, 216n20
blindness, motif of
  in *Gesta episcoporum,* 22–23
  in *Life of Gerald of Aurillac,* 53–54
Bloch, Howard, 132
Bloch, Marc, 169
Bouvines, Battle of, 178
Brut (Wace), 123
  romances of Chrétien de Troyes inserted
    in manuscript of, 166
burial regulation, 27

Calin, William, 173
Cambrai, Diocese of, 14–17. *See also Gesta
    episcoporum Cameracensium;* prince-bishop
    of Cambrai
  attempts to exploit complex identity of,
    15–16
  castellan of, 16
  Cathedral of Notre Dame
  —consecration, 13–14, 18–19
  —and power of the prince-bishop, 34
  —rebuilding of by Gerard, 13

Cambrai, Diocese of (*cont.*)
  charismatic founding, 21
  contemporary legitimacy through
    chronological continuity, 22
  location of, 14–15
  monasteries and, 35–36, 38, 44
  and power of the prince-bishop, 34
  as symbol of Christianity, 33
Caradoc of Llancarfan, 120, 165
Carmen de Hastingae proelio (Guy of Amiens)
  on Harold's burial, 70
  on Harold's death, 68–70
Carruthers, Mary
  on cognitive fictions, 31–32
  on memorability, 9, 40
castellans, emergence of, 16
Cathedral of Notre Dame (Cambrai)
  consecration, 13–14, 18–19
  and power of the prince-bishop, 34
  rebuilding of by Gerard, 13
Cazelle, Brigitte, 242n39
Chaitivel (Marie de France), 153–56
Chanson d'Aspremont, La, 172, 186–95
  Girart de Vienne compared to, 195–96
Chanson de Girart de Roussillon, La, 173, 185–86
  king's supremacy in, 205
  love story in, 204–6
Chanson de Roland, La, 169, 172, 191
  king's supremacy in, 205
  portrayal of Charlemagne, 183
chansons de geste. *See also Girart de Vienne;*
    Chanson d'Aspremont; Chanson de Girart de
    Roussillon; Raoul de Cambrai
  assimilation to Homeric epic, 169
  Bédier on origin of, 251n22
  as contemporaries of romance, 9, 167
  epic mode as deliberate choice, 170
  and feudalization of the realm, 208–9
  as form of resistance to royal
    administration, 207
  and new conditions of governance,
    172–73

as opposed to romance, 168, 169
social formation represented in, 202
Charroi de Nîmes, 170
Chenu, Marie-Dominique, 33
Chevalier au Lion, Le (Chrétien de Troyes),
    8, 126–50
  broken world in, 139–41
  claim to truth, 162–63
  discourses of desire in, 133–36
  Harpin de la Montagne episode, 135–36,
    139
  ideology of adventure, 141–48
  inconclusiveness in, 148–51
  intertextual relationship with *Chevalier de
    la Charette,* 166
  and *iudicium dei,* 142
  —assimilated to the chivalry topos, 143–44
  —in Lunete's trial, 144–45
  —opposed to chivalric honor, 145–46
  magic spring episode, 127–29
  —Arthur's reaction to, 130–31
  —Yvain's reaction to, 130, 131–32
  Pasme Avanture, 133, 138, 140–41,
    245n54
  political marriage in, 136–39
Chevalier de la Charette, Le (Chrétien de
    Troyes), 140, 141, 142
  continuator of, 165
  intertextual relationship with *Chevalier au
    Lion,* 166
Chrétien de Troyes. *See also Chevalier au Lion;*
    Chevalier de la Charette; Cligés
  claim to truth, 161–62
  Conte du Graal, 242n39
  romances inserted in manuscript of Wace's
    Brut, 166
  underplaying of the marvelous, 248n76
church (building)
  in *Acta synodi Attrebatensis,* 32
  as sacred place, 29, 30–31
church (institution), secular power of.
    See prince-bishop of Cambrai

Cligés (Chrétien de Troyes)
  canon list at beginning of, 165, 168
  claim to truth in, 161–62
  opening of *Pseudo-Turpin Chronicle*
    compared to, 167
  theme of *translatio imperii et studii* in, 164
cognitive fictions, 31–32
Conte du Graal (Chrétien), 242n39
Council of Chelles, 223n67
Crowland Abbey, 100, 102
Crowland Chronicle, 91
Curtius, Ernst Robert, 167

de Certeau, Michel, 50
Deeds of the Bishops of Cambrai. See Gesta episcoporum Cameracensium
De gestis pontificum Anglorum (William of Malmesbury), on Waltheof of Northumbria, 96–97
De inventione sancte crucis (chronicle of Waltham Abbey), 71–72
  criticism by author of *Vita Haroldi,* 84
  refutation of oral tradition on Harold, 73
  veneration of Harold in, 82
Denis, Françoise, 177–78
double figures
  in *Guigemar,* 152
  in *Historiae regum Brittaniae*
    —Arthur and Lucius, 111–12
    —Cadwallo and Edwin, 117
    —followers of Modred and of Arthur, 116
  in *Vita Haroldi,* 83
double perspective in *Chevalier au Lion,* 127
double plotting
  in *Historia regum Brittaniae,* 115
  in *Vita Haroldi,* 83
double scene in *Raoul of Cambrai,* 179
Douglas, David, 233n58
Duby, Georges, 17
  analysis of Gerard's speech in *Gesta episcoporum,* 19
Dupront, Alphonse, 237n4

Eadmer, 71
Empire, Cambrai and, 15
England
  as continuous political entity, 89, 90
  end of British sovereignty, 119
  territorialization of countship and identity, 234n72
"Epilogomena to Mimesis" (Auerbach), 240n28
Erec et Enide (Chrétien de Troyes), 166–67
erotic affective relations
  amour courtois, 109–10
  in chansons de geste, 203–6
  —in *Girart de Roussillon,* 204–6
  —in *Girart de Vienne,* 204
  in *Chevalier au Lion,* 133–36
  in *Raoul de Cambrai,* 178–79
Estoire des Engleis (Geoffrey Gaimar), 123
  claim to truth, 161
  place in manuscripts, 250n13
ethnic categories
  Geoffrey of Monmouth and, 112, 238n13
  Orderic Vitalis and, 98–100
  Waltheof of Northumbria and, 97–98
Eucharist
  folk beliefs on, 28
  and power
    —in *Chanson d'Aspremont,* 193
    —of the prince-bishop, 27–31, 34
  practice and appropriate use of, 27–28
excommunication
  Gerard on, 34
  new uses of, 27
  as tool of government, 29

feudalism
  in chansons de geste, 208–9
  —*Raoul of Cambrai,* 182
  —representation of royal administration in *Girart de Vienne,* 195
  —status of noble lords, 202
  Gerard I, bishop of Cambrai, and, 16–17

feudalism (cont.)
  Reynolds on creation of, 202, 207
  William the Conqueror and, 77
Florence of Worcester. See Worcester Chronicle
Flori, Jean, 151
Foreville, Raymonde, 260n72
  on Guillaume de Poitiers, 67
Foucault, Michel, 4, 209
France
  Cambrai and, 15
  castellans in, 16
  chansons de geste on royal administration,
    195, 207
Fulbert of Chartres, 7
  as author of Vita Autberti, 35

Gaimar, Geoffrey. See Estoire des Engleis
Ganim, John, 66
Geoffrey of Monmouth. See also Historia regum
    Brittaniae
  designation of successor, 120, 165
  Robertson on, 250n10
Gerald of Wales, 79–80
Gerard I, bishop of Cambrai. See also Gesta
    episcoporum Cameracensium
  and castellan as vassal, 16–17
  inquisition of heretics, 29–30
  and Walter of Lens, 16–17
Gerbert, archbishop of Reims, on
    Eucharist, 27
Gerí, Saint
  life of, 18
  relics of, 13
Gesta episcoporum Cameracensium, 6–7,
    17–22, 105
  beginning of narrative, 19–21
  book 1, 21
  book 2, Vita Autberti compared to, 35–36
  book 3, 21–22, 24
  climax of, 18–19
  epitome of the Vita Autberti in, 36
  organization of, 17–18

and ritual of homage, 214n13
textual archive for, 18, 35
writing of, 18
Gesta regum Anglorum (Simeon of Durham),
    93–94
Gesta regum Anglorum (William of
    Malmesbury), 94–96
Girart de Vienne, 172, 195–202
  love plot in, 204
Gishlen, Saint, Vita Autberti on, 37
Glaber, Rodolphus, 54–57
Godefroi de Leigni, 165
Gormond et Isembard, 173
Guigemar (Marie de France), 8, 151–53,
    156–58
  conventional love language in, 178
  prologue, 159, 163–64
  Yonec compared to, 156–57
Guillaume de Poitiers, on death of Harold,
    67–68

hagiography. See also Vita Autberti Cameracensis
    et Atrebatensis
  conventional, 49–50
  Geoffrey of Monmouth and, 119
  versus history, 8, 106, 107
  representations of death of Harold and, 72
Hanning, Robert, 110
Harold Godwinson
  body of
  —ignorance about in Roman de Rou, 77, 114
  —as sign of spiritual victory, 72
  burial of
  —in Carmen de Hastingae proelio, 70
  —in De inventione sancte crucis, 71–72
  —Guillaume de Poitiers on, 68
  —in Roman de Rou, 76–77
  —William of Malmesbury on, 72
  death of
  —in Bayeux tapestry, 67
  —in Carmen de Hastingae proelio, 68–70
  —chronicle accounts, 7

—Guillaume de Poitiers on, 67–68

—Henry of Huntingdon on, 228n30

—in *Peterborough Chronicle,* 67

—in *Roman de Rou,* 75–76

—William of Malmesbury on, 72

—in *Worcester Chronicle,* 67

Hastings, Battle of. *See also* Harold
    Godwinson, death of

dismissal of significance, 77, 114

as trial by combat, 88

Havelock, Eric, 168

Heidegger, Martin, 169

Heidelberg Colloquium of 1961, 169

Henry II (England)

embodying unity of English and Normans,
    73–75

political mythology of court, 80

Henry II, Emperor, 16, 23

Henry of Huntingdon, 120, 165

Herluin, Bishop of Cambrai, 16

Heroides (Ovid), 124

Hill, Christopher, 89

Hincmar of Reims, 215n6

Historia ecclesiastica (Orderic Vitalis), 105–6

on Waltheof of Northumbria, 93, 97–103

Historia regum Brittaniae (Geoffrey of
    Monmouth), 8, 108–20, 123–25

and appearance of romance, 116

Arthurian section, 108–16

—Arthur and Lucius as mirror images,
    111–12

—ceremonial crown wearing, 108, 123–24

—civil war in, 115

—combat of Gawain and Lucius, 112–14,
    123

—justification for conquest, 109

—settlement of inheritance dispute,
    147–48

—war against Lucius, 112–14

dating of, 240n26

ending of, 120

—in translations, 120–22

fiction modeled on history, 106–7

and Ovidian disenchantment, 124

reign of Cadwallo, 117

on Saxon conquest of the British, 117

story of Brian, 117–19

Historia rerum Anglicarum (William of
    Newburgh), 107

historiography. *See also Carmen de Hastingae
    proelio; De inventione sancte crucis;
    Gesta episcoporum Cameracensium; Roman
    de Rou; Vita Edwardi confessoris et regis;
    Vita Haroldi*

appearance

—cause of, 2

—simultaneous with romance, 1

association of writers with community of
    literate clerics, 164

English, 66

versus hagiography, 8, 106, 107

and justification for the state of present
    affairs, 105

as opposed to chanson de geste, 167

as opposed to oral tradition, 166

and representation of own circulation as
    text, 165

versus romance, 8, 106, 107, 211n2

use to assert power or to oppose power, 7

Holt, J. C., 257n54

Hult, David, 242n40, 243n42

Huon de Bordeaux, 173

Hyde Chronicle, 87, 88

on transfer of power in England, 89

images as Bible of the illiterate, 220n48

Institutiones (Lactantius), 20

intertextuality

of *Chevalier au Lion* and *Chevalier de la
    Charette,* 166

of *Girart de Vienne* and cycle of Guillaume
    d'Orange, 259n68

Itinerarium Cambriae (Gerald of Wales),
    79–80

iudicium dei
  in *Le Chevalier au Lion,* 142, 143–46
  parody in *Chanson d'Aspremont,* 189

John of Salisbury, 208
Jordan Fantosme, 123, 250n13
  and form, 253n31

Kay, Sarah, 182
Kelly, Douglas, 167
king
  portrayal of
    —in Oxford *Roland,* 183
    —in *Raoul of Cambrai,* 182, 183
  power of, 184
    —in *Chanson d'Aspremont,* 192
  relationship with his nobles
    —in *Chanson d'Aspremont,* 186–95
    —in *Chanson de Girart de Roussillon,*
      185–86
    —in *Girart de Vienne,* 195–202
kingship, sacredness of, 70
Knight, Stephen, 241n33
Köhler, Erich, 125–26
  on audiences of epic and romance, 169

Lactantius, 20
Landes, Richard, 29
landscape in *Vita Haroldi,* 84
Lanfranc, 27
Lawman
  and ethnic difference in *Historia regum*
    Brittaniae, 238n13
  as translator of Geoffrey of Monmouth,
    120–21
Leupin, Alexandre, 173
Life of Edward (Aelred). *See Vita Edwardi*
  confessoris et regis (Aelred)
Life of Gerald of Aurillac (Odo of Cluny),
  51–54
Life of Louis the Fat (Suger), 33

Life of St. Guthlac, 100, 102
Life of St. Martin (Sulpicius Severus)
  and preface to *Vita Autberti,* 57
  and preface to *Vita Haroldi,* 85–86
Life of St. Remi (Hincmar of Reims), 215n6
Life of St. Vaast (Alcuin), 224n78
  as source of *Vita Autberti,* 37, 59
Life of William of Volpiano (Glaber), 54–57
Little, Lester, 212n8
Lukács, Georg, 169

Making of the Middle Ages, The (Southern),
  8–9
Manisi, David, 171
manuscripts
  compilations as continuous cycle of
    secular history, 123, 165, 166
  of *Raoul de Cambrai,* 173
Marie de France
  on authority of her text, 165
  Chaitivel, 153–56
  claim to truth, 159, 161, 163–64
  on community of literate clerics, 164
  and conventional love language, 178
  Guigemar, 8, 151–53, 156–58
  —*Yonec* compared to, 156–57
  and naming, 151–52
  prologue to the *Lais* and to *Guigemar,*
    159, 163–64
  underplaying of the marvelous, 248n76
Matarasso, Pauline, 182
McNamara, Jo Ann, 27
medieval aristocratic family organization,
  247n70
medievalism, 65–66
medieval state, conventional story of
  development of, 207–8
merchants, treatment of, in *Girart de Vienne,*
  200, 201
Metamorphosis (Ovid), 124
Mimesis (Auerbach), 125

miracles
  in *Gesta episcoporum*
  —book 1, 21, 22–23
  —book 3, 24–26, 28
  in *Life of Gerald of Aurillac,* 54
  Life of William of Volpiano and, 55–56
  linked to Waltheof of Northumbria,
    102, 103
  in *Vita Haroldi,* 83–84

Nicolas of Senlis, 167
Norman conquest
  denial of
  —in Aelred, 73
  —by Wace and Aelred, 79
  Tolkien and, 232n55

Odo of Cluny, 51–54
Old French Epic of Revolt (Calin), 173
Opland, Jeff, 171
oral tradition
  in Africa, 171
  chansons de geste and, 168, 171
  on Harold, 73
  historiography and romance in opposition
    to, 166
  Parry-Lord thesis and medieval epic,
    168, 171
  versus writing in Prologue to *Lais,* 159
Orderic Vitalis. *See also Historia ecclesiastica*
  mentions of self, 98–100
Otter, Monika, 23
Otto I, 62
  and Cambrai, 214n4
Ovid, influence on Geoffrey of Monmouth,
  124

Parry-Lord thesis of oral formulaic
    composition and medieval epic,
    168, 171
Perceval, 245n53

Peterborough Chronicle
  on death of Harold, 67
  on Waltheof of Northumbria, 90–91
Philip Augustus /Phillipe-Auguste, 178, 182
philology, fundamental assumption of, 65–66
plots
  double plotting
  —in *Historia regum Brittaniae,* 115
  —in *Vita Haroldi,* 83
  love as structural element in epics, 203
political theory, medieval, 108–9, 183–84
primitivist myth of origin in *Gesta episcoporum,*
    19–21
Prince (Machiavelli), 209
prince-bishop of Cambrai, 15
  polemical position, 34
  power of, 24–27
  —Eucharist and, 27–31
  —institutional legitimacy of, 21, 24, 49
  secular use of spiritual weapons, 24
Prise d'Arles, 191
Prise d'Orange, La, 259n70
Pseudo-Ingulph Chronicle, 234n66
Pseudo-Turpin Chronicle (Nicolas of Senlis), 167
public penance, new uses of, 27

Raoul de Cambrai, 173–81
  computer-assisted lexical study of, 177–78
  conventional love language in, 178
  date of composition of, 255n38
  placement into the epic cycle, 174–75
  as reflection of contemporary political
    situation, 182
  secularization of territorial power, 256n44
  self-conscious epic writing, 176
  versification of, 173
repetition. *See also* double figures; double
    perspective in *Chevalier au Lion*; double
    plotting; double scene in *Raoul of
    Cambrai*
  in *Guigemar,* 156

Reynolds, Susan, on creation of feudalism, 202, 207

Rhetorica ad Herennium, 49
  introduction of *Vita Autberti* and, 57

Richard, abbot of St. Vaast, 13

Richard, Duke of Normandy, 23

Robertson, Kellie, on Geoffrey of Monmouth, 250n10

Robert the Pious, 15, 16, 17, 23

romance. *See also Chevalier au Lion; Guigemar; Historia regum Brittaniae*
  appearance of
  —cause, 2
  —simultaneous with historiography, 1
  association of writers with community of literate clerics, 164
  Auerbach on, 125, 126
  characteristics of, 107–8
  constant variation as fundamental principle of structure, 129–30
  versus history, 8, 106, 107
  immersion in the contemporary secular world, 8, 182
  Köhler on, 125–26
  in opposition to chansons de geste, 168
  —in audience, 169
  in opposition to oral tradition, 166
  presented as historical work, 161–62
  Vita Haroldi and, 83

Roman d'Eneas, 201

Roman de Rou (Wace), 75–79
  claim to truth, 161
  compared to *Historia regum Brittaniae,* 114

Roman de Thèbes, 169

Rubin, Miri, 27

Rychner, Jean, on *Lais,* 248n76

sacred history, Aubert as incarnation of, 62

Simeon of Durham. *See Gesta regum Anglorum*

Simmons, Clare, 66

Sot, Michel, 216n20

Southern, Richard, 8–9

sovereignty. *See* king

Spiegel, Gabrielle, 33

spiritual weapons. *See* Eucharist; excommunication

states
  conventional story of development of medieval, 207–8
  diversity of European, 5
  ideological fiction of nationality of, 4–5
  language and nation, 65–66
  Tilly on formation of, 3

Stephen of Blois, 79

St. Ghislain, Abbey of, reformation by Bishop Gerard, 24–25

Subrenat, Jean, 245n54

symbolization in *Vita Autberti,* 61

Three Orders, The (Duby), 19

Tilly, Charles, on state formation, 3

Tolkien, J. R. R., and Norman Conquest, 232n55

Tovi le Preud, 71

Trachsler, Richard, 211n2

tradition. *See also* oral tradition
  epics as voice of, 9
  and resistance to new forms of governance, 208

transitional literacy, 171

truth, claim to
  by Chrétien de Troyes, 161–63
  of epics, 172
  by Geoffrey of Monmouth, 161
  by Marie de France, 159, 161, 163–64
  in vernacular narrative, 161
  by Wace, 161
  by William of Malmesbury, 161

Vaast, Saint, 37

Valenciennes, Count of, 23

van Mingroot, Erich, 18

veiled figure, image of, in *Vita Haroldi,* 86–87

vengeance
    in *Chanson d'Aspremont*, 188–89
    in *Raoul de Cambrai*, 181
Vienne, town of, 201–2
Vincent Madelgarius, *Vita Autberti* on, 37, 48
Vindicien, Saint, 22
    stories about as meditation on history,
        23–24
Virgil, influence on Geoffrey of Monmouth,
    123
Vita Aldegundis as source of *Vita Autberti,* 37
Vita Autberti Cameracensis et Atrebatensis
    (Fulbert), 7, 18, 35–38
    context of, 35
    dating of, 35
    emphasis on Autbert in the rewriting of
        Vita Landelini, 42–43
    and historical justifications for the
        dependence of monasteries on
        Cambrai, 38
    introduction and *ad Herennium,* 57–58
    as narrative of apostolic succession, 58–59
    organization of, 37
    and politics, 36
    preface, 57
    public reading
        —and manuscript tradition, 222n56
        —and text divisions, 36
    radicalism of, 50–51
    on secular activity of the bishop, 49
    sources of, 37
    Vita Landelini and, 38–44
    Vita Waldetrudis and, 44–49
    writing of, 36–37
Vita Edwardi confessoris et regis (Aelred), 73–75
Vita Fursei as source of *Vita Autberti,* 37
Vita Ghisleni as source of *Vita Autberti,* 37
Vita Haroldi, 7, 80–87, 105
    hagiographic exemplarity redefined in,
        81–83
    oral tradition and, 73
    story, 81

Vita Landelini
    rewriting in *Vita Autberti,* 38–44
    —angel's speech, 40–42, 43
    as source of *Vita Autberti,* 37
Vita Lietberti, 18
Vita Vincentii Madelgarii as source of
    Vita Autberti, 37
Vita Vulmari as source of *Vita Autberti,* 37
Vita Waldetrudis
    rewriting of in *Vita Autberti,* 44–49
    as source of *Vita Autberti,* 37

Wace, 75–79
    and claim to truth, 161
    and ethnic difference in *Historia regum*
        Brittaniae, 238n13
    and form, 253n31
    as translator of Geoffrey of Monmouth,
        120, 121–22
Waldetrude
    treatment in *Vita Waldetrudis* and *Vita*
        Autberti compared, 46–47
    Vita Autberti on, 37
Walter of Guisborough, 172
Walter of Lens
    and Count of Flanders, 16
    and Gerard, bishop of Cambrai, 16–17
Waltham Chronicle. See De inventione sancte
    crucis (chronicle of Waltham Abbey)
Waltheof of Northumbria, 7
    Crowland Chronicle on, 91
    De gestis pontificum Anglorum (William of
        Malmesbury) on, 96–97
    Gesta Regum Anglorum (Simeon of Durham)
        on, 93–94
    Gesta Regum Anglorum (William of
        Malmesbury) on, 94–96
    Historica ecclesiastica (Orderic Vitalis) on,
        97–98, 100–103
    Peterborough Chronicle on, 90–91
    in twelfth-century Latin histories, 91
    Worcester Chronicle on, 90, 91–92

war. *See also* Hastings, Battle of
  discourse of just war, 186
Western European development, traditional
  narrative of, 4
William of Jumièges, 67
William of Malmesbury
  criticism by author of *Vita Haroldi,* 84
  on death and burial of Harold, 72
  Geoffrey of Monmouth and, 120, 165
  on Waltheof of Northumbria, 93
  —in *De gestis pontificum Anglorum,* 96—97
  —in *Gesta regum Anglorum,* 94—96
  on William the Conqueror, 89
William of Newburgh, on Geoffrey of
  Monmouth, 107

William of Poitiers, on William the
  Conqueror, 89
William the Conqueror
  claim to the English throne, 71, 88
  as feudal lord, 77
  between Hastings and coronation, 87—88
  as lawgiver, 77—78
  William of Poitiers on, 89
Worcester Chronicle
  on death of Harold, 67
  on Waltheof of Northumbria, 90, 91—92
writing, importance of, in *Chanson
  d'Aspremont,* 188—89, 190—91

Yonec (Marie de France), 156—57

ROBERT M. STEIN

is professor of language and literature at Purchase College,
State University of New York, and adjunct professor of
English and comparative literature, Columbia University.